Vital Relations

Publication of this book and the SAR seminar from which it resulted were made possible with the generous support of The Paloheimo Foundation and The Brown Foundation, Inc., of Houston, Texas.

School for Advanced Research
Advanced Seminar Series

James F. Brooks
General Editor

Vital Relations

Contributors

Laura Bear
Department of Social Anthropology, London School of Economics and Political Science

Barbara Bodenhorn
Division of Social Anthropology, Pembroke College, University of Cambridge

Fenella Cannell
Department of Social Anthropology, London School of Economics and Political Science

Janet Carsten
Social Anthropology, School of Social and Political Science, University of Edinburgh

Gillian Feeley-Harnik
Department of Anthropology, University of Michigan

Michael Lambek
Department of Anthropology, University of Toronto

Susan McKinnon
Department of Anthropology, University of Virginia

Danilyn Rutherford
Anthropology Department, University of California, Santa Cruz

Elana Shever
Sociology and Anthropology Department, Colgate University

Sylvia J. Yanagisako
Department of Anthropology, Stanford University

Vital Relations

Modernity and the Persistent Life of Kinship

Edited by Susan McKinnon and Fenella Cannell

School for Advanced Research Press

Santa Fe

School for Advanced Research Press
Post Office Box 2188
Santa Fe, New Mexico 87504-2188
www.sarpress.org

Managing Editor: Lisa Pacheco
Editorial Assistant: Ellen Goldberg
Designer and Production Manager: Cynthia Dyer
Manuscript Editor: Merryl Sloane
Proofreader: Kate Whelan
Indexer: Catherine Fox

Library of Congress Cataloging-in-Publication Data
Vital relations : modernity and the persistent life of kinship / edited by Susan McKinnon and Fenella Cannell.
pages cm. — (Advanced seminar series)
Includes bibliographical references and index.
ISBN 978-1-938645-01-3 (alk. paper) — ISBN 978-1-938645-06-8 (ebook)
1. Kinship—Cross-cultural studies. I. McKinnon, Susan, 1949-
GN487.V58 2013
306.83—dc23
2012038509

Library of Congress Catalog Card Number 2012038509
International Standard Book Number 978-1-938645-01-3
First edition 2013.

Cover Image: *All Hands on Deck*, copyright The Singh Twins: www.singhtwins.co.uk

The School for Advanced Research on the Human Experience (SAR) promotes the furthering of scholarship on—and public understanding of—human culture, behavior, and evolution. SAR Press publishes cutting-edge scholarly and general-interest books that encourage critical thinking and present new perspectives on topics of interest to all humans. Contributions by authors reflect their own opinions and viewpoints and do not necessarily express the opinions of SAR Press.

Contents

Figures

Vital Relations

1

The Difference Kinship Makes

Susan McKinnon and Fenella Cannell

What difference does kinship make to our conception of the conditions of "modernity"? Why should kinship matter in an analysis, for instance, of the ways Italian textile and clothing manufacturers outsource the production of their fashion lines to China? How might attention to kinship illuminate our understanding of the Argentine nation-state and its oil industry? What does it mean that even high-tech, scientific workplaces—such as blood banks and pathology labs in Penang, Malaysia—are thoroughly domesticated by relations of kinship and marriage? Can Indian shipyard workers' ideas about kinship, reproduction, and the divine tell us something unexpected about the presumed secular nature of productive labor in the global economy? How do Mormon understandings of kinship and adoption help us reflect on mainstream Protestant and even ostensibly secular ideas of kinship? What can kinship perspectives add to current discussions on "secular ethics" and claims that we are living in a modern, "secular age"?

Why are these provocative questions? For the past 150 years, at least, theories of social evolution, development, and modernity have been unanimous in their assumption that kinship organizes simpler, "traditional," prestate societies but not complex, "modern," state societies. And they have been unanimous in their presupposition that within modern state-based societies, kinship has been relegated to the domestic domain, has lost its economic and political functions, has retained no organizing force in modern political and economic structures and processes, and has become secularized and rationalized. *Vital Relations* challenges these presuppositions.

This is a book by anthropologists. Indeed, it is because of our historical and ethnographic inquiries across the globe—in North America, Mexico, Argentina, Europe, China, and Malaysia—that we have been compelled to reconsider the significance of kinship for comprehending the political, economic, and religious relations of "modern" societies. But this is not a book about anthropology alone or for anthropologists only. It will be of interest to anyone who wishes to gain a different perspective on the concept of modernity itself and on the place of kinship and "family" in modern life. It will also be of interest to anyone who wishes to consider, with us, how our ethnographic investigations call into question the validity of long-standing ideas about what counts as modernity.

THE IDEA OF MODERNITY IN THE SOCIAL SCIENCES AND THE PROBLEM OF DOMAINS

Vital Relations brings anthropological understandings of kinship to bear on a critique of the narratives of social evolution, development, and modernization that originated in the West but now circulate widely across the globe as a powerful ideology that shapes both individual and national aspirations. Susan McKinnon (chapter 2, this volume) traces a genealogy of explicit and implicit ideas that give form to these narratives of modernity. She argues that a wide range of social theorists share a critical set of assumptions about what they see as the main lines of social development and differentiation, even as these assumptions are expressed in quite different theoretical terms. The point is not to single out or stereotype particular theories and theorists but rather to draw into plain view the often unspoken, limiting assumptions about the place and significance of kinship in so-called modern societies.

These assumptions include not only a temporal or typological dimension that differentiates *between* societies but also a structural dimension that concerns the relative differentiation of institutional domains *within* societies. Along the temporal/typological dimension, so-called premodern or kin-based societies are seen as organized by reference to kinship status, relations between groups, and religious ideas and ritual ceremonies. By contrast, "modern," state-based societies are seen as organized by reference to territory and market, relations between individuals, and rationalized, secular contracts and laws. Along the structural dimension, in kin-based societies, kinship is understood to constitute the fundamental structure in terms of which all other social relations—political, economic, and religious

—are organized; indeed, all kinship relations are simultaneously and inextricably also political, economic, and religious relations. In "modern," state-based societies, however, kinship is understood to be relegated to the domestic domain and divested of its political and economic functions—which are separated into distinct institutional domains. Thus, in kin-based societies, kinship provides the underlying structure and organizing force of political, economic, and religious relations, whereas in "modern," state-based societies, kinship is assumed to have lost its organizing force and, instead, to be subject to the constraints of political, economic, and religious relations. Such assumptions, we argue, have had a collective rhetorical impact on the conceptualization of modernity in the social sciences that exceeds the determinism of any individual author and that has created unhelpful silences in our discipline and beyond.

MODELS OF MODERNITY AND HISTORICAL CHANGE

We hasten to stress that our purpose is not to suggest that there has been no historical change, nor that these social science models do not address what have been historically significant transformations in the history of the world. To take the United States as an example of these transformations, it is clear that between the Revolutionary War and the Civil War, massive social transformations occurred in the structures of kinship, marriage, and family life and their relationships to economic and political structures and processes. Nancy Cott notes:

> The period between 1780 and 1830 was a time of wide- and deep-ranging transformation, including the beginning of rapid intensive economic growth, especially in foreign commerce, agricultural productivity, and the fiscal and banking system; the start of sustained urbanization; demographic transition toward modern fertility patterns; marked change toward social stratification by wealth and growing inequality in the distribution of wealth; rapid pragmatic adaptation in the law; shifts from unitary to pluralistic networks in personal association; unprecedented expansion in primary education; democratization in the political process; invention of a new language of political and social thought; and—not least—with respect to family life, the appearance of "domesticity." (Cott 1977:3)

In the midst of these broader social transformations, many dimensions of kinship and family life also changed. Although John Demos (1986) cautions against an overly rigid interpretation of these changes, there is general agreement among historians on certain points: a demographic decline in family size due to changing patterns of fertility; a decline in parental control over marriage choice and family formation; a rise in both gender equality and individualism that challenged patriarchy; and the disembedding of production from the domestic domain and the constitution of the latter as a unit of consumption rather than production (e.g., Cott 1977; Demos 1986; Dolgin 1997; Grossberg 1985:6; Hall 1977, 1978, 1982; Mintz and Kellog 1988:xvi; Shorter 1975; Smith 1973).

Despite the historical accounting of these social transformations, the idea of what constitutes modernity—and its conceptual counter, "tradition"—is reiterated in a kind of stereotypical contrastive frame, the acceptance of which is as unquestioned as its empirical foundation is untested. Philip Abrams (1972) has argued persuasively that although one of sociology's main goals is to understand the transition to industrial, modern society, sociologists have dealt more in "structural types," with the mechanisms of social transformation from one type to the other assumed rather than demonstrated (see also Kumar 1991). Abrams observes that "logically ordered contrasts between structural types have been treated, quite naively for the most part, as though they effectively indicated chronologically ordered transitions. On this basis a sociological past has been worked up, a past which is linked to the present not by carefully observed and temporally located social interaction but by inferentially necessary connections between concepts" (1972:20). Conceptual polarities between structural types (such as status and contract) thus have evoked beginning and end points without requiring an empirical account of the transition between them. Abrams suggests, "The point after all was not to know the past but to establish an idea of the past which could be used as a comparative base for the understanding of the present" (28; see also Smith 1973). This "idea of the past" as a particularly configured structural type—and its implications for understanding the present configuration of the "modern" family—was widely accepted by sociologists and historians alike (see Cott 1977; Demos 1986; Dolgin 1997; Grossberg 1985; Hall 1977, 1978; Mintz and Kellog 1988; Shorter 1975; Smith 1973).

To take one example, in the article "The American Family: Its Relations to Personality and to the Social Structure" (1955), Talcott Parsons paints a picture of the American family as a kind of prototype of what becomes of the family in modern societies—an isolated unit with drastically reduced social functions. Taking up the classic contrast between kin-based and state- or market-based societies, Parsons argues that in "primitive" societies, kinship "'dominates' the social structure; there are few concrete structures in which participation is independent of kinship status. In a comparative perspective it is clear that in the more 'advanced' societies a far greater part is played by nonkinship structures. States, churches, the larger business firms, universities and professional associations cannot be treated as mere 'extensions' of the kinship system" (1955:9). This development of independent institutions outside the family entails, he suggests, a "loss of function," through which the family "has become a more specialized agency than before, probably more specialized than it has been in any previously known society" (ibid.). The family remains an important institution, Parsons suggests, but its functions have been radically circumscribed to two: the socialization of children and "the stabilization of the adult personalities of the population of the society" (16).

In the end, Parsons outlines the unambiguous separation of the familial and occupational (or economic) domains. The familial domain is a solidary and holistic unit in which "membership and status are ascribed, and the communalistic principle of 'to each according to his needs' prevails" (Parsons 1955:11), and gender hierarchy is evident in the role of "the husband-father as the 'instrumental leader' of the family as a system" (13). The economic, or "modern occupational," system, by contrast, is based on achieved status, individual merit, and equality of opportunity—at least for males, who are seen as the agents in the economic domain (11–12). Critically important for our interests here, Parsons suggests that the "loss of function" both in our own recent history and as seen in broader comparative perspective, means that the family has become, on the "macroscopic levels," almost completely functionless. Except here and there, it does not engage in much economic production; it is not a significant unit in the political power system; it is not a major direct agent of integration in the larger society. Its individual members participate in all these functions, but they do so "as individuals," not in their roles as family members: "The most important implication of this view is that the functions of the family in a highly differentiated society are not to be interpreted as functions directly on behalf of the society, but on behalf of the personality.... [Families] are 'factories' which produce human personalities" (16).

Although, obviously, much has changed in the structure of the family since the time that Parsons wrote, the received wisdom about the place of kinship relative to other domains in society has not. Delimited as a unit of socialization, the modern family is understood to be subject to economic and political forces but irrelevant to the structure and dynamics of the "macroscopic" domains of economics and politics.

This perception of the particular role and place of the family in modern life is, interestingly, reflected in the importance of family history as the fastest-growing hobby in the United States—and one of the most popular in Europe, Canada, Australia, and beyond. The enormous popularity of both the US and UK versions of the TV genealogy series *Who Do You Think You Are?* speaks to the significance placed on "family" in contemporary life (Cannell 2011). On the one hand, we think of it as a key to identity, morality, and personal and social wholeness. On the other hand, at the back of most people's minds is an idea that, in the past, life was organized around and through kinship more than is the case today. Recognition of the institutional complexity of modern life easily shades into the feeling that modernity is a space in which kinship is constantly under threat of being lost. We may feel that we have to work to sustain, and sometimes to recover, those ties of relatedness (Basu 2006; Nash 2008). Genealogy and family or local histories may be ways in which people engage in the work of creating and maintaining those bonds of memory and practice.

Thus, both popular and classical scholarly accounts of the specific role and place of kinship or "family" in modern life tend to coincide: the larger organizing force of kinship in economics and politics has been lost; kinship has been progressively restricted to socialization and the development of personality, identity, and a moral compass; and, indeed, the continuity and relevance of kinship appear threatened by and at odds with modernity.

TOWARD A CRITIQUE OF THE NARRATIVES OF MODERNITY: CROSS-DISCIPLINARY RESONANCES

One can hardly argue with the fact that the historical development and diversification of institutions—such as hospitals, schools, orphanages, and banks—resulted in the takeover of several functions that had been previously the purview of the family. However, in *Vital Relations*, we argue that models of social evolution, development, and modernity have been overdrawn in such a way that it is nearly impossible to assess, or even consider, the ways in which kinship actually operates beyond the domestic domain in so-called modern societies. Although the understandings about the place of kinship in the modern world obviously relate to many fundamental institutional changes in the organization of modern life,[1] they also relate to the *myths* of modernity—the narratives that we all tell ourselves about how modern social life is different from, and differently structured than the past.

Historians have long recognized the ways in which these myths can be at odds with reality, and the complex effects of culturally formed expectations on how we understand what is happening. The historian Jay Winter, for example, has shown us that the catastrophic death rates of young men during the 1914–1918 war, which were experienced as creating a "lost generation" in many families, were actually lower than the rates of loss of children to diseases in most British families only a few generations earlier (Winter 2005[1985]; see also Cannadine 1981). It was not only the trauma of war but also the recently raised expectations about the survival of children (ca. 1900) that created the sense of an unprecedented loss of young life. Similarly, social historians of early modern England have traced the relative mobility of the workforce—especially of young people—before the Industrial Revolution, and they have modified our idea that life before the factory age was securely fixed in place and ruled by tradition. Indeed, one discovery made by many amateur family historians is that modern families are often more rooted and stable than those of the nineteenth century and even the early modern past, because they are less subject to being divided by early deaths, economic pressures to migrate, forcible evictions, and so forth (Gittins 1993[1985]; Laslett 2004[1965]; Wrightson 1982). The transition between past and present thus cannot be reduced in any simple way to the "loss" of kinship in modernity. Nor, as we show in this volume, does kinship decline in importance in any automatic way with urbanization, industrialization, or other processes associated with modernity in non-Western settings.

In reflecting on the myths of modernity, the issue of domains, and the place of kinship in modernity, anthropologists are in the good company of not only many distinguished historians interested in these matters but also colleagues in social geography, demography, sociology, feminist theory, social policy, and other disciplines. An introduction such as this wholeheartedly acknowledges but could never pretend to summarize the variety and importance of this work. We hope, however, that the distinctive contribution of this volume will offer multiple points of engagement for these colleagues and will begin a number of conversations.

Among the many possible examples worth mentioning, let us consider some contributions in sociology that intersect with the themes of this volume. Viviana Zelizer has offered a fascinating series of studies that demonstrate the persistence of economic factors in family relationships, which are often thought of in North America and Europe as being about "love" and not "money." In *Pricing the Priceless Child* (1994[1985]), Zelizer unravels the assumptions in different legal codes and practices of adoption in Canada, the United States, and Europe over the twentieth century, arguing inter alia that the widespread contemporary claim that children are "beyond price" is as much of an objectification as earlier views that children should be valued (and adopted) according to their potential labor contributions to family farms and other enterprises. It both misleads (since economic costs are always attached to adoption) and carries its own risks for children when they are cast as economic dependents rather than as valued contributors to households. In *The Purchase of Intimacy* (2005), Zelizer continues to question the widely held view that love and money are separate spheres in modern Western life. She argues that personal relationships are constructed as much through the careful deployment of money as through its avoidance, although people may build symbolic boundaries between different kinds of expenditure in daily life, and these are often instantiated in complex forms in the law. A connected theme is taken up by Allison Pugh (2008), who gives a nuanced and illuminating account of the ways that American parents, rich and poor, take decisions about how to spend money on their children. Pugh shows that apparently "irrational" spending decisions actually represent a recognition by parents of the need to balance the purchase of items that give their children certain kinds of immediate social acceptance against items that may offer longer-term investments in social mobility. Thus, like Zelizer, Pugh clearly recognizes that intimate relations are made *through* economic interactions and not apart from them.

Zelizer's larger conclusions are in tune with our own here in recognizing that popular and scholarly assumptions about a differentiation and an incompatibility between the spheres of economics and family life have long taproots. "Since the nineteenth century social analysts have repeatedly assumed that the social world organizes around competing, incommensurable principles: *Gemeinschaft* and *Gesellschaft*, sentiment and rationality, solidarity and self-interest" (Zelizer 2005:23). The difference between her project and ours is that we ask not only how economic relations penetrate and shape relations of kinship in the domestic domain but also, and perhaps more important for the purposes of this volume, how relations of kinship penetrate and shape political and economic relations in the public domain.

One might think also of the sociological classic *Habits of the Heart* (Bellah et al. 2007[1985]). The tensions between "individualism" and "commitment" in contemporary American life are approached with a catholicity of attention to the ways in which political, economic, personal, and intimate relations are interconnected, but its rich account is framed with a pessimistic view of the difficulty of moving beyond the self in search of modern community.

The current volume approaches these areas of deep mutual interest—including those relating to secularism, discussed below—from the distinct perspective of anthropology, which is fundamentally an attitude of sustained and radical comparison between different parts of the world. Anthropologists tend to start from the assumption that there is nothing universal or natural about the way change has unfolded in the history of the West.

We might sum up the heart of this attitude with reference to the classic anthropological thinker Marcel Mauss's most famous essay, *The Gift* (1990[1950]).[2] As Jonathan Parry (1986) argued in unforgettably incisive style, it is a mistake to take from Mauss's essay (as many commentators have done) the central message that "primitive" peoples have "magical" or superstitious forms of gift exchange (the famous "spirit of the gift") that contrast with the familiar reality of ordinary economic exchange. Rather, the central message is that it is only in Western late capitalism that we acquire the superstitious notion that "gifts" and "commodities" are two separable and distinct forms of object with correspondingly distinct registers of exchange that operate in distinct domains. In most other kinds of human society, in other times and places, the fact that there is no clear dividing line between gift and commodity exchange has been considered apparent (Parry 1986). Or, as Bruno Latour (1993) puts it, modernity can be diagnosed as the insistent attempt to create "purifications" between categories, which are, in fact, impossible to sustain.

The comparative reflections that we bring to bear in this volume therefore do not in any way deny the complex historical changes of the industrial period and later, but they do start from the assumption that the relationship between institutional change and the ideological or mythical aspects of modernity is a question to be empirically determined. We take kinship as our central topic because we each found through our empirical research that what we knew about particular cases did not seem to fit well with the claim that kinship is replaced by other structuring forces in modernity. This empirical work, moreover, led us to the assertion that the Gemeinschaft-Gesellschaft split is, above all, an ideological feature of modernity, not an entirely structural one. Indeed, we collectively propose that the *avoidance* of the term "kinship"—and the presupposition that kinship is irrelevant to matters of Gesellschaft—is one of the ways in which all sorts of implicit claims are made about Western modernity.

Thinking about the category of kinship in the contemporary world is one way to reason against the grain of modernization myths and to ask, with an open mind, what is happening in each case. If, as Zelizer says, it is actually impossible to keep "money" out of "love" relationships in modern America, we also ask how far the modern "economy" continues to be structured both by kinship institutions and by kinship sentiments. In looking anew at the place of kinship in relation to contemporary politics, economics, religion, law, and science, we attempt to move beyond the theoretical marginalization of kinship and family in the landscape of what counts as modernity. In the process, we mobilize the particular resources of anthropological thinking against the "domaining" practices that have been so key to the narratives of modernity.

In the chapters that follow, we examine more closely the ways in which kinship has been situated—indeed, often erased—in narratives of modernity relative to the domains of economics, politics, and religion. We point to scholarly work that suggests that there is cause for questioning not only the received wisdom of the placement of kinship in these narratives but also the fundamental validity of the narrative structure of modernity altogether.

THE LIMITS OF DOMAINING: KINSHIP, POLITICS, AND ECONOMICS IN "MODERN" SOCIETIES

Vital Relations questions the core presumption in narratives of modernity: that kinship has been effectively cordoned off in the domestic domain and has become irrelevant to the operations of modern economic and political institutions. We build on several decades of work at the intersection of kinship, feminist, and gender studies in anthropology, which, beginning in the 1980s, critiqued the analytic separation of the domestic domain as it related to understandings of both kinship and gender. This analytic separation had at least two sources, and the challenges to it had slightly different but interlinked trajectories.

On the one hand, in the 1970s, feminist anthropologists attempted to understand what was perceived as the universal asymmetry in gender relations and the subordination of women in terms of a number of distinctions—deriving from various analytic perspectives—including domestic (kinship) and public (economics and politics), nature and culture, reproduction and production, and women's and men's consciousness (Rosaldo 1974; Rosaldo and Lamphere 1974; see Yanagisako and Collier 1987 and Comaroff 1987 for overviews). It was not long, however, before a number of anthropologists (Carsten 1995b, 1997; MacCormack and Strathern 1980; Strathern 1980, 1984, 1988; Yanagisako and Collier 1987) challenged the universality of this analytic framework. They demonstrated that these categorical distinctions were not cross-culturally universal and, in any case, could not be shown universally to correlate with gender relations. It became evident that these analytic distinctions were reflective of cultural categories that were central to Western, industrialized societies and were most relevant to the analysis of gender in relation to the rise of states, class divisions, and, especially, industrial capitalism (Rapp 1979; Reiter 1975; Sacks 1975). Much later, others questioned their utility even in describing Western societies (e.g., Yanagisako 2002). The lesson here was that the separation of domestic (kinship) and public (political and economic) relations should not be presupposed but rather should be a matter of historical and ethnographic inquiry.

On the other hand, the anthropological study of kinship was built, particularly in Britain, on a distinction between the domestic domain and the politico-jural domain (Fortes 1958, 1969; Fortes and Evans-Pritchard 1940) and, more broadly, on the analytic separation of kinship, politics, and economics as the building blocks of social organization, with religion and symbolic systems seen as both reflective of and a force for the integration of social organization. Although these domains were deemed inseparable in kin-based societies (if not in state-based societies), the rationale for their analytic separation rested in their distinctive underlying constitutive forces and institutional functions. In the case of kinship, the constitutive reference for the domain was the biological relations of procreation and the genealogical grid. David Schneider (1984) and a number of scholars who built on his work called into question the assumption that kinship was everywhere ultimately based on relations of procreation and biology—an assumption that was deemed to be tied to Western understandings of kinship that were not universally shared cross-culturally. Kinship, anthropologists showed, could be created through processes of doing as much as being and by reference to such processes as exchanging valuables, laboring, worshiping, residing, or eating together as much as sharing blood or other biological substances (Bodenhorn 2000; Carsten 1997, 2000b, 2004; McKinnon 1991; Schneider 1984; Weston 1991). If kinship could not universally be constituted by reference to biology and procreation, then the rationale of kinship as a distinct domain was also necessarily challenged (Schneider 1969, 1984:181–201). Anthropologists explored the problematic consequences of using Western analytic distinctions (in particular, the separation of kinship, politics, economics, and religion), which skew our understandings of other cultures (e.g., Collier and Yanagisako 1987; McKinnon 2000). Again, the lesson here was that the nature of kinship—and forms of relatedness (Carsten 2000b, 2004; Franklin and McKinnon 2001a, 2001b) more broadly—should not be presupposed but rather should be the focus of historical and ethnographic inquiry.

These two lines of inquiry inevitably overlapped because many of the scholars who were opening up new lines of inquiry for the study of kinship were also feminists exploring new lines of inquiry in the study of gender. In the introduction to *Gender and Kinship: Essays toward a Unified Analysis* (1987), Sylvia Yanagisako and Jane Collier mounted an integrated challenge to the ways in which gender and kinship had been analyzed. Analyses of both categories were mutually entangled, they noted, and both were assumed to be founded on relations of procreation and biology (Yanagisako and Collier 1987:31–32). Rather than take either gender difference or kinship relations as inherently given in the nature of things, the authors argued, anthropologists should attend to the ways in which the categorical differences in gender and kinship are culturally and historically produced and, moreover, how they are differentially valued in culturally specific systems of inequality (35–40; see also Strathern 1988). In the process, Yanagisako and Collier also rejected the utility of separate analytic domains: "We do not assume the existence of a gender system based on natural differences in sexual reproduction, a kinship system based on the genealogical grid, a polity based on force, or an economy based on the production and distribution of needed resources. Rather than take for granted that societies are constituted of functionally based institutional domains, we propose to investigate the social and symbolic processes by which human actions within particular social worlds come to have consequences and meanings, including their apparent organization into seemingly 'natural' social domains" (1987:39). Not only did this allow anthropologists to explore other cultural understandings of gender and kinship without imposing Western analytic separations, but it also opened up the exploration of the ways in which Western domaining practices themselves were part of a culturally specific system of knowledge and power.

In *Naturalizing Power: Essays in Feminist Cultural Analysis* (1995), Yanagisako and Delaney emphasized how cultural categories and domains—and their differential valuation and power—are naturalized and essentialized by reference to either the order of nature (as revealed by science) or the order of the divine (as revealed by religion), both of which are understood to transcend culture and human agency. The unassailable quality of these categories—as outside human agency—is further enforced by taboos on reading across domains in ways that would denaturalize or desacralize their hierarchical order. Thus, for instance, "religion seems to be about god rather than about gender; the family seems to be about reproduction and childrearing rather than about gender and religion" (Yanagisako and Delaney 1995:12). But if one reads across domains, one sees how specific notions of gender and kinship are naturalized—indeed, sacralized—by reference to religious ideas about divine creation. For Yanagisako and Delaney, it is precisely by reading across domains that it is possible to reveal the processes of naturalization and sacralization that hold particular relations of power, knowledge, and social hierarchy in place.

In the context of this volume, the idea of the modern—and the hierarchical order of social relations that is entailed in the distinction between modern and traditional social orders—is founded on the assumptions that modern societies are marked by a separation between the domains of kinship, economics, politics, and religion and that these domains are distinguished by fundamentally different forms of social relations. In *Vital Relations*, we ask what happens when we defy the taboo on reading across these domains and follow the trail of kinship relations as they lead us into what are supposed to be the discrete domains of economics, politics, and religion. How might such explorations challenge the domaining distinctions that have indeed naturalized the differences between what counts as modern and traditional and the hierarchies of power that are based on these naturalized differences?

One way to explore this question is to focus attention on the institutions that are understood to be quintessential social formations of modernity. Below, we take two such institutions—the economic corporation and the nation-state—to consider how kinship has generally been ignored in anthropological models of these institutions and virtually erased from accounts of economic and political domains, structures, and processes. Going further, we point to the work of scholars who have begun to question these received models and to the work of the authors in this volume as they develop alternative models to account for the vitality of kinship relations in economic and political institutions and processes.

Kinship, Economics, and the Corporation

Since most narratives of modernity locate kin relations either in "kin-based" (but not "market-based") societies or, within market-based societies, in the domestic (but not in the political or economic) realm, it is not surprising that few scholars have actually asked what kinship means and does in the realm of "modern" economics—and one of its key institutions, the corporation—particularly in those European and American societies presumed to be the font of the "free market" (Marcus 1998; Watkins 1995; cf. Yanagisako 2002). On the whole, investigations of the significance of kinship for the economy have focused either on the past or on those places deemed to be "backward," where economic relations are still presumed to be embedded in kinship relations.

With regard to the past, attention—primarily of historians but also of anthropologists and sociologists—has been focused on the relationship between kinship, the economy, and the rise of capitalism both in premodern Europe (Adams 2005; Davidoff and Hall 1987; Grassby 2001) and in seventeenth- to nineteenth-century America (Faber 1972; Farrell 1993; Hall 1977, 1978, 1982). Adam Kuper (2001, 2009) has written accounts of the importance of kinship and cousin marriage to the formation of both the Rothschild transnational banking empire in Europe and the intellectual and corporate elite of Britain primarily in the nineteenth century. As McKinnon (chapter 2, this volume) shows, various American historians have provided ample evidence that extended family networks and dense webs of kin marriages helped consolidate not only the wealth of plantation owners in the American South but also the capital resources of the rising merchant elite—such as the Boston Brahmins—and the key banking and investment houses in the American North.

Yet, remarkably, this historical work has, on the whole, neither troubled the developmental narrative that places kinship and contract in antithetical temporal and social dimensions and domains nor precipitated much curiosity about the place of kinship and marriage in contemporary markets and corporations. It is true that, in Europe and the United States, certain legal instruments were put in place in the eighteenth and nineteenth centuries that made it possible to separate the finances of family and business and marginalized such institutions as cousin marriage from their once central role in capital formation (Hall 1977, 1978, 1982; McKinnon, chapter 2, this volume). However, rather than provoke an inquiry into the newer configurations of kinship and economy, this fact has, as Yanagisako (2002:21) noted, been translated into an a priori assumption that kinship and economics have been, effectively, separated.

To the extent that anthropologists have studied family firms in contemporary societies, they have tended to focus on non-Western societies (for instance, Birla 2009; Ong 1999; Oxfeld 1993) or on recent immigrants to the United States or Europe (for instance, Glenn 1983; Liu 2005; Ong 1999), precisely in those places where kinship is presumed still to predominate. But, as Elana Shever (chapter 4, this volume) demonstrates in her account of the Argentine oil industry, the force of kinship for economic institutions and processes continues to be "underestimated even in the places where it is widely recognized as important."

Although works delving into the kinship coordinates of contemporary corporations and financial markets in Europe and America are rarer (see Colli 2003 for an overview), there are notable and important exceptions. There is, of course, extensive research on family firms, which primarily comes out of business schools and specialized research institutes devoted to the topic (see Stewart 2003, 2008, for reviews). The chief concern of this literature is the analysis of the organizational problems deemed to be specific to family firms and the development of strategies to deal with these problems.

Within anthropology, several scholars have taken on the cultural and social dimensions of the entanglements of kinship and economics in contemporary family firms. George Marcus and Peter Dobkin Hall in their book, *Lives in Trust: The Fortunes of Dynastic Families in Late Twentieth-Century America* (1992; see also Marcus 1980), explore the role of legal instruments not only in conserving "patrimonial capital" but also in creating the organizational structure (oriented around shared wealth) for intergenerational and extended family relations among American dynastic families (Marcus and Hall 1992:15, 48). Marcus and Hall note the irony: "American business dynasties...have achieved durability as descent groups in a bureaucratized society by assimilating, rather than resisting, characteristics of formal organization which are usually assumed to be antithetical to kin-based groups" (15). Antónia Pedroso de Lima (2000), in her account of elite Portuguese family firms, articulates a kind of double dynamic that characterizes the interplay between kinship and economics typical of family firms. On the one hand, "familial values—the ways of being and living in a family—are crucial elements in defining the ways in which the economic group works and continues through time" (152). On the other hand, "the enterprise itself becomes a cultural symbol of kinship. Its effectiveness in bringing people together attributes greater power to the enterprise by maintaining active kinship relations than to the sharing of a common substance: 'blood'—one of the most important Portuguese cultural symbols of the family" (153).

Sylvia Yanagisako, in particular, has articulated a trenchant critique of the analytic domaining practices of Weber, Parsons, and others who characterize "modern" societies by their separation of domestic from economic domains; kinship from business relations; affect, emotion, and sentiment from instrumental economic rationality; communalism from individualism; and other social actions and desires from strictly economic actions and desires (Yanagisako 2002:9, 19–21; and chapter 3, this volume). As Yanagisako notes, the "study of family capitalism—a form of capitalism that has been marginalized in both Marxist and Weberian theories—enables us to see that its marginalization is itself part of the hegemonic process through which capitalism is made to appear as an economic process that is autonomous from family and kinship processes" (13). In the space opened up by this critique, Yanagisako has provided a remarkable ethnographic account of family firms in the Italian textile and clothing industry, analyzing "the sentiments, desires, and meanings of kinship, gender, and capital that are crucial to the production of the industry at a particular historical conjuncture" (4). "As sentiments in play at different moments in the developmental histories of family firms, trust and betrayal shape the character of technological diffusion, firm competition, and the creation of new firms. They are, on the one hand, products of the workings of Italian family capitalism. On the other hand, they operate as *forces of production* in Italian family capitalism" (11). In the Italian textile and clothing industry, then, kinship sentiments and relations are neither contrary to nor separated from contemporary capitalism but rather count centrally among its forces of production.

The chapters in this volume by Laura Bear, Janet Carsten, Elana Shever, and Sylvia Yanagisako not only critique the separation of kinship and economy in contemporary modern societies but also question the implicit developmental framework that supposedly differentiates premodern, modern, and neoliberal capitalist formations. Yanagisako challenges the "absence of kinship in metanarratives of transnational and global capitalism [that are fueled by] an evolutionary model of modernity that posits a steady, global march away from the fetters of family and kinship bonds" (chapter 3, this volume). The authors in this volume take up this challenge from the perspective of both the owners (Yanagisako, Shever) and the workers (Shever, Bear, Carsten), and their chapters demonstrate the persistence and importance of kinship ties in contemporary transnational and neoliberal economic formations.[3]

Yanagisako argues that family sentiments continue to drive the transnational expansion of the Italian family firms that dominate the textile and clothing manufacturing industries as they form joint ventures with Chinese firms and outsource production to the cheaper Chinese labor markets. This transnational expansion into global markets has not resulted in the predicted "managerial revolution," or what the Italians call the impetus to *managerializzare* businesses. On the contrary, it has been accomplished, on the one hand, by an intensification of the symbolic and managerial centrality of the proprietary families in Italy and, on the other hand, by the strategic use of a set of (explicitly nonfamily, but Italian) managers to oversee offshore production in China. These Italian managers and their allied Chinese entrepreneurs (all of whom have been trained in business schools to take the separation of kinship and economy as a normative ideal) find themselves confronted with what Yanagisako calls a "kinship glass ceiling." In what might be read as an ironic turn, Chinese entrepreneurs are surprised to find themselves in business with Western firms that are organized by the communal sentiments of kinship and family rather than the supposedly "modern," rationalistic, managerial logic they learned about in business school.

Building on the work of Yanagisako, Elana Shever (2008, 2012, and chapter 4, this volume) investigates the dense interpenetration of kinship and industrial relations that characterized both the state-owned oil company in Argentina and its subsequent offshoots, generated by the neoliberal privatization of the industry in 1990s. The state-owned company not only fostered kinship sentiments and family life as a way of civilizing the Patagonian frontier and countering an anarchist labor movement but also explicitly built the industry on a paternalist model in which the company provided fully for the lives and livelihoods of its workers and their families. The relation between kinship, economy, and nation was multiply intertwined: the national industry was organized as a (national) paternalistic family; relations between workers were simultaneously relations between kin; and—in accord with Pedroso de Lima's observations about the importance of enterprise in the constitution of kinship—oil itself came to be seen as a cultural symbol and the very substance of (familial/national) reproduction as much as (economic/national) production. Shever shows how Argentine oil workers continued to draw on kinship relations to forge the small businesses they were compelled to establish in the wake of the industry's privatization. Unlike the managers of the foreign oil companies—who saw the continued emphasis on kinship relations as a liability—the oil workers saw these relations as critical to their survival in the newly restructured, global oil industry. Indeed, they continued to value kinship relations as *the* standard by which economic relations should be judged and implemented.

The same is true of the workers in the shipyards along the Hooghly River in India. Through these workers—skilled builders of massive ice-class vessels—Laura Bear (chapter 7, this volume) broadens our theoretical understanding of the nature of "productive power" within a context that must be read as utterly typical of the contemporary corporate structures of global neoliberal capitalism. Focusing on the contradictions in the market logic of wage transactions—which highlight tensions between short- and long-term social debts and relations, as well as radically different understandings of the sources of productivity—Bear argues that because "Marx and Arendt solved these problems with a naturalist, secular explanation of the fertility of capital, they could not anticipate the significance of kinship and ritual to the lived experience of the institutions of capitalism." Bear elegantly shows that workers understand their productive powers in terms of a transfer of their own life force into the form of the ship they are creating. She goes on to elucidate how—in opposition to short-term relations, which they characterize as causing a "burning of the stomach"—shipyard workers see models of trust and long-term relations between kin and friends, who live, work, eat, and perform religious *pujas* together, as critical to life-sustaining relations and (re)productivity in the shipyard as much as in the family household. Through ritual pujas in the shipyards, workers materialize the desired flow of (re)productive powers and life forces, and they elicit evidence from managers of the long-term social and ethical obligations that workers see as critical to their sustenance—that is, to maintaining and replenishing their (re)productive powers. The failure of owners and managers to recognize these claims is experienced by workers as constituting the conditions for a dangerous diminishment of life force—for ill health, despondency, or death.

The impossibility of disentangling relations of kinship from those of work is evident in another site of specifically "modern," capitalist production: the scientific or medical laboratory. In chapter 5, Janet Carsten's fine ethnographic exploration of the high-tech clinical pathology labs and blood banks in Penang, Malaysia, reveals the "seepage" of kinship relations into the workspace and life of modern scientific and medical practice, which, by definition, is supposed to be constituted as a space above and beyond social relations. Carsten documents the multiple ways in which these labs undergo processes of "domestication": as people make the space and time to eat together both within and outside the labs; as actual kinship connections and marriages are forged between co-workers; as families come in and out of the labs; as family health, illnesses, pregnancies, postpartum practices, and childrearing are discussed; as workers and their families donate their own blood; as co-workers offer advice on life, marital relations, and financial problems. In the context of an ideology that stresses the separation between scientific and social relations, the impossibility of drawing a line between kinship/social relations and the workplace provokes a sense of ambivalence that is manifested in the ghosts that haunt the workers and mark the breach of a tabooed separation. By contrast, in Danilyn Rutherford's account (chapter 11, this volume) of the logics of contemporary American environmental politics, kinship is invoked in the form of the spectral presence of future children, whose claims on present generations campaigners must struggle to articulate through established economic rhetoric that would otherwise discount them.

In the end, it is impossible to say that contemporary global capitalism is entirely structured by kinship (as economic relations supposedly are in "kin-based" societies), but it is also impossible to say that kinship is irrelevant to its structures and processes. Resituating family firms in the overall landscape of contemporary capitalism helps us to rethink the assumed inevitability both of the separation between kinship and economy in modern economic systems and of the evolutionary logic of the stages of capitalism and its ultimate transcendence of kinship. Revisiting the entanglements of kinship and work, reproduction and production, and long-term and short-term debts and obligations in contemporary economic systems helps us to understand that these need not—indeed, ultimately cannot—be separated under capitalism. It behooves us to examine the particular configurations of kinship and economy that are manifest in various contexts. Reassessing the differentially configured claims of owners, managers, and workers helps us comprehend the centrality of ideas about long-term kinship relations and their (re)productive powers to the dynamics of capitalist relations of ownership and production—as, for instance, owners ground their proprietary claims (vis-à-vis managers and workers) or as workers assert their own claims (vis-à-vis managers and owners). Here, the ethics and ideologies of kinship have, perhaps, a special place in articulating and contesting the "managerial revolution" that values the idea of corporations as autonomous individuals and an economic imperative that achieves, for workers, only the "burning of the stomach."

Kinship, Nation, and the State

Another of the key categories and outcomes of the modernist narrative—whether the frame be evolution, development, or modernization—is the nation-state, with its corresponding emphasis on territory, property, equality, individualism, secularism, and legal and market rationality. Richard Handler's account of nationalism in his 1988 book, *Nationalism and the Politics of Culture in Quebec*, perfectly captures the critical relation between the idea of nationalism and (possessive) individualism. The "primary reality" of the ideology of the nation is "individuated being," defined "in terms of choice and property" (Handler 1988:50). Handler draws upon Louis Dumont's formulation that the nation "is in principle two things at once: a *collection of individuals* and a *collective individual*" (Dumont 1970:33, qtd. in Handler 1988:32). As a "collective individual," the nation is territorially bounded, self-contained, independent, equivalent to other nations, and possessed of autonomous will/choice and self-determination (Handler 1988:40–43). As a "collection of individuals," the nation is composed of a type (like a natural "species"), the members of which are equal and equivalent and possessed of the same attributes, common origins, and history (43–47).

In various accounts, the fully realized modern nation (as described more or less in Handler's terms) is juxtaposed against something that is prior, more primordial, and ultimately to be transcended. These accounts—and the very ideal of "nation" entailed by them—reproduce (often inadvertently) the familiar evolutionary distinctions of the modernist narrative. For instance, Clifford Geertz's work (1963, 1973b) on the "new nations" project makes use of a distinction between "two conflicting tendencies" (1973b:258–259): "primordial sentiments" (kinship, religion, particularistic languages and customs) and "civil politics" (universalistic rationalities of the modern market and nation-state). As McKinnon (chapter 2, this volume) notes, although Geertz does not see these tendencies to be temporally discrete, he nevertheless implicitly resurrects an evolutionary frame that contrasts kin-based societies (in which primordial sentiments predominate), "new states" (which are characterized by an unresolved tension between primordial sentiments and civil politics), and fully modern states (which have supposedly contained primordial sentiments in favor of civil politics) (see Kelly and Kaplan 2001:431).

Benedict Anderson (1991[1983]) conceptualizes the nation and its precursors in different terms from those of Geertz but clearly in line with the narratives of modernity (see Kelly and Kaplan 2001:433, 434). In contrast to religious communities and dynastic realms—organized as unbounded, centripetal, high centers with porous borders and by reference to sacred languages and texts and to cosmological hierarchies—nations are understood by Anderson (1991[1983]:6–7) to be organized as bounded, sovereign, autonomous, self-determining communities constituted in terms of horizontal, egalitarian, individualistic comradeship and by reference to secular, vernacular languages and texts, as well as print capitalism. Because he is focused on other distinctions, kinship rarely enters his account. When it does—for instance, as he discusses the difference between the kinds of solidarities created by pre-bourgeois ruling classes (royalty and nobility) and the bourgeois elites of the modern nation—Anderson notes that kinship and marriage are critical tools of the former but claims that they are irrelevant to the latter. "Factory-owner in Lille was connected to factory-owner in Lyon only by reverberation. They had no necessary reason to know of one another's existence; they did not typically marry each other's daughters or inherit each other's property. But they did come to visualize in a general way the existence of thousands and thousands like themselves through print-language" (76–77). This is a good example of the way in which contemporary theorists have erased kinship and marriage from the "reverberations" of contemporary political economy. It is not a question of *whether* but a presupposition *that* they are irrelevant.

The dominant portrait of "nation" has been critiqued from various perspectives. A number of scholars have questioned the assumption that the nation must necessarily be tightly bounded, egalitarian, or defined by ideologies of possessive individualism, singular national identity, or autonomous will and choice (Kapferer 1989; Strong and Van Winkle 1993). Others have critiqued the focus on nation and sought to transcend altogether the framework of modernity within which it is situated, preferring rather to concentrate on the workings of (neo-)imperial power (Kelly and Kaplan 2001) or the uses of "primordialisms" "in the project of the modern nation-state" (Appadurai 1996:146) and of ethnic "culturalisms" in the transnational movements and diasporic publics of the postnationalist political order (147).

What is remarkable is that, no matter whether scholars have sought to explicate the making of national cultures (Foster 1991), to critique and transcend the centrality of the idea of nation, or to focus on transnational disaporic publics, rarely has kinship been considered relevant to the topic at hand (see below for notable exceptions). The relative invisibility of kinship in relation to nation may be due, in part, to the fact that kinship studies went out of fashion about the same time that the study of nationalism came into vogue (Franklin and McKinnon 2001a). But it is more likely that the absence of kinship in studies of the nation-state is due precisely to the fact that kinship has been a priori defined as a pre- or sub-nation-state formation. As David Sutton observes, kinship's "significance in the study of modern nation-states has been underplayed, particularly because, as Herzfeld put it, 'the absence of kinship [in political and economic formations and processes] seems to be one of the defining characteristics of the West's view of itself' (1992:148)" (1997:416).

Vital Relations contests the idea that kinship is a social formation that can be understood exclusively as either historically prior or structurally subordinate to the nation-state and that the nation (or state) can be conceptualized apart from its entanglements with kinship. Building on other work in kinship studies noted below, chapters in this volume by Barbara Bodenhorn, Fenella Cannell, Michael Lambek, Elana Shever, and Sylvia Yanagisako suggest that the reigning understanding of what counts as the nation-state needs to be queried in several different ways.

First, we posit that ideas about kinship and nation are inextricably bound together. What is at issue here is not simply a "metaphorical" relation (the nation is "like" a family) but rather how particular cultural understandings about kinship, marriage, family, and relatedness organize, inform, and naturalize what will count as the nation and citizenship and how these intersect, as John Borneman (1992) has attempted to document, with contrasting visions of the state. Since David Schneider (1969) called attention to the shared distinctive features of kinship, nationality, and religion in American culture, several works have begun to survey this terrain, including explorations of the different generative qualities of paternity and maternity in the parallel constitution of ideas concerning kinship, nation, and state (Delaney 1995; Heng and Devan 1992; Lampland 1994). Other works have analyzed the tension between ideas about nature and about law/naturalization—birth and choice—that shape laws, debates, and policies about immigration and citizenship in the United States (Chock 1999; Coutin 2006[2003]). And still others have investigated the relation between understandings of kinship and marriage and those of nation and citizenship that focus on the forms of inclusions and exclusions, hierarchies and equalities, movements and restrictions, and shared essences and essential differences they entail (Alonso 1994; Bear 2007a; Carsten 2004; Das 1995; Delaney 1995; Heng and Devan 1992; Kim 2003, 2010; Mauer 1996; Nash 2008; Rutherford 2003; Sutton 1997).

Several chapters in this volume continue in this vein to explore the relations between ideas about kinship, nation, and national identity. Yanagisako (chapter 3) shows that the authenticity of Italian fashion brands—indeed, their essential "Italian-ness" (*italianità*)—is tied to the rootedness of proprietary families in their provincial homes and towns. Thus, the continuity of the family line—and its unbroken connection to its home place in a specifically Italian landscape—becomes a way of anchoring and differentiating the national authenticity and vital Italian-ness of brands that are produced offshore and in the flux of global economic relations. The deployment of nonfamily managers to oversee production in China makes it possible for proprietary families to guard the purity of their Italian-ness (through their presence in Italy, their consumption of Italian food, and their participation in an Italian lifestyle) and avoid compromising it by residence and work abroad in China. Shever (chapter 4) examines the ways in which kinship and nation are mutually constituted through the generative power of oil and oil work in the context of the paternalism of the state-owned oil industry in Argentina. Shever notes, "National sentiments meshed easily with kinship ones because both rest on a trope of familial bonds as the authentic basis for solidarity, care, obligation, and sacrifice. Kinship offered a language to talk about many kinds of affinity, most importantly, those that bound people together as company employees, town residents, and national citizens."

One worker's statement, "I am a petroleum product," points to the fact that sentiments of kinship, national belonging, and company loyalty were inextricably intertwined through a national industry that seamlessly articulated both familial and national aspirations.

Second, the dominant assumption that the individual is both the unit and the model for the nation-state makes invisible the kinship (and religious) correlates of those nations that are assumed to conform most to the ideals of a progressive, individualistic, secular, democratic nationalism, let alone those of nations that explicitly do not conform to this logic. Fenella Cannell (chapter 9, this volume) articulates this point as she follows Sarah Gordon's (2002) argument about the constitutional crisis posed by Mormon polygamy and its prohibition in the United States. Gordon suggests that this model of the nation-as-individual is actually grounded in Protestant (read as progressive, secular) notions of kinship—including the nuclear family, monogamous marriage, and individual autonomy and choice—in contrast to the Mormon theocracy of extended polygamous families and the presumed lack of individual autonomy and choice (specifically of wives and daughters).

The kinship and marriage coordinates of Western liberal, supposedly secular, individualistic, democratic states—and their connection to claims to sovereignty—are therefore unmarked and invisible. Various chapters in this volume demonstrate that they come into focus only when the underlying cultural politics of difference are made evident by the state's suppression of contrasting forms of kinship and marriage and of divergent claims of sovereignty. Thus, Cannell (chapter 9) shows how the US government simultaneously suppressed Mormon aspirations to secure rights to plural marriage and to religious sovereignty in the Utah territory. Shever (chapter 4) elucidates how the Argentine state's suppression of Native people centrally involved its support of particular forms of family (marital, nuclear, settled, with particular gender configurations) in its attempts to colonize and "civilize" the Patagonian frontier. And Bodenhorn (chapter 6) describes American colonial efforts to stigmatize and actively suppress certain indigenous forms of relatedness that were considered "morally suspect"—including open and extended families created through acts of labor and nurturance and correspondingly high rates of fosterage and adoption—at the same time that Americans suppressed indigenous forms of sovereignty (for parallel cases in Hawaii, Guam, and Native North America, see Modell 1998; Monnig 2008; Schachter 2008; Ungar 1977). In the state's attempt to deal with the "native problem," children from Native Alaskan families were resettled far from home in order to combat tuberculosis (in distant sanatoriums), to foster Western, Christian values (in distant missionary and boarding schools), and to implement assimilation into the dominant culture (through nonnative adoptions in distant places). Ultimately, Bodenhorn argues, the intention was not simply to deal with "morally suspect" forms of kinship and relatedness but also, and in parallel, to "breed out" nativeness altogether (a goal that would inevitably lead to the eradication of claims to sovereignty and separate nationhood). Similarly, Judith Schachter (2008) and Laurel Monnig (2008) show us that in Hawaii and Guam, respectively, precisely those forms of kinship and relatedness that were suppressed in the colonial order have been revalorized as the sign of new sovereignty movements, becoming the means for the restoration of indigenous cultural integrity and for alternative visions of the relation between kinship and sovereignty (McKinnon 2008).

If one can assume that all nation-states have some kinship (and religious) correlates, then the operative questions become when and how models based on different forms of kinship and marriage (or on the individual) are mobilized and made visible and when and how they are erased and made invisible. What we are interested in here is the politics of their different valuation and of their different visibility. Why and when are some kinship or religious configurations made evident as an example of backward primordialism and tribalism, and why and when are others made to stand for progressive secular democracy (see McKinnon, chapter 2, this volume)?

Third, Michael Lambek (chapter 10, this volume) makes a larger argument about the relationship between kinship (and religion) and the state. He suggests that in so-called modern societies, the state asserts the right to define, control, legitimate, and authorize acts of kinship and the making of new persons and kinship relations. But he queries the extent of this state control and its implications for the "encapsulation" and privatization of kinship presumed in the metanarratives of modernity. Powerfully, Lambek suggests that this encapsulation of kinship by the state does not result in the separation of kinship and state into discrete domains. On the contrary, "kinship is not separate, because it is embedded in the fundamental actions of the state, and it is not subordinate, because it is part and parcel of what the state is and means. The state is constituted in and through such acts as making citizens, providing birth and death certificates, registering property, taxing households, and, more generally, producing and authorizing the means by which people are related to one another as parents, offspring, spouses, siblings, and the like" (Lambek, chapter 10, this volume; see also Carsten 2007; Mody 2008). Although the state and kinship are intertwined and marked by the state's efforts to establish bureaucratic clarity, exclusivity, singularity, and the referential identity of persons and relations, Lambek argues, the nature of kinship inevitably exceeds the grasp of the secular state. On the one hand, the state is almost never the only agent capable of authorizing and legitimizing kinship relations; religious and other cultural agents and agencies retain powers to do so, and they operate with goals and values that contrast with those of the state bureaucracy. On the other hand, kinship itself, Lambek contends, is immodern in the excesses of its very nature—which are evident in the superfluity of who can count as kin, in kinship's "surfeit of meaning, feeling, and presence," and in its immoderate demands for care and love.

In different ways, Bodenhorn (chapter 6, this volume) also questions the relationship between kinship and the state. First, she suggests that "the state" is not singular but rather multileveled. In Alaska, for instance, the federal, state, regional, municipal, and tribal governments often operate with quite distinct laws and customary understandings, practices, and goals—which at times are at odds with one another.[4] Furthermore, she is concerned to broaden our historical and ethnographic appreciation of the multiplicity of social boundaries—racial, ethnic, religious, territorial, cultural—that people negotiate within, between, and beyond those imposed by the nation-state. And she points to the ways in which marriage, in particular, is inherently an institution that effects transboundary crossings at these multiple levels. Indeed, marriage and kin ties are among the few legal ways of penetrating restrictive immigration policies and crossing borders, and they are everywhere mobilized to this end (Constable 2005; Freeman 2005, 2011).[5]

It is evident that the narratives of modernity—which presuppose the temporal and structural transcendence of the nation-state over kin-based social formations—do not do justice to the interpenetration of kinship in the political units of contemporary societies. In revisiting the ideologies of the nation-state, we find kinship and marriage central to the conceptualizations and practices of this quintessentially "modern" institution, even in its most individualistic forms. In reexamining the ways in which contrastive forms of kinship and marriage articulate different claims to sovereignty, we reveal how they have articulated the dynamics of colonial subordinations and postcolonial contestations. And in reconsidering the entanglements of kinship and the state, we understand how critically intertwined and inseparable they are, even as kinship in its immodernity perpetually exceeds the constrictions of the state.

KINSHIP, RELIGION, AND THE "SECULAR"

We began by discussing a range of models that claim that modernity is defined by a move from status to contract—from social organizations structured by kinship to those dominated by the state and by rationalized economic and legal processes. One central contribution of this volume is to bring these claims into conversation with a key paradigm that identifies the modern by its relationship with religion rather than with kinship. Many forms of secularization theory—or, more recently, framings of the secular—have proposed that the modern state is characterized by its annexation of functions previously belonging to formal religion. One strand of secularization theory claims that as these functions are annexed, the power of religious experience also wanes and religious indifference becomes a universal feature of modernity (e.g., Bruce 2002). Other writers have taken divergent positions, and the literature is extensive (see Cannell 2010; Martin 2005). The most teleological versions of secularization theory have subsequently been rejected. José Casanova (1994) famously declared that such theories were a myth, and he reexamined changes in the public role of European and American religion without assuming a necessary link between these and religious indifference. Charles Taylor (2007) focused instead on the phenomenology of the "secular" and how it was historically constructed.

Narratives of modernity and modernization—whether centered on kinship or on religion—have been understood sometimes as empirical claims about changes in institutions and sometimes as descriptions of changing ideologies. Both accounts of modernity have been articulated not only by academic social theorists but also by actors in the larger social world. Thus, whether or not we believe them to be truthful descriptions of social processes, they come to have an "ethnographic reality" of their own. They become articles of faith to many people in contemporary society and therefore a basis upon which people may act (Cannell 2011).

Despite deep connections, the kinship-to-contract and the secularization models have often been discussed in isolation from each other and by different academic constituencies. Debates about secularization have been led by political scientists, sociologists, and philosophers, among others for whom the language of kinship is not an everyday tool (Cannell 2010). It may seem unremarkable, therefore, that kinship does not figure in the important accounts of secularization given by Casanova (1994) or Taylor (2007), for instance. Yet, where these discussions come closest, as in Casanova's work, we see a reaching for the terminology of the "family," the "private," and the "domestic" (Casanova 1994:41–43). It almost seems as if, in concentrating on the problem of supposed secularization in modernity, many writers have let the parallel claim about kinship—including its attenuation and its separation from the domains of politics and economics—pass under their guard.

In this collection, several authors explicitly ask what happens when kinship—which, following Collier and Yanagisako (1987), may be understood in terms of its particular conceptual potentials for evoking contexts of connectedness between different aspects of social action and formation—is put back into play in the debates about religion and secularity in the contemporary world. We ask this question at the level of empirical institutional changes. We also ask it in relation to modernization myths: how are kinship and religion said to be related to each other, for example, as competing stories are told?

Certain versions of "domaining" already discussed in this introduction link kinship and religion as two subordinated domains in a world where economic and other material, causative dynamics are supposed to prevail. As Lambek (chapter 10, this volume) points out, this connection is reinforced to the extent that kinship has often been identified with ritual or religious acts (marriage, the naming of children), which are understood to create and sustain kin relations. Cannell (chapter 9, this volume) considers the case of American Latter-day Saints, whose present-day kinship subverts ordinary expectations in ways rooted in their history. Nineteenth-century Mormonism asserted the religious value of kinship through explicit teachings on the divine value of plural marriage (Gordon 2002). For the developing US federal state and its legal system, the specter of Mormon theocracy became a key target and a persistently haunting threat. Both religion and kinship, when not defined and placed exactly as the state would have them, become subversively charged with "primitive" associations, and the alliance of the two all the more so.

However, in other strands of modernization stories, kinship and religion may be treated as different in kind. As Cannell (chapter 9, this volume) argues, when kinship is considered within the domain of "science"—for instance, with a focus on reproduction, heredity, and DNA—the idea of its material reality is often privileged, and religion may be contrastively viewed as having no ultimate material basis and therefore being less real. Janet Carsten's account of laboratory blood work in Malaysia (chapter 5), Danilyn Rutherford's description of the polemical linkage of contemporary US kinship discourse to both economics and the environment (chapter 11), and Gillian Feeley-Harnik's recuperation of the "science" of genealogy in the mid-nineteenth-century eastern seaboard (chapter 8) trace different attempts to anchor kinship in what is "scientific," that is, truth understood as ultimately material. Each also attests to the impossibility of achieving this fixed meaning for kinship, which continuously overspills the boundaries set for it. Although this is well recognized in the context of the fluidity of the social meanings of kinship (e.g., Edwards 2000; Franklin and McKinnon 2001b; Strathern 1988; Weston 1991), the chapters in this volume each suggest ways in which kinship also exceeds the implicitly secular definitions that have been set for it in social theory and in social action (Cannell, chapter 9). In bringing secularization and kinship-to-contract narratives of modernity together, therefore, *Vital Relations* permits each to illuminate the limitations of the other.

Indeed, in relation to Yanagisako and Delaney's observation (1995:12) noted above, about the taboo against reading across scientific and theological contexts of kinship, several chapters in this volume illustrate the inevitability of violating that taboo, even if the breach is temporary, muted, or denied. Rutherford's reading (chapter 11) of Cormac McCarthy's endtimes novel, *The Road*, as a text about kinship and futurity brings out such taboo-breaking moments, in which the notion of divinity is threatened with the same collapse as the notion of genealogical continuity and the survival of each inheres in the other. In *The Road*, Rutherford suggests, the "man's orientation to his son verges—but only verges—on the religious. He knew only that the child was his warrant. He said: 'If he is not the word of God, God never spoke'" (McCarthy 2006:6). The prospect of world destruction—like the contemplation of world creation (Feeley-Harnik 2001a)—brings religion and kinship into intense contiguity, even in contemporary American settings, where each is otherwise supposed to reside within a clearly demarcated ("secularized") space.

Talal Asad's *Formations of the Secular* (2003) offers one of the most influential accounts of the secular constitution of modern society. Lambek (chapter 10, this volume) notes that Asad offers acute insights into "the retraction, objectification, and subsumption of religion by the state"—especially, perhaps, into its objectification. For Asad, it is crucial to understand the limits of secular liberalism and the forms of human experience that are cast as antithetical to its political projects. Certain conceptions and self-conceptions of human "nature"—particularly those that value "passionate agency," including, in some cases, the ascetic and religious valuation of physical pain—are excluded from the dominant national and international forms of recognition, including human rights law. Religious traditions that do not reproduce the values of the secular nation-state are deemed "irrational" and are cast (once again) as primitive forms to be superseded by the modern. Contemporary forms of governance are predicated on a "secular ethics," which sidesteps the potential claims of religion on the state, and other evaluations of the "ethical" (or the religious) are to be tolerated only where these are underwritten by the state as legitimate "private" arenas.

Asad devotes the final chapter of *Formations of the Secular* to changes in the regulation of Egyptian marriage, to the shift away from polygamy, and to the gradual encompassment of *shari'a* courts and principles by state law. For Asad, it is inadequate to see these changes in terms of European imperial agency pitted against local resistance or accommodation or even in terms of the expansion of the Egyptian state: "There was more at work here than a single project of increasing state power. There was also the question of how liberal governance (political, moral, and theological) was to be secured during the different phases of state building" (Asad 2003:218). Asad is concerned with how specific forms of experience (such as companionate marriage) came to be desirable or imaginable as a social goal, creating the conditions under which the secular demarcation of private from public, by law, would take root. He contrasts these secular demarcations (a form of what we have been discussing as "domains") with an ethical and legal order associated with Islamic "traditional discipline," in which "the moral subject is not concerned with state law as an external authority. It presupposes that the capability for virtuous conduct and the sensibilities on which that capability draws are acquired by the individual through tradition-guided practices" (250). These practices, which Asad also sometimes refers to as "habitus," are at odds with "the liberal concept of the right to self-invention" (ibid.).

The historical specificity of Western concepts of agency is a point well taken from both Asad and Foucault. Put simply, historical change is multifarious and more than the sum of any personified intentions. As Lambek (chapter 10, this volume) suggests, "there is no critique of the place of kinship in narratives of modernity that could be completely objective." Much depends on which aspects of the problem a particular analyst seeks to illuminate. Asad's "secular ethics" and Saba Mahmood's "secular religion" (2006:341) have shed much light on progressivist myths, especially in relation to European attitudes toward Islam. One could, however, argue that Asad's Foucauldian approach also casts other areas into shadow. In drawing on a contrast between historical Islamic—or, occasionally, European early medieval (Asad 1993:123)—bodily traditions and the secular law–ethics split, Asad risks creating an impression of oversimplification. Veena Das (2006) has remarked that there are more views of "human nature" to be found in the world than those that might be labeled either the Islamic traditional view or the Western liberal Enlightenment view. Indeed, India offers one rich source of alternatives, as Bear (chapter 7, this volume) writing on Hindu Kolkata also observes. Further, Asad's dichotomies sometimes skirt a reductive view of European and American experiences as primarily defined—from the early nineteenth century on—by their supposed secularity, which would appear to suggest that contemporary Western experience does not partake of embodied ethical meaning. Asad (2003:87–89) does offer one concrete counter-example of embodied ethical meaning, in citing Pamela Klassen's (2001) description of the meaning found in childbirth by home-birthing women in North America, but he does not develop this line of inquiry.

Various chapters in *Vital Relations* contribute to the problematics of "secular kinship" in several ways. Lambek (chapter 10) builds on Asad's insights but seeks to enlarge them by thinking more explicitly about kinship as such and what makes it more than a subdivision of the secular state's constitution. Lambek distinctively views kinship as a series of "performative acts" and the histories they create. Kinship terms themselves are a form of kinship act because they have the quality of invoking a relationship and implying further webs of relatedness beyond the speaker and the person named. Although fully accepting that objectified categories of law, religion, kinship, and so forth, are mutually constitutive in contemporary life, Lambek gives a more dynamic and less occluded place to kinship. He suggests that we can observe a particular freighting of meaning and value onto kinship, as onto religion, in modern secular constitutions. Kinship, Lambek argues, becomes a "romanticized object," using Hannah Arendt's (1958b) term, loaded with inexhaustible, multiple significances. However, for Lambek, the signifying potential of kinship is not simply derived from its heightened role in modern sensibilities; in agreement with other contributors, he suggests that too much has been made of the division between the place of kinship in "traditional" and "modern" contexts. For Lambek, Foucault's characterization of governance through "biopower" as a modern hallmark seems to miss the fact that traditional states, too, have attempted to rule through intervention in the reproductive and kinship lives of their subjects, albeit with different technologies of knowledge. Furthermore, Lambek argues that kinship always has profound utopian and dystopian potentials of signification in any polity or culture. Thus, for him, kinship is both immoderate and "immodern"; it always has multiple and distinctive powers to signify, and, although historical variation is wide-ranging and crucial, these powers do not ultimately originate from one particular historical order of knowledge or another.

Gillian Feeley-Harnik's work (chapter 8) articulates an invitation to provincialize the historical and geographical heartland of status-to-contract theory as one way to establish a broader theoretical foundation for the study of kinship and capitalism. One of the many ways to read her richly wrought account is as a counterpart to Lambek's chapter in rethinking "secular kinship." Her investigation proceeds, first, from a meticulous examination of the historical specificities of thought and action about family at the time of Lewis Henry Morgan and his brother, the amateur genealogist Nathaniel Morgan. Like the battle over Mormon polygamy discussed by Cannell (chapter 9, this volume), developments in the eastern United States in the mid-nineteenth century were heavily influenced by the British withdrawal from the slave trade and, later, by US abolitionism. For Feeley-Harnik, one fundamental element in American kinship practices during this period was the energy invested in making clear one's status as a free person (and not a freed person). At the same time, shifts in political economy were prompting new patterns of investment and the development of urban property among the middle class, who thought of themselves as highly respectable but self-made, having fortunes based on success in gentlemanly trade and scientifically informed, "improved" agriculture. At stake was the creation of a particular sense of persons as made through their own and their family's merit, work, and skill—a model tacitly opposed to both "aristocrat" and "slave." It is out of this highly specific historical and geographic milieu that the idea of the move "from status to contract" as a universal marker of progress can be seen to emerge.

Like other contributors to this volume, Feeley-Harnik also calls on comparisons with societies outside the modern West to illuminate what kinship can be and do.[6] Her familiarity with Malagasy kinship and secondary funerals leads her to recognize the development of nineteenth-century American genealogy—and associated changes in the organization of cemeteries—as a change in the way that the living make ancestors, underwriting the assertion of a certain reading of personhood. A series of erasures is involved: the new urban poor are excluded from the communities of both the living and the dead; the elimination of Native American communities is both effected and symbolized by the mass destruction of forests and their replacement by commemorative groves in the parkland cemeteries of rich white Americans. Class formation proceeds through both the making and the breaking of kinship ties—through both "kinning" and violent "dekinning."[7] This kind of comparative "provincialization" characteristic of anthropology is sometimes evoked by Asad (2003:17). However, it seems in tension with a Foucauldian view of historical change, in which it would be difficult to hold steady any term or category across periods or cultures in order to make a meaningful comparison. "Immodern" kinship is not, in this sense, a Foucauldian concept.

Weber defined modernity, in part, by the pervasive experience of disenchantment, by which he meant that modern people would increasingly feel that the world was fractured. He himself was divided between vitally important but incompatible value spheres, including, but not limited to, an incompatibility between "science" and "religion" (Kippenberg 2005; Weber 1946).[8] In Feeley-Harnik's account of the world of the Morgans (as also in Cannell's and McKinnon's chapters), we see aspects of a particular nineteenth-century moment in which this incompatibility was increasingly being felt, without yet having the status of the obvious. Thus, Lewis Henry Morgan's publisher's refusal to include Morgan's memorial to his dead daughters in a "scientific" work is balanced against Nathaniel Morgan's view that genealogy itself is a science and compatible with conventional Christianity. This moment, and the social science thinking it engendered, has a continued legacy both in contemporary scientific discourse on kinship as materially determined and in the resurgence of forms of ethical kinship thinking that have, as Lambek notes, a countersecularist tendency.

We have already observed that the modern preoccupation with what Latour has called "purification" is a doomed endeavor. Although we may believe that religion and science are incompatible—indeed, Weber argued that it may be the central fate of our time to suffer under and wrestle with that conviction—we cannot, in practice, keep them separate as we live our lives. It is unclear, therefore, whether kinship can ever be wholly secular even in the contemporary West, and we know that it is not so in other times and places. The tensions and multiple meanings of kinship experience at key moments in the formation of modern American sensibilities of kinship are instructive. They counterbalance the tendency—exemplified in the work of Asad—to cast Western spheres of action as "already" secular with a vivid sense of the lived contradictions and inherent incompleteness of secular experience. For Weber (1946), the possibility of joining up the different orders of value in modern life was a lost hope, belonging to the historical past; courage and clear-sightedness in the face of this existential dilemma—and the avoidance of self-deception—were what he mainly urged on himself and, at least publicly, on others. Nevertheless, Cannell (chapter 9, this volume) notes that even Weber sometimes perceived a utopian potential of kinship in modern times. As Robert Bellah (1997) has shown, Weber sometimes argued that altruistic fellow-feeling in salvationist religions was a generalization of kinship sentiment; Weber (1978b, 1998) also wrote as though kinship is not, itself, subject to rigid objectification (domaining) in modernity, unlike erotic love, which is. Whether or not one wishes to use Weber's categories, it remains possible to consider, as Cannell suggests, that in a "secular age," people may place in "kinship" discourses and practices a range of meanings that defy and exceed neat categorization. Thus, if Pamela Klassen's (2001) ethnography of home-birthing hints at an "unsecular" register in contemporary American kinship, then Cannell and the chapters in this volume by Feeley-Harnik, Lambek, Bear, and Rutherford indicate that there may be a much wider range of practices and contexts in which this is the case. Home-birthing is, in multiple ways, coded as a "private" sphere of action, as Asad's conception of the limits of secular ethics would predict. But the case of American Mormonism discussed by Cannell points to the fact that elements of the more public, historical refusals of the "secular constitution" persist into twenty-first-century life also.

Finally, among the chapters that converge on the theme of the secular, Bear's account (chapter 7) of the productive life of Indian shipyard workers addresses what she calls "theologies of materiality." In tune with Veena Das's observation (2006) that there are more than two understandings of human nature in the world, Bear explores the construction of ships as an act of labor inseparable from the ethics of kinship and divinity, which Bengali workers understand to power it. For Bear, in this context, labor retains an ethical dimension through its longer-term interpolations with social relations, especially the relations of kinship, which are partly made and remade through exchanges with the Hindu gods. Thus, in India, where the history of the secular is widely divergent from Western concepts of the same (Cannell 2010), kinship appears to be "secular" neither in a Western nor yet in an Indian sense of the term.

Myths of modernity and modernization continue to resurface in unexpected places. In this introduction and in the chapters by Cannell, Lambek, and Bear, it is suggested that there is a crypto-progressivism in the approaches taken by Foucault, among other theorists. Despite his radical skepticism about the advances made by liberal modernity, Foucault, like many other writers, tacitly assumes that kinship has no place in modern constitutions, being instead replaced by "biopower," which operates on the capacity of its citizens for physical reproductive, rather than for social and imaginative, life. This thought has been taken up by many constituencies, including scholars writing on the important issues of "biocitizenship" (e.g., Novas and Rose 2000). But as Bear (2007a; see also Cannell 2011) has demonstrated elsewhere, genealogy is not, as Foucault would have it, just a metaphor, but a lived reality. It is now widely accepted that religion has not simply drained away in modernity; it may have taken different forms. We suggest that it may soon seem as obvious to draw attention to the continued life of kinship in the vital relations of modernity.

CONCLUSION: THE VITALITY OF KINSHIP RELATIONS

As we wrote the final paragraphs of this introduction, one episode in a major scandal was unfolding in the United Kingdom. Rupert Murdoch and his vast international company, News Corporation, were in trouble with the British Parliament and police over allegations of phone hacking, corruption, obstruction of the course of justice, and attempts to intimidate members of Parliament. On the eve of being granted permission to increase his share in the biggest British pay-TV company, BSkyB, from 40 to 100 percent, Murdoch saw a severe check to his ambitions. He, his son, and his lieutenant were summoned to appear before a Select Committee of the British House of Commons, and public inquiries and criminal investigations were under way. The scandal held the potential to spread to the United States, where Murdoch owns Fox News, among other major media interests.

One of the key debates was over the relationship between the possibility of large-scale corruption in a global company of this stature and the "clan" organization of Murdoch's business. Also under fire with Rupert Murdoch were both his youngest son, James Murdoch (chair of BSkyB), and Rebekah Brooks (former CEO of News International), who—because of the closeness of her relationship to Rupert Murdoch—has regularly been described as being "like a daughter" to him. Other major shareholders in BSkyB have complained of feeling "shut out" by the inner core of the family.

The central issues of the scandal are related to the structure of global capital and to the ability of vast monopolies to dominate national media and, allegedly, to direct decisions of national governments that are otherwise meant to be answerable to their electorate. These issues are, in fact, similar to concerns that have been raised in relation to the dominant power of international finance and speculative banking and its effect on the economic crises of both the United States and Europe in the 2000s.

Whatever the sequel to the Murdoch drama, this moment alone is surely enough to remind us of the fallacy of assuming that kinship—either literal or figurative—is a spent force in the contemporary world. Here, we see deeply entwined relations between kinship, economics, and politics that have fueled both the rise and, potentially, the downfall of one of the most powerful corporations in the world (if not also its allied government in Britain). Here, we observe the tensions between claims of status and contract, kinship and meritocracy, which have not been resolved, as predicted, under the conditions of modernity. And here, we witness the critique of a family's corporate organization as nepotism in an attempt to assert a properly modern separation between kinship, economics, and politics—as if the corruption derived from their kinship alone and not from the structures of capital and governance.

Precisely these kinds of compelling entanglements are what we explore in this volume and what motivate us to question deeply the narratives of modernity that have been so central to our scholarly and popular cultural understandings of the world for so long. Indeed, the goal of this book is to consider ways of thinking about kinship in contemporary societies that escape the constraints of the evolutionary imperatives and domaining practices that have structured our ideas of the modern and to reach toward more complex and nuanced accounts that reveal the vitality of kinship in contemporary social life.

Acknowledgments

We are deeply grateful for the generous support and exquisite hospitality of the School for Advanced Research, which made possible the week-long advanced seminar "The Difference Kinship Makes: Rethinking the Ideologies of Modernity" (March 20–26, 2010), on which this volume is based. SAR's staff and facilities created an atmosphere that was gracious and nourishing (both literally and figuratively) of our intellectual project. We are also greatly appreciative of the intense intellectual energy, engagement, and camaraderie that the participants brought to the discussions of one another's work and to the project as a whole, throughout the week of the seminar and long thereafter. This is the best of what we all hope for in the work of intellectual exchange. We dedicate this volume to Olivia Harris, whose presence in our lives is profoundly missed, as it was, indeed, during our week in Santa Fe.

Notes

1. For a review of seven aspects of institutional change relevant to an understanding of the transition to modernity, see Reed and Adams 2011; for an extensive account of the history and future prospects of historical sociology and its analysis of modernity, see Adams, Clemens, and Orloff 2005.

2. Interestingly, Mauss (unlike Durkheim or Weber) rarely seems to be invoked by colleagues working in sociology or historical sociology. Perhaps this is because they have been given the impression that his work is less relevant because it appears not to speak directly about Western developments.

3. Work on transnationalism and globalization has attended to the ways in which the bounded integrity of core units of so-called modern society—the nation, the corporation—have been called into question by the movements and migrations of people,

capital, and culture (e.g., Appadurai 1996; Basch, Schiller, and Blanc 1994; Schiller, Basch, and Blanc-Szanton 1992). This work has rarely called into question either the larger metanarrative of modernity or its presupposition about the separation between kinship and economic processes. However, a few anthropological studies have theorized the ways in which kinship organizes transnational economic ventures (see, for instance, Ho 2006; Ong 1999; Ong and Nonini 1997; Oxfeld 1993; Ratanapruck 2008).

4. Viewing sovereignty from the margins of the state, Thomas Blom Hansen and Finn Stepputat have pointed out that a number of figures and networks of "informal sovereignty"—whether these are of chiefs, big men, strong men, mafia, masons, warlords, gangs, traitors, terrorists, brigands, bandits, pirates, outlaws, or elite families—"operate within, beside, or against formally sovereign states" (2006:306; see Heyman 1999). As David Nugent (1999) shows for Peru, the illegal networks of kin and patronage that constitute "shadow states" can quickly become the legal structures of the state. No one has yet theorized more generally the extent to which such figures and groups are organized in configurations of kinship, such as families, brotherhoods, or fraternities.

5. Nicole Constable's edited volume, *Cross-Border Marriages* (2005; see also Freeman 2005, 2011), explores the paradoxes of gender, class, and nation in the proliferation of transnational "hypergamous" marriages. Caren Freeman (2011) paints a striking portrait of the brisk market in the creation and documentation of fake kinship ties that help move ethnic Koreans out of the cold winters of Harbin, China, into the warmer economic climes of South Korea. The worldwide manufacture of fake kinship ties is a testimony to the force of kinship in transnational movements and in claims to citizenship in the current global political economy.

6. From among the chapters in this volume, we think, in particular, of Rutherford's juxtaposition of US politics with Melanesia (chapter 11) and Yanagisako's examination of Italian family firms in China (chapter 3).

7. Signe Howell (2006) coined the terms "kinning" and "dekinning," which she used in her discussion of transnational adoptions. By kinning, she means "the process by which…a previously unconnected person…is brought into a significant and permanent relationship with a group of people that is expressed in a kin idiom" (63), and dekinning refers to the opposite process (9).

8. Weber did not, of course, mean, as is sometimes said, that no belief in magic or religion was possible in the modern world (although sincere belief in traditional religion might be difficult).

2

Kinship within and beyond the "Movement of Progressive Societies"

Susan McKinnon

> Every anthropological investigation of kinship sets out from one variant or another of the idea that kinship is somehow more important to the working of simple societies than of complex ones, and that in the course of their development complex societies have substituted something else for kinship. If Maine was not the first to come up with the idea, he gave it its motto. "From status to contract" might well adorn the family crest of anthropology.
>
> —*Thomas R. Trautmann,* Lewis Henry Morgan and the Invention of Kinship

On September 28, 2003, John Tierney published an article in the *New York Times* entitled "Iraq's Family Bonds Complicate U.S. Efforts." Tierney painted a portrait of two worlds sharply distinguished by their forms of kinship and marriage and the supposed consequences of these differences for nation-building and modernization. He saw Iraq as a place dominated by patriarchal extended families, clans, and tribes—a place where marriages were arranged and "nearly half of marriages were between first or second cousins" (Tierney 2003). By contrast, he saw the United States as a place dominated by nuclear families, gender equality, "outbreeding," and autonomous individuals who were free to choose their marriage partners—the latter being, inevitably, nonkin.

Tierney followed the lead of several conservative commentators, such as Stanley Kurtz (2002) and Steve Sailer (2003), who had pointed to cousin marriage and the extended family structure as the most important factors explaining Iraqi resistance to US nation-building. According to their analysis, people who live in kin-based societies and "inbreed" are inherently prone to clannishness, feuding, and fighting, not to mention cronyism, nepotism, corruption, and even terrorism (Kurtz 2007).[1] Supposedly incapable of autonomous individual agency, such people are also incapable of economic modernization and favor "authoritarian government dominated by kin, cronies and religious leaders" (Tierney 2003). "Outbred people"—who eschew cousin marriage and have been freed from the ties of clan and tribe—are presumed capable of the unity, patriotism, and cooperation necessary for the formation of a modern nation-state (ibid.). As autonomous individuals, they naturally embrace a "free" market economy and shun authoritarian government dominated by kin, cronies, and religious leaders.

I call attention to this representation—appearing as it did in the context of US neocolonial nation-building efforts in Iraq and elsewhere—because it perfectly reproduces the significations of kinship in the narratives of social development and modernization that have dominated Euro American popular and academic discourse for the past 150 years and indicates kinship's continuing cultural salience in debates both within the academy and beyond.

The particular landscape of kinship that I explore in this chapter is envisioned through accounts of the evolution of "civilization" and the development of "modern" society that feature, as a primary trope, the subordination and transcendence of kinship. That is, some social relations, specifically those of kinship, are constituted as more "natural," whereas others, notably those of politics and economics, are presumed to be the result of cultural improvements on nature and therefore to be transcendent of and superior to kinship. The conditions for modernity are conceptualized in terms of the separation and subordination of kin-based regimes and their characterization as prior, more primitive, and more deeply primordial. This twofold division is, in fact, doubly articulated: comparatively, it marks the difference between kin-based societies and states; within more "advanced" societies, it distinguishes the domestic domain from the domains of politics and economics. I argue that what we mean by "kinship"—in the social sciences as much as in the cultural discourses of Euro American societies—is given form and content by this particular conceptual framework and, inversely, that this conceptual framework is articulated by reference to kinship and its transcendence.

This configuration and placement of kinship emerged as a precipitate of a contrastive logic that was rooted in earlier narratives but brought to full florescence in the second half of the nineteenth century as the central organizing trope of evolutionary theory. Whether Maine's "status" became the ground to the figure of "contract," or Morgan's "societas" revealed the particular shape of "civitas," or Tönnies's *Gemeinschaft* formed the counter to

Gesellschaft, a set of cultural distinctions remained central to the organization of the developmental trajectory imagined by social theorists: kinship versus territory/state; group versus individual; status versus contract; communal versus private property; religious ceremony versus legal and secular rationalization. Yet, with the demise of nineteenth-century evolutionary theory and the rise of twentieth-century functionalist, structuralist, and other theoretical paradigms, these distinctions were not abandoned; rather, they were transferred from evolutionary to typological frameworks with remarkable conceptual consistency.

My argument about the place of kinship in these narratives unfolds in three parts. In the first, I trace the persistence of this contrastive logic through a set of texts that have been central to the history not only of kinship studies in anthropology but also of social theory more generally. This is familiar terrain, but I revisit it with an eye to comprehending how kinship becomes a prime signifier in these narratives and how different affinities and alignments are established between kinship, religion, politics, and economics. In the process, I ask what the consequences of these alignments are for our understanding of what counts as kinship and where kinship can be counted. In the second part, I consider the stigmatization of kin marriages in the late nineteenth- and early twentieth-century United States as an example of one of the mechanisms that has served to establish the truth value of the modernist presupposition of the separation of kinship from politics and economics. Finally, in the third part, I argue that the force of this persistent dichotomous rendering has produced models of "modern" politics and economics that have rendered invisible the meanings, functions, and structural force of kinship in these processes. As anthropologists have turned their attention to "modern" societies and global phenomena, they have unquestioningly accepted the assumptions about the place of kinship embedded in these models. This chapter challenges what Shils (1970) called the "tyranny" of this model and suggests that we build a different foundation for analyzing the workings of relatedness in the contemporary world.

THE TRANSCENDENCE AND SUBORDINATION OF KINSHIP

Maine's "Movement of Progressive Societies": From Status to Contract

Thomas Trautmann was right: "If Maine was not the first to come up with the idea, he gave it its motto. 'From status to contract'" (1987:180, 163; see also Pina Cabral 1989).[2] I argue that Henry Maine's account in *Ancient Law* (1970[1861])—which contains the essential blueprint for narratives of modernity, or what he called the "movement of progressive societies"—involves not so much the replacement as the de-encompassment of key elements (territorial contiguity, the individual, and contract) that were contained within the original kinship corporation of status-bound societies.

Maine envisioned territorial contiguity as initially encompassed by kinship, not simply subsequent to it.[3] Indeed, he saw the Roman family as an "artificial" unit founded precisely as an assemblage of members who were related by various criteria besides "blood," such as adoption, enslavement, marriage, and the absorption of displaced foreigners (Maine 1970[1861]:46, 59–60, 125–129; see also Coward 1983:22–23). Thus, whereas contiguity already existed as a de facto principle of organization, "kinship" was the encompassing conceptual framework for all relationships—whatever their origin or nature. A critical step toward "civilization" was taken when the "older theory" of social organization—based on this legal fiction of kinship—was, as Maine put it, "vanquished and dethroned" (1970[1861]:128) and supplanted by the new theory of territorial organization, which he deemed critical for the movement of progressive societies.

In tandem with the shift from kinship to contiguity or territory, Maine outlined the transition from the corporate kin group to the individual as the unit of society and from religious ceremony to legal contract as the dominant form of social relation. When Maine talks about "kinship," he is referring to agnation, which he defines quite explicitly: "The foundation of Agnation is not the marriage of Father and Mother, but the authority of the Father. All persons are Agnatically connected together who are under the same Paternal Power.... In truth, in the primitive view, Relationship is exactly limited by Patria Potestas. Where the Potestas begins, Kinship begins; and therefore adoptive relatives are among the kindred. Where the Potestas ends, Kinship ends; so that a son emancipated by his father loses all rights of Agnation" (1970[1861]:144).

The definition of kinship, therefore, resides not in *biological* relatedness but precisely in submission to the power of the father. Moreover, all rights of individual persons and property are encompassed—or, as Maine puts it, "swallowed up"—by the group and by the authority of the father (1970[1861]:133, 136, 177–178). Similarly, contract was encompassed by religious ceremony. Maine envisioned the possibility of contracts in ancient society, but they were between families, not individuals, and were "encumbered" by the formalities of ceremony (263, 302–303). Just as the (male) individual had to be liberated from the family group and the power of the father, so, too, the kernel of legal contract had to be liberated from the technicalities of religious ceremony (263, 269–271, 303–304, 307–308,

312, 327–328). Once broken away from the "external shell" of ceremony, the "nucleus" of the contract was free to be expressed in rational legal language (304).

These movements of de-encompassment create a narrative trajectory that ultimately separates and opposes kinship and territory, status and contract, families and individuals, religious ceremony and secular law. In the end, Maine constitutes kinship as a historically prior and more primordial social formation that is organized through relations between groups (not individuals), through the workings of paternal power (not individual equality), and through the form of religious ceremony (not legal contract). He simultaneously constitutes unfettered contracts and territory as later, transcendent, and progressive social formations that are organized by secular, legal, and market rationality rather than religious ceremony and by the rights and power of the individual rather than those of the corporate kin group or its patriarch. The momentum of Maine's "movement of progressive societies" is generated by the displacement, transcendence, and subordination of kinship as an organizing structure, after which the individual stands alone and free to contract for *himself* in the marketplace, unfettered by the kinship group, paternal authority, or religious ceremony. Kinship has no status, as it were, in the political economy of progressive societies, no place or dynamic worthy of consideration. It belongs to the past.

From Maine to Tönnies and Weber

It is worth sketching briefly here a line of theoretical elaboration that builds on Maine's distinction between status and contract, since the contrast between Gemeinschaft and Gesellschaft, which was developed by Ferdinand Tönnies and then Max Weber, became central to social scientific typologies and histories in the late nineteenth century and the twentieth. Among the many influences on Tönnies's thought, it is clear that his conceptualization of Gemeinschaft and Gesellschaft drew heavily on Maine, while extending it far beyond Maine's original formulation (Harris 2001:xxi ; Shils 1991).

In *Community and Civil Society*, Tönnies saw Gemeinschaft, or community, as "having real organic life": it was to be understood as a genuine, enduring "living organism" (2001[1887]:17, 19). As a holistic community, it was built, in the first instance, from the "primal unity of existence" (27) derived from the more natural, instinctual ties of kinship (in particular, maternal, spousal, and sibling bonds) (22). Although rooted in a "community of blood," Gemeinschaft developed to include a "community of place" (the relations of neighbors) and a "community of spirit," or shared work, belief, or religious worship (the relations of friends, fellows, or comrades (27–28). Gemeinschaft is characterized (31–34) by shared language and customs, memory and history, communal ownership, mutually binding sentiment, fellow feeling, and consensus and by the hierarchical relations of authority (patriarchy, etc.) and reciprocal services that emanate from primordial divisions of functions based on sex, reproduction, and physical strength (Harris 2001:xix). A particular form of human will—natural, organic, essential will, or *Wesenwille*—defines relations of Gemeinschaft, or community (Tönnies 2001[1887]:95). Wesenwille is embedded in physical, material being: "It is the psychological equivalent of the human body; it is the unifying principle of life, conceived of as the pattern of material reality to which thinking itself belongs" (95). Inherited and inherent, it entails "natural talents or tendencies [that] become practical capabilities" (96, 98). More "'natural,' spontaneous and unreflecting," Wesenwille "fostered development of the human 'self' (a mode of identity wherein human 'subjects' were in harmony with their habitats and closely identified with, rather than differentiated from, other human beings)" (Harris 2001:xvii).

By contrast, Tönnies saw Gesellschaft, or civil society, as "a purely mechanical construction": it was to be understood as a "transient and superficial thing," a "mechanical aggregate and artefact" (2001[1887]:17, 19). Gesellschaft is composed of a multitude of individuals who, whatever interactions they may have, remain detached from and independent of one another (63–64). The "common good" "*can* only exist by means of a *fiction*," is constituted in the form of contract and market exchanges, and "lasts as long as the time taken for the 'transaction'" (53). Another form of human will—calculating, arbitrary, abstract will, rational choice, or *Kürwille*—defines the self-interested and profit-oriented relations of Gesellschaft, or society. Kürwille fostered the "development of the human 'person' (whereby human 'subjects' created or invented their own identities, were abstracted and estranged from their natural selves, and perceived other people and the external world as mere things or 'objects'" (Harris 2001:xvii).

Harris notes that there is a tension between three different themes or aims that are central to Tönnies's *Community and Civil Society*: "At the most obvious level the work aimed to provide a systematic, atemporal framework for analysis of the major building-blocks of any human society.... At a second more tentative level, and one that was to generate much misinterpretation, the study sketched out a theory of general historical change.... And at a third, less conspicuous...level, it was an essay in the logic of the social and moral sciences, designed to reconcile the competing theories of perception and epistemology that had riven European philosophy since the early seventeenth century" (2001:xv–xvi). This tension between a typological analytical framework and a theory of social evolution or historical transformation has characterized most social theories since the demise of nineteenth-century evolutionary theory. On the one hand, a set of ideal types—primordial kin groups versus individuals; hierarchy versus equality; more natural and embedded social relations versus more abstract and detached relations; historical customs and religious ceremonies versus rational market contracts and calculations—was meant to define a range of differential forms of social relations, not a temporal sequence. On the other hand, as part of efforts to understand distinctive social formations and the historical transformations that linked them, they stood in place of, and presupposed, an actual analysis of historical change. It is often difficult to disentangle the two.

Just as Tönnies drew upon and greatly elaborated Maine's core contrast between status and contract, Shils (1991:161–164) argues, Weber drew upon and significantly expanded Tönnies's conceptualization of the contrast between Gemeinschaft and Gesellschaft. "The fundamental contrast between, on the one hand, the self-sufficient household and the moneyless economy—the economy of the *Gemeinschaft*—and, on the other, the extensive money economy oriented towards the urban translocal, national and world economies—*Gesellschaft*—is certainly a central feature of Weber's work" (Shils 1991:162). In numerous places, Weber outlines a contrast between fundamentally different types of social order that are distinguished by their dominant form of social relations, their forms of social action, and their constitution of authority. Politically, these social orders are defined by a contrast between those societies based in personal relations of kinship, clanship, caste, and clientship and founded on the authority and sanctity of tradition—in particular, religion, magic, and ritual—and those societies based on more abstract, rational, legal relations of citizenship in the state and founded on the authority of a rational, legal, and bureaucratic administrative order, as well as on science and technology (Weber 1978a:217–228, 370–379; 2003[1927]:312–354; Shils 1991:162–163). The two types are distinguished by the contrast between social relations that are "communal" (*Vergemeinschaftung*) and are "based on a subjective feeling of the parties, whether affectual or traditional, that they belong together" (Weber 1978a:40) and social relations that are based on "associative action" (*Vergesellschaft*), which "rests on a rationally motivated adjustment of interests" (ibid.). In "the purest cases," these interests "are constituted in terms of (a) rational free market exchange...; (b) the pure voluntary association based on self interest...; [and] (c) the voluntary association of individuals motivated by an adherence to a set of common absolute values" (40–41; see Yanagisako, chapter 3, this volume).

Although these differentiated forms of social action were ideal types and, moreover, could be found in different configurations in most societies, it is also clear that, for Weber, there is a historical transformation that shifts the primary orientation of Western societies in particular.[4] Beginning with the great medieval business houses in Florence and elsewhere, a "significant, and *uniquely* Occidental, transformation of domestic authority and household" (Weber 1978a:378) initiated the separation of business from the family household. This separation played out both legally, in terms of obligations and responsibilities, and financially, in terms of accounting for assets and debts (379). And these economic separations are mirrored by those in the political realm, as bureaucratic offices and official functions, assets, and liabilities are separated from the private household and private property (ibid.). Here, we have the beginnings of an account of both the historical transformation of social forms and, within Western society, the functional differentiation of the public economic and political domains from the private domain of kinship and family. Although Weber's accounts of both the historical transformations and the functional differentiation of Western society are far more sophisticated and nuanced than his predecessors', they nevertheless remain structured by the same set of fundamental contrasts: personal relations of kinship versus more abstract and individual relations of state citizenship and market contract; the authority of traditional customs, religion, and rituals that support communal action versus rational legal structures that support self-interested utilitarian action, the free market, and the political administrative bureaucracy.

Lévi-Strauss's Comparative Typology of Marriage Systems

The tension between social typology and the historical account of social evolution that we have observed in the works of Tönnies and Weber is also evident in theoretical writings in anthropology. The shift from nineteenth-century evolutionary to twentieth-century typological frameworks, significant as it might have been, nevertheless did not involve a radical rethinking of the categorical distinctions that were the foundation of evolutionary narratives. These distinctions were—as both Meyer Fortes (1969:37) and Adam Kuper (1982, 1983, 1988) have noted—simply transposed to a comparative order, which retained an implicit temporal trajectory. Moreover, they have remained relatively consistent across a wide range of theoretical paradigms.

I begin with Claude Lévi-Strauss's alliance theory because the continuities of his paradigm with earlier models are more direct. Lévi-Strauss is best known, in kinship studies, for his monumental *Elementary Structures of Kinship* (1969[1949]). In this work, not only does he articulate his vision of the transition from nature to culture through the institution of reciprocity in the marital exchange of women, but he also masterfully outlines the distinctive structural consequences of different types of cousin marriage. Here, however, I am interested in his larger contrast between the elementary and complex structures of kinship.[5]

For Lévi-Strauss, the elementary structures of kinship were characterized by alliances between groups, by the positive determination of the preferred spouse—with reference to specific kinship status, or category—and by the operation of a system of ceremonial gift exchange. The complex structures of kinship, by contrast, were characterized by marriages between individuals (not alliances between groups), by the negative determination of marriageable categories—leaving the field open to nonkin determinations such as race and class—and by the operation of choice and individual contract in a social system organized by principles of the market and capital (Lévi-Strauss 1969[1949]:xxxiii–xxxix). He notes the distinctive characteristics of the European marriage system: "freedom to choose the spouse within the limit of the prohibited degrees; equality of the sexes in the matter of marriage vows; and finally, emancipation from relatives and the individualization of the contract" (477). If the incest taboo and the organization of kinship reciprocities marked the transition from nature to culture, then, for Lévi-Strauss, the transcendence of kin marriages altogether marks the transition from the elementary to the complex structures of kinship.

Despite Lévi-Strauss's disavowal of an evolutionary framework, he represents the elementary structures as secure, repetitive, and limited to reproducing the same social structure. He sees the complex structures as risky, adventurous, and speculative, creating "unprecedented alliances, and new coalitions [that] stir up the dynamics of history" (Lévi-Strauss 1984:74). In short, they are the conditions for the movement of progressive societies.

As with Maine's shift from status to contract, the advent of the complex structures is marked by the "emancipation" of the individual from the kin group, of contract from religious ceremony, and of political and economic relations from both kinship and religion (Lambek, chapter 10, this volume). By tying the elementary structures of kinship conceptually to religious ceremony and gift exchange, it becomes impossible to conceptualize how kin marriages (or kinship itself) might be integral to the political and economic dynamics of market-based societies. Conversely, as

James Boon pointed out, Lévi-Strauss's framework makes it impossible to discern how marriages of individual choice might be integral to systems of marital exchange (Boon 1977:119–144; Boon and Schneider 1974). The elementary structures mark that which is temporally prior, more primordial, and historically static in contrast to the progressive dynamism of complex structures, in which kinship is structurally invisible and subordinated to the political and economic dynamism of individuals released from the constraints of kinship and religious ceremony.

Fortes and Evans-Pritchard's Comparative Typology of Political Systems

The other main line of kinship theory in mid-twentieth-century anthropology was British descent theory, most often identified with the work of Meyer Fortes and E. E. Evans-Pritchard. Adam Kuper (1982, 1983, 1988, 1991) has argued that Fortes and Evans-Pritchard's comparative political typology is a reinvention of Maine's distinction between kinship and territory and Morgan's societas and civitas. Although the overall contrast holds, I would contend that the distinction is quite differently configured due to the particular alignments Fortes and Evans-Pritchard establish between group and individual relations and to their emphasis on the emergence of differentiated social domains. Moreover, attention to the work of Fortes and Evans-Pritchard provides an opportunity to consider how a developmental trajectory (or, in this case, typology) articulates with the differentiation of social domains that is understood to be a hallmark of modern society.

When Fortes and Evans-Pritchard laid out their overall typology of political systems in 1940, they did indeed replicate the earlier distinction between kinship and territory. However, one of the main differences between Fortes and Evans-Pritchard and the other theorists we have been considering is their assertion that the emergence of this distinction is the result of the progressive differentiation of domains rather than of the workings of either property (à la Morgan) or reciprocity (à la Lévi-Strauss) (Fortes 1969:40, 72–73, 87–100, 103, 180–189). And, rather than a progressive de-encompassment of the individual or more individuated forms of social relation from larger kin groups, Fortes and Evans-Pritchard reverse the sequence: they begin with individual dyadic relations in the natural bilateral family and gradually encompass those relations within successive layers of differentiated social domains. "Types of society," then, "differ in the number and character of the domains incorporated in their social structure" (99).

Thus, small-scale societies, or "kinship polities," are defined precisely by their lack of differentiated domains. Fortes notes, "Simple, or primitive societies are often said to be distinguished from complex societies by the fact that kinship, political, economic, religious, etc., relationships and spheres of activities are not differentiated from one another in the former as they are in the latter" (1969:99; Fortes and Evans-Pritchard 1940:6–7; see also Mauss 1990[1950]). This lack of differentiation is the essence of what Fortes calls "kinship polities."

By contrast, "stateless societies" are defined by the emergence of a distinction between the domestic domain (the original dyadic relations of the bilateral family) and the politico-jural domain (the system of unilineal kinship groups)—a distinction that Fortes and Evans-Pritchard first articulated in their introduction to *African Political Systems* (1940:6) and considered a major advance in anthropological understandings of "kin-based" social systems (Fortes 1969:72).

A further differentiation of domains distinguishes kin-based societies from territorially organized "primitive states." Here, the addition of a politico-jural administrative structure that transcends kinship formations altogether is the critical feature. In Fortes's formulation, the administrative and territorial structure that constitutes the political domain sits on top of and encompasses, even as it transcends, the structure of unilineal kinship groups upon which citizenship is still dependent in primitive states (see Fortes 1969:143, 155). Presumably, Fortes and Evans-Pritchard envision the eventual emancipation of the individual in the modern nation-state, but they are largely silent on this matter.

Unlike their forebears, therefore, Fortes and Evans-Pritchard begin with dyadic relations between individuals and undifferentiated domains, but they quickly move to larger corporate lineage groups and differentiated domains; then, falling back into line with their predecessors, they ultimately trace a line that transcends kinship. This transcendence of kinship in the political and economic domains is paralleled by a transcendence of religion in political or territorial relations. Although territory might exist in primitive states, stateless societies, or even kinship polities, Fortes deems it to be structurally irrelevant to the extent that it is unbounded and defined by religious rather than secular or utilitarian values (1969:38, 103, 105, 126, 129). The movement of progressive societies—or, at least, their typological differentiation—is thus accomplished by the de-encompassment of territorial relations not only from those of kinship but also, specifically, from those of religion (see both Cannell and Lambek, chapters 9 and 10, respectively, this volume, on the relation between kinship and religion).

In the end, the structure of the progressive temporal or typological differentiation *between societies* is reproduced as a progressive structural differentiation *between domains within societies.* The same logic underlies both frameworks: bilateral kinship marks either a temporal phase or a functional domain that is more natural, prior, subordinated to, and ultimately separated from the transcendent domains of politics and economics.

Geertz on Primordial Sentiments and Civil Politics

The paradigm we have been following is also evident in the early work of Clifford Geertz (1963, 1973b) in the context of the "new nations" project. Echoing the categorical distinction between Gemeinschaft and Gesellschaft, Geertz makes a more general case for the relevance of "two conflicting tendencies," which he characterizes as "primordial sentiments" and "civil politics" (1973b:258). However, he is clear that this tension is particularly relevant to the situation of the "new states" that emerged in the 1950s and 1960s from the strictures of colonialism. This, he argues, is because "the new states are abnormally susceptible to serious disaffection based on primordial attachments" that stem "from the 'givens'...of social existence: immediate contiguity and kin connection mainly, but beyond them the givenness that stems from being born into a particular religious community, speaking a particular language,...and following particular social practices" (259). Here, we have the classic characterization of "prestate" peoples as bound by primordial sentiments of kinship, religion, and particularistic languages and customs. Their attempts to don the cloak of civil politics and the universal rationalities of the modern market and nation-state are seen as wanting. Hardly a cultural evolutionist, Geertz nevertheless reanimates the tension between social typology and temporal sequence that is characteristic of the models we examined earlier. His analytic frame contrasts kin-based societies—in which primordial sentiments predominate—not only with new states, which are characterized by this unresolved tension between primordial sentiments and civil politics, but also with fully modern states, which have supposedly contained primordial sentiments (in the domestic domain) in favor of civil politics (in the political domain) (see Kelly and Kaplan 2001:431).

Making Kinship Invisible

For more than a century and across a wide array of theoretical paradigms, the oppositional framework that Maine first articulated in terms of status and contract has remained exceptionally productive, both conceptually and historically. It entails a set of categorical distinctions that are not simply opposed but also emergent and, most often, ranked: that which comes later culturally transcends and is more developed than that which is prior, primordial, and more natural. This framework formed the foundation for a set of narratives about what counts as the "movement of progressive societies" in nineteenth-century evolutionary texts, twentieth-century typological treatises, and, as we shall see, more contemporary accounts of "modernity" and "modernization."

The presumed truth value of this conceptual framework has two effects: on the one hand, it makes certain associations seem inevitable; on the other hand, it makes certain questions seem inconceivable. Kinship becomes—inevitably, essentially—associated with that which is prior, primordial, or more natural; with status rather than contract; with the group rather than the individual; and with the authority of religion and ceremony rather than that of secular and legal rationality. This makes it inevitable that we look for kinship in certain places and with regard to certain questions. This also makes it inconceivable to look for kinship in other places and with regard to other questions. We look for kinship in kin-based societies or the domestic domain of "modern" societies but not at the heart of capitalist market economies, whether these are local or global (Schweitzer 2000:11). We presuppose the relevance of kinship in what are called "tribal areas" or pockets of "backwardness," such as Appalachia or Afghanistan, but do not think to ask how it might work in the heart of political and economic institutions of "modern" nation-states.

KIN MARRIAGE AND THE MAGICO-PURIFICATORY INJUNCTIONS OF MODERNITY

If, in the modernist tale of evolution and development, a clear distinction is imagined between the stasis of backward societies and the "movement of progressive societies"—between status and contract, group and individual, the domains of kinship and those of politics and economics—then a boundary-making technology must articulate the point of transition and transcendence to clarify the oppositional frame. I argue that the revaluation, stigmatization, and prohibition of several historically prevalent forms of kinship in the late nineteenth-century United States were part of a larger "magico-purificatory" move (Latour 1993; Strathern 2005:95) that *brings into being* modernity's constitutive, if also illusory, claim concerning the separation of kinship and marriage from the domains of politics and economics. The targets of this stigmatization and prohibition were precisely those institutions and practices—such as kin marriage, nepotism, polygamy, and even slavery—in which kinship and political economy were densely intertwined. In this section, I take as an example the institution of kin marriage—in particular, cousin marriage—and argue that the stigmatization of cousin marriage was not an inevitable consequence of the objective conditions of economic development and industrialization. Rather, it was one of the means by which this separation between kinship and economy was articulated ideologically, and, in the process, a line was drawn between what would count as primitive or as civilized, backward or modern.

What strikes me about Tierney's and Kurtz's accounts of the conundrum of development in Iraq is not simply the significations of kinship in their narratives of modernization but also how completely the history of kin marriage in the United States has been erased. If marrying kin and attending to the concerns of extended family make one backward, tribal, antidemocratic, and incapable of economic development, then we have to rewrite the history of the United States because kin marriages were ubiquitous in American families right up through the Civil War and the turn of the century. In fact, the history of the United States suggests that kin marriages were central both to capitalist development and to the politics of nation-building. In order to appreciate the power of the taboo on cousin marriage, it is critical to understand first the dramatic shift in its status from a widely accepted and highly valued institution to one that became deeply stigmatized and reviled.

Kin Marriage and Political Economy in the Antebellum United States

In looking at the historical record, what stands out is the prevalence of kin marriage from at least the seventeenth century through the nineteenth in the United States.[6] During this time, kin marriage—including both cousin marriage and sibling exchanges (for instance, two brothers from one family marrying two sisters from another)—was a central force in the American social landscape. This was the case among the yeomen and aristocrats of the planter South, among the artisans and merchant elites of the industrializing North, among the members of religious groups migrating to the West, and among the emergent professional classes of lawyers, doctors, bankers, and entrepreneurs who remained in the East. The world of extended family and kin marriage was multilayered, weaving emotional intimacy through the fabric of social relations and forming the foundation for the consolidation of both political alliances and great landed wealth and investment capital.

It is amply evident that complex patterns of cousin marriage and sibling exchange were common throughout the planter and yeomen classes across the South, with alliances repeatedly tying and retying together networks of families across the generations. Take a family like the Hairstons, whose empire totaled forty-five slave plantations across four states, primarily straddling the Virginia–North Carolina border (Wiencek 1999). Their position as perhaps the wealthiest family in the country in the early nineteenth century was established through slave labor and maintained through a series of patrilateral cousin marriages—often combined with sibling exchanges—that created double and triple Hairstons and a tightly interconnected system of landed slave estates (76–77). Or consider the families of the "founding fathers," such as Thomas Jefferson, whose genealogy was densely intertwined with the Randolph and Lewis families of Virginia (for genealogies, see Daniels 1972; Kierner 2004; Merrill 1976, Wyatt-Brown 1982). So prevalent were cousin marriages (both patrilateral and matrilateral) and sibling exchanges among these families that, in the generation of Jefferson's grandchildren, Peter Field Jefferson married a woman who was his triple first cousin (see Merrill 1976:420n34, and genealogies on 344–347; Wyatt-Brown 1982:219).

Just as families in the agricultural South were marked by a multiplicity of cousin and sibling exchange marriages, so, too, were artisan and merchant families in both the South and the North. Bernard Faber (1972), Peter Dobkin Hall (1977, 1978), and Betty Farrell (1993) have demonstrated the importance of kinship ties and cousin marriage among the artisan classes in Salem, Massachusetts, and among the emerging merchant elites of Salem and Boston—in particular, those who came to be known as the Boston Brahmins—from 1700 into the 1900s. Faber and Hall note that the marriage of a man with his father's brother's daughter was favored by lower socioeconomic status families in Salem because they "had more need for manpower than for financial capital" and such marriages "tied sons back into the paternal enterprise" (Hall 1977:44). By contrast, Hall argues, merchants in places like Boston favored exogamous cousin marriages and sibling exchanges because these "tended to tie together previously unrelated males, bringing their capital and their skills into family firms, enlarging their capital, and, as a result, increasing their potential for success" (ibid.). It is also clear that cousin marriages and sibling exchanges were key to the formation of the German Jewish family firms that began in merchandising across the United States in the mid-nineteenth century and gradually consolidated their wealth in the investment banking houses that came to dominate Wall Street (Supple 1957; see also Birmingham 1967). Indeed, a number of these houses—such as Goldman Sachs and Kuhn, Loeb (which later merged with Lehman Brothers)—bear the name of marital alliances.

In the United States, as in England, cousin marriage and sibling exchange were widely practiced across economic sectors and social classes into the nineteenth century. They were, in essence, the unmarked and unremarkable coin of the realm. Cousin marriages, sibling exchanges, and extended family relations were not set apart from politics and economics but rather were the central means by which the development of political alliances and the consolidation and expansion of capital were achieved from the seventeenth century through the nineteenth century.

The Prohibition of Kin Marriage and Its Entailments

Against this background, it is remarkable that over the course of several decades after the Civil War, cousin marriage began to be prohibited and became a deeply stigmatized social institution—one of the prime markers of the primitive, the economically backward, and the politically regressive.

Many factors contributed to the decline in kin marriages. Michael Grossberg notes, "The economic moorings of the household shifted from production toward consumption. Generational influences on family formation declined. New fertility patterns resulted in declining family size [and thus fewer cousins]. A new domestic egalitarianism emerged to challenge patriarchy" (1985:6). Hall (1977, 1978) makes an economic argument for the decline in kin marriages, suggesting that before the development of corporate and testamentary structures, family capital and business capital were intertwined and indistinguishable. The creation of testamentary trusts beginning in the 1780s effected a separation between family capital and corporate capital at the same time that it circumvented the problem of partible inheritance and its cross-generational dispersal of family wealth (Hall 1977:47–48; 1978:105). The result was the creation of a legal structure that simultaneously accommodated and separated the needs of corporate capital accumulation and family inheritance. Cousin marriage and sibling exchange, Hall (1978:113) suggests, were no longer the most effective means of accomplishing the ends of capital accumulation, consolidation, and expansion.

Hall's account gives us a rationale for the *waning* of cousin marriage and sibling exchange as primary instruments of capital accumulation, but it does not tell us why cousin marriage came to be stigmatized, prohibited, reviled, and erased from popular historical memory. Nothing about cousin marriage and sibling exchange is inherently incompatible with the emerging "modern" world of the nineteenth and twentieth centuries. I suggest that it was precisely because cousin marriage had encompassed relations of both kinship and capital, status and contract, group and individual, that it became inappropriate—indeed, scandalously out of place—in a world whose progressive modernity was measured by the standard of their presumed separation. In the absence of any otherwise objective rationale, the stigmatization, prohibition, and erasure of cousin marriage should be read as one of the central injunctions or taboos that *creates* the modernist illusion of the separation of kinship and economy into distinct and hierarchically ordered domains. Indeed, just as Lévi-Strauss argued in his narrative of the origin of society that the incest taboo and the institution of reciprocity marked the passage between (and the separation of) nature and culture, so, too, I argue that in narratives of the evolution of modern society, the taboo on cousin marriage marks the passage between (and the separation of) the "traditional" and the "modern."

In the mid- to late nineteenth century, several narrative strands came together to naturalize this transformational trajectory and the distinctions and separations it entailed. One narrative strand involved hugely defective but highly popular and widely accepted "scientific" studies of the consequences of cousin marriage, which were published in the nineteenth century in the United States and Britain. For example, in the United States, the 1858 Bemiss Report, despite its many evident flaws, had the effect of convincing people that cousin marriage presented profound risks to the health of offspring (Ottenheimer 1996:53–57). A second narrative strand, evident in Lewis Henry Morgan's *Ancient Society* (1877), built upon this assertion of the biological dangers of cousin marriage and wove it into an evolutionary account of the origins of civilization. Despite the fact that Morgan himself was married to mother's brother's daughter, he maintained that over the course of evolutionary history, people gradually had recognized the "evils" of close marriage. Those who failed to recognize these evils were left behind in the sweep of evolutionary history. A third narrative strand appeared during the same years that Morgan was writing his evolutionary history, when Americans began to frame certain areas of the country, such as Appalachia, as backward and comparable to "primitive" societies elsewhere. Henry Shapiro (1978) describes the "discovery" of Appalachia after 1870, when the presumed stasis of the region was characterized as antithetical to the emerging institutional changes in the United States. He notes that it "was only in the context of such new notions about the nature of America...that the southern mountains and mountaineers became Appalachia, a 'strange land and peculiar people'...and that what had earlier seemed normal or at least explicable came after 1870 to seem nonnormal and inexplicable" (xi). As Appalachia became America's internal primitive—a counterimage to the prevailing picture of modernization and progress—cousin and close kin marriages became prime markers of the perceived backwardness of Appalachia, whether or not people were actually marrying their cousins.

The historical transformation of cousin marriage from an emotionally resonant, legal, commonplace, validated, and economically productive institution to one seen as emotionally repugnant, illegal, rare, stigmatized, and economically backward thereby became one of the central tropes in nineteenth-century American accounts of progress. It marked not only the internal distinctions that divided the North and South after the Civil War but also the external cultural distinctions that justified US political and economic ascendancy in the global order. I argue that the prohibition of cousin marriage—together with the nearly simultaneous prohibition on the "twin relics of barbarism" (polygamy and slavery) and, somewhat later, nepotism—formed the central injunction that articulated and symbolized the separation of kinship from political and economic institutions—a separation that, itself, became a sign of progressive modernity.

THE INVISIBLE LIFE OF KINSHIP IN MODERN POLITICS AND ECONOMICS

The narrative framework that I have been analyzing and its attendant taboos have the effect of rendering invisible the workings of kinship in "modern" politics and economics. I am not suggesting either that there has been no historical change in what kinship is and does over the past 150 years or that there are no cultural differences in how kinship is situated relative to other social institutions. Rather, it is my contention that the dominant analytic framework that came into being some 150 years ago—and continues under various guises to this day—has made it virtually impossible to ask questions about kinship in particular places. If, by definition, kinship is irrelevant to the workings of modern politics and economics, it hardly makes any sense to go looking for it in these processes, let alone ask questions about what it means and does.

In what follows, I explore the marked invisibility of kinship and the absence of theorizing about kinship in works that have more recently reinvented this developmental narrative in theoretical accounts of modernity and modernization. Further, I point to some of the work that has challenged this invisibility and absence by investigating the entanglements of kinship and modernity. My goal here is to envision an analytic terrain that is finally outside the modernist framework within which kinship has so long been confined and for which kinship has constituted the naturalized origin point and foundation.

The Movement of Progressive Societies, Redux

Reinvented on the bedrock of the old narratives of evolution, theories of modernization (and development) have, on the whole, presupposed rather than critiqued the contrastive logic that has long been embedded in this narrative trajectory. Indeed, these theories continue to be structured by a series of unexamined assumptions that modernization unfolds as the egalitarian individual is released from the hierarchical restrictions of kinship, as relations of (secular) market and contract supplant (ceremonial, religious) relations of family and status, and as nuclear families and marriage with nonkin replace extended families/tribes and kin marriage.

Anthropological critiques of modernity and modernization have taken a variety of forms. Much effort has gone into deconstructing the universality of the narrative and its supposedly universal correlates, making space for "alternative modernities" but preserving the alterity of the traditional-modern framework (Knauft 2002:18; see also Gaonkar 2001; Sivaramakrishnan and Agrawal 2003). This reveals the evident tension between the impetus to denaturalize and deconstruct the terms of the narrative altogether and the inclination to study "the force of the modern as an ideology of aspiration and differential power" that has the ability to bring particular, culturally mediated effects into being (Knauft 2002:33; see also Rofel 1999). Other work has attempted to refine the theoretical apparatus through which we understand what counts as modernity (Adams, Clemens, and Orloff 2005; Foster 2002; Inda 2005). Yet others wish to deconstruct the modernist master narrative altogether to seek, as John Kelly puts it, "not...alternative modernities but alternatives to 'modernity' as a chronotope necessary for social theory" (2002:262; see also Appadurai 1996; Englund and Leach 2000; Tipps 1973). Whatever the critique, the power of the master narrative is such that a consideration of kinship is conspicuously absent—whether the investigation concerns modernity, alternative modernities, or alternatives to modernity.

In contrast to the marked absence of accounts of kinship in theories of modernization, a number of works have taken on the issue of kinship and modernity more directly. Some have shown how this dominant analytic framework has made it impossible to conceptualize differing forms of kinship and marriage as integral to modern society—including its political and economic order—thus pointing, in essence, to "alternative modernities." Others, in critiquing the overall framework of modernity, have attended to the manner in which the operative distinctions have (or have not) been brought into being, primarily as artifacts of colonial governance and state power.

Scholars of colonial India have been particularly astute in their critique of the master narrative of modernity. Rochona Majumdar, in her book *Marriage and Modernity: Family Values in Colonial Bengal* (2009), makes several important, interrelated arguments. She calls into question the assumption that there is an inherent connection between modernity, individualism, equality, contract, choice, the nuclear family, and companionate marriage, on the one hand, and between tradition, familialism, patriarchal hierarchy, status, the extended family, and arranged marriages, on the other (Majumdar 2009:15). Indeed, she argues that the contemporary presence of arranged marriages and the continued validation of extended families in India are not holdovers of a stagnant, unchanging tradition but rather the result of a vibrant debate in the late colonial era about the relative value of liberal understandings of person, kinship, and marriage. In the midst of this dynamic historical process, Majumdar suggests, "the institution of arranged marriage was reconstituted and rearranged under modern conditions" (2). The revaluation of arranged marriage and the joint family as an integral part of modernity in India therefore "makes the descriptive template of this modernity different from the Western one" (14) and ultimately undermines the universality of the modernist frame.

Ritu Birla (2009:3, 8) not only critiques the universality of the supposed transition from status to contract, Gemeinschaft to Gesellschaft, but also goes on to demonstrate that colonial law in India brought this very distinction into being. Her book *Stages of Capital: Law, Culture, and Market Governance in Late Colonial India* (2009) traces how colonial market governance *produced* two exclusive economic arenas. One was coded as a local, vernacular, premodern (and ultimately illegitimate) form of capitalism that was embedded in kinship relations, was subject to "customary" norms of "culture," and was "placed under the purview of personal law that governed what were considered private concerns" (5). The other was coded as a universal, modern (and legitimate) form of capitalism that was extracted from kinship relations, was subject to formal relations of contract, and was placed under the purview of law that governed public concerns, in which social relations were modeled on market relations (3). By "highlighting the *making* of the distinction between contract and kinship," Birla's analysis "emphasizes the ways in which market governance *produced and managed* two general modes of community: state, civil society, and market, on the one hand (as gesellschaft), and family, caste, and culture on the other (as gemeinschaft)" (27; emphasis added). Such an analysis demonstrates that this distinction should be understood as a historical artifact of colonial power relations rather than as a necessary precipitate of modernization.

Indeed, the presence in India of social theorists such as Maine—who "was appointed legal member of the Viceroy's Council, effectively becoming the head of the Indian legal system" (Kuper 1988:34)—suggests that their social theories served to shape social realities on the ground as much as, if not more than, to reflect them (Birla 2009; Kuper 1988:33–35; Mody 2008:61–102).

In *Expectations of Modernity* (1999), James Ferguson provides a thoughtful analysis of the power of presuppositions about kinship and modernity to inform not only anthropological accounts but also government policies concerning development in the Zambian Copperbelt. Beginning in the 1940s and 1950s, the assumption was that urbanization and industrial wage labor would entail a shift from extended to nuclear families, from multiple, varied, and shifting sexual and marital relations to stable, monogamous, companionate marriages (170–171). Although ethnographers continued to note the disjunction between these "modern ideals" and the complexities of "actual living arrangements," their complete faith in the modernist narrative shaped their insistence on the inevitability of the emergence of the "modern family." As Ferguson notes, in the late 1980s the modern forms of kinship and marriage had failed to emerge, despite civil laws of inheritance, welfare, and pensions that both presupposed and supported them. Countering more recent accounts that pathologize contemporary kinship formations in the Copperbelt (blaming either the persistence or breakdown of "traditional family formations"), Ferguson argues that "taking apart the fiction of the modern family and the master narratives into which it is woven is therefore a necessary part of the process of reimagining the domestic as a site of political struggle" (205–206). Inversely, I would suggest that this is also a necessary part of reimagining political struggle as inextricably bound up with ideas about kinship and marriage.

Finally, Edward Schatz makes a strong argument for attending to the place of kinship in the modern political order in his book *Modern Clan Politics: The Power of "Blood" in Kazakhstan and Beyond* (2004). In the case of Kazakhstan, Soviet modernization efforts were extensive and dramatic, transforming a society based on "nomadic pastoralism to one based on large-scale mechanized agriculture and extractive industry" (15) and introducing widespread electricity, mechanization, literacy, and education. Yet, Schatz contends that "shortages of goods, services, and access to power that were endemic to the state socialist economy" (17–18) ultimately enhanced clan relations. It was precisely because clan relations were concealable that they became the key access networks in the political economy of shortage (14, 19). Making the argument more broadly, Schatz notes:

> It is becoming increasingly clear—contra the assumptions of modernization perspectives—that low-aggregate identities such as clans remain very much a part of the modern political condition. These are affiliations that are neither slated for social oblivion nor doomed to political insignificance. Moreover, we should not understand the ongoing political expression of subethnicity in the modern period as evidence of failed or incomplete modernization.... The specific mechanisms of modernization may themselves preserve and even strengthen—rather than render obsolescent—these lower-aggregate attachments. (Schatz 2004:6–7)

These studies shift the focus of our attention as we examine the master narrative of modernity. On the one hand, they point to its power, in certain contexts, to bring into being the kinds of social distinctions and processes that conform to its logic. On the other hand, they point to the widespread failure to realize its supposedly universal logic as it collides with the realities of other cultural orders. The question then becomes, under what circumstances, and under what conditions of power and agency, are the terms of this narrative realized, defied, endlessly deferred, or transcended altogether?

BEYOND THE MOVEMENT OF PROGRESSIVE SOCIETIES

Looking forward, my argument is that we must finally divest ourselves of the narrative framework that has, over different epochs, articulated the various guises of the story we have told ourselves about the "movement of progressive societies." The trope of kinship and kin-based societies has formed the natural base and mythological origin point for this narrative. Dislodging kinship from its entrenched place in these narratives has at least two critical effects.

First, it finally removes the presumed natural foundation of these narratives and troubles the tropes of transcendence that gave them their form. That these narratives of the movement of progressive societies have stayed with us for so long is perhaps a function of the way in which we grounded their origins in a naturalized kinship that seemed so obviously given in the nature of things, a perfect foil for the message of the transcendent progress of culture. By denaturalizing the foundation of these narratives, it is possible to consider them not as accounts of the universal and inevitable effects of the movement of progressive societies but rather as manifestations of a culturally and historically specific—yet globally circulating—"ideology of aspiration and differential power" (Knauft 2002:33), the effects of which are desired or deferred, realized or resisted, in the complex entanglements of diverse cultural understandings and differential powers.

Second, it finally removes the constraints that these narratives have placed on our understanding of the place and force of kinship and allows us to follow the myriad forms of human relatedness wherever they take us historically, cross-culturally, and in the structures of contemporary societies and the global political economy. Much has already been done—by David Schneider and those who came after him—to set the stage for this move. Analysts have critiqued not only the presumed objectivity of a universal biological base of kinship but also the domaining practices that have located kinship in some places but not others (Schneider 1984; Yanagisako 2002; Yanagisako and Collier 1987; Yanagisako and Delaney 1995). Yet, even as many of the "new kinship studies" have explored new kinds of relatedness and new ways of creating relatedness in new places (labs, clinics, transnational arenas), their focus has remained remarkably "domestic." By dismantling the metanarrative of modernity, it is possible to make visible what has been rendered invisible and to reveal the persistent force of kinship within political and economic worlds, where it has, for all too long, been presumed absent.

Acknowledgments

I thank the National Endowment for the Humanities for a fellowship (FA-52089-05) in 2005 that allowed me to begin to think through the ideas in this chapter. I am especially grateful to the participants in the SAR advanced seminar "The Difference Kinship Makes: Rethinking the Ideologies of Modernity" for their inspiring intellectual company during our week together and, more specifically, for their thoughtful commentaries on a much longer version of this chapter. I also acknowledge the able assistance of Erin Golden and Sena Aydin, who helped research certain aspects of cousin marriage that appear here, as well as the astute comments on an earlier version of this chapter that were provided by my colleagues Ira Bashkow and Lise Dobrin.

Notes

1. In 2007, Stanley Kurtz narrowed his focus to patri-parallel cousin marriage and its supposed "self-sealing" effect, which, he claimed, was the cause of terrorism not only in Iraq but also across the Muslim Middle East.

2. Morgan's distinction between societas and civitas clearly echoes Maine's status and contract. Morgan's evolutionary trajectory involves a gradual shift from group to individual relations, from communal to private property, and from matrilineal to patrilineal relations. These shifts are worked out through a change in gender rather than through a complete transcendence of kinship—as the supposedly more natural,

maternal and matrilineal relations are replaced by paternal and patrilineal ones—and through a radical reduction in the scope of kinship and marriage ties, in what Morgan calls an "individualizing" process. I have provided a detailed analysis of Morgan's evolutionary trajectory elsewhere (McKinnon 2001).

3. Kuper (1982, 1988, 1991) has focused on Maine's categorical opposition between kinship and territory or contiguity, rather than on the temporal process of encompassment and de-encompassment.

4. For an astute examination of the slippage between an analysis of ideal types and one of historical transformation, see Abrams 1972; see also the discussion of Abrams's point in the introduction to this volume.

5. Elsewhere, I have argued that the specific logic of Lévi-Strauss's *Elementary Structures* is the inverse of that in Morgan's *Ancient Society* (McKinnon 2001). Here, I draw attention to the similarities between the categorical distinctions evident in the evolutionary narratives of Maine (and Morgan) and those that organize Lévi-Strauss's larger typological framework, which contrasts elementary and complex structures of kinship. In other places (McKinnon 1991, 1995, 2000), I have also explored Lévi-Strauss's (1982:186–187; 1987:152) positioning of "house societies" as an intermediate form between societies organized in terms of kinship status and ceremonial gift exchange and those organized in terms of individual contract and the political and economic forces of the market.

6. For sources on cousins and cousin marriage in the United States, see, among others, Cashin 1990; Censer 1984; Faber 1972; Hall 1977, 1978; Kulikoff 1976, 1986; Ottenheimer 1996; Smith 1980; Supple 1957; Wiencek 1999; Wyatt-Brown 1982.

3

Transnational Family Capitalism

Producing "Made in Italy" in China

Sylvia J. Yanagisako

At the firm's sleek and ultramodern headquarters in Shanghai, Gu Shiyao, assistant director and translator for the top managers, explained to us that after the Chinese partners entered into their joint venture with an Italian clothing brand, they decided not to hire any more relatives. It had been a different story when the Chinese partners initiated their clothing manufacturing business in a small workshop with ten sewing machines. At that time and for the next fifteen years, the three brothers who owned the firm employed numerous relatives and also drew heavily on the labor of their wives. Since forming the joint venture and becoming an "international firm," however, the Chinese owners could no longer give "special treatment" to their relatives. In addition, the eldest brother had decided that it was better that the Italian partners hire the general manager of the firm, not only because they needed a professional who had studied business management but also because this would resolve disagreements that had arisen among the brothers about who should lead the firm.

More than 5,000 miles away, at the Italian partner firm's original manufacturing plant in northern Italy, the current chief executive officer (CEO), Alessandro Bossi, offered his ideas about how to keep a family business intact in an increasingly global world. According to Bossi, who is the great-grandson of the firm's founder, he and the cousins who manage the firm have agreed upon a policy of respecting both family values and corporate governance by laying out clear rules for the next generation. Each member of the fifth generation must become "a world citizen" before he or she will be considered a serious candidate for a job in the firm. This includes English-speaking ability, a university degree, and success at working outside the family firm for at least three years.

Transnational business collaborations between Italians and Chinese in the textile and clothing industries are, as this example shows, shaped by crosscutting currents of kinship. Yet, kinship rarely makes more than a fleeting appearance in popular and scholarly models of transnational capitalism, global capitalism, postindustrial society, or the "knowledge economy." If kinship appears at all, it is commonly as a metonymical representation of the distinctive local cultures that are being transformed into homogeneous sites of capitalist production and consumption. Both neoliberal celebrations of the global triumph of capitalism and antiglobalization critiques of its dehumanizing consequences tend to portray capitalism as a relentless and overpowering economic force that acts on local communities, which are represented as the sites of culture (Harvey 1989; Pred and Watts 1992). By locating capitalism in the rarefied realm of "the economy," these models conjure a spare social dynamic in which rational actors are driven solely by the pursuit of profit and accumulation, thus breathing new life into economic determinism.

One might expect better of anthropologists. Yet, despite the centrality of kinship studies in the history of our discipline—or perhaps because of it—since we broadened the scope of our inquiry to include capitalism and global transformations, we have paid scant attention to the beliefs, practices, and relations we recognize as constituting kinship. Susan McKinnon (chapter 2, this volume) points to the puzzling absence of studies of and theorizing about the constitutive power of kinship and marriage in the literature on transnationalism and globalization. She calls into question our lack of curiosity about the connections between kinship and corporations in spite of the fact that many leading corporations in the United States and elsewhere are both publicly traded and family corporations. I agree with McKinnon that underpinning the absence of kinship in metanarratives of transnational and global capitalism is an evolutionary model of modernity that posits a steady, global march away from the fetters of family and kinship bonds.

An unintended consequence of the inattention to kinship in research on transnational economic ventures is the endowment of capitalism with reproductive powers independent of kinship sentiments and bonds. In this progressivist account, professional managers and stockholders emerge as the rational seekers of profit in corporate capitalism. Family businesses, in contrast, are treated as archaic survivals of an earlier stage of capitalism. As is the case in social evolutionary models, a narrative of lag discounts and marginalizes social forms that diverge from the "modern firm"—that is, the multi-unit, professionally managed corporation in which ownership is separated from control (Chandler 1980; Daems 1980).[1]

In this chapter, I show how the transnational projects of Italian family firms collaborating with Chinese entrepreneurs are motivated and shaped by kinship sentiments and commitments to family unity and intergenerational succession, as well as by critiques of and struggles over them. My research demonstrates that family ownership and control persists in Italian firms that have expanded transnationally to forge partnerships with Chinese firms—and so do the tensions and struggles over the incorporation of nonfamily managers into these firms. Far from spawning a "managerial revolution" and resulting in a shift from family capitalism to managerial capitalism, the transnational expansion of these firms has drawn on and strengthened both the symbolic and managerial power of the proprietary families. I also explore the parallels between managers' critique of the messy interplay of family and business in these Italian firms and Max Weber's concept of "modern capitalism" to show that the separation of the domain of kinship from the domain of economy is central to the managers' and Weber's evolutionary models of capitalism.

This chapter draws on ethnographic research that I have undertaken with Lisa Rofel on twenty-first-century Italian-Chinese collaborations in textile and clothing manufacturing and distribution. Since 2002, we have been investigating the formation and transformation of transnational relations of production among Chinese and Italians in the unique historical context of China's shift to a market economy and the relocation of manufacturing by US, Japanese, Italian, and other European companies to China.[2] Our research has been conducted primarily in two sites: the eastern coast of China around Shanghai, which has served as one of the central locations for foreign investment in China, particularly in labor-intensive industries such as textiles geared for export,[3] and northern Italy, in particular, Milan, which is the center of the Italian fashion industry. My focus in this chapter is on the Italian family firms that have pursued these transnational ventures.[4]

PRODUCING "MADE IN ITALY" IN CHINA

When Italian textile and clothing firms began moving production to China in the late 1990s, China was already becoming known as the workshop of the world. Like capitalists in other countries, the Italian manufacturers were lured to China by its cheap labor and, subsequently, by its huge potential domestic market. Investment in production and sales in China was a dramatic shift in the strategies of the Italian fashion industry. Throughout the 1980s and early 1990s, Italian textile manufacturers viewed China as a source of inferior products and unfair competition. By the late 1990s, however, the increasingly favorable environment for foreign investment and trade created by the various levels of the Chinese government made China the most favored nation for the outsourcing of some or all of the phases of production of Italian textiles and clothing.

The Chinese central government was at first hesitant about allowing foreign direct investment in China. Initially, all foreign firms doing business there had to be joint ventures with the Chinese government—whether municipal, provincial, or central. But in the late 1990s, China began to build an economy heavily dependent on foreign investment, and in 2001, China began allowing wholly foreign-owned enterprises (WFOE), thus making China a central player in the growth of the global economy.[5] After 2000, these shifts in policy, along with the growth of the Chinese domestic market and the end of import quotas established by the Multi-Fiber Agreement, led to a further increase in Italian textile and clothing firms engaged in manufacturing and distributing their products in China through various forms of collaboration with Chinese partners.[6]

The Italian firms in these transnational collaborations are small- to medium-size firms that are owned and controlled by family members. Their presence in China parallels the predominance of family firms in Italy's economy. At the beginning of the twenty-first century, family firms constituted 75–95 percent of all registered companies in Italy, and nearly 50 percent of the top hundred Italian corporations were family controlled (Colli 2003:16). The Italian firms also reflect the predominance of small- and medium-size foreign companies engaged in direct investment in China (Huang 2003).[7] These firms produce and distribute fabric and clothing priced for the middle and upper levels of the fashion market, including well-known luxury brands.

In the 1980s, many Italian firms began to take advantage of the market reforms and the lower cost of labor in China by exporting phases of the manufacturing process to China and other Asian countries.[8] By the beginning of the twenty-first century, these firms had become interested in forging joint ventures with Chinese entrepreneurs in hopes of maintaining their favorable position in the global commodity chain by controlling the phases of design and marketing. Their vision of the future included plans to transfer the prestige and market value of "Made in Italy" to "Designed in Italy." At the same time, China's textile and clothing industries looked to Europe—in particular, to Italy—for models of how to transform their enterprises from being Third World suppliers of yarn, undyed cloth, and inexpensive clothing to being producers of fashionable, finished clothing.

The Italians and Chinese arrive at these collaborations through very different histories of kinship, capital, labor, and the state. As a result, they bring to their encounter different historically shaped sentiments, different ideas of family and business, and different access to forms of capital, including financial capital, cultural capital (such as brand reputation), and social capital (such as access to distribution networks in China, Europe, and the United States). The organizational structures and management dynamics of Italian capitalist firms and their Chinese collaborators also differ. Perhaps the most significant difference is that the vast majority of Italian textile and clothing firms are family firms, whereas only some of the Chinese firms with which they collaborate are owned and managed by individuals or families. Although China has steadily moved from a centrally planned economy toward a market-based, decentralized, and somewhat privatized one since the beginning of economic reforms in the late 1970s, the Chinese government—whether central, provincial, county, or municipal—remains a dominant figure in the market economy. Local government subagencies operate corporate-style enterprises, often competing with other local government-run enterprises (Oi and Walder 1999; Pieke 1995; Wank 1999).

Among the ten Italian firms we studied that are engaged in these transnational collaborations is the fourth-generation family firm mentioned above, which has forged a joint venture with an up-and-coming Chinese family firm to manufacture and distribute a new brand modeled on the Italian one. Another is a first-generation Italian clothing firm owned and managed by siblings, which has outsourced the manufacture of its leisure wear to a Chinese factory formerly owned by the state but privatized when its employees were offered (and pressured to buy) its stock. Other cases include first-, second-, and third-generation Italian family firms that have outsourced the production of textiles and clothing to China, as well as family firms rushing to take advantage of the rapidly expanding domestic Chinese market by opening up brand-name retail stores in major and secondary cities. Finally, the firm that has been characterized by the most intense family drama was forged by an Italian entrepreneur who had initially arranged outsourcing for Italian and US firms but then opened factories in a joint venture with his Chinese wife.

Although the histories, business strategies, and practices of Italian family firms vary and are shaped by a multiplicity of factors—ranging from the phase of manufacturing and distribution in which they engage to the extent of their capital investment—the Italian bourgeois families who own and manage these firms share kinship and gender ideologies and sentiments that operate as forces of production of both firm and family (Yanagisako 2002). Among these family firms, the strategies of capital accumulation, reinvestment, company expansion and diversification, and management organization are shaped by ideas, sentiments, and commitments of family, gender, and personhood. At the headquarters—whether in Milan, Como, or Rome—these families' fashion strategies of transnational expansion are spurred by their hopes for the survival of the firm and its passage to the next generation. Indeed, their primary motive for relocating production to China, forging transnational joint ventures, and developing transnational distribution chains is to enable the firm to survive and expand, thus providing the next generation with both the means of production and the means of family unity. (See Shever, chapter 4, this volume, for an account of how kinship sentiments in the Argentine oil industry likewise operate as a powerful productive force to mold business practices among workers in both the state company and the private ones that succeeded it.)

The goals of Italian firm owners are also usually linked to ideas about the masculine self and men's desire to retain authority in their families. Fathers' goals of handing the firm over to their adult sons (and, to a lesser extent, their adult daughters) are motivated by their desire to provide their sons with the means to remain independent of other men (employers) and, at the same time, to provide themselves with the means of maintaining their authority and centrality in the family. These firms are generally organized according to a patriarchal structure in which the head of the firm (usually the father) makes decisions in consultation with his adult children (usually sons, but increasingly daughters), who manage divisions of the firm. By the time the second generation has taken over, the siblings co-direct the firm according to a managerial division of labor that often places one in charge of production and others in charge of sales and client relations. Most family firms do not survive to the third generation, but those that do are commonly directed by an executive committee composed of siblings or cousins, each of whom manages a section or branch of the firm.

Whether family firms survive beyond the first, second, or third generation, they are frequently the breeding grounds for managers and technicians who eventually leave to start up their own firms. This has been a crucial dynamic of the "flexible specialization" of the innovative small firms in the industrial districts of northern and central Italy, which were trumpeted in the 1980s as offering a promising alternative to Fordist mass production (Piore and Sabel 1984). These networks included small, specialized firms alongside larger, more vertically integrated firms. The latter relied on the former for subcontracting services. Many of the owners of subcontracting firms, moreover, began their careers working as technical directors or managers in other firms, often with the clear intention of learning their employers' techniques and acquiring the practical training that would prepare them to open their own firms.

The transformation of technical directors and managers into the owners of subcontracting firms has been a well-established pattern of upward mobility in industrial districts such as Como and an integral part of the process of the reproduction of subcontracting firms (Yanagisako 2002). It has also meant that a firm's employees, especially its managers, can become its competitors. The thin line between on-the-job training and industrial espionage has reinforced owners' disinclination to place nonfamily members in upper-level management positions, creating a "kinship glass ceiling" beyond which nonfamily members do not rise (Yanagisako 2002:138). The cap on advancement, in turn, fuels the frustrations of ambitious managers, who leave to found their own firms. This process thus generates a constant supply of new subcontracting firms. In addition to the demand for their services by larger firms, the continual generation of new firms is spurred by the desire of Como entrepreneurs, who are mostly men, to be their own bosses.

The expansion of Italian family firms into China and other countries has created a new wrinkle in the relations between proprietary families and the managers they hire. The establishment of manufacturing divisions, joint ventures, and distribution offices abroad has created overseas managerial positions that family members are unwilling to fill. As lucrative as China has become for these firms—as a site of cheap labor and as a growing market for their products—it is still considered by Italian firm owners to be a cultural hinterland and a difficult place to live. Whether they are members of the senior generation of the family, who hold the highest-level positions in the firm, or members of the up-and-coming generation, who manage departments or regions, family members limit their stays in China to short visits of up to two weeks. During these trips, they visit their firm's headquarters in Shanghai, meet with its Chinese partners or the entrepreneurs who outsource production to Chinese factories, inspect factories, and grace the opening ceremonies of new ventures and retail outlets. But we have found only one member of a proprietary family who lives in China.[9]

As a consequence, Italian family firms expanding their activities to China have been forced to rely on nonfamily managers.

The growth of production and sales abroad has increased the opportunities for nonfamily managers, who can now rise to higher managerial levels, such as director of production in China, director of a joint venture with a Chinese partner, or director of the company's operations in Asia. Some family firms have even hired CEOs from outside the family to head the entire firm, although executive positions are still usually reserved for family members. Of the ten Italian family firms in our sample that have expanded to China, only two had nonfamily managers at the executive level.

MANAGING "MADE IN ITALY" IN CHINA

The Italian managers who have moved to China to work in these transnational ventures in the textile and fashion industries occupy a range of positions: working with Chinese partners to set up the management structure of a new joint venture, directing production in a joint venture's manufacturing plants, marketing franchises to sell an Italian designer brand, and finding and recruiting Chinese manufacturers to collaborate in joint ventures with an Italian firm that produces several middle-market brands. Managers on the production side work closely with Chinese factory managers, shift supervisors, accountants, technicians, and office staff, but they rarely supervise Chinese factory workers. Those involved in distribution and sales, by contrast, work with Chinese franchise managers, retail clerks, warehouse managers, and office staff. A few use the services of Chinese translators—who translate from Mandarin or a regional dialect to Italian—but more often, the Italian managers communicate with Chinese staff in what is called "business English."

These managers are predominantly male, although not exclusively.[10] Two-thirds are married or have a steady partner, and they are, on the whole, young—all but a couple are between the ages of twenty-six and forty. Most have the Italian equivalent of a bachelor's or master's degree in business;[11] others have degrees ranging from psychology to chemical engineering to Chinese language and literature. Two managers initially came to China to continue their study of Chinese language and literature and only later began working in business; a couple of the women came to China because they were engaged or married to another worker in the firm.

Approximately half the managers had worked for their employer in Italy before being transferred to China either to initiate operations or to join an already established office. For example, Paolo Rinaldi, who heads the Italian management team in a joint venture with a Chinese manufacturing firm, worked for the Italian company at its headquarters, managed its operation in Turkey, and became the director of finance and management in its Mexican operations. He then returned to the home office in Italy, where he was responsible for industrial production in Europe and China for one of the company's brands, before being assigned to the Shanghai office, where he took the place of the previous manager. His wife also worked for the firm, in both Mexico and China, with a break after the birth of each of their two children. The other half of the managers arrived at their positions through more circuitous routes, for instance, by working for other firms in the same sector or as global supply-chain managers in other sectors.[12]

Most managers consider living and working in China to be a daunting experience. Even Shanghai, with its international restaurants, large European expatriate community (including a sizable Italian community estimated at around a thousand people), glittering shopping malls, international schools, and decent Italian restaurants, is considered to be a formidable challenge. As one manager put it, "it is more interesting than beautiful." The air pollution, the communication difficulties, the different cultural environment, and the lack of beauty of the surrounding countryside are most frequently cited by managers as the primary challenges. Very few managers speak Mandarin or the local dialect, although the recruitment of Italians trained in Chinese language and literature programs in Italy has increased since around 2008. In comparison with other cities or townships where textile and clothing factories are located, however, Shanghai is considered a paradise. A manager who had recently been transferred to Shanghai after living and working in a large industrial city in another province compared his former assignment to being sentenced to "twenty years of life imprisonment." The absence of an Italian or even a European community, of international restaurants, and, above all, of Italian food is a further hardship. Another manager, who had been working and living in a provincial city for two years, exclaimed, "The body needs pasta and pizza!" But he added, "You get used to it. Humans can get used to anything."

In spite of these complaints about life in China, Italian managers view the career opportunities offered there to be far superior to what is available to them in Italy. Almost all of them candidly admit that had they remained in Italy, they would never have obtained positions or salaries as good as their present ones. They point to the 10 percent growth rate in China's gross domestic product—in contrast to the slow rate of economic growth in Europe and the United States—and to the commensurate growth of their firms' business in China. One manager said, "There's no way I would have the opportunity to open thirty stores a year in Italy." He added, "Here, if you make a mistake, you can recover." Another compared the pleasure of participating in the 20 percent annual growth in his firm's production in China to his previous work in Italy, which had consisted primarily of downsizing and working with the labor council to fire people.

Italian managers pride themselves on providing these transnational collaborations with crucial knowledge and skills that are beyond the capabilities of both their employers and the Chinese they work with. They position themselves between the Chinese-ness of their local partners and the provincialism of Italian firm owners. While acknowledging that their Chinese partners have invaluable knowledge of the Chinese market and the indispensable know-how to negotiate the multiple levels of Chinese governmental bureaucracy, Italian managers have a bevy of complaints about their shortcomings. Among these are poor planning skills, lack of professional training in management systems (including information technology), lack of creativity, and lack of initiative in problem solving. The oppositional terms in which Italian managers portray the differences between Chinese managers and themselves are hardly unfamiliar. Although Italy did not have colonial projects in China or any other area of Asia, Italians are well steeped in nineteenth- and twentieth-century orientalist discourse. Thus, it is not surprising that oppositions between tradition and modernity, despotism and democracy, collectivity and individualism, and authority and creativity pervade much of what they have to say about their experience working with Chinese.

In addition, given their assessment of the undeveloped state of Chinese understanding of Western fashion, Italian managers view themselves as crucial to guaranteeing quality control, brand management, and effective marketing. Whether they are overseeing production in a joint venture, arranging for subcontracting by Chinese factories, or setting up franchise retail outlets, Italian managers feel they must be constantly vigilant to maintain the quality and prestige of the brand. Above all, Chinese cannot be trusted to preserve the brand's *italianità*—its Italian-ness. This includes not only the quality of the manufactured product but also the design features that convey its italianità. In the view of Italian production managers, Chinese production supervisors and workers simply do not have the ability to recognize the small but crucial details of italianità, such as the positioning of a pocket or the alignment of a zipper. Likewise, in the view of Italian distribution managers, Chinese retailers and clerks do not have the capability to set up a retail store that effectively conveys the italianità of the brand.

Italian managers' criticisms of the failings of Chinese managers and entrepreneurs must be situated in the history of the transnational production of "Made in Italy" clothing and the marketing campaign that has shaped its value since the 1980s. Just as it did when it was launched in the 1980s, the current "Made in Italy" promotional campaign, which is sponsored by the Italian Trade Commission, trumpets the Italian-ness captured in commodities that have been produced in an imagined, culturally saturated, "Italian" location. The evocation of Italian artisanal and craft traditions that can be traced back to the Renaissance endows these commodities with a rich cultural heritage, which, in turn, legitimates their high price. For example, the Salvatore Ferragamo Fashion House celebrated its eightieth anniversary with an exhibition inaugurated in Shanghai that displayed two shoemakers crafting shoes by hand in a workshop. Ermenegildo Zegna employed an identical theme during Milan Fashion's Night Out in 2009, featuring a tailor's workshop in its flagship store on Via Montenapoleone (Segre Reinach 2010). As fashion studies scholars such as Simona Segre Reinach (2010) have noted, however, such advertising campaigns rely on a historical falsehood: since the 1980s, "Made in Italy" has relied on a form of industrial fashion that was created by substituting artisanal production with industrial manufacturing.

Given that the exchange values of the commodities produced are inextricably linked to their Italian-ness, it is hardly surprising that the Italians would view their labor as more crucial than the labor of Chinese. Less expected is the finding that, in the production of "Made in Italy" in China, Italian managers have become the surrogates of Italian workers. Although the "Made in Italy" marketing campaign highlights the artisanal craft and skill of Italian workers, in the transnational production and distribution process, the Italian managers have become responsible for infusing commodities with Italian charm. Through their managerial practices—which are shaped not only by past and present discourses of italianità and orientalist discourses of China but also by the asymmetries of power in their relations with Chinese—managers come to view themselves as embodying the cultural powers of italianità. For them, like the managers and workers in the shipyard on the banks of the Hooghly River in India (Bear, chapter 7, this volume), work entails a polyvalent idiom of surplus meaning that is not contained in conventional analytic domains of economy, kinship, or religion. For Italian managers, the surplus of meaning spills over into their conceptions of themselves as cultural beings endowed with particular cultural powers.

In addition to appropriating the fetishized powers of the commodity as their own labor power, this new generation of Italian transnational managers has forged a critique of the "provincialism" of firm-owning families. As one nonfamily manager in Shanghai put it, the Italian bourgeoisie are hardly willing to give up pasta and parmigiano to live in China.

THE PROVINCIALISM OF OWNERS

Managers' characterization of the proprietary families as "provincial," while clearly self-serving, is not cut entirely out of whole cloth. All the Italian textile firms and many of the clothing firms doing business in China originated in small towns and semi-rural provinces rather than in the major urban areas of northern or central Italy. These sites were, after all, close to the raw materials (silk, wool, linen), land, and labor power they needed for industrial manufacturing.[13] The most successful of the textile firms initiated clothing manufacturing divisions, thus moving up the commodity value chain. The most successful of these, in turn, transformed themselves into luxury designer brands or national—and now international—retail chains.

Despite the ascendance of these family firms over the course of three to four generations, their provincial roots are still apparent and, indeed, celebrated alongside claims of their contributions to "global fashion." Even those proprietary families that have offices and homes in major cities such as Milan and Rome maintain homes and reside part of the time in the small cities or towns in which their family's business originated. Whereas in Milan or Rome they are recognized as members of the upper class, in their communities of origin they are nothing short of aristocracy. A family's enduring connection to its provincial origins is, moreover, a testament to the authenticity of the brand and its Italian origins. Indeed, the marketing of these luxury brands commonly employs images of rural aristocracy and gentry. For example, the book *Italian Touch* (Sartorio 2009)—sponsored by the Italian luxury brand Tod's—displays photos of Italian families, friends, and dogs in their elegant homes and gardens (Segre Reinach 2010). Their informal but stylish dress is, according to Diego Della Valle, the head of Tod's, intended "to promote not products but a lifestyle of good taste, high value, and understated refinement" (Triptree 2009).

The display of the familial and provincial origins of these firms has become all the more important given the resentment and anger that have been incited in Italy by the overseas production of "Made in Italy" fashion. Since the 1990s, numerous campaigns against the unlawful exploitation of the "Made in Italy" label have been launched by a number of regional governments, labor unions, and business associations in Italy. This anger over outsourcing production to China is exacerbated by, and often confounded with, the circulation of "counterfeit" products, some of which have fake brand labels and others of which falsely claim "Made in Italy." Partially in response to this outrage, in the spring of 2010, Italy passed the Reguzzoni-Versace law, which requires that two of the four production phases take place in Italy for the "Made in Italy" label to appear on shoes, leather, textiles, and clothing.

A founding family's continuing residence in its site of origin symbolically grounds the claim to the italianità of the brand even though it is being manufactured abroad. The prolonged presence of family members in China could conceivably undermine the provincial essence and national purity of the brand, which is protected by hiring nonfamily managers to oversee the firm's operations abroad.[14] The occasional visit of firm owners to China, by contrast, serves to publicize the brand. The growing buying power of Chinese consumers—in particular, wealthy Chinese consumers—has made China "the privileged theatre" of Italian fashion (Segre Reinach 2010). Marketing strategies, consequently, underplay the manufacture of Italian brands in China while celebrating their success in sales there. As Segre Reinach notes, in 2007 and 2008, the "images for the Pirelli calendar were shot in Shanghai with garments designed by John Galliano for Dior, inspired by an Orient of Saidian memory, a mix of costumes from China and Japan, sartorially described as a cross between *qipao* and *kimono.* Ermenegildo Zegna created [its] corporate catalogue in Beijing, printed on a paper recalling the rice paper used for ideograms, in a sophisticated, rarefied setting, a mixture of exoticism and modern recognition of the grandiose Chinese culture" (2010:206).

Although half the Italian managers in our sample come from the same communities or surrounding areas as their employers, they view themselves as professionals who are able to overcome the provincialism of firm owners. The longer they live abroad, moreover, the less they feel they have in common with family and friends back home. The work and social life to which they grow accustomed in China is a far cry from their experience growing up back home. Not only do they become habituated to having drivers, maids, and nannies, but also their social life in Shanghai is centered on the European expat community. Those who are single go out to dinner frequently with friends and participate in the lively expat night scene. Those who are married with children usually live in expat compounds, which one woman self-consciously described as their "own international ghetto," a kind of Club Med for families. Although they have some Italian friends, their social life includes a mix of European, Australian, and North

American friends.[15] When managers return to Italy on vacation, many find their old friends to be rather unsophisticated and close-minded.

Managers may be cautious about openly criticizing the provincialism of their employers, but squiring around members of the proprietary family and playing intermediary between firm owners and their Chinese partners enhance managers' sense of themselves as cosmopolitan cultural interpreters. They are, moreover, painfully aware of the family sentiments and commitments that shape the strategies and decisions of firm owners, including decisions about managerial promotion and succession. These they view as unfortunate impediments to the transformation of the firm into an efficient business that can compete successfully in the global market. They speak of their desire to restructure the firm along the lines of the management schemes they were taught in business school, in which there is a CEO, a chief financial officer, and division heads, each with a clear job description, domain of responsibility, and place in a chain of command of reporting and accountability. Managers commonly complain about the impediments to their attempts to *managerializzare* the firm (that is, to institute a managerial organizational structure) and to rid it of the "extraneous" family emotions and dramas that get in the way of increasing the company's efficiency and its profits.

The argument about the need to further managerializzare family firms is not limited to transnational managers working in China. It has been in wide circulation in Italy for at least the past thirty years. One can hardly open an Italian business journal without encountering discussions about the competitive advantages of transforming family firms into more "modern" business organizations. The owners of family firms themselves participate in these discussions. Rather than challenge this vision of modern capitalism, however, they speak of the ways in which they have incorporated modern management techniques and organizational forms into their firms to forge a modern family capitalism. Many owners and their children, after all, have degrees in business and finance, information technology, marketing, and economics.

WEBER AND THE OXYMORON OF MODERN FAMILY CAPITALISM

Were Max Weber privy to this debate between Italian transnational managers and firm owners, he might well be skeptical of the owners' attempts to develop a "modern family capitalism." According to Weber (1978a), there is a fundamental divide between modern capitalism and other forms of capitalism—including the pariah capitalism of European Jews and medieval

Italian capitalism. The orientation of family firms toward communal commitments of family unity and continuity disqualifies them from modern capitalism, which is, by Weber's definition, oriented exclusively toward the rational, calculated pursuit of profit and accumulation. Although he located the *origins* of modern Western capitalism in the deeply felt moral sentiments of Calvinists, Weber emphasized its emergent ethos of rational calculation, thus tracing this fusion of religious subjectivity and economic action to a historically and culturally specific conjuncture (Weber 1992). Calvinists' striving for the continual accumulation of wealth impelled them to pursue a distinctive mode of economic action that integrated ascetic self-control with disciplined accumulation. When capitalism took its place as the "modern economic order," Weber argued, it quickly became detached from the specific religious motivations that initially produced it. What was once an entrepreneurial practice driven by a spiritual ethic became a *secular* logic of rational calculation (Yanagisako 2002).

The binary between modern and premodern forms of capitalism was laid out most clearly in Weber's mammoth work *Economy and Society* (1978a). At the core of this treatise is the concept of "economic action," which rests on the distinction between action oriented toward the satisfaction of a desire for utilities and action oriented toward the satisfaction of other desires (68). While Weber recognized that actions may be oriented toward multiple ends and shaped by multiple considerations, he argued that they could be analytically differentiated on the basis of their "conscious, primary orientation" (64). Modern capitalism—with its calculative spirit and singular goal of profit and accumulation—is accordingly distinguished from the premodern capitalism pursued by the large capitalist households of the medieval cities of northern and central Italy (359). Because these households were committed to a principle of solidarity in facing the outside and to a "household communism"—in other words, a communism of property and consumption of everyday goods (ibid.)—Weber considered them to be based on "direct feelings of mutual solidarity rather than on a consideration of means for obtaining an optimum of provisions" (156). Hence, he concluded, they had a "primarily noneconomic character." Weber's model of modern capitalism, consequently, rests on the analytic dichotomy between the rational pursuit of utilities and the sentiments of mutual solidarity—in other words, between the domain of economics and the domain of kinship. For Weber, "modern family capitalism" is an oxymoron.

Managers' attitudes toward the family sentiments and commitments that shape their employers' goals and strategies are hardly surprising, therefore, not only because these sentiments and commitments are obstacles to their career advancement but also because they have been trained in business schools whose models of business management are predicated on Weber's dichotomy between economy and kinship. Like comparable institutions in the United States, Italian business schools have promoted the professionalization of business management and financial strategies employing business models informed by the social sciences, especially economics. In the United States, professional management became hegemonic in the first half of the twentieth century with the increasing concentration of capital in corporations (the product of capitalists' strategies to reduce uncertainty by reducing competition) and the incorporation of business education into research universities (Khurana 2007).[16] In Italy, in comparison, the continuing predominance of medium and small family firms throughout the twentieth century checked the power of professional managers, muting their challenge to owners' authority and the legitimacy of owners' rights to control firms. Even big business in Italy has been labeled as "oligarchic family capitalism," in which the controlling shareholders are members of a small number of families (Brioschi, Buzzacchi, and Colombo 1990:165).

The continuing discussions in business journals and among Italian owners and managers about the need to managerializzare firms reveal that "managerial capitalism" is far from hegemonic in Italy. Neither has it become accepted as a universally efficient form of business organization for all market sectors. In spite of the career opportunities that recent transnational expansion and attempts to "globalize" Italian fashion have created for nonfamily managers, there has not been a managerial revolution in the Italian textile and clothing industry, nor is there any indication that there will be. According to economic historians such as Andrea Colli (2003), who specializes in family business, the medium-size Italian enterprises that are expanding into certain global market niches—such as clothing, luxury goods, machine goods, and the various branches of "Made in Italy" enterprises—have been "managed by the creation of hierarchical structures based upon a multi-subsidiary system" that remains firmly in the control of the family (62). Colli argues that the "family's influence is reflected in the composition of the board, which is dominated by the founder's immediate family or close relatives. The family is, in many cases, the source of skill that has always been relied upon to provide finance, labor, and know-how. The structures of these groups mirror their historical evolution. The first, original nucleus of the enterprise has transformed itself into a family-controlled financial holding company, presiding over a large number of unincorporated subsidiaries active in the core, but also in very diversified fields" (63). At the end of Colli's history of family businesses in the United

States and Europe from 1850 to 2000, he concludes that the family firm is not merely a "transient state on the way to more developed and sophisticated organizational forms." Rather, it has proved to be resilient and capable of adapting to rapid shifts and changes in the market (65).

KINSHIP LESSONS FROM WESTERN CAPITALISM

My focus so far in this chapter has been on the Italian family firms engaged in transnational collaborations. But what of the Chinese who participate in these transnational ventures in textile and garment manufacturing?[17] The first thing to be noted is that the Chinese "entrepreneurs" who collaborate with the Italian firms are individuals and also social entities that are not conventionally included in this term. Only a few are individuals or families who own private firms, such as the brothers who own 50 percent of their joint venture with an Italian firm or the married couple whose factories specialize in producing Italian clothing. Others are middlemen or middlewomen whose small companies specialize in connecting Italian firms with sources of raw materials or with factories that produce yarn, fabric, and garments. Among Chinese, moreover, the category of entrepreneurs blurs into the category of managers: some are employees of import-export trading companies that are run by the state, others are managers of state-owned factories, and still others manage formerly state-owned factories that have been privatized. Finally, there are Chinese who are employed as managers of Italian-owned factories or as overseers of quality control. Many of these individuals and social entities are engaged in multiple business activities, sometimes combining work for an employer with their own profit-seeking activities.

Because the shift toward a market economy has taken place only recently, these Chinese entrepreneurs are, for the most part, young. Most of them are in their twenties and thirties. The Feng brothers, whose joint venture with an Italian firm is mentioned above, are the old men of the group; they are now in their early forties. Like other entrepreneurs from Wenzhou[18]—a prefecture on the coast in Zhejiang province, 375 miles from Shanghai—these brothers began their business with a small amount of capital and by relying on family labor. Although none of them had worked in clothing manufacturing, they set up a workshop by buying ten sewing machines and bringing in a tailor from Shanghai to teach them garment manufacturing. Over the next fourteen years, they expanded to employ a thousand workers, with upper-level management positions reserved for the brothers and their wives. One brother was the director of sales, another was in charge of design, and the third managed production. Their respective wives worked as head of the accounting department, as the shop floor leader, and as the assistant director of sales. Thus, when the brothers formed the joint venture with their Italian partners, Italian family capitalism encountered Wenzhou family capitalism to forge a truly transnational family firm. Whereas the Italian family is in its fourth generation of family ownership and control, like the other entrepreneurial families that have emerged in China, the Feng brothers are too young and their firm too recent to have produced a history of family succession.

Family firms, however, are only one type of entrepreneur with which Italian firms collaborate. Most of the young Chinese managers and entrepreneurs who work for and with Italians are not yet involved in family firms. This is understandable because the opening of China to capitalist enterprise is too recent for their parents to have participated in it. Instead, this cohort of freshly minted college graduates has entered into business eager to learn from Western capitalists. Those in textile and garment manufacturing are especially keen on learning about branding, retailing, advertising, and how to design fashion that appeals to Western tastes. Many have degrees in business—including from the former textile university in Shanghai, Donghua University, where Marxist economics quickly gave way to Keynesian and neoliberal economic theory. Many of them explain their decision to go into business as motivated not only by a desire to make money but also by the desire to avoid the inefficiencies, constraints, and burdens of the social networks that they view as dominating the state sector. Rather than rely on their parents' kinship and friendship networks, they prefer to rely on their peer networks of classmates and work colleagues to forge their own paths to success.

Indeed, these young entrepreneurs look askance at the use of family and kinship ties, which they associate with the socialist past from which they want to distance themselves. They are aware of the widespread, ongoing discourse in China about corruption among government cadres, which emerged in the early 1980s with the beginnings of economic reform. In both official and popular discourses, this corruption is said to be the result of the degradation of political power during the Cultural Revolution, when cadres were viewed as using their power (instead of wealth) to gain access to privileged positions and resources for themselves and their families. Thus, a frequent critique among Chinese entrepreneurs is that state agencies continue to be characterized by this kind of behavior, which undermines effective profit making and weakens the company as a whole. Chinese managers and entrepreneurs contrast the lax work ethic of cadres—who represent various levels of the Chinese government—to their own hard work.

As they work for Italian clothing and textile firms, these young Chinese entrepreneurs are realizing that the Western, capitalist rationality they were taught in business school is not always what occurs in practice. In particular, they are learning that Italian capitalism itself is fettered by "communistic" bonds of family and kinship. Emily Shu, for example, is a bright, ambitious, and personable young woman in her early thirties who has worked for several years with an Italian entrepreneur who arranges garment production in China for several European designer brands. As the middlemen in a transnational production chain, Emily and her boss seek out Chinese factories that can be relied upon to produce the desired quantity and quality of garments within the time constraints of their European clients. Emily's hope had been that when her boss—who is now in his early seventies—retires, she would take over his clients. But to her dismay, a couple of years ago her boss brought his son into the business. Emily's complaint—that the son knows little about the business and has lived the life of a playboy rather than developed the disciplined work ethic of an entrepreneur—is an all too familiar one, voiced repeatedly by nonfamily managers employed by Italian family firms in both Italy and China. Like them, Emily is learning the painful lesson of hitting the kinship glass ceiling.

CONCLUSION

The Italian family firms that have expanded their production and distribution to China have been propelled headlong into transnational capitalism in the global era by the very "household communism" that Weber associated with premodern capitalism. I argue that their "noneconomic" communal commitments of family unity and continuity have been central to their efforts to become transnational. Thus, it is hardly the case that Western capitalist firms are exporting to China a Weberian modern capitalism forged by economic action oriented solely toward the satisfaction of a desire for utilities. Instead, a rising generation of aspiring Chinese entrepreneurs is encountering communistic family sentiments and commitments in what they have been taught is the core institution of Western modernity—the capitalist firm.

These encounters offer an ironic twist to Sahlins's (1994) historical analysis of the cosmologies of capitalism in which the precapitalist "other" that is pulled into the orbit of the Western capitalist "world system" is enabled to enrich and develop its own premodern cultural logic of hierarchy and value. In the current case of the transnational encounter between Chinese and Italians in textile and garment manufacturing, the agents of Western capitalism—namely, the Italian capitalist families—aspire to enrich and develop a cultural logic that does not fit comfortably into evolutionary models of capitalism. How all of this will work out over the long run remains to be seen. I suspect that the goals, strategies, and cultural logics of both the Italians and the Chinese will be reimagined and reformulated through this encounter, as will the sentiments, commitments, and bonds of kinship with which they are interwoven.

But what of our theories of modern capitalism—in particular, our theories of kinship in the age of transnational and global capitalism? As McKinnon (chapter 2, this volume) argues, these, too, must be reimagined and reformulated rather than merely enriched to salvage evolutionary models of kinship and capitalism.

Acknowledgments

The research on which this chapter draws was supported by grants from the National Science Foundation, the Wenner-Gren Foundation for Anthropological Research, and the Clayman Institute for the Study of Gender at Stanford University. I am grateful to Susan McKinnon and Fenella Cannell for their incisive comments and suggestions on an earlier draft, as well as to the other participants at the SAR advanced seminar "The Difference Kinship Makes: Rethinking the Ideologies of Modernity."

Notes

1. There is a large body of literature on family businesses to which economic historians, economists, sociologists, psychologists, management specialists, and a few anthropologists have contributed. In this chapter, I do not attempt to summarize the debates and issues of this literature, which are especially unwieldy because there is no single definition of a family business (nor, I would add, should there be). The attempt to come up with a universal definition of a family business is as futile as the attempt to forge a universal definition of the family, an enterprise that anthropologists have long abandoned. For useful reviews of the interdisciplinary scholarship on family businesses, see Colli 2003; Colli and Rose 2003.

2. Our research has focused on four types of transnational collaborations between Italians and Chinese in the textile and garment industries: joint ventures with active collaboration in management; joint ventures with a division of managerial labor; wholly Chinese-owned enterprises that provide subcontracting for Italians; and wholly Italian-owned firms in China.

3. Since the late nineteenth century, the lower Yangze River delta, where Shanghai is situated, has served as one of the central locations for foreign involvement in China (Honig 1986; Skinner 1976, 1977).

4. A monograph based on this research will be co-authored with Lisa Rofel as part of the Lewis Henry Morgan Lecture series of the University of Chicago Press.

5. In compliance with the World Trade Organization (WTO), which China joined in 2001, the Chinese government has allowed foreign entrepreneurs to establish WFOEs rather than joint ventures with the government. The liberalization of foreign direct investment became a driving force in the decline of China's state-owned enterprises (Gallagher 2005).

6. At the turn of the twenty-first century, China's textile and garment industries accounted for more than one-fifth of all Chinese exports, garnering an increasing share of this global market since China's entry into the WTO (Lardy 2002).

7. Foreign direct investment (FDI) in China has certain characteristics not shared by FDI in other countries. In contrast to other countries, where FDI is usually concentrated in a few industries, in China, FDI is spread throughout many industries and regions.

8. Italian designers, of course, are not the only ones to have outsourced production to China; so have labels such as Donna Karan, Ralph Lauren, and Victoria's Secret, as well as retail chains such as Banana Republic, Levi Strauss, and the Gap.

9. This exception is the owner of an Italian textile firm who has opened a factory in China with a combination of Chinese and Japanese investors. He lives at the factory for several months each year. This firm owner is unusual: first, he is not from a family with roots in one of the provinces, and, second, he is married to an Asian woman.

10. Of the sixteen Italian managers in our sample, twelve are men and four are women. I should note that there is an obvious bias to our sample (in addition to the bias of the firms' self-selection in being willing to be studied). Our study includes only firms that have been successful in forging joint ventures or other forms of collaboration in China. We do not have good figures on the percentage of textile and clothing firms that fail in these transnational ventures in China, but one director of the Italian Trade Commission in Shanghai estimated that 75 percent fail.

11. These include degrees in economy and commerce, management economics, and fashion business administration.

12. There has been a marked shift in recruitment and hiring from an earlier period (2000–2004), when Italian firms found it difficult to recruit Italians to work in China. In the earlier period, the pool of Italians living in China or willing to work there was so small that firm owners were even willing to hire scholars who had studied Chinese language and literature but had no background in business. This changed significantly around 2005 as job opportunities in Italy shrank while those in China grew.

13. Until World War II, the main source of labor in these areas was peasant households that engaged in a mix of farming, petty entrepreneurship, and wage labor.

14. I thank Susan McKinnon and Danilyn Rutherford for pointing out that nonresidence in China increases the symbolic capital of proprietary families.

15. Few Italian managers socialize with Chinese, and when they do, it is with Chinese from Taiwan, Hong Kong, Singapore, or the United States—in other words, with Chinese who are expats.

16. According to Rakesh Khurana, "the goal of the professionalization project in American management, carried out by the university-based business school, was to achieve control in a specific area—the large, publicly traded corporation—and protect that control from competing groups, namely, shareholders, labor and the state" (2007:10).

17. A full discussion and analysis of the Chinese entrepreneurs involved in these transnational collaborations will be published in a monograph I am currently writing with Lisa Rofel.

18. Wenzhou was a vibrant site of private entrepreneurial activity in China even before the initiation of market reform in 1978, perhaps due to the region's relative autonomy from the control of the central government (Chen 2008). Hence, Wenzhou entrepreneurs had a head start in capitalist enterprises, and many have been highly successful over the past thirty-five years.

4

"I Am a Petroleum Product"

Making Kinship Work on the Patagonian Frontier

Elana Shever

Carolina Lucano introduced herself to me as "completely a petroleum product" the first time I met her. She explained that her father came to northern Patagonia as a teenager to take a job with Yacimientos Petrolíferos Fiscales (YPF), the Argentine state's oil company, met his wife in the company town Plaza Huincul, and continued to work for YPF in the Neuquén oil fields for more than twenty-five years, until the state enterprise was converted into a private company in 1992.[1] Carolina was born in the YPF hospital in Plaza Huincul and raised in a workers' cooperative housing complex in the adjoining town, Cutral Có. "My siblings and I grew up in the bosom of YPF during its most benevolent era," she recounted. Carolina particularly credited YPF with the education—from elementary school through a professional degree—that enabled her to become the articulate, successful, and gregarious professional woman I met in 2005. Carolina's self-description illustrates that processes of capitalist production and filial reproduction are tightly linked. She calls attention to the dual meaning of labor as the act of giving birth and of alienated work. Her life illustrates that the Argentine state, through its oil company, produced not only oil but also modern family structures, kinship sentiments, and national belonging on the Patagonian frontier. Kinship bonds among the residents of the oil towns enabled petroleum production in northwest Patagonia from the founding of the state company at the beginning of the twentieth century through its privatization at the century's close. In recounting this history, this chapter reveals the mutual constitution of modern kinship, familial sentiments, disciplined labor, state governance, and industrial capitalism.

The history of YPF in northwest Patagonia indicates that company towns and their residents blur the assumed divides between kinship, labor, industry, and state. The history of Plaza Huincul and neighboring Cutral Có illustrates that a particular kinship form and attendant sentiments emerged in conjunction with the national oil industry and state rule over Patagonia. The creation of places like Plaza Huincul and people like Carolina needs to be viewed as resulting from polyvalent projects of generating modern families, industrial laborers, capitalist production, and sovereign nation-states. The intertwined paternalism of state and company has been central to this project. Paternalism undergirded the development of the oil industry but then came under attack during the neoliberal restructuring. Yet, it hardly disappeared. Relationships among workers, and between them and the state, have continued to be understood and organized in terms of kinship, sometimes as brotherly dedication and intergenerational care and other times as filial constraint and paternal discipline.

The centrality of kinship for the oil industry has been unrecognized. In revealing the generative force of kinship in one of the most powerful engines of modern capitalism, I seek new theoretical ground that fuses the study of affective states, modern biopower, kinship sentiments, and capitalist labor. This examination builds on Sylvia Yanagisako's (2002) argument that kinship sentiments are forces of production that shape business enterprises and, through them, capitalism. Affect is not a force of reproduction incarcerated in the domestic domain but a force of production that shapes industrial and commercial processes. Sentiments are, therefore, both "resources that are used in production" and "cultural forces that incite, enable, constrain, and shape production" (11). Yanagisako's analysis of struggles over inheritance and succession in Italian family firms shows how men's desires for filial continuity shape business strategy and the relationship between labor and capital. My analysis of YPF demonstrates that we cannot fully understand the productive power of kinship sentiments without paying attention to state institutions, their agents, and the national discourses they deploy. This chapter shows that kinship and nationalism come together to constitute a particularly powerful but unrecognized force that has been fueling oil production in Argentina and molding the people who have done the labor of producing petroleum—first for the state-owned company and then for the privately owned ones that succeeded it.

I expand insight into the generative power of kinship sentiments in four related directions. First, I extend Yanagisako's analysis of entrepreneurial owners of family firms to reexamine workers, who were the subject of the initial feminist critique of the analytical divorce between capitalist production and filial reproduction. Long before privatization of the oil industry encouraged workers to become small business entrepreneurs, their familial sentiments were crucial for oil production. The processes—first of developing a national oil industry and then of privatizing it—led workers both to construct kinship bonds and to break them. The twin practices of "kinning" and "dekinning" (Howell 2006:8–9) remind us not to romanticize kinship as other to capitalism but to recognize kinship as part of it.

Second, my attention to YPF workers highlights the sustained importance of the state in molding both family form and kinship sentiments. Anthropologists have long envisioned kinship—particularly men's desire to preserve property over time—as a substitute for a state rather than as central to it (Kuper 1988; McKinnon, chapter 2, this volume). Whereas the state is largely absent from Yanagisako's examination of family firms in Italy, it is central to my analysis of YPF in Argentina. Like Ann Stoler's (2004) study of Dutch rule in the East Indies, my examination of Argentine rule in Patagonia demonstrates that state agents were deeply concerned with settlers' sentiments because they recognized that cultivating, managing, and regulating domestic desires and familial attachments were necessary for governing the population. Stoler shows that the Dutch state's assessments of the "settled dispositions" of whites born in the Indies informed policies such as the criteria for civil service appointments, yet she underestimates the centrality of economic concerns for the state's affective projects. The history of YPF makes clear that creating proper family relationships and attendant sentiments was crucial not merely for extending state rule to the inhabitants of the Patagonian territories and generating national belonging there but also for promoting national economic development. Paternalistic practices—such as job inheritance, company housing, education, and medical care—were the mechanisms through which the state and its company governed oil-rich Patagonia and industrialized the national economy.

Third, this chapter links kinship to nationalism in a new way by showing that kinship bonds are more than a "foundational fiction" (Sommer 1991) or a metaphor for the "imagined community" (Anderson 1991[1983]) of the nation. Kinship sentiments not only dictated state social policies, economic projects, and political calibrations but also worked in combination with feelings of national belonging to reinforce and justify discipline on the Patagonian frontier. National sentiments meshed easily with kinship ones because both rested on a trope of familial bonds as the authentic basis for solidarity, care, obligation, and sacrifice. Kinship offered a language to talk about many kinds of affinity, most importantly, those that bound people together as company employees, town residents, and national citizens. We will see below how kinship sentiments glossed discipline and hierarchy in positive terms of loyalty, dedication, and love. Moreover, paternalism aimed to mold workers into model citizens of a modern nation-state.

Finally, I argue that kinship sentiments have proved to be a particularly flexible productive force that transcended the dramatic transformation of the oil industry from state to corporate ownership and management. Although YPF's privatization was intended to replace state and company paternalism with independent entrepreneurship, familial bonds and kinship sentiment continued to be powerful forces in the privatized industry that succeeded the national one. After YPF Estatal no longer existed, former state oil workers continued to refer to themselves as "YPFianos" and to work to maintain "the YPF family" through new business ventures. These terms emphasized the continued importance of oil workers' shared labor experience—and the sentiments that grew out of this—even when they no longer worked for the state oil company. Indeed, kinship sentiments were what the newly minted entrepreneurs credited with enabling them to sustain subcontracting microenterprises within the privatized oil industry.

The continued salience of family in South America is frequently contrasted with the supposed rise of the autonomous individual in the United States and Great Britain. This chapter joins others in this volume not only in illustrating how kinship is crucial at sites where it has remained unnoticed by previous scholars but also in demonstrating that its force is underestimated even in the places where it is widely recognized as important. As Laura Bear (chapter 7, this volume) points out, studies that counter widely held assumptions of the subservience of kinship to labor and the separation between the domestic and the economic domains have not become part of the theorization of capitalism. I, too, argue that kinship is not an atavism of peripheral persons and places but deeply formative of capitalism. The oil industry provides a particularly striking instance of the relevance of kinship to global circuits of capitalism. As Sidney Mintz (1986) demonstrated for sugar, the enormous rate of consumption of petroleum and its derivatives in those places that most closely follow the ostensibly universal trajectory of capitalism (Chakrabarty 2000) depends on oil production in those places that have been erroneously theorized as not fully part of capitalism. In addition, the theoretical positioning of the economic domain as determining relations within the domestic domain erases the work of kinship in producing oil. I join others in this volume in asserting the need to recognize the important role of kinship in capitalism and modernity.

In highlighting the polyvalent work of kinship in the history of YPF, I refuse both the romanticism of kinship as a domain outside capitalist power relations and the economic reductionism of kinship as yet another sphere being newly exploited for financial gain. I also aim to expand the examination of how kinship is materialized and stabilized. Anthropologists have scrutinized the rhetorical and material uses of blood, houses, legal documents, and biotechnical procedures in generating kinship but have largely ignored how industrial objects and labor are used to make kinship manifest. The significance of industrial materials is hinted at by Carolina's description of herself as a "petroleum product" and supported by the history of the mutual constitution of filial reproduction and industrial production on the Patagonian frontier.

CIVILIZING PATAGONIA

The petroleum industry was established in Argentina within the context of the annihilation of Native peoples, the encouragement of European immigration, and the incorporation of the southern territories into the nation and state.[2] By the time of Argentina's independence from Spain, missionaries had been working for almost two centuries to "civilize" the indigenous tribes, particularly to end their nomadism, polygamy, and idolatry. Although most Native inhabitants of Patagonia did not take to sedentism, they did take to capitalism.[3] Yet, it was not until after the military campaigns of the 1880s that state agents and *criollos* (people of Spanish descent) were able to assert control over commerce in the southern territories. The indigenous people were not entirely wiped out, as the dominant national narrative suggests, but survivors joined poor criollos in either becoming laborers on farms and ranches or becoming *fiscaleros*, precarious occupants of the semiarid grasslands and arid plains retained by the national state because they were undesirable for settlement. The state designated the area that would become the Neuquén oil region for ranching, but it was too dry for this use, so most criollo settlers abandoned their allotments (Nicoletti and Floria Navarro 2000:81). The spot known as Huincul stood amid the arid plains as an isolated way station for land travelers across the Andes, purportedly run by a woman known as "the Green Pasture" (la Pasto Verde; Contreras n.d.). That changed when the railroad was extended through the area in order to bring livestock and agricultural commodities from the interior of the Neuquén Territory to the Atlantic coast (Nicoletti and Floria Navarro 2000:89). At the same time that an enormous influx of immigrants arrived in Argentina, Huincul became a stop on the new southern train line. Patagonia became more densely colonized as Italian and Spanish farmers, aided by the railroad, ventured south from Buenos Aires in search of land and Syrian and Lebanese immigrants extended their filial merchant networks across Patagonia.[4]

After drilling the first oil well in 1915, the state's oil company took over the project of repopulating the region and governing it through biopolitical means. As oil exploration turned to oil extraction in the Neuquén Territory, Huincul was transformed into a work camp called "the Octagon" (Contreras n.d.). The state's hastily established camp soon grew into a company town, dotting the windy desert landscape with administration buildings, employee barracks, and other facilities. The population grew as the availability of jobs and the promise of above-average salaries drew people to the oil enclave (Nicoletti and Floria Navarro 2000:126). The residents were largely migrant, highly mobile, and mostly male. Scores of Chilean, Syrian, Lebanese, and Argentine migrants came to capitalize on the effort to extract petroleum, by selling goods and services to the state agents working in the Octagon and to the private oil companies working outside its boundaries. Men found jobs as manual laborers in the oil fields, and women worked as domestic servants for the male geologists, engineers, and other professionals who lived in the camp. Over the next two decades, more administration buildings, sturdier barracks, a hospital, and other facilities were constructed in the northern part of the Octagon, and nonstate employees were permitted to build houses and operate small businesses in the southern part (Favaro and Bucciarelli 1999:230; Palacios and Paris 1993:321). The first residential area "was erected as an emblem of progress and prosperity in the midst of a landscape dominated by dryness, cold and wind" (Mombello 2005:156).[5] Luxuries such as electric lighting and heat, which were unheard of in the region only a few years before, were now available in Plaza Huincul. YPF became not only the state's economic development agent but also its medical and educational arm. The company operated the only hospital and school in the area until the rise of Peronism in the 1940s. The oil camp thus enacted the state's "civilizing" mission in Patagonia and helped fulfill the liberal statesman Juan Bautista Alberdi's famous dictum: "To govern is to populate" (1979[1852]). It was in this context of the extension of state rule to Patagonia and the initiation of oil extraction that the particular form of YPF kinship emerged.

BUILDING HOUSING, DISCIPLINING WORKERS

The railways and meatpacking plants central to Argentina's export-oriented economy depended on British capital and on fuel imported by foreign companies. Military leaders, nationalist economists, and other nationalists argued that Argentina would not be able to industrialize—and thus would never become the modern nation-state that they desired—without state control of the domestic oil supply (Belini 2006; Solberg 1982). The military general who would become YPF's first director, Enrique Mosconi, articulated a vision of "petroleum nationalism" in which the state would supply energy, security, and sovereignty through its ownership and management of a vertically integrated, national oil company (Solberg 1979). By 1918, the state was extracting petroleum at two national oil reserves in the Patagonian territories. Mosconi aimed to vastly expand this effort.

YPF's company towns made manifest the productive powers of territory and labor in the name of personal and national improvement, as the agricultural fields of the Pampa had done before the hydrocarbon turn. Nationalist discourse contended that state oil workers were laboring for the well-being of the nation, and, in exchange, the state must care for them and their kin. General Mosconi recounted: "The General Directorate proposed watching over and subsidizing the general welfare of the organization's staff in the most complete manner possible, so that the family head would not feel his energy or work capacity decreased by the worries inherent in the necessities of a home" (1984:71–72). Moreover, company housing symbolized the aim to create a "patriotic and highly moral" workforce. As Gillian Feeley-Harnik (chapter 8, this volume) notes, the conquering of the US frontier was often measured in the number of houses built. Just as family residences were seen to demonstrate the "improvement" of the North American forests, so, too, houses followed rigs as signs of "civilization" in the high desert plateau of Patagonia. In both cases, indigenous land occupancy was erased, and urbanization was defined as progress. Also, the nuclear family, patrilineal descent, and a strong linkage between family and house were idealized.

Housing was a principal instrument through which the Argentine state, its oil company, and its union generated both oil and modern kinship. This dual project was significantly advanced in reaction to the anarchist and communist unions that emerged in the oil fields in the 1930s, was accelerated as Juan Domingo Perón rose to prominence under the military dictatorship of the early 1940s, and was further extended after he gained the presidency in 1946. Perón assisted trade unions that supported his program of state-managed labor relations and censured those he found to be disloyal. In the oil fields, he fostered the Sindicato Unidos Petroleros del Estado (SUPE) as the sole legitimate union in exchange for SUPE abandoning its adversarial stance against YPF. While the military brutally repressed anarchist and communist movements, YPF more subtly tried to discipline the workforce by offering housing in exchange for "an inflexible discipline and an absolute rigidity in the completion of their duties and obligations" (Gorelik 1987; Mosconi 1984:71). Company housing thus provided material substantiation of the rewards of aligning with the emerging paternal state.

Housing was used to create YPF families in the double sense of workers positioned as children in relation to the state and of children raised to replace their parents in positions in the oil industry. The housing YPF architects designed for oil towns like Plaza Huincul was not simply an extension of the barracks for single male workers that the state had been providing since the first oil well gushed in 1918. Now, YPF built housing complexes composed of row homes and bungalows, which differentiated employees by rank and family size, and communal athletic and social facilities. These residences were highly prized by worker families because they were equipped with "modern conveniences" such as electricity and indoor plumbing. Numerous YPFianos told of having company employees come to their homes to do even minor repairs, including to replace a light bulb when one burned out. As YPFianos vied to gain access to this housing, it reinforced hierarchy, enforced labor discipline, and fostered a particular form of familial sociality in Plaza Huincul.

An YPFiano named Franco Vincente explained to me that amid the chronic housing shortage, company housing grew to have "a family logic." That is, YPFianos eased their sons into company jobs, bequeathed them their company housing, and thus were able to stay in their homes once they retired. Franco argued that this "recycling of the same house within the same family" was one of the reasons that many YPFiano families, including his own, never lived in company housing, despite YPF's emphasis on its practical and moral importance. Franco remarked on the inequitable distribution of resources, but seen in another light, his comment indicates that a filial relation to an YPF worker gave a young man access to a job and a house and thus secured the continuity of individual families and the state company's labor force. This access was assisted by YPF hiring policies that gave preference to the children of employees and guaranteed positions to the relatives of YPFianos who were injured or killed at work. For example, Carolina Lucano's uncle Freddy began working for YPF because his father died in a work accident when Freddy Garza was a teenager. I also heard numerous accounts of men who eased the way for their nephews, sons-in-law, and other relatives to take positions in YPF. Feelings of filial love, a dedication to kin, and a desire for family continuity motivated fathers to try to ensure the well-being of their children and other kin through both sanctioned and unsanctioned means. In this way, fathers provided economic stability and a measure of prosperity for their sons, but they also constrained their sons' livelihood and living arrangements. The state oil company's labor regime helped organize families along lines of patrilineal descent, whereby houses and jobs were not only central forms of inheritance but also tools of familial and national continuity. They ensured conjugal fidelity, domestic stability, patrilineal descent, labor discipline, and state productivity in a region previously characterized by polygamy, nomadism, unlawful land occupation, extralegal trade, and enterprise unregulated by state institutions.

FROM THE "DANGEROUS NEIGHBORHOOD" TO THE NEW TOWN

The state played a more ambivalent role in developing the familial settlements that grew outside the official company town. After a 1932 fire in two oil tanks in Plaza Huincul was attributed to sabotage, the YPF director evicted the nonstate agents from the Octagon. Evictees described being thrown into an YPF truck and moved three kilometers away to an area that became known as Barrio Peligroso (Dangerous Neighborhood, now part of Cutral Có), where there were already approximately fifty households (Palacios and Paris 1993:321). Barrio Peligroso was one of several scattered settlements where manual laborers ineligible for company housing lived alongside domestic servants and peddlers in adobe and cardboard shacks around the few available water wells. There, an unpublished town history noted, "these families lived, with their little ones, in an exceedingly miserable manner" (Contreras n.d.). Officials in Plaza Huincul feared that Barrio Peligroso was "breeding uncouth people," including gamblers and prostitutes who took advantage of the state workers for unsavory purposes. In response, some YPF administrators refused the settlers' requests for assistance and discouraged their employees from going there, but others wanted to normalize these settlements. Víctor Ezio Zanni, the director and doctor at the YPF hospital in Plaza Huincul, was among the latter. He set out to convert Barrio Peligroso from a haphazard encampment into a proper town, with the cooperation of one other YPF professional, a state judge, and the chief of the civil registry stationed in Plaza Huincul, but without the consent of the YPF directorate or the national land office in Buenos Aires.

On a few Sundays in June 1933, Dr. Zanni and his like-minded colleagues measured, sketched, and pegged a grid for a new town for oil workers in the sandy desert soil. They renamed it Barrio Nuevo (New Settlement) and gave out lots to the men who lined up for them. When an YPF director, on a visit from the distant capital, objected that "it would have been better to attack the uncouth people who take shelter there than to give them benefits," Zanni countered that giving men landed property within a town grid was introducing "civilized" family structures into Patagonia (Contreras n.d.). Whether or not convinced by Zanni's paternalist argument, the YPF director did not order the settlement razed, as his predecessor had done to the one in the Octagon the prior year.

This unofficial company town outgrew the official one next to it to become the second-largest urban center in Neuquén Territory by the mid-1930s. Most of its more than 2,500 inhabitants were newcomers and included numerous Argentines from other regions and immigrants from Italy, Spain, Syria, and Lebanon, in addition to the Chileans who had long inhabited the region. Several prominent Lebanese and Syrian families relocated their businesses to Cutral Có to supply the oil companies with equipment and to capitalize on the commodity desires of the oil workers and their kin (Bandieri 2005; Favaro and Iuorno 1999:64–66). Although these families employed transatlantic kinship networks to achieve economic and then political success in Patagonia, they did not become YPF employees and thus served as a foil to the Argentine oil worker families. Yet, they helped build a schoolhouse (Palacios and Paris 1993:322) amid the brothels and gambling halls in order to make it a better place to raise a family.

At an inauguration ceremony on the morning of October 22, 1933, officials recognized Barrio Nuevo as an official Argentine town. A short time later, it was renamed Cutral Có, ostensibly an Araucanian term meaning "firewater," thus discursively placing the region's indigenous occupation as the prehistory of the extractive industry of the future. Although Zanni was credited as the town's founder, he asserted that the hardworking laborers were the ones reformed the settlement into a proper town in which a male worker could support his kin. In an interview conducted half a century later, the doctor related that the men who moved into the grid "erected their dwellings in only a few days, by stretching almost beyond their means, in order to relocate their families," and they created a "very modest but at least decent and forward-looking town" (Contreras n.d.). In a speech at the inauguration, Dr. Zanni projected: "Water, lights, heating, trees, aesthetics and much proper love: everything is possible when…the inhabitants of this new town, most of them humble soldiers of work, grab shovels and hoes to selflessly contribute to the common welfare" (ibid.). Neuquén's military governor concurred with Dr. Zanni's portrait of Barrio Nuevo as fulfilling a "civilizing mission." They both suggested that the labor of the town's male inhabitants made it possible not only to introduce "modern conveniences" but also to generate "selfless" sacrifice, "proper love," decency, and other signs of civilized kin relations. Although women's work went unmentioned at the inauguration, the event marked the initiation of a process through which marital desires were encouraged and women's remunerated labor in Plaza Huincul barracks was replaced with their unremunerated labor in Cutral Có homes. We will see below how the sentiments of dedication and sacrifice, and a gendered division of labor, became crucial aspects of the "YPF family" in Patagonia.

The prominent Argentine author Fernán Félix Amador published an article, "El pueblo sin nombre," in the Buenos Aires–based newspaper *La Prensa* in honor of the town's second anniversary on October 28, 1935. The article underscored the understanding that Cutral Có's development was the result of its residents' commitment to family and nation. Amador pointedly noted that state agents developed "the most valuable sources of petroleum deposits in the country" but failed to provide the "colonizing action of the state" to house those involved in petroleum production or to support their families. He argued that the "pertinacious existence of this remote urban center" represented "a valiant example of what can be done with goodwill, the spirit of colonization and love of the land." The town, he wrote, "has arisen from among the desert brush, by virtue of a social imperative: the institution of the family." When Amador named the family as a "social imperative," he hinted at how kinship sentiments, such as love, dedication, and the desire for family stability, articulated with state and industrial forces of production to carry out the projects that enabled the creation of worker families on the Patagonian plateau. The doctor's, governor's, and writer's narratives also combined military metaphors of discipline with a masculine settler ethos of hard work and love of the land to represent the nation on Argentina's remote southern frontier.

It is important to point out that both Zanni's statement about the connection between "proper love" and "the general welfare" and Amador's comments about the productive effects of "goodwill, the spirit of colonization and love of the land" drew on long-standing notions of an intimate connection between family and nation in Argentina. In literary and other representations of the nineteenth century, Latin America's nascent nations were portrayed in kinship terms, sometimes as brotherhoods and other times as nuclear families (Anderson 1991[1983]; Plotkin 2003:121;

Sommer 1991). The Argentine nation was repeatedly envisioned as springing from the marital union of the strong gaucho with the fertile fields of the Pampa. With increasing industrialization, the petroleum-rich territory on Argentina's southern periphery joined its agriculturally rich center in providing the grounds for enacting this ideal of the nation as a marriage. The workers were encouraged, following the model of the gaucho, to embody the union of male labor coupled to the natural riches of the land. The history of the oil towns illustrates how the mission of the state shifted from merely populating the frontier to encouraging "modern" living arrangements and family structures there. Whereas the former project was primarily expressed through a trope of the marriage of masculine labor and feminine land, the latter was expressed through one of marital desires and filial bonds between fathers and sons. Ideas of the nation as a brotherhood remained pervasive in both.

Peronism gave these ideas about labor, family, and the nation new meaning as workers were positioned as dependent children in relation to a paternal state, as well as part of the national brotherhood. As with the socialist regimes in Eastern Europe, the national imaginary that developed in Argentina "posited a moral tie linking subjects with the state through their rights to a share in the redistributed social product," in which citizens "were presumed to be grateful recipients—like small children in a family—of benefits their rulers decided upon for them" (Verdery 1996:63). Yet, at the same time that Peronism infantilized citizens, it promoted their rights to employment, commodity consumption, and public services. The promise of increased consumption and services depended on replacing an export-oriented economy with one centered on domestic production. This, in turn, rested on the production of sufficient and inexpensive energy from Argentine sources.

Petroleum nationalism was manifest not only in presidential speeches and state policy but also in the spaces of Patagonia and the lives of people in the oil towns. Public works connected with oil extraction—such as roads, refineries, and water and gas lines—became symbols of national modernization (Nicoletti and Floria Navarro 2000:118). YPF workers and their spouses saw themselves as sacrificing for the advancement of the nation and thus as deserving to be rewarded with the "goods" that corresponded to their role in delivering modernity to their fellow citizens. However, the reality of everyday life unsurprisingly fell short of the ideal. On the one hand, the YPFianos served as harbingers of modernity when they installed natural gas heaters and stoves in their homes, bought new cars and then quickly replaced them with the latest model, or traveled for leisure by plane or car. On the other hand, the ugly underbelly of this modernity became visible when they experienced gas explosions, plane crashes, and the isolation of living far from family. In all these instances, kinship sentiment was both motivation and remedy for men's labor in the oil fields.

THE DEVELOPMENT OF THE YPF FAMILY

Fernando Castillo was described to me as the man who best knew YPF's "social mission," for he had worked for many years in its social services (*obra social*) division. He insightfully explained—using his own experience as an illustration—that the YPF family developed through the combination of YPF policy and worker initiative. Fernando was born and raised in a tight-knit immigrant family in Buenos Aires. After finishing high school there, he sought one of the highly coveted positions in YPF. A friend of his mother helped him land a job in the Neuquén oil fields, but his parents opposed his leaving home to take it. Fernando was one of the many YPF workers who told me that although their parents took great pride in their son's working for the company, parents disapproved of a son's moving to "the end of the earth." Fernando recalled how hurt he had been that his father helped him prepare for his move but "didn't go to the send-off because for him it was not acceptable for sons to separate from the family." However, soon Fernando and his workmates forged kin relations among themselves to supplement, or replace, their natal families living far from the oil fields. This is one example of how the construction of YPF families in Patagonia involved both dekinning and kinning relations.

Upon arriving in Plaza Huincul in 1964, Fernando traded filial kinship for avuncular and later marital relations as YPFianos incorporated him into their web of kinship. He recounted, "The first thing that happened when it came out that you were from far away was that they invited you home to have a barbeque [*asado*] or some *mate*." His first Christmas exemplified his immediate incorporation into YPFianos' filial bonds. He always had celebrated Christmas with his extended family in Buenos Aires, but, he explained, he started working for YPF just before the holiday: "Therefore, I didn't even think about going to Buenos Aires to be with my family." He rhetorically asked, "Can you believe that there were *compañeros* [workmates] who invited me to celebrate Christmas with them, as if I was part of their family." These "as if" kin relations were soon replaced by ones legitimated by their intersection with the state's legal regime (Lambek, chapter 10, this volume) and its economic apparatus.

Fernando's incorporation into an YPF family was fully realized when he married Claudia, the daughter of a high-ranking YPFiano. Claudia was an office intern at YPF's base in Plaza Huincul when she and Fernando met. More important, she belonged to one of the many families in which all of the men worked for the national oil company. Fernando related that his marriage to this daughter of a prominent YPF family was possible only because he had spent his first eight years in Patagonia working at the Catriel oil camp even after his obligatory rotation at the camp ended, rather than taking a job at the Plaza Huincul base. YPFianos received a 10 percent bonus for working at oil camps like Catriel because, Fernando explained, "it was removed from everything that was civilization. Let's say, it was the Far West."[6] The financial reward for suffering Catriel's "inconveniences" enabled Fernando to save money for a marriage to an YPF daughter. When I asked him to further explain his prescient planning, he instead told me about its results: "When I became engaged, with the years that I spent in Catriel, we bought the refrigerator, we bought the tiles...we bought out the whole commissary." YPF policy encouraged workers to purchase on credit and repay their debts through deductions from their future salary, thus further binding them to YPF. Fernando bought his house this way. He went on to say, "When I had finished paying for everything, then I asked [Claudia] if she wanted to get married, and she said yes, and that was that." His marital desire thus necessitated his continued work for YPF, but, once wed, he was well positioned to take a job at the Plaza Huincul base and spend more time in his new home. Many other YPFianos were not so fortunate and continued to spend long periods in the distant oil camps in order to support their families in the oil towns.

The importance of a house in the company town equipped with the comforts the petroleum industry brought to Patagonia became clearest to me when I mistakenly asked Fernando a question about the eight years he lived at Catriel. Fernando interrupted me to explain that although he spent fifteen days at a time at Catriel, he did not *live* there, he only worked there. "We lived here," he said with a small laugh as he pointed out the window of the old YPF warehouse in which we were sitting. "Do you see that block of buildings, that house that has silver trim? Well, those...were bachelors' dormitories. I stayed there until I got married. When I married, I had my own little house." For Fernando, "living" meant having a residence in the company town where he engaged in familial practices like holiday meals, first as the adoptive kin of established YPF families and then as the head of his own family. In contrast, working in the social services division meant addressing the problems that arose because YPF required its workers to spend long intervals at sites they compared to the "Far West" they saw portrayed in the cowboy-and-Indian movies shown at the YPF theater in Plaza Huincul.

Although state employment was often contingent on extended absences from one's family, this did not mean that kinship bonds were eliminated, or even neglected. State institutions reworked familial attachments to make them support national concerns (Stoler 2004:17). YPF did this by providing its largely male workforce with the pay and benefits that enabled men to support their wives and children, and it thus encouraged the formation of families in which labor was strictly gendered. As was typical at that time, YPF restricted women to a limited number of office jobs at the Plaza Huincul base, paying them far less than male workers. Women were expected to leave these positions when they married, although some continued to work until they gave birth to their first child. Women's ability to maintain homes, raise children, and take care of husbands was made possible by YPF pay scales that increased a man's salary with the addition of each new family member. YPFianos also derived material and symbolic benefits from the package of cradle-to-grave services provided by YPF and SUPE to worker families in the oil towns. In addition to housing for some, YPFianos and their immediate families had access to high-quality health care, transportation, education, commissaries, sports and recreation clubs, and paid vacations at SUPE-owned hotels. As Carolina Lucano's mother saw it, "if you became engaged to someone from YPF, everything was solved, as far as your ability to construct a house, to have a family, to have children. All of that was guaranteed." She was among the many her age whose experience of the privatization led them to be nostalgic for the security and intimacy that the state oil company had provided.

A frequently repeated, bittersweet love story illustrates how familial sentiments assuaged the difficulties of the oil industry and blurred the boundaries among worker solidarity, friendship, and romantic love. A young single YPFiano named Carlos was offered a transfer from the Plaza Huincul base to a distant oil camp, where he would earn a bonus. But when he learned that Juan, a friend and workmate who had married recently, had not received the same offer, Carlos offered Juan the transfer in his place because he felt that Juan could use the extra income more than he. Juan accepted, but on his first trip home at Holy Week, his YPF transport plane crashed and everyone died. When Fernando Castillo repeated this story to me, he emphasized that it demonstrated how YPF was bound by familial sentiments: "The whole town felt the pain that they suffered because [the victims'] cousins, siblings, in-laws are here. Everyone lives here. Perhaps they didn't get along, but they know that his cousin lives over there, you see." Yet, the story does not end here. Following company policy, YPF provided Juan's young widow with a job as a secretary in one of YPF's offices in Plaza Huincul. She got to know Carlos while working there; they fell in love and married. Fernando was not the only one to recount this linked funeral and marriage to me as exemplary of the power of YPF kinship in its "golden days," when YPFiano families received material and ideological support from the nation-state.

The history of YPF in northwest Patagonia illustrates that a concern with kinship informed the practice of government. Whereas Stoler (2004) finds the "affective state" in educational and other social policies, the history of YPF demonstrates that affective concerns were central to the state's economic projects. The educational, medical, and social functions of the state in the company towns cannot be separated from its economic mission; they worked in concert to generate modern capitalist subjects as, for example, both sons and workers. Paternalistic policies (such as job inheritance and survivor benefits) and programs (such as housing and commissaries) were employed to discipline citizen-workers, their forms of liaison, and their sentiments through seemingly nurturing acts of encouraging family life. These biopolitical actions were naturalized by drawing on national discourse and religious idioms. In the story above, this entailed intertwining petroleum nationalism with Catholic ideas about brotherhood and sacrifice. Furthermore, the discourse of the company as parent subtly drew on religious metaphors of hierarchy and power to cloak discipline in compassionate cloth. One also can see the productive work of familial and national sentiments in Fernando Castillo's narrative about celebrating Christmas in the oil town. Kinship is repeatedly framed as the antidote to the ills and hardships of frontier capitalism and thus is understood as a crucial ingredient in the recipe for national development in the twentieth century. This history made kinship particularly rich material for dealing with neoliberalism as the newest capitalist frontier at the turn of the twenty-first century.

FATHERING NEW COMPANIES

The Lucano family's experience producing petroleum and children in northwest Patagonia reveals the importance of kinship in the oil industry under both the national regime and the neoliberal one that replaced it. Like the vast majority of residents of the oil towns, the lives of the men and women in the Lucano family were intimately tied to YPF. Carolina's father, Alberto Lucano, started working for YPF Estatal in Santa Fe province as a teenager and was transferred to Neuquén at age twenty-two. He came to the town of Plaza Huincul with his brother, who also worked for YPF, and five years later married Teresa, who was the daughter in an YPFiano family and a secretary at the YPF offices in Plaza Huincul. As in most YPF families, Alberto continued to work for YPF, and Teresa left when she was pregnant with their first daughter. Teresa's two brothers, her parents, her uncles, and several other family members were also YPFianos. "Because of this," Teresa's brother-in-law Freddy Garza concluded, "everything revolved around YPF, everyone, all the families."

YPFianos like the Lucano men expected to work for the state company until they retired and to be compensated for their dedication and sacrifice with lifelong financial and social support for their families. When YPF Estatal was converted into YPF SA, then bought by the Spanish firm Repsol, four out of every five employees were eliminated: 43,000 people in total. Alberto Lucano was fifty when he was dismissed and was thus among the enormous number of YPFianos who were "too old to find new jobs but too young to retire." With no other employment options, they followed the advice of their YPF bosses and union representatives that workers should convert their YPF units into *emprendimientos*, special oil service microenterprises that were collectively owned, managed, and staffed by former state oil workers.[7] The emprendimiento program was included in the national law that converted the state-owned YPF Estatal into the privately owned YPF SA, intended as a temporary measure to help ease the transition of state workers in isolated oil regions from dependence on the state and move them toward entrepreneurial independence.

Alberto Lucano and a few other skilled workers in YPF's exploration division formed Napalco, an emprendimiento offering oil well maintenance services to the privatized company. They continued to do the same work they had done for the state enterprise, only now without the guarantees of stable employment or the benefits that they once had as state workers. The emprendimiento worker-owners also assumed new responsibilities for which they were unprepared, including negotiating contracts, managing large cash flows, and paying business taxes. As the senior member of the group that formed Napalco, Alberto became the emprendimiento's manager. His partners recognized him as the "father," and later the "grandfather," of the company, yet he described himself to me as an "overalls manager, not a briefcase manager," who continued to work in the field alongside the others.

One way that people around the world have coped with recent political-economic changes is by adapting preexisting principles of descent to pursue new business ventures (Ellison 2009), yet kinship is not merely a new resource for capitalist exploitation. In the Argentine oil industry, nuclear families organized around patrilineal descent formed the model for oil field services subcontracting firms. Kinship was, moreover, the ideal against which contractual relationships were judged and often found to fall short. Although the YPFianos used kinship sentiments to articulate a moral critique of the separation of economic and familial domains that is supposed to characterize neoliberal formations, they were also constrained by their kin obligations and the paternalism entrenched in the oil fields.

Only a few years after Alberto and his partners founded Napalco, Carolina returned home from the university to find the company on the brink of bankruptcy. Its only client was YPF SA; it was deeply in debt; the person the YPFianos had hired to manage the office had taken another job; and their accountant was mismanaging funds. By this time, most of the other forty-four emprendimientos founded in the Neuquén region during privatization had closed, and the handful that remained were in as bad financial shape as Napalco. What is more, they were being pushed out by giant transnational oil services companies. As a professional who owed her education to her father's work at YPF, Carolina told me that she felt obligated to assist her father and his partners in saving their emprendimiento. She went to work addressing Napalco's financial and administrative problems while they continued to work at the wells as they had been doing for decades. Kinship bonds were more than a metaphor for business in the emprendimientos; they were crucial to their operation, especially in the face of crisis.

Carolina's action hints at how the kinship bonds that developed within the state oil industry were put to work in the private domain in order to rescue YPFianos from destitution. Yet, kinship *qua* paternalism was widely seen as the root of their problems. Business consultants hired to teach the emprendimiento owners how to be "entrepreneurs" identified the YPFianos' filial relationships as the cause of their failures. One consultant told them that many of the emprendimientos went bankrupt because their owners did not "understand that one can no longer depend on the state, on the paternal state, on 'Dad the State.'" He urged them, "Instead, it depends a lot on you guys now, on great ingenuity, intuition, on being go-getters...on having the mentality of an entrepreneur, having a vision for business." Kinship—here in the form of "Dad the State"—stood for an atavistic and juvenile dependency, in contrast to the individualism, self-sufficiency, and competition of the market. It was not an accident that the process of structural adjustment made the state into a neglectful, even abusive parent, as its new configuration was supposed to teach its "children" to grow up quickly and become independent adults. The apologists for the new privatized economy saw a stark division between filial relations and business acumen, and they used kinship as the ruler against which economic reason was measured.

The emprendimiento owners worked to overcome the tension between outsiders' infantilization of state workers and their own celebration of the bonds between fathers and sons. Unlike the business consultants, they understood kinship and business as mutually reinforcing. They acknowledged that their filial relationship with the state had changed, but they did not agree that familial bonds should be replaced by an entrepreneurial mentality that stressed individualism. Instead, the successful emprendimiento owners credited kinship bonds with sustaining their business ventures. When I asked Alberto what he thought separated Napalco from the emprendimientos that had gone out of business, he repeated what numerous surviving YPFianos-turned-emprendimiento-owners had told me: his company was a family. He frequently spoke of his junior co-workers as sons, for instance, remarking:

> My sons, well, we have known them for years. I call them kids [*pibes*], you see, because they arrived young at...our sector of YPF. I was an operator when they arrived. Thus, I was given them so that I could direct them and show them things first. It must be twenty years that we have known each other. Most of them have married standing by our side. The last of them, Julian, just got married. Ramiro just had his first kid, and he had him while with [Napalco].... When we get together, the wives, the daughters come...over to my house, and they are just one more family member.... And we are not going to get rid of anyone, because we are going to be [one of] the four or five [emprendimientos] that remain. We are going to defend [Napalco] for sure.

Alberto passed quickly from his description of the familial bonds within the emprendimiento to his justification for not dismissing any worker-owners, even during periods in which they did not have revenue to cover their pay. Most of the emprendimientos continued to employ all their partners—despite subcontracting agreements with YPF SA that did not cover the cost—pushing many into debt and then bankruptcy. Whereas this led the business consultants to see familial bonds as the cause of their financial problems, YPFianos like Alberto saw the roots of their dire economic situation in the terms of their contracts with YPF SA and in the structure of the global oil industry. He was among many YPFianos who pointed out that the privatized company used the emprendimientos to improve their negotiating position with transnational oil field service firms by maintaining the possibility of "local" options at lower cost. The irony was that state officials, corporate managers, and business consultants criticized the state-workers-turned-small-business-owners for maintaining the very filial practices that enabled them to offer less expensive services than their competitors (Shever 2008).

Alberto explicated the difficulties of his emprendimiento's affective bonds by telling me about a truck Napalco had inherited from YPF. The privatized YPF SA had sold the Napalco partners the truck they had used in YPF Estatal, overcharging them for it and then extracting money each month from the fees it paid for their services until the debt was settled. "We paid with our labor," Alberto told me, only to have YPF SA declare the truck too old to enter the oil fields a short time later. The Napalco partners planned to place the retired truck on a pedestal mound as a monument to how their emprendimiento was born, but Carolina convinced them that they should sell it instead. It was a very difficult decision for them. Alberto explained, "We had sold other things...but it's fucked up to sell [the truck] that got you started" [and that] "we loved so much." Napalco's truck was not mere property whose worth could be assessed in monetary terms but was a part of the Napalco family and thus owed an honored resting place that recognized its dedicated service. But this attempt to re-create YPF kinship in the emprendimiento was obstructed by the inflexible rules of the privatized company.

The Napalco partners were more successful in translating YPF kinship into familial bonds in their emprendimiento when it involved young employees rather than old trucks. After they regained financial stability and began to hire employees, Carolina analogized, "The new ones are under [Alberto's] wing, like chicks," much as Alberto's partners had been when they first joined his YPF unit. By the time Napalco started expanding, Alberto was shifting from an active, paternal role to becoming the "grandfather of the company." As a demonstration of his new, more indulgent position, he frequently picked up pastries (*facturas*) on his way to work as a treat for his team, because he could not provide the generous meals YPF Estatal once had offered him. While he spoiled them with sweets, Carolina pointed out, he also made sure that each of the "boys" got three doughnuts, checking that "no one ate one more unless someone gave it to him." It was this familial disposition that Alberto and his partners credited with saving Napalco when many other emprendimientos had failed.

The YPFianos understood the emprendimientos as creations of the state oil company and extensions of YPF kinship. The emprendimientos maintained their preexisting kinship bonds as the strategy that offered them the best chance for survival in the reorganized circuits of the global oil industry. Affective bonds among workers were an especially crucial legacy because most YPFianos lost the majority of their financial and material assets, including their homes. Alberto envisioned Napalco as a family constructed out of long-standing attachments that could not be broken by market forces, and he called Napalco his "adoptive son." Yet, this son had caused him many more problems than his loyal daughter, Carolina. Although YPFianos paid close attention to the links between fathers and sons, in many cases, their daughters maintained the intergenerational continuity in the oil industry. Napalco thus illustrates a change in gender dynamics with the reconfiguration of the Argentine oil industry (Shever 2012). While Alberto imagined the connection between the productivity of family life and industrial labor through adoptive sons and trucks, Carolina effectively enacted this connection through her financial management of the business. She performed the productivity of the domestic domain, in its double meaning of national industry and household kinship. The obligation of kinship thereby constrained Carolina's career path as much as it extended Alberto's. The Lucano family's experience also suggests that the notion of the domestic can signify both the space of kinship and the space of the nation, both the intimate family and the national public. It therefore offers rich ground for continued analysis of the diverse articulations of personhood, household, the state, and the global.

CONCLUSION

Kinship occupies a crucial yet ambivalent position within capitalism. This chapter highlights the uses of kinship, first, to construct the petroleum industry and the modern nation-state and, second, to refuse the dominant understanding of entrepreneurship in neoliberal discourse and policy. It illustrates how kinship enabled workers to build a national oil company and an urban enclave in Patagonia and, later, to reincorporate themselves within the privatized oil industry. Kinship bonds and familial sentiments have proven to be particularly flexible forces of production that have sustained both the national and private oil industries in Argentina and enabled the transition between them. The surviving emprendimientos show that an effective business strategy can include the maintenance, even the strengthening, of filial relationships. Yet, as YPFianos tried to translate the nurturing role of YPF into their emprendimientos, they were restrained by their far more limited resources. Kinship both enabled the YPFianos to make a place for themselves in the privatized industry and constrained their actions within it. Whereas this chapter emphasizes the challenges of preserving kin relationships in a rapidly changing world, others in this volume (for instance, Rutherford, chapter 11) remind us that breaking kinship bonds can be as desirable, and difficult, as maintaining them.

The YPFianos' nostalgia for familial wholeness comments on the realities of a neoliberal economic regime in which dekinning is a necessity for survival. Most of the emprendimientos that refused to limit their staffs/families went bankrupt. Moreover, the YPFianos' nostalgia overlooks the fact that the formation of the YPF workforce and YPF families had long been as much about dekinning as about kinning. Their life histories reveal that they needed to break the bonds of their natal families in order to form new families in the oil towns, then to abandon their new families in order to maintain them, and finally to downscale kinship in order to survive as subcontractors. Given this history, it seems that the family has taken on new salience in the aftermath of the wave of privatizations enacted around the world at the turn of the twenty-first century. The moral right to a stable family is being particularly vigorously asserted even as its conditions of possibility are being undermined. Although company towns like the one that engendered Carolina's life were part of a historical moment of industrial capitalism that has largely passed, the social forms they created—worker subjectivity and kinship, state and company paternalism, and petroleum nationalism—will continue to have a significant influence in the future. The reconfiguration of the Argentine oil industry only underscores the analytical necessity of recognizing the mutual constitution and transformation of kinship, labor, industry, state, and nation.

Notes

1. I use the designation "Patagonia" to refer to the southern region of Argentina, despite the fact that Patagonia encompasses both Chile and Argentina, in order to avoid the awkward repetition of "Argentine Patagonia" throughout the chapter. I use "YPF" or the anachronistic term "YPF Estatal" to refer to the state-owned oil enterprise that existed from 1922 to 1992. "YPF SA" refers to the privatized oil corporation from 1992 to 1999 ("SA" stands for *sociedad anónima*, which is equivalent to "incorporated" in English). In 1999, Repsol, the former national oil company of Spain, purchased controlling shares of YPF SA and renamed it YPF-Repsol, or Repsol-YPF outside Argentina. In May 2012, the Argentine government seized control of Repsol's stake in the company, thus renationalizing it. Yet, this was not the political and economic reversal that it may seem. The new YPF will still be a joint-stock corporation, not a state entity, and through it, the government will be able to control only a small part of the oil production industry in the country. This is not a return to the YPF of the preceding century.

2. Some parts of this historical narrative also appear in Shever 2012.

3. They bought and sold livestock, and they frequently were accused of stealing animals from the settlers who moved into the land that indigenous people had inhabited for centuries. Nearly all of the heterogeneous indigenous groups in Patagonia became incorporated into the Mapuche nation, whose chiefs (*caciques*) managed dealings with outsiders, including the livestock market and trade across the Andes (Nicoletti and Floria Navarro 2000:54–55). The government in Buenos Aires attempted to repopulate the land with European settlers by rewarding soldiers with land grants and facilitating the creation of enormous farms and ranches.

4. Although official state discourse spoke of "Argentizing" the new settlements by building primary schools in order to "educate to sovereignty" (*educar a soberano*), Catholic missionaries were the ones who provided what formal education there was in the Patagonian territories (Nicoletti and Floria Navarro 2000:90–92).

5. All translations from Spanish sources are my own.

6. Although speaking Spanish, he used the English term "Far West."

7. *Emprendimiento* is a term coined from the verb *emprender*, "to embark or launch." These emprendimientos might have been called "start-ups" in English if their owners had been much younger, wealthier, and more formally educated. Of the more than 3,000 YPFianos in Plaza Huincul and Cutral Có who were let go during the privatization process, approximately 1,700 formed emprendimientos.

5

Ghosts, Commensality, and Scuba Diving

Tracing Kinship and Sociality in Clinical Pathology Labs and Blood Banks in Penang

Janet Carsten

I had been observing life in the clinical pathology labs and blood banks for three or four months before I began to notice the ghosts. Having become apparent, however, they seemed hard to avoid. One morning in the blood bank, I was talking to Sharon, one of the medical lab technologists, as she was preparing equipment to take on a mobile blood campaign the following Sunday. Sharon mentioned that she would not be able to attend the blood drive because she would be on call in the lab. She preferred blood campaigns to being on call, she said, because the latter meant being on duty at night. When I asked whether she slept at the lab, Sharon said she did not—she was scared to because of the ghosts. "Are there ghosts in the blood bank?" I asked. On this matter, Sharon's reply was equivocal: "Temporarily. It's OK."[1]

The first account I heard of ghosts concerned particularly unsettling events at the house of the recently deceased grandmother of a lab trainee. There, relatives had gathered the night before the funeral. Such stories, told with considerable relish and excitement, would often trigger longer discussions to which others would contribute their experiences of uncanny events—some had nothing to do with the hospital, labs, or blood banks. As I listened more closely, however, I caught traces of ghostly presences in the workspaces of the labs and blood banks. One day, I heard a senior medical lab technologist, Siu Meng, telling a small group of trainees about working in the hospital: the different kinds of work available and the opportunities for training; the importance of time management, shifts, and on-call duty; and that they should not listen to ghost stories. I interjected a query about ghosts in the lab, and Siu Meng said that there were no ghosts in the present lab but, yes, in the old one, she had "felt the presence of evil."

Others were more matter of fact. One medical lab technologist reported that she would "normally [turn] on the radio and listen to music" when she felt something strange going on at night. Several agreed that ghosts had been prone to appear in the lab's old premises in the hospital but when it was moved upstairs some months before, things had improved. Another medical lab technologist, Kamariah, told me that she had once heard a little girl laughing in the old lab. When she went to look, a little girl was jumping over a drain, playing. Kamariah looked at the clock; it was 3:00 a.m. She shut the door and turned up the radio. Normally, she said, she did not listen to the radio. Downstairs was dirty, Kamariah added, and also it was open to the outside and to thieves.

One afternoon, as I was talking to someone in the Immunology Department, I noticed an animated discussion on the other side of the lab, where several medical lab technologists and a perfusionist were gathered around a workbench. When I went to investigate, I found them excitedly talking about an Indian nurse who had apparently seen a headless man in the old building of the hospital. The perfusionist brought up a story of a patient who had requested a transfer from a third-class ward to a first-class one because noise prevented him from sleeping. He was then given a separate room, but during the night, he felt children playing with his feet and then abandoned the room to sit at the nurses' station instead. Another patient, the perfusionist related, an Indian lawyer, had also complained about children running around in the night. I asked whether there were ghosts in the lab, and he replied that there were none yet but they were close by. And he added, "The blood bank is here." I asked whether ghosts were attracted by the blood bank. They were, he replied, and went on to tell me about the ghosts of women patients who had "hung themselves using their own blouses in psychy ward toilets."

In this chapter, I have chosen what may seem a rather unlikely entry into laboratory life. The hospital blood banks and clinical pathology labs where I conducted fieldwork in Penang in 2008 were highly technologized working environments. They housed sophisticated, up-to-date machinery for screening blood and for carrying out the hundreds of diagnostic tests on blood samples that are common in any modern clinical pathology laboratory setting. The main part of these workspaces was closed to patients and the public, and this was made clear by notices at the entrances to these departments. Apart from the designated areas where donors came to give blood or where blood samples were taken from outpatients, only lab staff and hospital personnel were permitted in the labs and blood banks. The working environments were air conditioned, calm, and quiet as white-coated medical lab technologists engaged in a multitude of detailed tasks associated with blood grouping, diagnostic testing, screening, and cross-matching. So what kinds of entities are these ghosts? And what attributes of social relations might their presence indicate?

The starting point for the research described here was blood as a site of biomedical procedures. There is, of course, a rich social science literature on idioms of blood in religious, political, and familial life (Feeley-Harnik 1981; Karakasidou 1997; Knight 1991; Schneider 1980; Starr 1998). In Malaysia, as elsewhere, blood is a dominant idiom for kinship relations and for ethnicity. An interest in the links and separations between biomedical knowledge, cultures of kinship, and other facets of identity has led me to investigate not only the working lives of those who deal with blood in everyday hospital settings but also the ways in which different idioms and practices of sociality—which ostensibly have little to do with the work that goes on in blood banks or clinical pathology labs—may coexist in these spaces. I seek to understand what kinds of workspaces blood banks and clinical pathology labs are, what sorts of boundaries operate between them and the outside world, and how professionals with medical, scientific, and technical expertise negotiate these boundaries when carrying out routine procedures.

This chapter focuses on some seemingly small ways in which laboratory life and everyday life in Malaysia coexist in the lab. I describe how those who work in the clinical pathology labs and blood banks endeavor to make these spaces sociable. Within this highly technologized working environment, we can discern a process of "domestication"—involving food, friendships, and kin relations—that is set in motion by the medical laboratory technologists and lab technicians who work there. But besides delineating the *forms* of this sociality, I suggest *how* they matter. I present stories in which the boundaries between the lab, the blood bank, and the world outside seem to have become a bit fuzzy. There are, of course, several levels on which this might be significant. One is how such boundary crossings affect the working lives of lab technicians and medical lab technologists; another is what they indicate more generally about how these employees experience the work processes that go on in these spaces; and a third might be what they tell us even more generally about social relations in Malaysia.

There is another obvious set of questions, however, which I mainly leave to one side in this chapter. They concern how the forms of sociality described here impact directly the way actual work tasks are carried out in these spaces—the taking of blood, its screening, and the many hundreds of diagnostic tests that are run every day in these labs. Partly because it is not possible to deal adequately with all aspects of a complex ethnography in one chapter, in what follows, I am not directly concerned with the processes of taking blood from patients or donors, screening, or diagnostic testing. Nevertheless, I would argue that the processes of domestication I describe—in contexts that are apparently unambiguously "modern"—suggest the possibility of "uneven seepage," to use Rayna Rapp's term, "in the traffic between biomedical and familial discourses" (Rapp 1999:303; see also Lock et al. 2006). Just what is meant by "seepage"? For the moment, I suggest that the circulation of different kinds and idioms of sociality in these spaces reveals that the separations between "laboratory life" and "everyday life" in Penang are uneven and incomplete. Such idioms and forms of identification circulate in the same spaces, sometimes directly colliding, often apparently coexisting without obvious consequences for work practices. This, in turn, might lead us to reflect not only on the nature of "domaining practices" central to the institution of kinship as an analytic field—and to its assumed isolation within a domestic sphere in modern societies—but also on the related symbolic importance of science as a "sacred domain" that "supposedly transcend[s] human agency" (Yanagisako and Delaney 1995:13; see also Carsten 2004; Schneider 1984).

In terms of scientific practice, Bruno Latour (1993:30–31) and others have argued that laboratory life proceeds *as if* it were wholly separate from the rest of life and that "the work of purification," which is central to the lab, involves separating nature and society. But this is a pretense, because nature is actually *constructed* rather than *discovered* in the laboratory. The connections between nature and society—the denial of which, Latour suggests, is crucial to the project of modernity—are actually central to how science works. Relating this insight to the themes of this chapter, and this volume more generally, the presumed isolation of kinship within a domestic sphere and its separation from such pursuits as scientific and laboratory work are seen as equally foundational to the project of modernity. The co-occurrence of a world of kinship and intimacy alongside a rigorously enforced regime of laboratory work suggests, at the very least, some fractures and wobbles, some gentle mergings and crisscrossings, between these supposedly separate domains. But domestication may not necessarily be a smooth or unproblematic process. Having delineated some of the contours of sociality among staff in the labs and blood banks, in the final parts of this chapter, I return to the matter of ghosts and probe the significance of their presence.

CONVIVIAL RELATIONS

During the time I spent based in two private hospitals in Penang, I tried to establish what kinds of social connections existed among the staff members who worked in the clinical pathology labs and between these workers and staff in other departments of the same hospital. Because what I was doing was, in many respects, a workplace ethnography, I did not have direct access to people's home lives—although almost all the people I talked to told me about their families and homes. I built up a sense of people's lives through their work and the things they talk about with their colleagues. Some of these colleagues have known each other for a very long time; they are also friends, or even spouses, and they would often tell me about each other. Many incidents in the everyday running of the labs revealed quite a lot about the staff's family lives, backgrounds, and concerns and their opinions on matters that went beyond the workplace. But I had the sense that what I was learning was quite fragmentary—in the same way that, in any modern institution, what we know about most of our colleagues is always fragmentary. By placing some of these vignettes side by side, it is nevertheless possible to get a sense of the texture of the lives and social relations of those I studied.

Much of what I gleaned was learned in one way or another over food. Food, as any Penangite will relate, is an important part of life there. Penang is renowned for its wonderfully diverse culinary culture (encompassing Chinese, Malay, Indian, and Western cooking traditions, among others) and the huge number of excellent restaurants and street stalls. People in Penang love to talk about food and do so constantly, swapping recipes and recommendations about favorite eateries. Food is, of course, not allowed in the labs, and this fact was displayed on the walls of the labs that I visited, where eating areas were strictly separated from work areas. It thus seemed paradoxical to discover the degree to which food was a fundamental part of collegial relations and a major topic of conversation. Both clinical pathology labs that I studied had areas separated from the workspaces so that staff could bring food and eat. In one lab, this was a small table and seating area screened off at the end of the main laboratory space and equipped with a refrigerator, sink, and kettle. In the other, it was part of an outside area adjacent to the lab and connected to a storeroom and an on-call room where staff could sleep or rest. This space, also equipped for very simple cooking, had been made pleasant by an elaborate arrangement of plants and a series of fishponds with water flowing between them that had been constructed and maintained by some of the lab staff.

The eating areas in both labs were well used by the staff. Some would bring breakfast and eat there before starting work in the morning; some would bring food from home, outside stalls, or the hospital canteen and eat there at lunchtime. Drinks could be made using kettles or could be brought in. Quite often, someone would bring in a special snack—such as fruit, cookies, or cake—to share with colleagues, and this was especially common during the major festivals, such as Chinese New Year. Lab staff would also go in groups of two or three, or more, to eat lunch together—to the hospital canteen, to outside stalls not far from the hospital, or occasionally to a reasonably priced restaurant. Because the same colleagues tended to eat together regularly, I was quickly absorbed into these commensal patterns.

On an informal and spontaneous basis, small groups of friends would sometimes go out together in the evenings—to see a film, eat a meal in a restaurant, or visit a karaoke bar. These events tended to involve younger, unmarried staff and especially those without young children. Occasionally, more formal eating occasions were organized by the lab staff. Until relatively recently, I was told by the staff in one lab, they had once a year cooked a large meal outside together. In the other lab, I was told that in the past, senior staff would organize this kind of annual event in their own homes. Large celebratory events away from the lab were considered somewhat difficult to organize because of the requirements of shift work and on-call duties, which made it impossible for all staff to attend. But there were also ways around these constraints. Biotech companies installing large, expensive items of equipment might be encouraged to order in a meal for the lab, which would take a recognizable Malaysian form, or food would be ordered in to mark a colleague's leaving to take a new job. The choice of menu would be a matter of much discussion and some anxiety for the person organizing it. For occasions when all the lab staff was involved, the menu had to take account of different dietary restrictions—especially the prohibition of pork for the Muslim members—although most of the staff were Malaysian Chinese. This is a normal and accepted part of contemporary Malaysian life in ethnically diverse settings.[2]

Thus, although it is true to say that food was not allowed in the lab, one could say that relations between colleagues were established and maintained through everyday and festive commensality. This might involve something as simple as a shared bag of mangos brought from a visit to parents in the village, a box of cookies baked at home, or perhaps something more elaborate, such as a full meal involving a small group of friends or even the entire staff. When young student trainees arrived successively in batches over a period of weeks in one lab I studied, they would at first eat lunch together. But, gradually, the trainees established tentative commensal relations with the permanent staff, and groupings were established through gender, age, ethnic, or other connections and sometimes crisscrossed these in different ways.

Food and commensality thus marked spatial and social separations in the hospital and the labs: one could eat in the hospital canteen with other hospital staff or eat in the designated space attached to the labs that was available only to clinical pathology and blood bank staff; one could go out to eat at lunchtime or (more rarely) in the evening with one's chosen group of friends; and one could bring home-cooked food or homegrown produce to work, either for sharing or to eat alone. In all these cases, staff would wash their hands at the designated sinks in view of colleagues after finishing their work and before eating. Occasionally, it was possible to observe seepages in the boundaries between eating and non-eating areas of the lab. A special meal ordered in and served in a "clean" meeting room that was too small for all staff members might necessitate colonizing the manager's office or other workspaces to eat; occasionally, a few sweets or a small snack might be quickly eaten in a work area, but not at a lab bench or in any space where samples were collected.

Certain groups of workplace friends would eat together almost every day; others were more flexible in their eating arrangements. It was noticeable that those who regularly ate together were often of the same ethnicity (this could partly be explained teleologically through adherence to different food proscriptions)—though, once again, one could also regularly detect seepages across ethnic lines. Since co-eating was a mark of friendship and, as I experienced, could also initiate friendships, temporality was folded into commensal work relations. Collegiality could be transformed from something transient into warm friendship through regular co-eating; conversely, fractures in work friendships were marked through the cessation of such relations. Sometimes, as I describe below, co-eating could be transformed into more long-lasting ties involving household members or even marriage.

Food thus marked spatial, social, and ethnic separations and seepages; it was an indicator of cleanliness and purity; it was a barometer of the warmth and strength of connections; and it articulated temporal accretions and fractures among colleagues.[3] In short, as many anthropologists have described (Appadurai 1981; Carsten 1997; Douglas 1966), it was a moral barometer of social relations.

LABORATORY CONNECTIONS

Over lunch with small groups of colleagues, I learned many of the most interesting things about the lives of staff in the clinical pathology labs and blood banks. On one occasion, over a Kentucky Fried Chicken lunch,[4] I asked one young couple, a medical lab technologist and a hospital administrator, how they had originally connected. With some laughter and embarrassment, Stephen, who worked in the human resources department, first told me to ask Mr. Khoo, the lab manager. But he then related that Mr. Khoo had invited him to come on a mobile blood drive four years previously, where he met his fiancée-to-be. It took him about a month after this event, Stephen told me, to ask her out on a date. Blood donation campaigns are serious work events, but they sometimes have the air of an office outing since they involve going in a group of ten or more staff in hospital vehicles to places outside the hospital, such as temples, factories, Chinese association halls, or shopping malls. These may be elsewhere on the island or some distance away on the mainland. Such excursions may take most of the day and can involve a lunch along the way. Stephen told me that Mr. Khoo now claims that he arranged their match. I asked whether Stephen knew that he was being set up before he went on the blood drive, and Stephen told me he did. Meanwhile, his partner was looking more and more surprised as she listened to this exchange. She told me that until I asked about it, she had not heard that her fiancé knew about the matchmaking intentions of her boss before their first meeting—although she had known that her boss was somehow involved. This young couple was planning their wedding a few months hence, and it was expected that, as when others in the lab held their wedding celebrations, they would invite all their colleagues.

Over the months I was there, I came to know of several marriages involving staff from the lab and staff from other departments. Also, quite a few people had other relatives, distant or close—in one case, a twin brother, in another a mother—working elsewhere in the same hospital. In one hospital, this was so much the case that I was advised never to say anything about staff working elsewhere in the same hospital, just in case they turned out to be a relative of the person to whom I was talking. One senior medical lab technologist was married to a colleague in the same lab, another's husband had previously worked in the same lab, but he had recently left the hospital to take up further studies. Although it took me some time to learn about these connections, they were not particularly hard to find when I started looking. In the case of the identical twin brothers who somehow kept popping up in each other's departments, it was hard to miss—especially after the twin who worked in physiotherapy came to donate blood in the blood bank while his brother was working close by.

Children and babies were another source of connection between staff members. They were often the subject of conversations between colleagues, who would relate problems they were having, discuss issues about feeding and diet, tell funny stories, or mention their children's achievements. During lulls in the work, they also often showed each other recent pictures of their children, which they carried on their mobile phones. Babies were regularly brought into the hospital for health checks and blood tests, which were available to staff at reduced rates, so they might be brought to greet colleagues in the lab. Similarly, elderly parents of staff were eligible for treatment at reduced rates at the hospital, so colleagues were usually familiar with one another's parents, spouses, and children.

Medical lab technologists and other staff in clinical pathology labs and blood banks often talked about their own and family members' ailments and possible cures in terms of the different kinds of medical knowledge (Chinese, Ayurvedic, and Malay) that circulate in Malaysia. Some of these conversations and references were quite fleeting and cropped up when a relative was ill or somebody had back pain or the flu. Different ways of dealing with these everyday problems might then be discussed with colleagues, and, depending on the background and nature of the problem, a Chinese remedy for sore throat or a particularly skilled specialist in Chinese massage might be recommended.

A more consistent theme in discussions about health matters related to babies and childbirth. Many of the medical lab technologists were married women with young children. When I asked them individually about their childbirth experiences, I was surprised to learn that almost all of them had gone through a lengthy period observing postnatal restrictions and taboos involving diet and bathing, and applying heat to their stomach. These practices are widespread in Malaysia, and I had encountered the Malay version of them in the 1980s when carrying out fieldwork in a rural Malay village (Carsten 1995b, 1997). In urban contexts in contemporary Malaysia, it is common to hear middle-class people talk of a period of "confinement" (using the English term) after childbirth, and in Penang, there are a number of private "confinement homes" where women can spend this period if it is more convenient than being looked after at home. The women I asked in the labs, however, spoke about being under the care of their mother-in-law or their mother during confinement, and they often attributed their following these practices to the strictness of their senior kin.

One reason I had not expected that medical lab technologists working in clinical pathology labs would follow these postnatal practices is that, in both the Malay and the Chinese cases, they focus on matters to do with blood (as well as wind)—precisely their area of technical or scientific expertise. The central idea is that giving birth involves the loss of blood and is a "cooling" process. This means that after giving birth, in order to restore the body to its normal state, women should stay in the house and should avoid various foods that are thought to be cooling (especially raw fruits and vegetables and iced drinks). They should also avoid bathing in cold water, and they may have heat applied in various ways to their body, specifically to their stomach. The confinement period is arduous in a tropical climate because it lasts for forty-four days in the Malay case and for at least one month, I was told, in the Chinese and involves subjecting the body to heat. One medical lab technologist, Hwa Min, told me that she had followed these prohibitions but had not enjoyed it. She could not wash her hair with water for a month and had to use alcohol instead, which would evaporate, and herbs. "But," she said, "it works." To indicate this efficacy, Hwa Min referred to a colleague of hers who had not followed the proper restrictions and now had a problem with backaches. However, she told me that she thought her daughter's generation would not do it—she had already wavered. Asking me about scientific proof, Hwa Min told me that Chinese people also worry about "wind" (using the Malay term, *masuk angin*, literally, "wind enters"). She then asked what I had done after giving birth. Did I wash my hair? When I said that I did, she nodded and said, "Maybe Chinese [are] more susceptible." We agreed that these were somewhat mysterious matters.

There were many different ways, then, for kinship and other types of intimate relations to be the basis of connections between staff who worked in the blood bank and the clinical pathology labs. Sometimes these connections—such as the shared health concerns of women who have young children—might be quite loose. Or they might build up gradually between colleagues who have worked together over several decades, developing mutual interests in projects—such as the construction and daily maintenance of decorative fishponds—or making visits to each other's houses. In one case of colleagues who had worked together over a very long period, one of them had lodged for some time many years previously in the other's parental home. Sometimes the connections were direct and intimate, leading to marriage between colleagues within the lab in two cases I knew of and, in another, to an engagement between a staff member and a young woman who had formerly been a trainee in the lab.

In both sets of labs and blood banks that I studied, it seemed to me that relations were in many ways warm and usually harmonious—although in one lab, there was more obvious friction between colleagues than in the other. This was manifested in a general concern about "groupings" or cliques, and although this was not explicitly articulated in terms of ethnic differences, it seemed to me that this potentiality was present. This was partly because such distinctions, to some degree, underlay commensal patterns. My impression was that there was a higher density of social relations than one might find in similar settings in the United Kingdom and that this resulted partly from the considerable time that many colleagues had been working together and also from locally accepted cultural practices and norms.

If food was a way to initiate friendships between colleagues and underlaid temporal accretions and fractures in social relations, then over time it could also provide an avenue to transform collegial relations into bonds of kinship. The manner in which such transformations could be worked was recognizably Malaysian (without necessarily being exclusive to Malaysia)—an insistence on sociability and a strong curiosity and interest in different kinds of food and ways of cooking that could sometimes travel across ethnic boundaries. The density of sociality and the instances recounted to me in which workplace conviviality had been transformed over time into marital relations reminded me of the registers of sociability that I had encountered among Malay villagers in Langkawi in the 1980s, where eating proper rice meals together over time creates a bond of kinship (Carsten 1995b, 1997). Analogies between Indian, Chinese, and Malay ideas connecting food consumption, the body, and ties between persons suggest their translatability (Appadurai 1981; Daniel 1984; Lambert 2000; Marriott 1976; Stafford 2000; Thompson 1988). Despite the fact that food here, as in many ethnically plural urban settings in Malaysia, is an obvious marker of ethnic boundaries, I suggest that it is also a potential means of overcoming them—both temporarily and permanently. And this perhaps explains why food consumption in such settings can be the subject of considerable anxiety.

The symbolic potential of shared consumption in this case had a further twist in that those who worked in the blood banks and clinical pathology labs, like other hospital staff, were strongly encouraged to donate blood to the hospital blood bank in order to maintain supplies. And quite regularly, they persuaded their spouses, boyfriends, and connections elsewhere in the hospital to come to the blood banks to do so. Thus, it was not uncommon to find one colleague taking blood from another or from the spouse of a colleague. One might thus speak of a process of domestication of the workspace that could have transformative potential for bodies and kin relations and that operated not just through the sharing of meals, friendships, time, and conviviality but also, and in a unique completion of this cycle, through the shared donation of blood to the hospital blood bank.

LABORATORY LIVES

The interpenetration of work with other forms of sociality was not restricted to a register of commensality or kinship but sometimes took more explicitly ethical forms. Kamariah was a Malay Muslim woman in her thirties, married and with a baby. She had been working as a medical lab technologist for seven years. Thoughtful, sociable, and lively, she had come to work in the hospital in the 1990s as a lab technician before being sent for training as a medical lab technologist. When I asked what had drawn her into her chosen career, she said, "I like to serve, very interested in that." At school, she had been active in clubs, "serving the people," as she put it. She had wanted to study nursing, but at the time, she told me, nurses at this hospital were not allowed to wear trousers, "just [a] skirt and no *tudung*" (Muslim head covering). "I can't do that," she said. Kamariah was a member of the breast cancer support group in the hospital and also did visiting at the main public hospital in Penang. She was an active participant in hospital staff outings and social activities. Kamariah also told me about her husband's difficulties finding a post as an Islamic teacher in Penang and that they wanted to move to somewhere on the mainland. She said that Penang was not a good Muslim environment for her son and that she and her husband wanted to bring him up in a Muslim community.

Somewhat to my surprise, directly following this, Kamariah spoke about learning scuba diving during a three-month, full-time course on the east coast of Malaysia and being part of Penang's emergency search-and-rescue team. She explained that this meant diving to retrieve dead bodies—usually, people who have jumped from the Penang Bridge. Kamariah told me that the rescue service has only two women divers. Most suicide attempts, she said, occur in February—"Valentine's Day, love. And exam results." This, too, was part of her service ethic. "Serve whole life," she said. The ethics of Islam and service are central here, but they emerge in unpredictable ways. Kamariah, like a few other medical lab technologists, mentioned that originally she had wanted to go into nursing, and this seemed to be directly linked to her ethical and religious orientation. It was also reflected in her daily interactions with hospital patients: when taking blood, she often spent time talking to the patients.

My second example of the entanglement between work and the ethical aspects of life is Siu Meng. In her thirties, married, and with three young children, Siu Meng was a relatively senior person in the lab. Quirky, warm, and highly intelligent, she had a degree in biochemistry and microbiology and had been working as a medical lab technologist for fifteen years, mainly in the immunology section. Siu Meng was a Baptist Christian, and her religious ethos inflected many of her attitudes.

When I asked Siu Meng how she had come to take up her particular line of work, she said: "I just want to work in [a] hospital environment because both [of my] parents work in hospital. Growing up, [I] stayed in hospital quarters. So it's just family-*lah!* [I] always wanted to be in hospital. [But] since [I] studied science, [I] had to be in lab." Siu Meng's mother and sister were nurses, and her father had also worked in a hospital before his retirement.

Siu Meng was always concerned about her colleagues and especially about the young trainees who were carrying out internships in the lab. These concerns, however, were not restricted to work matters. It was not unusual to find her in deep discussion at her lab bench with her assigned trainees. But if one listened closely to these conversations, they were as likely to feature advice about family matters, choosing a spouse, careers, financial affairs, or medical insurance as to be instruction in the technical matters of testing for lupus, HIV, or syphilis. One day, while she was running some immunology tests on blood samples and we were talking, Siu Meng told me that she often woke up early in the morning and read. I asked her what she liked to read. "The Bible and finance," she replied. "Actually, there's a lot about finance in the Bible—how to manage, planning, partners, finance." Then she began talking about marriage and how finance is an important factor in divorce. "People have unreal expectations," she said. "Husbands spend a lot, gamble." She said that she tells the trainees about finance and personal matters and how important it is for them to learn. Finance, she said, is "the most important thing in marriage because it can lead to bad relations. The machines are all different in different labs, but this stuff, relations, personal stuff, is the same." On another occasion, she told me, "Actually, work is all the same. It's the people that make a difference, [who] are interesting."

Siu Meng clearly saw her role in the trainees' education as one of counselor—an advisor on life and relationships—rather than just as an instructor on specific aspects of the job. And this attitude was fully reciprocated by the trainees. When I asked Zunirah, who had been rotating between different sections of the lab over some weeks, which department she liked best, she immediately said, "Immunology. Because Madam Tan [Siu Meng] gives advice—about saving, insurance. [She] advises [us on how] to buy [a] house, a car. Very useful." So a question about work and departments was transformed into a response about quite other matters. Referencing other sections of the lab she had enjoyed working in, including Kamariah's, Zunirah said, "I like the people."

On another occasion, I heard Siu Meng quizzing a small group of trainees about tests for hepatitis B and C and premarital blood screening. The topic under discussion, however, was not the technicalities of these procedures but what the trainees themselves would do if confronted with positive results for a boyfriend or girlfriend. Later, I asked Siu Meng why she was talking to the trainees about this. She said that it was to "find out their seriousness." She told me that the nature of marriage and attitudes toward it have changed: "Now, young people don't take it seriously. They sleep around, don't look after their health. Marriage is not just about sex." She said, it is "about commitment," and today the young "just marry—without proper commitment." Siu Meng told me that she wanted the trainees to think seriously and this was particularly important for women—although, at the time, she had addressed her remarks to a male trainee.

When I asked Siu Meng what she most enjoyed about her work, she said without any hesitation: "The people. After working so long, work is just *part* of the job. People element [gives] some motivation—and in other departments [of the hospital]. Helping people—trainees, not just patients, attendants—[they're] all people. To me there is no division. But no division sometimes [is] also no[t] good."

I have described two staff members with a particularly sociable stance in their working lives. For both, religious and ethical attitudes, combined with a willingness to engage socially with patients and colleagues, strongly inflected their working lives and relations. It is certainly not coincidental that both were women—this reflects quite strongly the gendered aspects of sociality and working relations in the labs. Of course, many other staff in the lab—both men and women—were less sociable, concentrating more exclusively on their work tasks and maintaining stronger boundaries between work and social matters. But there is no doubt that having women in the lab like Kamariah and Siu Meng, for whom the relationships in the lab were of great importance, affected the quality of the working environment for everyone. Male managers often capitalized on these propensities by using those women to smooth over difficulties, ensuring good working relations and productivity. The domesticating effects of their sociability thus spread beyond their particular workbench or section.

UNCANNY PRESENCES

I begin this chapter with stories about ghostly appearances and the suggestion that the presence of ghosts in the labs and blood banks was the subject of considerable interest. Because of hospitals' association with death, it is widely acknowledged that they are places where ghosts are liable to crop up. Since blood is well known to attract spirits in Malaysia, it seemed obvious to attempt to follow these ghostly leads to the blood banks and labs. But, as I discovered, such matters were not straightforward. To understand the significance of their disputed presence, I have found suggestive Freud's (2003[1919]) emphasis on the link between the uncanny (*unheimlich*) and what was once well known or familiar.

During one discussion about whether ghosts might be present in the labs or blood banks, one medical lab technologist, Shanthi, stated that it was not safe for the hospital to let staff work alone in these spaces. Another agreed, adding that the ghosts did not show up on the security cameras. Shanthi mentioned that she, like others, had heard about strange knockings on a ward door. When the nurses tried to get out of the room, she said, they found that the door had been locked from the outside. Her colleague confirmed this, noting that the room in question had been their lab's on-call resting room: "Luckily, [we] don't use it." It was generally agreed that although nurses see many ghosts, they themselves are not subject to ghostly attacks because of their white uniforms. Another medical lab technologist mentioned that there were no ghosts in the nursing college because there were no patients. A colleague teased Shanthi that she wanted to hear more stories but was also scared by them, confirming my sense that these discussions evoked pleasurable excitement as much as fear.

On the following day, over breakfast, Kamariah and Shanthi were discussing the story of the nurses who had seen the headless ghost. Kamariah mentioned that General Hospital had "more ghosts." She said, "Because they have a mortuary there. Sometimes they hold a dead person for three months because no one claims [the body]. Here, not. [We] don't accept patient[s] if [their conditions are] very serious, or without deposit from family. [We] just have [a] holding area for corpses—[for relatives have] one day to claim." Agreeing, Shanthi then mentioned that she was due to be on call the next day and was scared to be alone.

We can discern running through these conversations a diagnostic of different spaces (in marked counterpoint to that governing the consumption of food)—with certain locations being more prone to attract ghosts. Everyone seemed to agree that the hospital wards and the old labs—which had been on the ground floor, exposed to the outside, near the hospital drains, and therefore dirty—were known for such events.[5] Other areas, not frequented by patients—such as the nursing college—were not. Abandoned wards, locked rooms, and, even more macabre, the "psychy ward toilets" were all likely venues for ghosts.

Stories circulated not only through the spaces of each hospital but also between hospitals. It was perhaps not surprising, then, to be told that the mortuary at General Hospital was a gathering point for ghosts. When I spent time in another hospital's labs, a more senior medical lab technologist told me that he had heard from a maintenance engineer in a medical technology company about the ghosts in the laboratory of the first hospital. There were none in the labs where he worked, Sam said, because they were located in a building separate from the hospital. But, of course, he added, the main hospital was a different matter. Sam went on to inquire about the working relations between colleagues in the other set of labs—as if sensing that there might be some connection between the quality of these relations and uncanny occurrences. His colleagues, however, did not seem quite so certain of the security of their own workspaces. One told me that their lab did get ghosts, even though it was housed in a separate building: "[The] lab is still in [the] hospital compound." She told me that she was scared in the compound at night: "First thing we should be afraid of is thieves. Second thing is ghosts." Another medical lab technologist told me that she was not frightened: "On [the] wards, [we] wear uniform[s]. Ghosts don't bother [us]—they know [we're] working to save lives." The connection between thieves and ghosts here is not, I think, coincidental. James Siegel (1998) has suggested that amid the social dislocations experienced in Indonesia under Suharto, new types of criminals emerged and replaced the more familiar haunting caused by ghosts. Whereas ghost stories were told "with amusement and satisfaction," newspaper stories of such new criminal types spoke of "trauma and shock" (Siegel 1998:100).

On another occasion, a medical lab technologist told a story about the mother of a friend of hers who was giving birth in the hospital and was disturbed by ghosts at night in her room. She related that a nurse came to the room and fainted. Her friend's mother just pretended that it was normal, she said, although she could actually see the ghost and pressed the alarm to get help for the nurse. A colleague listening to her story then asked whether ghosts were also attracted to the blood bank. "No," she said, "that's OK because the blood is all in containers. It's spilled blood or the blood of childbirth that's not OK."

These stories are permeated with various kinds of evaluation: the likelihood of ghosts correlates, as we have seen, with the different uses of a space in the present and past, with the kinds of people who frequent it, and with concerns about practices of containment of blood. Patients who are near death attract ghosts, as do spaces associated with death. It is significant, I think, that the use of the English term "ghosts" avoids any specificity about the ethnicity or particular type of spirits involved and thus fits the multiethnic character of these urban hospitals.[6] Dangers are left unspecified, but they are linked to death and to uncontained blood. In some (but not all) accounts, those who wear the white coats of doctors, nurses, and medical lab technologists, who are "working to save lives," are not disturbed. I was often asked by staff in one lab about the working practices, spaces, and social relations in the other labs in which I had spent time, and I was struck by their interest in what I might know about how matters stood in other hospitals.

It also seemed hard to avoid a connection between the more frequent ghostly appearances and discussions in one lab and the more difficult and sometimes tense relations that existed between colleagues there. In one lab, staff members seemed to work particularly well as a team. In the other, things were more complex, and some relations seemed strained. It was perhaps not coincidental that in the latter working environment, I encountered several cases of illness among staff, as well as considerable anxiety about dangers associated with the workplace, including risks of infection, fumigation systems that might not be working effectively, accidents, and the long-term hazards of working with chemical reagents. Explicitly or not, a connection between strained relations among colleagues and the presence of ghosts was indicated, too, by questions I was asked by those who worked in other hospitals. It was clear that different people had different opinions about the likelihood of encountering ghosts; these were matters for discussion and speculation. And it became apparent that some people were more likely than others to have such experiences. When I began asking about ghosts in the labs, I was told that I should speak to a particular medical lab technologist who had had many such experiences. When I talked to Thomas, he told me, "Only in [the] old lab. [I would] hear sounds going on. Hear footsteps. Feel…something eerie, cold on [my] head. Turn around and [I would] see nothing. One incident, I thought I saw something sitting in [the lab manager's] old office. Turned around, not there.

[I] think they're everywhere. Just where and when [they] manifest [themselves] is different." But, as in Sharon's account, which begins this chapter, any certainty about the new space of the lab seemed somehow provisional: "Sometimes [I] still get [a] feeling in this lab. In bewitching hour—3:00 a.m. or something. Some people [are] more sensitive. In [the] old lab, [I] heard similar stories. Here in [the] new lab, [I] haven't heard any yet."

These comments strongly suggest that the ghostly presences in the hospital might be only temporarily—or just—kept at bay outside the blood bank and clinical pathology labs. Some of the staff seemed sure that as long as these spaces were unfrequented by patients and blood was kept only in sealed containers, their boundaries would be secure; for others, these matters were uncertain. If ghosts had not yet been encountered, this did not mean there was no chance that they would be in the future.

I suggest that—like food but in a markedly different register—these traces of dangerous, transgressive, and uncanny presences can be seen as a moral barometer of social relations in the spaces they frequent and that they indicate the fragile status of the boundaries of the labs and blood banks. Although members of the public have only restricted access to these spaces and these are apparently well-ordered, high-tech, and ultramodern working environments, we have seen that nonwork kinds of sociality, which have their basis in kinship connections and religious and moral commitments, also leave their mark. The dangerous sense of the uncanny suggests that the domestication of the workspace may be seen as an ambivalent process. Boundaries between the labs and the larger world of the hospital might, after all, not be secure; the presence of death in the hospital might invade the labs; familiar forms of sociality between colleagues might break down. Work protocols and regulatory regimes cannot after all guarantee the health or safety of medical lab technologists—however meticulously these are implemented. The safety and familiarity of these zones are, at best, imperfect and provisional. Those who work in these spaces can perhaps all too easily imagine that morally calibrated social connections and their penumbra of memory, registered as the threatening presence of ghosts, might take precedence over the routine technological processes of the labs and blood banks.

CONCLUSION

I begin this chapter with tales about ghosts that possibly have breached the boundary of the labs. Ghosts, food, fishponds, relatedness, religion, ethics, scuba diving, childbirth, and Chinese, Malay, and Ayurvedic medicine—the story so far has involved some improbable juxtapositions. As

Emily Martin writes, the "space in which science and culture are coconstituted is discontinuous, fractured, convoluted, and in constant change. To traverse such a space, we need an image of process that allows strange bedfellows, odd combinations, and discontinuous junctures" (1998:36). Behind all of this is the routine work in the lab, the many hundreds of precise clinical pathology tests that go on there, and in the blood bank, the collection of blood from donors, the screening and separation into blood products, followed by storage and then cross-matching prior to transfusion. This is highly technical work, and the medical lab technologists are under strong pressure from the hospital management—enforced through rigorous regimes of standard operating procedures, protocols, and monitoring—constantly to improve their speed, standards, and accuracy.

In many ways, these stories about life in the lab may seem inconsequential; they concern matters that are sometimes fleeting or peripheral to the main work processes. What I highlight here is the visible and strong effort made by staff to domesticate the working environment and to make it a sociable space. Siu Meng's comment that "work is just *part* of the job" is at the heart of this. But why should this matter? What are the implications of the "uneven seepage" (Rapp 1999:303) between the world of everyday sociality, kinship, and life in the lab? My depiction of those who work in the labs and blood banks might appear simply to echo other ethnographies of the workplace (Mollona 2005; Yanagisako 2002). But the argument is different. The processes of domestication I outline can be understood as rendering a strikingly unfamiliar world familiar. For all the appearance of well-ordered laboratory efficiency, there is no disguising the fact that these workspaces are also hazardous, and this is clearly recognized by those who work there. Well-maintained boundaries between different spatial zones, standard operating procedures, safety protocols, and a concern with hygiene cannot ensure the health and safety of those who work in these spaces. Whether from needle pricks, infectious microbes, or chemical reagents, these personnel know all too well that their health can easily be put at risk—and this is underlined by the manner in which they speak of the potential dangers of their work. Beyond their own health, they are also aware of the potentially devastating consequences that mistakes in their work could have for the health of others. The effects of a diagnostic test misread or carelessly carried out, blood that has not been properly cross-matched for transfusion, or donated blood inadequately screened—the list of potential errors and their spiraling consequences is endless. The history of contaminated-blood scandals in France, the United Kingdom, and China, among other places, demonstrates that the stakes are very high indeed (Feldman and Bayer 1999; Shao

2006; Shao and Scoggin 2009; Starr 1998). It should be emphasized here that the regulatory systems in which Malaysian hospitals participate are both local and international. Managers continually reminded lab staff of the importance of accuracy and care in their work, and the regulatory practices of the labs and hospitals involved the routine collection and display of statistics to support this.

An emphasis on the sociality of the workspace undoubtedly renders it more enjoyably habitable and reduces the negative effects of the pressure to increase productivity or the sense of dangers just kept at bay. But the obligations of friendship and kinship can, paradoxically, have the opposite effect. It is not hard to imagine conflicts of interest over the reporting of colleagues' infectious illnesses or mistakes in procedures. Sociability can simultaneously make the world of the lab seem safe *and* potentially undermine regulatory regimes or standard operating procedures and thus contribute to the risky conditions. This suggests that, far from being inexplicable, the uncertain and threatening presence of the uncanny expresses the peculiar ambivalence and provisionality of processes of domestication. A "shadowy residue" left by the work of domestication captures just this sense of implicit danger. In this light, the overdetermined interest in whether ghosts might invade the labs makes clear that domestication cannot fully dissolve the risks associated with this kind of work.

Significantly, it has long been recognized that the entanglements of *commercial* interests might potentially undermine the safety of blood services. That the safety of donated blood rests on the disinterestedness of voluntarily donated gifts was exactly Richard Titmuss's point (1970; see also Rabinow 1999; Tutton 2002).[7] This concern connects directly to the issues discussed here: not only commercial interests but also moral and social obligations might conceivably compromise the safety of blood. Tellingly, Titmuss's argument dovetails neatly with that of Latour about the importance of the work of "purification" to perceptions of the validity of scientific endeavors. If the gift might not be disinterested or if the work of purification is only a mask, then the modern, scientifically valid, safe products of these workspaces may be compromised. Thus, the creation of an insulated, disinterested world in the labs and blood banks is apparently the guarantee of accuracy and safety and the availability of an adequate blood supply to meet transfusion needs; it also ensures public trust. Slippages are potential breaking points in perceptions about reliability that may undermine the trust of patients and publics.

The separation of the lab from the world outside and the many microprocesses of separation that are integral to the work in the lab are, at best, precarious. Such divisions are always unstable. And this is partly because they are maintained by people who, as I have shown, are fully embedded in nexuses of relations and are situated simultaneously in multiple, different social locations within and beyond the lab. It is because the consequences of incomplete separations or entanglements of obligation may be literally lethal and may pile into one another that doctors and blood bank staff are concerned, as they often told me, about their public image. Mistakes have the capacity to feed quickly and devastatingly back into the many domains in which blood participates—including the bodies of patients. Lapses in the procedures of labs and blood banks can have abundant material consequences for patients, and they simultaneously have extraordinary ideological propulsion to penetrate many realms of moral discourse, implicating trust in health care, in public safety, and ultimately in political regimes. In this sense, the projection of such slippages onto the external, dangerous, but simultaneously familiar agency of ghosts may, as Laura Bear (2007b) suggests, paradoxically provide a certain reassurance. In an ideal world—such as one in which the national and international regulatory regimes governing the procedures carried out in blood banks and clinical pathology labs are perfectly effective—kinship, "culture," and human interest would be banished from the spaces of the lab. But the work cannot proceed in a vacuum.

These ghostly presences, which are only provisionally kept at bay outside the blood bank and clinical pathology labs, speak of the fragile status of the boundaries of the lab and also of how much might be at stake. When Siu Meng told me that "work is just *part* of the job," she immediately followed up with a qualification: "No division sometimes [is] also no[t] good." The porous boundaries between work and social life, between the ultramodern labs and the world outside—with inescapable social obligations and haunting memories—are intrinsic to the way life is carried on in the clinical pathology labs and blood banks. But such seepages have the potential to disrupt work undertaken in these spaces—and lives lived far beyond them.

Acknowledgments

The research for this project was funded by a Leverhulme Trust major research fellowship, with additional funds for fieldwork in Malaysia provided by a British Academy small research grant. I am deeply grateful to these institutions and to the staff at the hospitals in Penang for making this work possible. Hospitals have been anonymized and the names and some details of personnel changed to protect the confidentiality of participants. I thank the participants at the SAR advanced seminar "The Difference Kinship Makes: Rethinking the Ideologies of Modernity," especially Fenella Cannell and Susan McKinnon, as well as an anonymous reviewer for the Press; the audiences at seminars at LSE and NYU, especially Emily Martin and Rayna Rapp; and in Edinburgh, Richard Baxstrom, Ian Harper, Toby Kelly, Rebeccca Marsland, and, as always, Jonathan Spencer for extremely helpful comments on previous versions of this chapter.

Notes

1. Quotations used in this chapter were noted down at the time of conversation; unless otherwise stated, conversations took place in English, which was the lingua franca and generally fluently spoken, though it was not the only language used in these workplaces. I have tried to retain some of the cadences of Malaysian English, which characteristically has a somewhat staccato rhythm, with missed pronouns and articles and with extensive use of the present tense, but the interviews have been edited for clarity.

2. Just as I was writing this passage, I received an email from one of the medical lab technologists whom I knew quite well, telling me that she had just been asked to organize the meal for the annual lab staff dinner. She wrote: "Really difficult to find a suitable place and time for all. Halal food and somewhere in town. Thinking [of] seafood."

3. I am particularly grateful to Gillian Feeley-Harnik for helping to draw out these ideas.

4. Such self-consciously "modern" venues were sometimes favored for lunch and had the advantage of not catering exclusively to any particular ethnic food preferences.

5. In *A New Criminal Type in Jakarta* (1998:88), James Siegel also notes how ghosts are associated with particular sites, especially those of death.

6. For an account of ghosts and spirit medium practices in the context of Chinese popular religion in Penang and for a more historical framing of these practices, see DeBernardi 2004, 2006.

7. As Thomas Laqueur has remarked, however, "there are no ambiguities in Titmuss" (1999:3).

6

On the Road Again

Movement, Marriage, Mestizaje, and the Race of Kinship

Barbara Bodenhorn

Early in 2010, a young man was picked up in one of the street sweeps that punctuate public spaces in much of the borderlands United States. He had been given to a Mexican family, legally resident in Texas, the day after his birth twenty-two years previously and formally adopted by them as a six-year-old. He was deported to Mexico, despite the fact that he knew no one there, spoke no Spanish, and had no documents establishing him as a citizen of that country (*Milenio*, January 16, 2010). The nature of the kinshipped relations of the actors was not being contested, but the degree to which those relations were deemed to elicit moral recognition from the state was warmly debated. How states "see" kinship as a moral category when they are concerned about the movement of people is one focus of this chapter. How, when, and to what effect people recognize state-like processes as a relevant factor when making kinship decisions is another. My ethnographic material comes from the mountains of Oaxaca, Mexico, and the North Slope of Alaska, two regions whose inhabitants perceive themselves as vulnerable to the arbitrary powers of the US government.

Models suggesting that the public domain of economics and politics and the private domain of kinship are analytically separable continue to carry rhetorical weight in some circles. Many anthropologists have, for some time, challenged any easy separation between kinship, gender, economics, and politics, instead tracing their connections through a focus on households, on consumption, or on the intersection of new reproductive technologies, the market, the desire for "one's own" child, and the regulatory apparatuses of state.[1] By the same token, it is by now commonplace to recognize the extent to which governmental processes (by states and suprastates) have, since the nineteenth century, increasingly intervened in the domestic domain. Thus, a clear public-private division is difficult to posit in analytical terms; a perceived tension between them on the ground, however, continues to invite anthropological attention.

The present chapter is concerned with the ambiguous ways in which the kinship-state relationship repeatedly comes into and moves out of view. I take the movement of people—in the form of the circulation of children and the cross-boundary movements of adults in marriage—as a central focus, not because movement in itself is particular to the twenty-first century but because a comparison between the circulation of children and the cross-boundary movements of adults in marriage, as they emerge in late modern contexts, brings into view contradictory tensions concerning the sorts of relations such movements are capable of producing.

My weak arguments are related: this material emphasizes the importance of acknowledging that "kinship" includes large universes of people whose relatedness may or may not have anything at all to do with notions of blood. On one hand, this challenges the still common assumption that modern families are nuclear. On the other, it invites us to acknowledge that we should recognize that languages of blood drive much more than kinship and that notions of kinship encompass much more than the reproduction of children—even when focusing on kinship in the United States. This material also points to another truism that warrants restating. In the relatively recent anthropological turn to the study of state like institutions, there is the danger of falling back into dualist modeling, which, by implication, assigns political processes to "the state." In the ethnographic contexts under discussion, important tensions emerge between federal, state, local, and tribal/communal governmental authorities. "The state" and "the order of law" are multiple and complex. In addition, the political ordering of kinned relations is a function of a number of institutional processes whose intersections with specific states are oblique.

My strong argument is that this material invites us to think about marriage, in particular, as exemplary in its transboundary (rather than transnational) capacities. People have always married across boundaries; it is what gives marriage its alliance potential. But recognition of the boundary-crossing nature of marriage has historically constituted the default model of the institution.[2] It is with the modern invention of categories such as "race" and "ethnicity," I suggest, that "intermarriage" becomes a marked rather than an unmarked relationship. In the context of Mexican and US national ideologies, this is rendered more complex by the concepts of *mestizaje* and "melting pot" as metaphors of national character—metaphors that do not reflect the essentialist nature of race thinking, particularly in the United States, but that have historically coexisted with such thinking. Thus, we find that languages of mixture-as-norm and of purity-as-desirable exist side by side but are deployed in different contexts. That marking—which is processual, in that it moves in and out of salience—has the implicit effect of muting the many other crossings that continue to produce kin. It is this relationship between the marked and the unmarked that I explore in the pages that follow.

Loïc Wacquant's (2009, 2010) most recent sociology of entrenched systems of inequalities in the United States juxtaposes what he defines as a bipartite and essentialist view of race, which has taken hold in mainstream Anglo American rhetoric, with a more fluid, French racial hierarchy, which historically meant that people could marry their way out of the categories they were born into. I take this categorical assertion critically as an entry point to my discussion.

Wacquant's position links provocatively with Gregory Rodriguez's (2008) work on Mexican-US relations: Rodriguez comments that 32 percent of second-generation and 57 percent of third-generation Latinos married "outside their ethnic group" in the 1990s. The Population Research Bureau in Portland, Oregon, projects that by 2100 twice as many Latinos will claim mixed heritage as single heritage (xv).[3] Such assertions pose analytical puzzles: Cubans, Peruvians, Mexicans, and Puerto Ricans are all classified as Latinos, but they are not of the same ethnic group. People who originate in the Sierra Norte may be Zapotec, Mixe, Mizteca, and Triqui, among others—or *mestizo*, the default category. Given the history of complex comings together throughout the Americas, it is unclear what constitutes "single heritage." These categories are deployed—and contested—by many people, mobilized as ideological and indeed sociological artifacts. But they are not self-evident, and, I suggest, an examination of the ways in which people move as part of their kinship universes clearly reveals the categorical ambiguities that infuse this particular intellectual landscape.

Although new ways of making and recognizing kin were central to late twentieth-century anthropology,[4] I propose to look at more conventional means of making kin: through marriage and adoption. In doing so, my analytical framework encompasses both Schneider's (1968) assertion that the "order of law" is an important domain of kinship and Foucault's (1991) insistence that the power of governmentality resides in the capillary actions of those who represent authorities. We begin with a consideration of the circulation of children—in particular, customary Iñupiaq practices that may ignore, elude, or engage with state processes—and then turn to specific state-directed strategies to manage the placement of children, including policies explicitly designed to "breed out" indigeneity.[5] This logic framed the Bureau of Indian Affairs (BIA) policy of removing Native American children from their natal families throughout much of the twentieth century and it is a clear example of assumptions concerning the malleability of race, which is thought to shift through adoption and subsequent marriage. Subsequently, I turn to marriage itself, examining miscegenation laws as they were enacted in the United States. Although the BIA proposed to breed out indigeneity over the course of a generation, miscegenation laws—many of which stated that "race" resided in a single drop of blood—were in place in many states of the union. Thus, what is needed here is a more complex view of the race-kinship nexus that can account for the ways in which race emerges as a category influenced by shifting and contradictory classificatory moves.

I ask, then, why some boundaries matter more than others; why some crossings may be more difficult than others; and why we must recognize the ways in which they change over time. It is now commonplace to assert (as I most certainly do) that race does not exist as a biological category but that racism does.[6] The analytical result is often to point out the process—for instance, with reference to the racialization of nationhood, such as "being Mexican"—rather than to engage critically with it.[7] Although work on kinship and gender within (particularly feminist) anthropology continues to interrogate "the biological" as a constitutive—but not necessarily determinant—component of social life, the same critical attention to the instability of social categories such as race is less prominent in the study of kinship.

MOVEMENT, MODERNITY, HYPERMODERNITY, THE STATE, AND BEYOND

My interest in movement emerges from my work in two major field sites over the past thirty years. On the North Slope of Alaska, the complexities of mobile household dynamics and state interventions were at the center of my efforts as the director of social services for the regional tribal government, the Iñupiaq Community of the Arctic Slope, between 1980 and 1983 and were the focus of my report for the Iñupiaq History, Language, and Culture Commission in 1988. My work in the Sierra Norte of Oaxaca is of much shorter duration, extending back only to 2004. There, kinship, marriage, and migration strategies mutually inflect social life at the community level. In the following discussion, I borrow from Tamar Wilson (2009), who uses the term "transborder," rather than "transnational," to describe the processes in question, recognizing that the movements under examination involve multiple and shifting categories, only some of which take on particular salience at national frontiers. This also makes conceptual space for considering the significant movement—of children and adults—that takes place within as much as between national boundaries.

The nation-state as an actor in these boundary-creating and boundary-crossing processes must, however, be kept in view. Ann Stoler (2005) discusses how the ideologies and practices of empire are furthered by the constant (and knowing) deployment of shifting legal goalposts, particularly in the ways in which entrance to the polity is gained. Deborah Bryceson and Ulla Vuyorela (2002:11) suggest that "changing immigration legislation continually redefines the nation-state by redefining the status of its inhabitants and their familial relations." Nowhere is this clearer than with US migration policies, which have the capacity to open up and close down entry simultaneously (Cornelius and Lewis 2006; Nevins 2002; Stephen 2009). These policies depend on the erasure of recognition (particularly in Texas and California) of just how much of the United States was originally part of the Mexican nation-state, thus rendering descendants of pre-Alamo residents as "interlopers" (Rodriguez 2008), and the policies frequently produce the opposite effect of what was intended by state initiatives. The passage of Proposition 187 in 1994, for instance, was meant to exclude undocumented people from taking advantage of California state services, many of which involved education and health care for children. An unprecedented number of documented Mexicans reacted by applying for citizenship, something that had been relatively rare. The net result was the formation of an active class of citizens who are not to be shouted down in the state legislature.[8] Thus, migration patterns invite us to view government policies not only in terms of governmental processes but also in recognition of elusive, unruly bodies and not simply compliant or resistant ones. In this, migration and kinship are both mutually constitutive and analytically distinct.

THE ETHNOGRAPHIC CONTEXT

As Roger Sanjek (2003) has pointed out, people have been on the move—en masse and individually—throughout most of human history. The historically informed ethnographic descriptions below illustrate the extent to which late modern mobilities are continuous and discontinuous with processes that have little or nothing to do with modernity itself.

The North Slope region of northern Alaska is homeland for Iñupiat, whalers who have traveled, traded, and warred throughout the northwestern Arctic for millennia.[9] Semi-nomadic to a significant extent—well after the establishment of schools and other forms of village infrastructure—individuals and families still maintain mobility today in search of hunted food, employment, schooling, and vacations. European colonial contact resulted in the drastic reduction of local populations, initially due to the conjunction of famine and disease. Indeed, according to Burch (1975, 1998, 2005, 2006), the late nineteenth century introduced an era when Iñupiaq nations became "mixed up" due to large-scale movements of people throughout the region in response to these traumatic conditions, and these movements brought people together in marriage in new combinations. My Iñupiaq grandmother, Mattie Bodfish, for instance, talked about her "mail-order husband," Waldo, who had traveled from several hundred miles to the southwest with his mother along the coast on a commercial whaling ship. Waldo was the result of a liaison between the ship's captain, Hartson Bodfish, and Waldo's Iñupiaq mother, the ship's seamstress. People who lived in Wainwright advised Mattie to marry Waldo, not because of his relationship with a prosperous whaling captain but because he would come minus kin and therefore would generate fewer obligations on her part.

Until the late 1970s, children wishing secondary education had to leave their homes, usually for years at a time, to attend BIA-run boarding schools. Indeed, the mid-twentieth century marked a period of considerable outmigration. Since the foundation of the North Slope Borough (a home-rule government with a terrain of some 88,000 square miles) in the early 1970s, the region has profited from the borough's authority to impose property taxes on oil installations such as those at Prudhoe Bay. As a result, Barrow (the hub) has acted as a magnet, attracting people from outlying villages and the mainland United States. Thus, by 2010, Iñupiat had participated in several sorts of mobilities: as a central aspect of their social organization; as a considered response to changing ecological, economic, and political conditions; and as a function of coercive relations with "their" nation-state. The speed, intensity, and direction of such movements—and their influences on marriage patterns and on where children find themselves—have all fluctuated significantly since the late 1800s.

The Sierra region of Oaxaca is abundantly represented in the anthropological literature. This is where Eric Wolf (1959, 1966) and Robert Redfield (1960) developed models of peasant societies, Laura Nader (1990) explored the role of dissent in what she calls "harmony ideology," and Lynn Stephen (1991) presented a gendered account of village artisanal specialist production as part of global economic processes. In 2010, *serrana* (Sierra) communities continued to be organized in a system of relatively autonomous local government in which members were required to fulfill jobs of increasing responsibility (*cargo/tequio*) in order to maintain their community membership. In Ixtlán de Juárez, membership in the commune is reckoned both by family (384 families make up the collective) and by individual members who represent those families. Whether Ixtlán is a Zapotec community, a community "with Zapotec roots," an "indigenous community," or a "mestizo community" depends on whom one is talking to and on the context.

Michael Kearney, who has made significant contributions to the study of migration, globalization, and transnationalism (1995a, 1995b), conducted his initial fieldwork (1972) in Ixtepeji, a serrana community about ten miles south of Ixtlán de Juárez, the site of my own fieldwork. His model of "revolving door" migration as characteristic of Mexican patterns was made explicit to me as people defined migration in terms of continual movement: going to the city of Oaxaca to study for a few years was counted as much as a trek to the northern Mexico city of Zacatecas or time spent working for the US Forest Service in Oregon. Tellingly, one young woman in Oaxaca City responded in the negative to my question about whether she had ever migrated: "Because I stayed." As a region, Oaxaca entered the migratory flow relatively late. By the late twentieth century, however, large numbers of Oaxacans had joined Mexicans from other states moving in search of work. Many of the serrana communities in the region are called "ghost communities" (*comunidades de fantasmas*) because of the scarcity of adults in residence. But, whereas people leave Ixtlán for the same complex of reasons as elsewhere, it departs from the norm in terms of its high rates of return. Ixtlán parallels Barrow in its relative prosperity, drawing sustainably on its communal forest reserves over the past twenty years. Like Barrow, it operates as a magnet community: the presence of a successful forestry enterprise attracts people from throughout the region. Defined in the state census as having a moderate level of outmigration, many of those who leave (and virtually every family I have met over the course of my fieldwork has at least one member who has either left and returned or has come from somewhere else) return at a strikingly young age. Ixtlán, they say, is a good place to bring up a family. I asked key informants (communal and municipal authorities, schoolteachers, and small business owners) which aspects of migration they thought represented the greatest advantages for and the most serious threats to the community in general. The most common answers were opposite sides of the same coin. Outmigration—whether for education, employment, or travel—represented the chance for the community to benefit from the formative experiences of young people, who could then put their knowledge to the service of the community. The greatest threat was the community's loss of its best and brightest young people through the same process.

THE CIRCULATION OF CHILDREN

The circulation of young people is thus a constant in both communities, although it is driven by different motives and takes on different patterns depending on the context. Because of our focus on the kinship-state intersection, I concentrate my discussion on the movement of North Slope children, who leave their natal homes as minors. This section consciously evokes the title of a paper by Jessaca Leinaweaver (2007), who considers the multiple strategies involved in moving children between households, which has customarily underpinned social relations in Peru. The movement, almost always an extralegal process, is not problematic unless it comes to the attention of the state, at which point the capacity or the propriety of particular people to care for particular children comes into question.[10]

Throughout much of the twentieth century, the settler nations of Australia, Canada, and the United States consciously adopted policies to resettle indigenous children in non-indigenous families or institutions to "solve" the "native problem." Children were removed not only from their natal homes but also from their native homelands. With a European upbringing, it was assumed, their "nativeness" could quickly be bred out. These child placement policies were reminiscent of the sixteenth- and seventeenth-century marriage strategies in Hispanic America, through which a family's race and social position could be changed over the course of decades (López Beltrán 2007). This was an inversion of the prevalent form of race thinking—particularly in the United States—which tended to lodge race in (very small amounts of) blood. As Pascoe (2009) has detailed, miscegenation laws persisted in the United States until 1967, when the US Supreme Court declared them unconstitutional.

Before turning to my examination of the capacity of state-like actions to intervene in contemporary North Slope family lives, I will provide a brief description of what local people continue to define as particularly Iñupiaq parenting practices.[11] Households are fluid, with children easily moving between extended family members for a meal or a night. Fosterage—an explicitly temporary shift in parenting arrangements—is common and deployed strategically. Iñupiat make a distinction between this sort of arrangement and adoption, which redefines the identity of the "real" parents as those who have taken in a child. In the 1980s, adoption was the norm rather than the exception, and the majority of Iñupiaq households in Barrow had adopted at least one child either in or out—some had done both. Stated reasons were multiple, but childlessness was one of the least common. Adoption was valued positively rather than looked on as a last resort; it often mildly intensified the relations between biological and adoptive parents and extended rather than substituted the kinship universe of the adoptee. It generated "real" rather than "fictive" kinship, and it assumed considerable agency on the part of children, who themselves could decide to shift households and to what extent to include their natal families in their adult kinship universes. Crucially, many of the responsibilities defined in US law as pertaining to those of a parent—under the general heading of "taking care of"—were spread among extended kin and community members. Bertha Leavitt, for instance, remembered her childhood in the 1940s: "I lost my dad when I was a little girl. Our brothers and uncles took care of us. At that time, everyone took care of the kids. In those days, our people took care of us, even when they didn't have much.... People always looked out for everyone else."[12]

Federal authority—in the form of magistrates and public schools—was introduced in the early twentieth century, almost simultaneously with the arrival of Presbyterian missionaries. Still, it was not until the 1950s that the last families moved to Barrow from the outlying villages of Piġnik and Nuvuk so that their children could more easily attend school. Despite virtually total conversion to Christianity, the notion that the status of children can depend on the marital status of their parents continues to bemuse. I have heard disappointed whispers among some (certainly not all) seniors that a young couple is living together out of wedlock, but "illegitimacy" is not a concept I have come across during my time in the region.

Although the customary institution of the *qargiich* (whaling captains' associations, which had considerable power to exert social control) was suppressed by Christian missionaries early in the twentieth century, other local institutions developed that kept significant amounts of political decision making in local hands. Village councils appeared in the early twentieth century, and in the 1920s and 1930s the Presbyterian Church produced sessions of elders, which regularly dealt with village concerns over social behavior. At the same time, the church sponsored mothers clubs in Barrow and Wainwright that are remembered as probably the strongest force of social control in both communities through the 1960s. Their powers ranged from inspecting houses for cleanliness in a bid to combat tuberculosis, to enforcing a 9:30 p.m. curfew for children and making sure that they attended school during the day. The BIA introduced "traditional councils" after the passage of the Indian Reorganization Act in the late 1930s; these provided a forum for the resolution of disputes following Iñupiaq, rather than federal, rules.[13] In 1959, Alaska shifted status from federal territory to state. Its constitution is explicitly antidiscriminatory, which, in effect, means that Native Alaskans are not recognized as occupying any position other than individual citizen. This legal language contradicts that of federal Indian law. Thus, the political domain has historically included multiple institutions that may be defined as state-like—including the nation-state, the state of Alaska, and regional and village tribal governments—in their capacity to affect Iñupiaq families, but it cannot be reduced to any one of them.

Beginning early in the twentieth century, active state measures that moved children away from their home communities and families were relatively coercive. According to Linda Green (2006), tuberculosis was endemic in the late nineteenth-century Arctic but then intensified as sedentarization brought families together in denser settlements. By the 1930s, she estimates, one out of three Alaska Natives suffered from the disease. By the 1950s, a multipronged campaign was introduced to combat the epidemic, which meant that many children were taken from their families and sent to inaccessible sanatoriums, where they remained for years. One Wainwright woman reported to me that during her childhood, her mother and sisters were sent out. This, along with the deaths of two other siblings, left the family in tatters and her father in a vulnerable state. At the same time, as already mentioned, any family wanting secondary education for its children had to be willing to send them out of the region to boarding school—again, for years.[14] According to the people I talked to in the 1980s, this happened crucially at the age—generally around eleven years old—when both linguistic and hunting skills would have been honed. Thus, governmentality was introduced in textbook Foucauldian fashion: populations were managed for the general public good; parental resistance was discursively interpreted as evidence of a lack of proper care for their children, so their compliance became part of the process. The rupture that was experienced was in many cases traumatic and in some cases permanent, but those anxieties could not be voiced with equal weight to the official rhetoric of care. In this case, "the state" was manifested in the authority of the BIA, which was seen as draconian in its ability to decree but not necessarily as an enemy.

The intentional transplantation of Iñupiaq young people to non-Iñupiaq settings began with the federal Urban Indian Relocation Program, instituted mid-century, in which young people were sent to families outside the state in order to transform rural Natives into an urban workforce.[15] It continued with the intervention of federal and, subsequently, state officials in "problem" families for which the solution was the removal of children—preferably to non-Iñupiaq families or to state child-care institutions—and the termination of parental rights.[16] In neither case was the political agenda behind these policies made explicit at the local level. The former depended on being able to convince people to enroll; the latter was coercive and experienced as such.

Two events occurred in the 1970s that had profound effects on these sorts of movements. The Molly Hootch case, settled out of court in the late 1970s, resulted in the state of Alaska ensuring that children have access to secondary education in their home communities. The federal Indian Child Welfare Act (ICWA), passed in 1978, explicitly rejected a policy that, in effect, promoted ethnic eradication by adoption. The ICWA requires individual states to notify tribal authorities before they remove a child from his or her home and to include those authorities in child welfare decisions and, if children have to be removed, to seek child placements first with family members and, if no family can be found, then with another family within the community. During my time working with the regional tribal government, it was the ICWA that we invoked to prevent the local school system from convincing the Alaska Children and Youth Services to send "problem" students to state-run children's homes in Fairbanks, an hour's plane ride away.

The ICWA recognizes the legitimacy of customary adoption, which raises the question of why a significant number of Iñupiat nevertheless opt for the formal state procedure. In some cases, young people who have adopted culturally and foresee no problems simply regard legal adoption as the "proper" way to proceed. In others, it is a strategy for ensuring that what is, in fact, a cultural adoption will be recognized by the state of Alaska (which does not recognize that Native Alaskans have rights not held by all Alaskan citizens), thus forestalling legal problems in the future. That Alaska does not recognize procedures allowed by federal law has, in the past, affected the right of culturally adopting parents to claim benefits from the state and has blocked the right of a culturally adopted child to claim inheritance. In addition, there is a relatively small number of cases in which aunts or uncles who have undertaken a cultural adoption insist on going through the legal procedure for fear that natal family members will change their mind and reclaim the child.[17]

Cultural adoptions are thus instigated outside the realm of the state (either federal or Alaskan) and then occasionally validated or contested by Alaskan state procedures. Occasionally, kin pressure parents to allow a cultural adoption if the extended family fears that parental behavior may attract the negative attention of the state. It can thus be strategically both an evasion and a deployment of state governmentality to ensure that the child remains unproblematically within the extended family's ambit. More often, it is simply a way of expressing the value that children are "good to share" and ensuring that state processes do not get in the way in the future. Occasionally, it is also a way of creating the sort of finality that legal adoption assumes in the mainland United States. In this, I would suggest, the state is seen not as an automatic adversary but as the source of strategic tools. Even though its rules are often perceived as arbitrary—in terms of who can claim benefits or inheritance—those same rules can also be evoked to contain that arbitrariness. What remains clear is the extent to which federal and state authorities cannot be considered different aspects of a single "state" and indeed must be dealt with or avoided in distinct ways.

With the formation of the state of Alaska in the 1950s, court-supported decisions to remove children from "problem families" were felt as a real danger to many of the families I interviewed during the 1980s. Today, an adversarial role is often assumed when the Alaskan (rather than the federal) state initiates the procedure. "It's like a foreign country over there! They don't understand anything!" fumed a friend of mine some time ago. She had just gone to court because her niece had been taken into custody; her frustration was not linguistic but systemic. The Division of Family and Youth Services (DFYS) can go to court to petition that parental rights be terminated. If successful, the child then becomes a ward of the (Alaskan) state and is put up for adoption. Even though the state today identifies "family" as the preferred adopters, complications abound. In fact, close kin often reject the invitation to "step up" because of the coercive implications involved in a state termination of parenthood, something that is antithetical to common Iñupiaq practice and therefore a likely source of intra-kin friction. Even in 1987, ten years after the inception of ICWA, one Alaska Legal Services attorney reported that of the fifteen "children in need of assistance" cases he was involved in that year, a third resulted in off-slope adoptions after long-term foster care.

Thus, we see an order of law that clearly is not monolithic and is effective only insofar as actors can make it so. I close this section with two final examples that illustrate both positive and negative aspects of the capillary nature of agency as it affects people's experiences of child welfare law on the

North Slope. The state of Alaska complies with the federal requirement to send notification of proposed child actions to tribal authorities throughout the state, but what happens beyond that is a function of local response. In the 1980s, the North Slope was fortunate in the presence of two key people. Raymond Neakok was the regional tribal council member designated to oversee ICWA-related cases because he had been trained as a paralegal and because of his extensive knowledge of North Slope families. He was my direct supervisor, and we collaborated closely; not once in three years did I see him promote a decision that was politically rather than socially driven. I am quite sure that the degree to which families approached the regional tribal authorities for ICWA help was a direct function of the trust they had in Raymond as a fair-minded person. On the other side, as it were, Rod Caskey was the state social worker who had primary regional responsibility to enact Alaskan state policy regarding child welfare cases. Married to a Sioux woman, he was sympathetic rather than resistant to the intentions of the ICWA. The approach of the Iñupiaq Community of the Arctic Slope to the Division of Family and Youth Services was to say, "Let's figure this out before it goes to court. Neither of our agencies wants to spend scarce funds and lots of time arguing these issues before a judge. We can help you find a solution that does not require sending a child off the slope." Thus, when we went into the schools—which we did through the authority of the ICWA—we went allied, at least in principle, with the state youth workers. The representatives of the school—who often thought that sending problem students away *was* the best option—found themselves confronting both tribal and state authorities who were looking for alternative solutions. Although, obviously, the positions of the regional tribal authorities and the Alaskan state were not always in agreement, the level of mutual respect between the actors meant that formal adversarial action was thought of as a last rather than a first resort. The positive outcomes of several of these cases were without doubt a function of the collaborative efforts of the individuals who represented different agencies. Because the tribal council has the power to intervene but not to enforce, it was seen by families as an advocate. Because DFYS simultaneously has the responsibility to provide assistance and the power to take children away, people (sometimes realistically) feel that approaching the agency for help could be held against them if their case is ever brought to court. The structural nature of the agencies therefore played an important role in the ways in which families engaged with them. Although individual actors displayed broad discretion in the actions they took, they were, at some level, constrained by the official policies of the agencies in which they were embedded.

It is important, then, to recognize that the circulation of children—like the circulation of adults—may take place for economic reasons, on political grounds, for emotional reasons, or a combination of the three. It may take place as a result of state or family initiatives, both of which depend on the recognition of extended kin as "family." Federal status, which is the subject of regional tribal council action, may be—but is not always—opposed by the policies of the Alaskan state. How the order of law is enacted and where "the state" resides in this is obviously complex: although state, federal, and tribal institutions are governmental at some level, they cannot be reduced to one another. And in important ways, each does not recognize the legitimacy of the others in some ways.

ADOPTION AND RACE

One way in which mobile kinship has been recently examined is the study of transnational adoption. Frequently, the assumption is that it is the adopted child who crosses the boundaries; the parents are a unit(y), bringing in a child that is somehow Other. In an exploration of China-US adoptions, for instance, Dorow and Swiffen (2009) suggest that for adopting parents, culture may be framed in essentialized assumptions about the "blood" of kinship and the "blood" of race, which, in turn, make the possibility of incorporation problematic. In many cases, race, culture, nationality, kinship, and biology become conflated into a single, unstable—or, to use Dorow and Swiffen's word, unintelligible—category. I began my discussion of this sort of adoption-marked-as-boundary-crossing by looking at the US policy to breed out Otherness by placing Native American children in non–Native American families. By contrast, I now turn to James Axtell's (1985, 2000) ethnohistorical work to think about the extent to which and the reasons that Native Americans historically adopted Euro Americans *in*.

During the British colonial era, such adoptions happened in two ways. First, as an official move between dignitaries, sons were temporarily exchanged so that each could learn the ways of the other in order to conduct diplomacy. Second, by far the greatest number of transfers took place as a result of raiding, when children were taken captive and then integrated into the captor society. Axtell (1985) notes that, when given the chance, most Native Americans returned to their natal communities; however, significant numbers of Euro Americans did not, opting to remain in their adoptive families. This mode of absorption was not particular to encounters with Euro Americans. Rather, it was part of a more general form of warfare—one in which captives could also be tortured and killed or turned into slaves. But Axtell's point was that significant numbers of Euro Americans became so absorbed into their adopted culture that they rejected the chance to return to their natal families. Although Leinaweaver's (2007) ethnography examines a form of child circulation that more or less encompasses a known kinship universe, we should recognize the frequency with which people whose custom it is to adopt incorporate outsiders as kin.

Closer to home, the twenty-first-century desire for transnational adoption does not emerge because there are no children in the United States who need homes, but because they are, more often than not, the "wrong" race. Other sorts of Others seem more absorbable; at the same time, however, the fetish of "culture" and of "race" renders the process of absorption as one to be managed rather than as one that is automatic. I hasten to add that this moral preoccupation is not universal in the United States. A few years ago, Mae Panigeo was speaking at the funeral of her son-in-law, a Euro American. "We were proud to have Eugene whale with us," she began. "How do you turn a *tanik* [white person] into an Iñupiaq?" She continued, "You let him work with you." Iñupiat talk of their kin as *ilya*—literally, their additions—and relations created through marriage and adoption are part of that expansive process. People have taken great pleasure in telling me about their relatives in Norway, New England, and Scotland, not to claim "whiteness" but to note expansion. National distinctions between potential spouses (which today include Filipinos and Samoans and Euro Americans living in Barrow) clearly exist, but the logic is just as much about boundary blurring as it is about boundary crossing.

OF MARRIAGE AND MESTIZAJE

Although transnational adoption is often thought to produce mixed families, many "mixed" people are produced in the entirely conventional way: their parents, grandparents, and even great-grandparents were the ones doing the mixing. The mixing of *what* is what I want to explore here.

In some quarters (see, for instance, Wacquant 2010), it is now common to challenge the notion of the United States as a melting pot. Racism, the argument goes, has created a caste system, with people of all colors other than pink kept in an undercaste that is difficult to budge. That is undeniably true. In the twenty-first century, if you are a young black man, you are much more likely to have spent time in jail than a member of any another demographic group in the United States. Once you have a jail record, you may often be denied the right to vote, which effectively disenfranchises a significant number of people who might be likely to vote against the interests of political and economic elites. Another example of this caste system is that Native Americans who reside on reservations are, as a demographic group, at the bottom of the socioeconomic scale.

But this ghettoization of poverty along racial lines does not negate the extent to which the melting pot *is* an integral part of the US historical landscape. To explore this, I turn briefly to Pascoe's (2004, 2009) work on miscegenation laws. These laws, passed by individual states, were initiated in the late nineteenth century, had been instituted in thirty states by 1948, and were overturned by the US Supreme Court as abrogating equal protection laws in 1967. The laws themselves reveal very particular moral panics. Twelve states prohibited marriage with African Americans, twelve with Indians, one with Native Hawaiians, one with Portuguese, and nine with Filipinos. At no point was there concordance as to what counted as miscegenation—bad mixing. The fact that a number of states declared a single drop of blood sufficient to place people in the prohibited category attests to the amount of mixing that had *already* taken place. If race is thought to be simultaneously written on the skin and in the blood, it becomes confusing when one cannot "see" who is who. Pascoe (2004) reviews a number of the many court cases that were initiated on the grounds of "miscategorization." Sometimes this was because a spouse wanted an annulment. More often, it involved disputes over inheritance: the family of the deceased claiming that the surviving spouse had no legal right because the couple had not been legally married in the first place. As with current controversies over same-sex marriage, the miscegenation laws—contradictory as they were in terms of who was included—were generally justified on the grounds of "natural law" or "God's law." Challenges were (ultimately successfully) mounted under the language of equal protection under the law. In one Arizona case, the claimant complained that under the one-drop rule, he "couldn't marry anyone!" In *Loving v. Virginia*, the case that ultimately made it to the Supreme Court, the couple had been instructed by a state judge that the only way to marry and avoid prison would be to leave Virginia—which they did for seven years. It was when they decided they should have the right to live at home—and were subsequently arrested—that they initiated the case against "their" state that would, in the end, be decided by the federal courts. Here is a conjunction of virtually all the issues I have been discussing so far. The rule of law, which defines what constitutes a proper kinship relationship, is not coherent even at the individual state level, and racial categories emerge as variable and strategic. Individual states and the nation-state approach the issue of what these categories mean for the status of citizens in radically different ways. And the actors involved can respond in evasive as well as confrontational ways.

The moral preoccupation with marking particular categories of people as transgressive in their marriage choices tends, as I suggested in the beginning, to obscure the extent to which other kinds of crossings continue to underpin marriages of all sorts, albeit unproblematically. My interest in this stems, in part, from weddings I have attended over the past several years. My first wedding in Ixtlán was by invitation of my neighbors, who had designated themselves as my *padrinos*—godparents with the responsibility of introducing me to important aspects of Catholic ritual life. On the eve of the wedding, a party took place that featured hours of "dancing the turkey" on the patio of the bride's house. The groom's family (which, in Ixtlán, pays for the wedding) provided the still living turkey and a stack of wood—both of which would be employed the following day in the preparation of the wedding feast. During the dance, the participants took turns twirling around the patio to the music of a local traditional band, the turkey cradled in their arms or held above their head. I later learned that dancing the turkey marks a wedding between two Ixtlán families. The second wedding I attended was a barrio event in which one of my colleagues from the preparatory school was padrino to the groom. The groom was *ixtleco* (someone from Ixtlán); the bride was from a neighboring village. They had been living together in Oaxaca—first as students and subsequently because of employment—and had a five-year-old son. The ceremony, greeted with obvious delight by the priest, was a joint wedding and baptism. After the festivities were over, the couple returned to Oaxaca. The third wedding was almost an affair of state. The in-marrying spouse was from an important family in Etla—a much larger community on the other side of Oaxaca City—and clearly no expense was spared to ensure that the Ixtlán family held up its side. The most endogamous marriage that can take place in Ixtlán is between two comunero families, and such marriages happen. But they are neither the rule nor the exception, simply one of a number of possible pairings.

My point here is basic. Mestizo is the unmarked category of twenty-first-century Mexican social citizenship, but the concept is anything but fixed. It was historically introduced, not with the arrival of the Spaniards, many of whom married local women, but (in a way resonating with Pascoe's material) several decades afterward when the inheritance of land came into dispute.[18] Mestizo is the historical consequence of several ideological moves—none of which encompasses the sorts of boundaries that were implied by the weddings I have just described. These marriages—which *may* express awarenesses of distinctions between comunero/non-comunero; ixtleco/non-ixtleco; serrano/non-serrano; Zapotec/Mixe—are familiar to anthropologists: they celebrate collective, perhaps uneasy, alliances; they reaffirm public statements of faith; they express political and economic positions; and they take place in that ambiguous space between family expectations and personal desire. It may well be that the pool of potential spouses is conceptually or demographically enlarged, in part because of the experiences migration brings. But to echo Yanagisako (1985) and Wilson (2009), we need to recognize in these ceremonies continuous elements that may well be rooted in pre- and postmodernities without assuming that they are necessarily in tension with those elements that are clearly present as conditions of rupture.

To return to the Alaskan material once again, what is striking is that many of these same categories exist: tanik ("bossy" = Anglo or Euro), Iñupiaq, *itqilik* (mostly Athapaskans, historic enemies of the Iñupiat), person of Barrow, Alaska Native (who can also be "half-breed"), "real" Iñupiaq (Bodenhorn 2004b). Many of the people who might be defined by those different terms get married to each other. But in contrast to the ixtleco material just considered, the Barrow weddings I have attended over twenty years have not invoked these categories as part of their performance. Rather, kinship is talked about in terms of "my additions," does not use the language of blood, and is not fixed with reference to parents or ethnicity (Bodenhorn 2000, 2004a, 2006). Iñupiaq weddings are about coming together; they are much less about the categories that contain the participants.

Residents of the North Slope—like those of the Sierra Norte—have participated in the various versions of modernity to emerge from the Euro American encounters in complex ways. Historically, this has involved a sense of rootedness coupled with considerable movement—voluntary and coerced—for marriage, work, trade, and play. It has involved aspirational desire and exasperated resistance—and it has involved a lot of simply getting on with it, assuming rather than asking for autonomous authority. In neither region does one find a clear-cut demarcation of tradition or modernity. Both need to be thought about in terms of American kinship. Despite the hard-edged hierarchies of citizenship that seem increasingly entrenched in both Mexico and the United States, taking a look at how people get married invites us to loosen things up a bit, to recognize the multiplicity of "trans-ing" that is involved in these processes of making relatives. In the Sierra, those boundaries are there to be mobilized or not, according to the wishes of the participants. On the North Slope, they seem not to participate at all in the vocabulary of becoming wed.

FROM MARRIAGE TO MIGRATION: THE SCOPE OF KINSHIP

In December 2005, a friend who teaches mathematics at the local preparatory school in Ixtlán asked me to work with a small group of her students who needed to think about research design and the relationship between "capturing" data and analyzing it. Since many people return home for an extended visit at Christmas, we agreed that trying to think about the reasons behind and the major impacts of migration would be an interesting topic. For about a month, we talked about the students' own experiences of migration in their families, designed and tested a structured interview format and worked on interview techniques. In teams of two, the students sallied forth to interview approximately a dozen randomly selected households each. I conducted a series of interviews with people who had specific views of "the community" because of the nature of their work, primarily as teachers and public officials.

So much excellent work on migration has been done in Oaxaca already that I did not expect to discover new information, although I was quite interested to find out the reasons local people would give for the relatively unusual pattern of return in the village. It was striking to hear the range of views expressed in this village of not many more than four thousand inhabitants.[19] We encountered only one household in which no members had ever migrated. Although, occasionally, young people said that they left for the adventure of it, by far the most common reasons were family related: someone was ill and extra money was required for medical attention; the family was growing and more space was needed; people wanted seed money in order to establish a small family business. Once a family was used to the extra income, a temporary sojourn was often worked into an annual cycle. People almost always went to places where some kinsperson could help them find work. Returnees said that they could not get used to the stress of illegal status, that they missed their families too much, or that life in the United States was too expensive. People had differing accounts of the sorts of reception they had experienced, relating encounters with racism but also telling of being well received or reveling in the relative freedom of conduct.[20] Some people returned with a heightened sense of appreciation for their own place; others missed the lights of the big city.

Tamar Wilson (2009) challenges the notion of bounded community that continues to influence much social analysis in rural Oaxaca. Thinking in transboundary rather than transnational terms, she follows the expansive networks that contemporary families develop, which are often dependent on intermarriage strategies and proliferate through the routes the migrants follow. Women act as what Bott (1971[1957]) calls "connecting relatives"—that is, as mothers, aunts, sisters—especially as they marry into "non-overlapping" families involved in transmigration networks. Bryceson and Vuyorela (2002:14, 24) speak of "relativizing" transnational families that draw on fluid intra- and interfamilial relations. Indeed, if we bring North Slope sharing networks into brief comparative view, it becomes evident that for a significant number of Iñupiat who move to Fairbanks or Anchorage, their sharing networks of "real," or hunted, food become larger rather than narrower (Fogel-Chance 1993).

Thus, this final section of my exploration of late modern family mobilities underscores the extent to which twenty-first-century kinship (in these contexts at least) is very much about extensions, additions, and incorporations of a wide range of relationships. They extend throughout national and international territories, and they entail a variety of transformations in which no form of state process is involved.

DISCUSSION

I begin this chapter by suggesting that circulation among adults and children can contribute to the study of kinship and modernity. Migration practices in the twentieth- and twenty-first centuries serve as a cautionary note to those who assume that modern families are nuclear. Elizabeth Bott's (1971[1957]) work details the importance of extended kinship networks in 1950s London. Late twentieth-century sharing networks expand when Iñupiat go to Fairbanks in search of full-time waged employment (Fogel-Chance 1993), and twenty-first-century Mexican households in Silicon Valley exhibit all manner of kinned combinations in their organization (Zlolniski 2006). We need to continue to recognize that kinship is broadly defined. One danger of Schneider's focus on the biological facts of reproduction—coupled with the sorts of fine-grained analyses that have emerged from his exhortation to take culture seriously—is to narrow the field. Kinship studies focus on questions of parentage (and childage) and occasionally of parenting but relatively infrequently on those kinship relations that have nothing whatsoever to do with birth, including those with aunts, uncles, godparents, and third cousins twice removed.

My comparison is between two regions that I define as equally American but in different ways. I want to return here to my original plea for more in-depth work on "inter"marriage. Bodies—citizen or alien, legal or illegal, laboring or in need, ruly or unruly, elusive or insistently present—preoccupy governmental regimes, which constantly institute strategies for imposing order by creating boxes to be checked, checkpoints to be crossed, and papers to be presented. The consequences, frequently, are not the intended ones. Marriage, which by definition crosses categories, has the capacity for encompassing relations that refuse easy definition. Much of the first-person literature I have read about the experience of growing up Mexican American seems to fall into quite different camps. Authors such as the poet Gloria Anzaldua (1987) and the academic Gilda Ochoa (2004) have produced powerful accounts of their experiences of racism, which led them to a position of pan-Latino solidarity. Others, such as Nicholas de Genova and Ana Ramos-Zayas (2003), examine the sharply expressed opinions put forward by Chicago Puerto Ricans and Mexicans about each other. And still others, such as Richard Rodriguez (1992), Carlos Velez-Ibañez (1980), and Christina Ceisel (2009), have written in a celebratory way of experiences that are more hybrid. But I have come across few accounts of the marriages (or, indeed, consensual unions of any sort) that might be considered composite in all sorts of ways.[21]

In this chapter, we have seen how both mestizaje and melting pot, as ideologies of nationhood, imply value in the dissolution of boundaries; the notion of such dissolution is then reproblematized as shifting categories of people are selected out of the "melting" process. Through my examination of the circulation of children and adults, we simultaneously see governmental notions of race as mutable, in that race can be "bred out"; as so essential that race defies the rhetoric of mixture; and as emergent, in the sense that "Mexican" has moved from a marker of national identity to one of racial identity. We see that these—and other—moves designed to manage mobile kinship through the rule of law reveal a multiplicity of political authorities that are often in direct contradiction with one another. And we see that the sorts of movements under discussion involve extra-state strategies and actions taken with state institutions in mind. By our recognizing the transboundary character that comes to the fore in so many different ways, the state-kinship-race nexus is revealed as both mutually constitutive and constantly shifting; as such, it is a perfect focus for twenty-first-century anthropologists.

Acknowledgments

As should be evident in the text, my intellectual debt to Raymond Neakok Sr. is enormous. He was the first to suggest that if I "wanted to understand what it means to be Iñupiaq," I should go camping with "their family," and he was the first to call me "a kid of some sort" within that family. The organizers and participants of the SAR advanced seminar "The Difference Kinship Makes: Rethinking the Ideologies of

Modernity" generated a stimulating and thought-provoking week. Benjamín Macias Pimentel, Carlos López Beltrán, and I have discussed questions of race in Mexico over the course of several years, and Linda Layne pushed my thinking about the order of law at a crucial moment of rethinking my overall argument. And finally, this chapter was largely written in memory of Mattie Aanavak Bodfish, who declared herself to be my *aaka* (grandmother), was an important touchstone in my life for decades, and passed away in 2006 at the age of 101.

Notes

1. This literature—much of it emerging out of second-wave feminist interventions in economic anthropology—is extensive. See, for instance, Collier and Yanagisako 1987; MacCormack and Strathern 1980; Strathern 2005; Yanagisako and Delaney 1995; Young, Wolkowitz, and McCullagh1981.

2. See, for example, Lévi-Strauss 1969[1949], but this assumption is by no means restricted to structuralist approaches.

3. This is the name of the organization as provided by Rodriguez. It is likely that he was referring to the Population Research Center at Portland State University.

4. Most of the contributors to this volume have played a central role in the development of these new directions, but see also Copeman 2005 on notions of blood and personhood in India; Franklin 2007 on genetic technologies; Howell 2006 on transnational adoption; Layne 1999 on motherhood; Rapp 1999 on conceptive technologies; Strathern 1991, 1992a, 1992b, 2005, for the ways in which her gaze consistently shifts.

5. This section is not comparative for reasons of space; moreover, my initial North Slope fieldwork was directly related to these issues, so my information is much more complete.

6. Although I thought that this was a common notion, the introduction to *Race in Cyberspace* (Kolko, Nakamura, and Rodman 2000) reveals continuing debate among academics about whether "race" reflects fixed biological categories.

7. Genova and Ramos-Zayas (2003), in their examination of how Puerto Ricans and Mexicans define each other in Chicago, were the first anthropologists I read who argued that "Mexicans" were defined as a race in the United States. The position was counterintuitive to me, but I have now been convinced that the category Mexican is deployed racially by at least some people and at certain ideological levels of government rhetoric. I continue to reject the conceptual logic of that definition.

8. Much has been written about this, but see Rodriguez 2008:240ff. for a sustained discussion of Proposition 187; Stephen 2009 for a considered analysis of shifts in border policing and its effects between 1995 and 2006.

9. *Iñupiat*, which means "real people," is the collective noun for the inhabitants of

the northwestern Arctic. The singular and adjectival form is *Iñupiaq*. *Inuit* is the plural for *inuk*, or "person," and is not employed as an ethnic marker in Alaska.

10. This process is by no means restricted to Peru. It has been documented cross-culturally, including in Ghanaian fostering practices (Goody 1982), the forced movement of women and children in postpartition India and Pakistan (Das 2007), the removal of "mixed" children in aboriginal communities in Australia (Wolfe 1999), and the recurrent incidents of foundlings in Europe and elsewhere (Panter-Brick and Smith 2000).

11. Because I have published extensively on this (Bodenhorn 1992, 2000, 2004a, 2006), I provide only a brief overview here. Life history interviews and extended household surveys conducted during my fieldwork provided information about individual lives from about 1908 to the present. Following Burch's observation that the late eighteenth and nineteenth centuries were times of turbulence and significant demographic changes, I am by no means positing a timeless, changeless Iñupiaq culture. The material here reflects the ethnographic realities of the 1980s, when I did my most systematic research on these issues; as far as I know, the values and the strategies I describe continue to shape social life in Barrow in the twenty-first century. For the most detailed presentation of these data, see Bodenhorn 1988, 1990; see also Worl and Smythe 1986; Chance 1990; the Burch references already mentioned. Briggs (1970, 1998) provides detailed accounts of Inuit family life in central Canada.

12. This testimony, translated by Raymond Neakok from its original Iñupiaq, was part of a session of the 1980 Elders Conference in which a proposed daycare center was being discussed. The question was, "How were kids taken care of when there weren't any of these social services programs around?" The original transcript is held by the Iñupiaq History, Language, and Culture Commission in Barrow. See Bodenhorn 1988, vol. 2, ch. 18, for a more detailed discussion of these issues.

13. See Brøsted 1985 and Klausner and Foulks 1982 for the appearance of councils; Bodenhorn 1988 for memories of the impact of the mothers clubs; Brower 1981 for the institutional processes of traditional councils.

14. This emerged during the life history interviews I conducted, but see also Barnhardt 1976 and, particularly, Kleinfeld and Bloom 1973. The potential familial rupture of these actions is, of course, not restricted to North Slope Iñupiat. See Briggs 1970 on central Canadian Inuit life; Basso 1990 on the anxieties of Apache parents when their children return home from boarding school.

15. See *Encyclopedia Britannica Online*, entry on Urban Indian Relocation Program, http://www.britannica.com/EBchecked/topic/1398461/Urban-Indian-Relocation-Program, accessed March 29, 2012.

16. Although the isolation of Alaska's indigenous populations meant that these

policies were never implemented with the same ferocity as with Native American families living in the mainland United States, many of the families I know recount losing a family member through these procedures during the 1950s and 1960s.

17. This information comes from Alaska Legal Services and from cases brought to the regional tribal government by parents wanting to use the ICWA.

18. See López Beltrán 2007 on seventeenth-century race categories; Rodriguez 2008 on marriage patterns from the sixteenth to nineteenth centuries. See also Lockhart's 1994 article, in which he argues that neither Nahua nor Spaniards were the Other for quite some time.

19. The views strongly resonate with Cohen 2002, 2004; Conway and Cohen 2003; Grishop 2006, which follow where people migrate on a regional, national, and international scale; why they go; what patterns they follow; and what sorts of flows are created and maintained by their movement.

20. For the most part, people from the Sierra tend to congregate in New Jersey, Oregon, and midwestern states.

21. Susan Benson's work—from her early (1981) ethnographic exploration of liaisons between West Indian, West African, and Anglo youth in London to her later (2006) more autobiographical work on names—is an exception.

7

"This Body Is Our Body"

Vishwakarma Puja, the Social Debts of Kinship, and Theologies of Materiality in a Neoliberal Shipyard

Laura Bear

A month into my fieldwork at Incorporated Shipyard on the muddy banks of the Hooghly River in Howrah, India, I noticed the men making a recurrent gesture. They would place their hand on the growing hull of the vast ice-class steel ship they were building for a Norwegian company and say, "*E shorir, amar shorir,*" or "This body is our body." They added that this was the most important thing I should remember about the yard. Some men expressed this as a mapping of functions onto parts of the ship. Others explained that the ship was a man lying down. Each time someone spoke of this, he would mark the ship onto his body, gesturing with his hands. These assertions were stronger than a claim that there was a similarity between the ship and a man's body. Men insisted that the ship was the "incarnation/form" (*roop*) of a man. This word carries with it the ritual and mythological associations of the "life force" (*shakti*) of gods or goddesses taking material form. This same concept applies to the ceremonies held with images of deities, when priests make them "alive" (*shojib*) by giving them life at the beginning of festivals. For the workers, the ship was a scaled-up body made vital by their acts of labor. When you are working inside or underneath the ship, you can feel this transference of energy because the ship shudders with the echoes from welding and hammering. Workers often remarked on these reverberations and smiled when I said that the ship felt "alive." This chapter explores this idiom of mobile productive life—which is human, divine, and part of the act of work—as it moved between the contexts of kinship, ritual practices surrounding the iron-working god Vishwakarma, and labor.[1] In fact, the idiom used by shipyard workers and their families asserted the irrelevance of these distinctions of context as they sought recognition for the long-term interconnections of "trust" (*bishash*) that would secure the continuous circulation of this life force.

As I will show, the use of this idiom by shipyard workers can be related to Hindu ritual concepts of shakti and to neoliberal work environments associated with outsourced, deunionized, and informal work. Yet, as I will argue, these concepts of the life force associated with labor also have a broader significance for our understanding of capitalism. They reveal the recalcitrant social debts of kinship and the mystery of productivity that haunts wage labor. I draw on the arguments of Karl Marx and Hannah Arendt that the act of labor is part of a fertile life process, but I suggest that their accounts are founded in a narrow domaining of kinship inside nature and of labor within the secular, material realm. Contrary to these segregations, I argue that the act of labor in capitalism often involves a polyvalent comprehension of productive powers that escapes such confinements.

My point about productive powers attempts to contribute to and push beyond approaches to life and work founded in the analysis of biopower or affective labor. Much important analysis has addressed colonial, paternalist, and neoliberal mobilizations of sentiment, religion, and ethical self-formations. At the center of these approaches are a focus on managerial strategies and the definition of a singular form of life or ethics. In this chapter, I take a different direction, one that takes seriously the complex paradoxes in the act of wage labor, which involves a transaction that cannot be confined to a single definition of life or be contained in managerial ethics. It crosscuts the domains of economics, kinship, citizenship, "nature," and the divine. There is always a surplus of meaning to the act of work that is not contained (not only a surplus value that is appropriated). In particular, work can provoke reflection on the forces that animate the world, produce material objects, and sustain human fertility. Our analysis of workplace relationships and capitalism will therefore always remain incomplete if we do not take seriously the various ethics of kinship, ritual, and human productivity that are conjoined in the act of labor. Marx and Arendt—with their emphasis on the act of work as part of a force of life—can help us begin to trace this complexity, but we will also have to move beyond their secular, materialist naturalism. It is to the limits and potential of their approaches for understanding acts of wage labor that I turn next.

Marx's conception of the act of wage labor was founded in a particular Protestant-influenced understanding of the source of productivity in a transcendent, fertile life force. It was Arendt who first made this point. She suggested that he was the last in an intellectual line of scholars—from John Locke through Adam Smith—who attempted to explain the phenomenon of economic growth by using metaphors of the life process and by focusing on labor as the source of growth. But she argued that Marx secularized and naturalized these earlier Protestant metaphors. Substituting life for God, he made labor into one aspect of a transcendent vital process. Arendt argues that, for Marx, terms such as "consumption," "production," and "reproduction" were meant as literal descriptions of a life process at work in the world. Labor's productivity comes from the human capacity to produce beyond immediate subsistence needs, and "laboring and begetting are merely two modes of the same fertile life process" (Arendt 1958a:106). For Marx, it was the fertility of this natural process that was appropriated by capitalists with the payment of wages and explained the expansive growth of capitalism.

Arendt deployed Marx's secular naturalism to make a distinct argument. She suggested that Marx wrongly subsumed all forms of work into labor, thereby unintentionally valorizing the never-ending and meaningless natural cycle of production and consumption. Arendt (1958a:115), like Marx, takes the existence of this cycle in capitalism literally. She assumes that all that is served in this world is a meaningless process of production and consumption that leaves no permanent trace. To this capitalist work of the body, Arendt counterposes the work of the hands, or of *homo faber*, that creates durable, permanent objects for use. For homo faber, the work process begins with an idea, a plan that will be realized and completed in a final product. This work is not oriented toward a repetitive process of consumption. Yet, it is ultimately limited by its ethical emphasis on utilitarianism. But Arendt's distinctions between the capitalist (animal) *homo laborans* and homo faber rest on the same initial domaining that Marx made in his definition of labor. The animal laborans's lack of ethical life and the homo faber's limited, utility-driven politics arise from the segregation of the act of labor into the realm of secular nature. However, what if labor within the institutions of capitalism has never been confined in this realm of secular nature? What if it has constantly exceeded this? I argue that this excess of the act of labor is often expressed by participants in wage labor within the ethical framing of kinship and ritual. Even though both Marx and Arendt significantly point us toward the relevance of life and fertility to capitalism, they cannot take us beyond the narrow boundaries of their analysis. Life and fertility for them belong to nature rather than to the ethical languages of kinship. Homo faber and homo laborans belong to the material world alone and are understood as governed solely by a natural life process. But, for participants in capitalism, these separations often make little or no sense. This, I contend, is for two reasons: one to do with the structure of wage labor, the other to do with the sensual nature of the work process.

What is it in the structure of wage labor that creates an ethical excess of kinship and endows the productivity of labor with a mysterious, excessive quality? To answer this, we can draw on Marx's analysis of the contradictions of the wage relation in volume 2 of *Capital*, but we must also move beyond his secular, naturalist interpretation of them. Marx argues, "In the relation between capitalist and wage-laborer, the money relation, the relation of buyer and seller becomes a relation inherent in production itself" (1992[1885]:19). So workers and capitalists meet each other as sellers and buyers of labor in a single wage transaction. But such a relationship is far from simple in its enactment or ethical conundrums. First, workers must treat their labor as a commodity in a single act of exchange, but in order to survive, they must repeat this act. Workers must attempt to make claims of a permanent relationship out of a short-term market transaction in order to sustain themselves. Second, the payment of wages to workers is not a recognition but a denial of the productive power of labor that workers give free to the capitalist. This is because wages recompense workers only for their means of subsistence, not for the full value of the labor they add to the production process. Third, workers are paid their wages out of the stock of revenue that their labor—or that of other workers in the past—has contributed to the firm. So the wage transaction takes on dualistic, contradictory features. It is a single marketplace encounter but must become a long-term relationship. It is both a monetary transaction and a free unpaid gift of productive powers. It is a payment for the subsistence needs of workers but does not acknowledge the full value of the productive power of human labor. The money payment passes from capitalist to worker, but the stocks of money are generated by the past and future fertility of workers' labor.

These contradictions, I suggest, stimulate workers' attempts to assert that the wage relation is more than a short-term transaction and that it should become part of the series of expansive, permanent social debts associated with kinship and ritual. Workers use these idioms to claim obligations—what employers owe to them is greater than a short-term wage transaction—and to assert their unacknowledged productive powers. Employers can also draw on these idioms in forms of state and individual paternalism that promise higher justice and permanent ties but still ultimately offer only the recompense of a capitalist wage relation. They also can forge claims that their acts are actually the source of the productivity of capital; the very denial of the productive powers of workers makes it necessary for employers to do this in order to account for the generative power of capitalism. The market logic of the wage transaction can never completely suffuse workplaces because its contradictions bring to the fore the problems of long-term social debts and contestations about the sources of productivity. Because Marx and Arendt solved these problems with a naturalist, secular explanation of the fertility of capital, they could not anticipate the significance of kinship and ritual to the lived experience of the institutions of capitalism.

Yet another complexity in the capitalist production process is hidden by Marx's and Arendt's assertion that labor belongs to the secular, material world of exchange: workers do not experience their acts of labor through exchange relations or as animal laborans. Both Marx and Arendt read the experience of labor in capitalism back from the context of the sale of commodities for consumption. Because commodities end up in a marketplace—where they find their value in relation to other objects and in the act of being consumed—Marx and Arendt assume that they are also experienced as commodities during the production process. The commodity fetishism that occurs within the exchange relationship of consumption is assumed to exist also in the relationship between workers and the objects they produce. Well-known arguments about alienation as part of the experience of labor, or the absence of alienation, due to processes of generating consent, have emerged from this assumption. But none of these approaches considers that, at the point of production, an object's exchange value might not exhaust its sensual form or meanings. We have rarely left it an open question as to whether industrial workers affiliate themselves to their products or through what theories of materiality and ethical idioms they might do this. Certainly, for shipyard workers, as we shall see, these affiliations are expressed in idioms of divine life forces, in theologies of the effectivity of ritual acts on the material world, and in the ethics of kinship. These are in fact, the opposite of the forms of the fetishism of commodities that Marx's and Arendt's theories would predict. Men claim ships as the product of a life force that is manifested in their acts of labor, and they let them go to their new owners through acts of launching on the river, in which this life dies. Therefore, shipyard workers do not see the commodities they produce as external, reified fetishes, which is what Marx's limited interpretation of the act of worship would suggest. Commodities have their existence only because of people's acts of giving life to them through labor. This is a logic that reflects the structure of Hindu ritual in which the community of worshipers gives idols their life force through acts of reciprocal and amplifying trust. It also exceeds the valuation of these objects in the act of market exchange as commodities.

My approach here differs from the cultures of capitalism argument and from the usual interpretations of ritual idioms in industrial workplaces. I am not arguing that capitalism is everywhere distinct and that diverse ritual and kinship idioms disrupt its universal logic. Instead, I am suggesting that internal to the structure of the wage relation and the work process are denied obligations and experiences, which reappear in the ethical idioms of kinship and ritual. Capitalist waged work constantly exceeds a materialist, secular, and economistic interpretation because of its own internal elisions. This is a different claim from that usually made about ritual, ethics, and industrial labor in historical and ethnographic analysis (Chakrabarty 1989; Nash 1979; Taussig 1980). Take, for example, the ways in which the Vishwakarma *puja* (festival) has been interpreted by prominent labor scholars. This festival is widely observed in India in industrial workplaces and in contexts where people work with machines. As explained later in the chapter, it involves the stilling of machinery and tools for one day each September and the collective celebration among workers of their labor, through the consumption of food and drink. Usually, the owners of companies or unions sponsor the celebrations.

This ritual has been understood as a problem: how to relate an anomalous religious consciousness to the secular, material realm of economics. Dipesh Chakrabarty (1989) wrote of the puja in the nineteenth century as a lingering element of precapitalist peasant religious consciousness that interrupted the secular time of capital. It also reflected the inegalitarian, precapitalist culture of the jute mill workers in Kolkata. Leela Fernandes (1997, 1998) importantly reversed this argument in her work in the 1990s in a jute mill in Howrah. She suggested that a religious festival under union patronage had been "politicized," producing a masculine space of labor in which workers could seize back control of the means of production by disrupting work schedules during the festival. So, she argued, a religious outlook could become the basis for the creation of class consciousness. But both of these interpretations preserve the domains of a secular, materialist economics, politics, and religion. I argue that the Vishwakarma puja and its affiliated domestic ritual, the Ranna puja, are importantly uncontainable in such domains, as are workers' interpretations of their acts of work. The Vishwakarma puja is a particularly interesting context in which to explore the issue of productive powers because it is an entirely urban ritual that developed within capitalism among people who have worked for three generations in industrial settings. The capitalism in Howrah emerged simultaneously with British industry and with many of the same participants. The Vishwakarma puja also continues to grow alongside more than twenty years of the Communist Party of India's Maoist- and Marxist-influenced rule in the state of West Bengal. It is neither a "culture" of industrial capitalism nor a provincialized form of it. It should instead be taken as a guide to our creation of a broadened theoretical understanding of productive powers.

Incorporated Shipyard provides a particularly significant site for the exploration of these issues. First, it is a workplace that is typical of the outsourced labor conditions of contemporary neoliberalism and its production from a global labor pool for a global market. Second, so insecure is this work environment that, for the participants in it, it makes manifest in an extreme manner the contradictions inherent in all wage labor. It is a temporary assemblage formed from a joining together of family, state, and international capital and is owned and run by two brothers. The work is outsourced from state agencies and international companies along chains of intermediaries. It is an informal "family" enterprise with no regulation or unionization. Here, 1,500 men work on orally arranged day contracts (only 50 are permanent staff, and only 40 are on monthly contracts) in five yards. They are provided by three brokers, who divide workers into separate "companies" of no more than 20 men to evade employment law regulations. The vast ship being built in Number 3 Yard for a Norwegian firm had been subdivided into blocks, each of which was being constructed by workers under separate brokers. Men work with leased machinery on the open mud of the shore; there are no permanent structures. Command in the yards is fragmented between contractual foreign managers, contractually employed middle managers, and supervisors of small teams of workers. Here, we have the highest realization of the logics of neoliberal outsourcing—a reduction of infrastructure, accountability, and labor cost to the minimum. The shipyard exists entirely beyond the limiting regulations of the state and politics since there is neither unionization nor any legal regulation of its practices. The productivity of risk and the productivity of debt are combined to create a particular form of disorganized, speculative, short-term capitalism (Roitman 2005; Zaloom 2004). In this environment, the problems of the sustenance of families, the continuity of wage relations, and the contrast between the value produced by labor and the wages paid for it are starkly evident to participants.

In addition, the work process itself is a mixture of elements that Arendt would have separated into the experiences of animal laborans and homo faber. It is oriented toward consumption but produces a product that has a bulky, permanent presence in the world: the towering hulls of ships. The work process is oriented toward an end product and starts with an overall plan known to all workers. Construction is carried out with tools rather than with large-scale mechanized processes and in an environment unprotected from the elements, so the rhythm of the work is guided much more by men and the events of the tide and weather than by the rhythms of capital. These circumstances, as we will see, provoke much reflection among the men on the work that they produce as agents in the world and their relationships to the products of their work.

At Incorporated Shipyard, we can trace in high relief the contradictions and experiences that Marx's and Arendt's analyses of capitalism can help us to understand, but only if we abandon their segregation of kinship into nature and of labor into the material, secular world. How, then, are work and the act of production understood by shipyard workers and their families? If idioms of productive powers incorporate ritual, kinship, and economics, through what practices does this occur? How are productive powers made manifest, and what happens when they are denied their polyvalent meaning? What can we understand from shipyard workers' idioms and practices more generally about the life of kinship as part of the productive powers in contemporary neoliberalism?

VISHWAKARMA AND RANNA PUJAS: PRODUCTIVE POWERS, EXPANSIVE RELATIONS OF BISHASH, AND THE IMMANENCE OF SHAKTI

The majority of the men who work at Incorporated Shipyard live with their extended families in established working-class neighborhoods along the Andul Road south of the second Howrah Bridge. Their fathers had been employed in state shipyards, on the docks, and in private manufacturing companies as permanent staff or as day laborers. Most private industries closed during the 1980s, and the state sector now takes on only limited amounts of contractual labor. Access to work has always been precarious for both generations, and most men have spent long periods unemployed. The social networks of neighborhoods are built around uncles and brothers in the male line who have settled along the same narrow lanes in one-room mud houses that were established gradually through a process of squatting on land. Women sometimes work nearby, stitching in small garment units, doing piecework at home, or providing domestic labor. Each neighborhood has three local party offices, but few of the shipyard workers are politically active. Political power has become a monopoly of certain families, and unions enroll only permanent workers. Almost all the workers in these neighborhoods are from scheduled and low-caste groups.

Families intermarry through arrangements due to male friendships at work or through love relationships struck up during festivals. Neighborhood networks are extremely important for collecting news of work opportunities. When contractors need workers, they always put out the word among existing employees so that they, in turn, will recruit family members, neighbors, and friends. The assignment may be temporary, but the personal relationships between workers are often long-term. Large numbers of workers are related to one another or are from the same neighborhoods or have worked together before in other places. Affection, tender caresses, and small signs of mutual care are regularly displayed between the workers. This is known as the "love of men" (*bhalobhasa*).

Kinship idioms are framed through ever-widening circles of connection between households that stretch outward to form neighborhoods, "types of people" (*jati*), and the world of the city. Each household is perceived as a segment—more or less complete—of a group of brothers born of the same father and mother and arranged in precedence by birth order. They share a common line (*bongsho*) linked by blood (*rokto*), out of which sisters move and into which wives are adopted. The ideal situation is for as many brothers as possible—with their productive power and that of their wives—to be grouped in a single household of connected one-room buildings. By contrast, the movement of sisters out of the household is seen as an evil that impoverishes the family's wealth and productive power. But it is a necessary movement because women's life force is realized only through their reproductive roles and their work as wives. As the proverb among these families insists, "a woman is born in one house and works in another." In addition, marriage importantly strengthens the productivity of the household in the sense of creating ever-widening networks of *kutum*—a term that is used to describe not only relatives by marriage but also close friendships in neighborhoods and workplaces. Friends become part of the kutum that can be mobilized for the metasociality of festive occasions and practical help; they become kutum by sharing in puja celebrations and, most important, by eating in one's house.

Neighborhoods along the Andul Road are described as an ever-widening sphere of ties of kutum, actual and potential allies through marriage and friendship. Making friends part of the category of kutum (wife takers) places them in a hierarchical relationship to oneself that can never be terminated. It is an incitement to a long-term connection and a constant flow of food, information, and affection between households. But, of course, the widening of these ties is limited by distinctions of ancestral origin (*gotro*), or what is usually described as caste status. Men describe bitterly their rejected approaches to neighboring families for marriage due to a difference in caste status. Similarly, the refusal to allow acquaintances to eat in one's house or to accept a relationship is interpreted as an illegitimate claim to higher-caste status. The widest expanse of the encompassing circles of connection is "type of person" (jati), which is understood on the model of a household of brothers and its ties of marriage projected outward. As such, it could have its boundaries marked by various social distinctions. The ones most commonly evoked are region, religion, and nation but not caste, which is seen as an illegitimate form of distinction in this widest circle of sociability. The city is seen as a collection of jatis arranged like the five fingers on one hand. Each is different but has both good and bad people in it. The ties between men—relatives by blood and marriage or friends—should, ideally, be marked by affection (*bhalobhasa*) and trust (*bishash*). Unlike the temporary ties created by money, these take time and effort to make.

The centrality of food to creating ties of trust cannot be understated. Its agency provides the wellness and fertility of individuals and households, and its offering and consumption signal acceptance of a relationship. But the appetite for food can be both productively social and individualistically antisocial. People would complain that the stomach and its selfish impulses have become the ruler (*mahajan*) everywhere. Diagnosing the lack of recognition of social obligations at work, Shankar Das, a forty-year-old heavy laborer (*khalasie*) in the shipyard, said that this was because relationships there were just guided by "the burning of the stomach." Collective eating and sociality, especially during rituals, provided the source and expression of life-sustaining relationships. It also dramatically displayed the productive fertility of households, neighborhoods, and companies in the numbers of people eating together and the quantities of food offered.

The rituals of the Vishwakarma and Ranna pujas make material these expansive idioms of productive fertility that are projected upward from households to social relations of every kind. These rituals link together all forms of productive power in a spectacular display of the work, fertility, and sociability that are necessary for their continuing realization. For families in the shipyard, the ritual season starts with these twinned pujas. The explicitly stated point is that they are the first in the cycle of pujas that will create joy (*annondo*) over the next few months and will make the family and its work stay well (*bhalo thake*). "Staying well" is an inclusive phrase that involves prosperity, *sukh* (individual good health and happiness), fertility, and the prevention of accidents. "Joy" is an equalizing, shared emotion is associated only with pujas and is amplified as more people take part in rituals together. The practice of these pujas exactly materializes the desired flows of productive power, or shakti.

I turn first to the Ranna, or cooking, puja. Unlike the management of daily budgets, brothers pool resources for the household Ranna puja, and women cook together with no selfishness (*hingso*). Preparations for both the Ranna puja and the Vishwakarma puja begin on September 16. Women who have married into the family and their mother-in-law clean the household with the usual domestic tools, Ganges water (*ganga jol*), and basil water (*tulsi jol*), which is associated with the man-god Siva. At the same time, men at work clean all their tools and machinery with Ganges water in preparation for the next day. Women make this cleaning a dramatic display of their usual routines, complaining to anyone who will listen about how hard and difficult it is. Every word is a claim for the legitimacy of their contribution of work and fertility to the household alongside that of their husband and his brothers. The work for the puja is indeed hard because multiple foods are cooked, although no meat. That is supplied to men in the yard by their employer on Vishwakarma day. These foods are laid out on the floor in a beautiful display, offered to the goddess Ma Monosha, and eaten by the people in the household and in the mother's uncle's house (*mamabari*), which together constitute a bongsho. When the women in the household wake up on the morning of the seventeenth, before their husbands leave for the shipyard, they carry out a puja to the goddess Monosha. On this day, one's kutum come to eat with you. In this puja, women's work and the powers of fertility and sociality of both the bongsho and the kutum are spectacularly enacted through the medium of food prepared and eaten in a collectivity. Houses on Vishwakarma day fill with people who are the materialized forms of these productive powers and who eat in an acceptance of the idealized relationships of mutual sustenance.

When men arrive at the shipyard, they celebrate the flow of these household-generated productive powers into their acts of work, and they demand recognition of them. Huge idols of the god Vishwakarma—each one paid for by a different key labor broker—are set up in the yards, and priests carry out a puja in front of them. All equipment, from cranes to welding torches, is cleaned, decorated with flowers, and stilled for the day. First, there is a short, solitary moment in which men sit with their tools in their place of work, offering these and their minds to Vishwakarma. Then, in their best clothes, the men wander freely through the yard, displaying their work to their children. The most anticipated moment is when the owner feeds the workers meat and alcohol. Ideally, he passes the packets of food around with his own hands. Men explained this ritual entirely in terms of a recognition of their productive powers, which make them Vishwakarmas who must be acknowledged on this day by brokers and, most important, the yard owner. We, they say, are Vishwakarmas, men of "iron" (*loha*), so that is why on this day we worship Vishwakarma, an incarnation of Siva, a man-god who gave us our tools and was the most skilled ironworker. The manager must show his recognition of his permanent debt to them as Vishwakarmas by feeding them the meat and alcohol that will regenerate their shakti. If he does this and the puja goes well, then the work through the year will stay well (bhalo thake), the workers will experience happiness and health (sukh), and there will be no mishaps or death in the yard.

These practices materialize the connections between the work and fertility of the household and the work and fertility of the yard, and they elicit social obligations that crosscut these spaces. The rituals materialize the social feeding and never-ending flows of life and the recognition of forms of social debt that workers and their families desire to be at the center of social life. For twenty-four hours, these are made present in spaces such as the yard that are always in danger of being ruled by the individualistic asociality and short-term ties of monetary relationships. Work should be an act that takes place as part of these longer-term forms of social debt and the flows of life between material forms.

The myths associated with these rituals link the trust (bishash) between humans and their exchanges of life forces to the reciprocity between humans and the divine. All shipyard workers and their family members asserted that the Ranna puja and the Vishwakarma puja were held on the same day because of the role of the man-god in the myth of Behula and Lokhindar. This is the story of the confrontation between the wealthy ship merchant Chandsadagar and Mother Monosha, the snake goddess. Monosha is thrown out of heaven by Siva, who tells her that she can return only if she rallies enough followers. She seeks the worship of Chandsadagar but is rejected by him. She persecutes him, killing all his sons and sinking all his ships. A last son is born, Lokhindar, who grows up and marries Behula. To protect Lokhindar from Monosha, Behula asks Vishwakarma to build an iron room for them to sleep in on their wedding night, but Vishwakarma is forced by Monosha to leave a tiny hole in the corner of the room. In the night, Monosha's favorite snake crawls in and kills Lokhindar. Behula takes his body downriver to the kingdom of the gods on a boat of banana leaves built by Vishwakarma. There, she promises to worship Monosha and to persuade Chandsadagar to carry out grand pujas for her.

Lokhindar is then restored to life. How did people relate this story of the importance of trust or mutual recognition between goddesses and humans for the continuance of life to the household and shipyard?

For both men and women, Chandsadagar became a great ship company owner like Gautam Chatterjee, the man who founded Incorporated Shipyard. When telling the story, women emphasized the struggle for recognition of Monosha as a female goddess and as a woman whose bishash was denied. Her actions were the stuff of drama, echoing the emphasis on women's fertility and productivity recognized in the Ranna puja. Men, on the other hand, were gripped by Vishwakarma's role in the tale. They often forgot that he had been intimidated by Monosha and instead emphasized that he had made the room "watertight" to protect a fellow man, Lokhindar, but for technical reasons—he had to get out of the room at the end of the work—a hole had been left. They also emphasized that bishash was at the core of the story, and it was in these conversations that the multiple contexts of trust were explicitly interlinked. Shankar Das explained: "See, Laura has been to my house about ten times! There is special trust. That is what is important. Without bishash, nothing can be. I have an unwritten contract with my contractor. My only contract with him relies on bishash. She has bishash in my family, so she comes to my house. Bishash is everything to a man and to the gods and goddesses too." For women, it was bishash as trust in the fertile power of female goddesses that was significant, linked to the recognition of women's work in the household. For men, the expansive social meaning of bishash as ties of obligation between men was most significant. Ultimately, the tale of Monosha and the pujas assert that flows of life (which generate fertility and productivity) can be maintained only if long-term ties of obligation or bishash are expansively created. If bishash is not forged, then the material world will disaggregate into vengeful acts that deny life and may cause death, and humans will be driven by individualistic desires. Acts of work, both female and male, should be part of this desired flow of life. But beyond these ritual settings, we need to explore how concepts of productive power were manifested in everyday work.

THE PRODUCTIVE LIFE OF INCORPORATED SHIPYARD: LABOR, SHAKTI, AND THE ROOP OF THE SHIP

Tasks in the yard where the vast ice-class vessel was being produced were divided between small teams that worked for different brokers on separate blocks of the ship. All the work involved tight dependencies within the groups. The welders' labor was the most individualized because each welder was put on a specific seam and enclosed in a mask through which he could see only the flame's blue spark. Grinders were similarly absorbed in avoiding bursts of sparks and metal dust and staying on the seam. But dependencies crosscut even these tasks: in each team, the older, experienced men were teaching younger helpers in their first jobs, and the older men were entirely dependent on the younger men for safety. For example, the young men watched out for electric wires falling into pools of water, warned welders inside the ship cavities when other workers were getting too close, and cautioned grinders when plates were approaching on cranes overhead. The three or four loftsmen, who lay out the vessel's form, and the markers they worked with were seen as the most technically skilled workers. Kalahasies (heavy laborers) were seen as the least skilled: they provided the muscle, helping cranes lift plates, doing other heavy lifting, and beating metal. But, reflecting the small differentials in wages and the mutual dependencies of tasks,[2] everyone insisted that within the yard, everyone was equal—*somman.* Men insisted that they all did work with their hands (*hater kaj*) and that this was a skill that could be learned by anyone, whatever his birth origin. They were also extremely proud that they were part of a world of universal technical knowledge. Skill and knowledge were unequivocally associated with the possibility of equality and social mobility for these low-caste and scheduled-caste workers. This feeling of the freedom of skill rather than the inequality of inborn essence was enhanced by the decentralized command of the yard. Workers in their small teams would negotiate and debate with their overseers the value of different technical procedures and often insist that the overseers accept their solutions.

The workers' only frustration was that their embodied skills were not recognized as valuable or modern work by managers and foreign supervisors because their skills were not associated with high-tech machinery or education. The workers were aware that their work environment was not—as they would have put it—as "developed" as the navy shipyard across the river. But they claimed strongly that they were part of a universal community with modern engineering skills. Viduth Samanta, a fifty-year-old skilled fitter, told me: "There is a box that we use with five compasses... and with this...all the things in the world can be constructed. People have BSc [degrees] and are engineers and can work abroad. We don't have this, but we have this box and this is exactly the same knowledge they use." The sense of a collectivity of the men at work on the ship—united in the labor of their hands to produce a final complete product—was expressed by men through projecting the model of the group of brothers and their kutum that form the household. This became clear to me because the shipyard workers often returned to the puzzling issue of why ships abroad were given women's names but in India were always (they insisted) given men's names. Shankar Das said: "But we associate the use of the women's name if the father is dead. Then the son will go to the mother's family. This is why here we give men's names to the ships. Otherwise, it would seem that the father is dead or something, that we who made the ship are no longer alive any more." This projection of kutum logic onto the workplace is a small fragment of a larger theology of how the ship's materiality is produced and what the act of work is. It draws on the idioms of the ritual actions and mythologies surrounding the Vishwakarma and Ranna pujas. This became clear in the shipyard workers' discussions of the yard as a space of life, the shakti that transfers from men to the ship, and the celebrations of the Vishwakarma puja and the launching of the ship.

Workers were insistent that the yard, in spite of the multiple dangers, was a space of productive life. One day, I was with Joydev Mandal (a young pipe cutter) and Shankar when we began to discuss ghosts (see Carsten, chapter 5, this volume). I asked how ghosts appeared. They both agreed that it was when people died in accidents and suicides. I wondered aloud whether people felt the ghosts of the three or so men who had died in the yards in accidents. Joydev said that sometimes when he was welding, he would feel something behind him but that, generally, places of work cannot accommodate ghosts. If they are there, they usually go away when he is in the act of working. I knew that a man's head had been cut off by a plate in the Number 5 Yard, so I asked about that. Both Joydev and Shankar insisted that people no longer work in the place where that happened. But then Shankar began to speculate that the reason the Number 5 Yard was so disastrous for work—and the cavity of mud they had tried to build there for a dry dock was always failing—was that, in the British times, it had been a hanging ground. He said that they used to throw all the bodies there, so it would always be *phaka* (empty, useless, unproductive) land, on which no good work could be done. Work is an act inherently associated with the forces of life; death repels and is repelled by its productive powers.

Shipyard workers also understood their work as a transaction in which their productive energy (shakti) left them and entered the ship iron as they worked on it. Viswanath, a forty-year-old welder, and Bipak, his seventeen-year-old helper, were discussing with me their acts of work as they sat, as usual, under the ship's belly. They talked about their work diminishing their shakti and their having to eat bananas (*kola*) and milk (*dud*) to take away the sting of the fumes in their lungs from welding and to revive their shakti. These are the foods associated with and offered specifically to Vishwakarma at puja time. Viswanath added: "When you are old and worn out [and] all your shakti is gone, then the company will not care. They will throw you away, and you will just not be able to get work." The life that disappears from a person through the course of his work enters into the ship itself and makes it alive. This is a giant, permanent body of iron that has taken on the form of Vishwakarma. The shipyard workers' claim that the ship is a scaled-up version of their own bodies (shojib) and an incarnation (roop) of their own life force (shakti) makes these transfers of life absolutely explicit. The commodity they produce is not fetishized, as Marx and Arendt would have predicted, but is seen as a form that is given life by their actions of labor.

The failed Vishwakarma puja that occurred in the yard during my fieldwork made this framework for the act of labor even clearer. On that day, men took possession of and displayed the product of their shakti and skill, the giant iron ship. They also claimed recompense from Gautam, the yard owner, for the expenditure of their shakti in his behalf. But this was not forthcoming, creating a fatal spiral of ill health and unhappiness (*osukh*). An excerpt from my field notes from that time traces the failed obligations of trust (bishash) and their consequent effects:

> Mohan Kholey (a young welder) and another, older friend called Aushik (a fitter) came up to us [my husband, Subhrasheel, and I] smiling. Mohan immediately said, "Let me show you all 'round inside the ship, all our work." As we walked through the dark passage into the first tank area of the ship, I asked Mohan why this was such a special day for them. He said, "Because we are Vishwakarmas. We are men of loha [iron, steel] who have made such a huge loha ship. So for that reason we celebrate today." Then, as we walked out of the ship, Mohan complained that this year the puja was much smaller than last year, when Gautam gave them meat. But this year he had heard that Gautam would just give them a small packet the day after the celebration.... I asked them what would happen if they did not worship Vishwakarma on this day...would it mean that their work would be spoiled? Mohan said, "No, not like that. This is a puja that makes our minds calm and focused so that we can do good work. It does not protect us. We worship Vishwakarma because he is a very highly skillful man, so he helps to make us skillful."

Talking the next afternoon under the ship with workers, I learned that they were bitterly disappointed because Gautam had given them just small packets of sweets, not meat and not even on Vishwakarma day. To add to the insult, he had not given the packets with his own hand; they had been passed around by the peons. As the day wore on, the workers grew more disappointed that joy (annondo) would not be realized fully. They complained that they felt unwell and unhappy (osukh), that Gautam was not giving them the strength of meat so that they could work, and that they were not recompensed for the shakti they put into the ship.

The spiral of osukh continued in the weeks afterward as more and more workers complained to me that the relationship between the workers' skill and shakti, which had gone into the ship, and Gautam's wealth had not been fully recognized at the Vishwakarma puja. They said that here was the final sign that the burning of the stomach—rather than the reciprocal sustenance of sociable relations—was in control in the yard. Men began to leave in groups as soon as they heard of work elsewhere, complaining that the yard's conditions and the lack of acknowledgment from the owner were making them unwell.

One important issue remains. Because the ship was the animate product of workers' shakti, how did they let go of it at the end of their work? Also, how did they make explicit that the ship was, in fact, the life-filled image of a god? When the hull was completed, there was a dramatic moment of launching. The ice-class ships had to be launched sideways from the bank into the river. This happened under floodlights in the small hours of the morning when the tide was highest. In their descriptions of this event, shipyard workers explained that the launching of the ship was exactly like the moment of immersion of the Vishwakarma idol, when people say goodbye to its lifeless container until the next year, when the festival is celebrated again and the life takes the form of another idol. Sukumar, one of the yard supervisors, explained: "The immersion time of Vishwakarma is like the launching of the ship. When you launch a ship and immerse an idol, you have the same emotions and feeling. You do the same things, singing and dancing and putting it into the Ganga at last."

So the men of iron produce a permanent ship of iron that is also Vishwakarma, a god, to whom you bid goodbye on the riverbank. All the workers said that at the launching of the ice-class vessel, they had experienced the greatest annondo of their lives. All the arrangements of the launching—which I saw on the DVDs that circulated among the workers—mimicked a cross between a puja and an immersion: the ship decorated with flowers, a coconut smashed on its hull by the ship owner, loudspeakers blaring Hindi film music, and dancing after the launch. Everyone spoke of how incredible it was because all the men danced together in joy. The workers' intense annondo came from the acknowledgment and evidence of their collective shakti, which had produced the ship and had now left it, only to be manifested again in the next cycle of building and launching a vessel. Their claims are, of course, the opposite of the fetishism of commodities assumed by Marx to be operational at the end of the production process for workers. Here, workers claim the product of their work as part of their life force and let it go only because it dies in its return to the Ganges. They never experience the commodity they generate as an external fetish. To do so, they would have to share Marx's impoverished understanding of ritual as the worship of an external Other, rather than as the generation of a reciprocal, life-giving relationship of trust between humans and deities. In addition, they would have to experience the act of labor as simply the production of a commodity for exchange, rather than as a sensuous process of creation.

Workers asserted that their acts of labor are part of a creative universe of expansive obligations and immanent flows of life that pass reciprocally between gods, humans, and objects. They are also simultaneously part of a global world of equalizing, modern technical skills. Idioms and ritual practices of kinship provide the mediating ethics that unite the worlds of production and social reproduction with the creative forces immanent in the material world. Labor power is never simply a commodity that can be paid for by wages. On the contrary, it is a creative, life-generating act that demands the recompense of long-term relationships of social obligation and mutual sustenance. These meanings of labor are close to Marx's and Arendt's valorization of labor as the source of productivity in their critiques of capitalism, but they are importantly distinct. They emerge from a combination of Hindu theologies of the material world and practices of kinship. The circumstances for their emergence characterize a specific kind of workplace—one in which the work process emphasizes the achievement of an act of work rather than the production of a commodity. That workplace is also a neoliberal one, without political or legal protection or secure employment. As a result, actual kinship ties have acquired a central role in the securing and enacting of work. In addition, any other potential overarching ethics of union politics or company paternalism have entirely disappeared. The emergent content of this ethics of labor is specific to a particular time, place, and work process. Yet, its emergence is built into the contradictory, repetitive structure of the wage transaction itself, which can never recompense workers for the expenditure of their polyvalent productive powers or renew anything more than their immediate subsistence needs. Workers' creative life force—and that of their families—can never be returned to them in its fullness but passes away without renewal. The ethics of kinship will always recur in public as the idiom and practice of the denied aspects of human creativity and obligation in capitalism.

THE PRODUCTIVE LIFE OF MANAGERS: DIVINE NATURAL RHYTHMS AND INDIVIDUAL TECHNICAL CHARISMA

There is another side to the wage relation: the position of the employer. Here, we have to analyze how a lack of obligation and long-term ties is produced in workplace transactions. Importantly, this was not achieved at Incorporated Shipyard by the claim that the wage relation is fair recompense for work. The managers knew that the labor was dangerous and made the men's bodies deteriorate and also that the wages were much lower than in the navy shipyard across the river. But, for managers, the productivity of the shipyard was not produced by the surplus labor or acts of work, which they described as unskilled. Instead, this was created by the individual technical charisma of managers who could master natural rhythms and their immanent divine force. Gautam Chatterjee, the original founder of the company, most manifested these qualities—in particular, through his technical projects and daring sideways launch of the vast ice-class vessel.

One morning, the rumor spread among the yard supervisors that Gautam was trying to build a hovercraft that would float fifteen feet above the ground. Managers were certain that he would be successful and discussed how this would lead to manufacturing the hovercraft for the Indian navy and, in turn, to the rising fortunes of them all. Later that day, I went to see the prototype Gautam was working on. All the middle managers from across the yards were clustered on a raised pallet, bent over the prototype, which had been cobbled together from a large industrial fan and plywood. They tenderly looked at the parts of the machine. The collective feeling of awe and excitement was palpable. It was also characteristic of the effect that talk of the spectacular past and future successes of Gautam produced. Like the figures of urban charisma discussed by Hansen and Verkaaik (2009), he was admired for his ability to bring foreign work and foreigners to the shores of the Hooghly. Managers often speculated about the opaque networks of influence through which he had achieved this. His inventions, like the hovercraft, were widely mentioned as evidence of his qualities of technical daring.

The admiration managers had for Gautam also rested on his ability to manipulate the rhythms of the Hooghly River, which was always called the Ganga and was strongly associated with the myth of Ma Ganga and the ritual uses of the purifying power of Ganga water. Commentary on the river's nature and Gautam's ability to tap into natural rhythms referenced their sense of the immanent divine in nature. In particular, they referenced Ma Ganga's force, which manifested during her descent to earth when Siva had to catch her in his locks in order to control her power. They also referred to the Ganga as a place for a good death. These idioms came together in the accounts of the launching of the Norwegian ice-class vessels.

The first time I met Gautam, he played a video of the launching—as did each of the managers in turn. When I later interviewed him, he began by insisting that the most important knowledge that a shipbuilder needs is that of the tides of the river Hooghly. To demonstrate this, he began an excited description of the launching. Gautam explained: "You can't pull the ship from the river, so instead you take the help of God [meant literally], which is called gravity." To emphasize his point about gravity and the river and how the vessel launches, Gautam said, "Everything is nature, not going against it, and how you can influence nature." I commented that knowledge of the river is vital for his work, and Gautam replied, "Yes, I know it very well. I have sat thirty feet from it for the past thirty years."

The manager of the Number 3 Yard, Somnath Banerjee, offered a description of the launch that combined these themes of expertise, the river, and the divine with the moment of death. Somnath suggested one day that I should write a novel about the yard. He said that to do this, I had to find the fierce beauty in the yard. The time he had seen that beauty was when the ice-class vessel was launched. He went on to describe the event: "For one hour before, not a pin dropped, so silent in the yard that was usually so full of hammering, welding, etc. The only noise was Gautam-da announcing instructions for the letting off of charges gradually, step-by-step, under the boat. All the VIPs were on a launch in the river. Everything was silent until the boat hit the water. Then, there was a spontaneous shout from every single worker in the yard. Everyone came out of the office and everyone danced with everyone else all together. That is fierce beauty and poetry." He added that the most intense beauty he had ever seen was in the Sundarbans at the place where the land ends and there is only water. He continued: "Here, there is a Bengali saying: 'This is where you go when the last blow of the broom comes down on you.' This is the place where there is the last blow of land before the ocean. This is fierce beauty, where death and beauty and the river are all mixed together." The sideways launch of the vessel into the river enabled the managers to combine the understanding of the Hooghly as a place for mourning the death of family members and as the place to go for a good death with the technical charisma of Gautam-da. For managers, the source of productive power is not the labor of shipyard workers but the divine rhythms of nature manifested in the force of the Ganga combined with individual technical daring.

The labor ethics held by workers and managers exist within the structures of contemporary neoliberal capitalism, which entails economic governance from a distance. This arm's-length control is sutured together by the circulation of paper contracts between the Norwegian firm and various intermediary firms in Cyprus and Mumbai. The contracts assert a stripped-down logic of market exchanges and wage payments for the services of brokering, laboring, and managing. For example, foreign managers on short contracts appeared in the yard—sent by an agent in Cyprus—to inspect the workers' labor. They spoke of the tremendous personal costs to their families and lives of this work, but they passed a distanced judgment on the workplace of Incorporated Shipyard—one devoid of any sense of social obligation. This disengagement is a direct product of the outsourcing structure that creates shallow, temporary market links along the chain of circulation of capital and disavows any obligation other than that of capital relationships. But, equally, this network of shallow obligations contributes both to the managers' experiencing sense of individual charismatic destiny in the figure of Gautam and to the shipyard workers' applying idioms of kinship and ritual to their acts of labor. Within this system, Gautam appears to middle managers as a free, creative agent who attracts capital and transforms it with his productive skill and intuition about divine rhythms. He is a man with amplified agency. On the other hand, shipyard workers demand recognition of their productive powers within idioms of kinship and ritual and refuse the denial of these by the market transactions of outsourcing contracts and the technical charisma of Gautam.

CONCLUSION: PATERNALISM, NEOLIBERALISM, AND PRODUCTIVE POWERS

Sennett (2008) has argued that Arendt was wrong in her assumption that animal laborans is confined to a domain of unreflective life. He suggests that acts of work within capitalism also contain an ethic that emerges from a slow, curious, skilled encounter with materials and the world. But my point here is a different one that supplements Sennett's argument: Arendt, following Marx, was unable to recognize that a recalcitrant ethic of long-term social debts and a mystery of productivity haunt wage labor because of its internal contradictions. These contradictions provoke ethical speculation among participants in wage labor that draws on diverse theologies and ethics of materiality, fertility, and human productivity. Marxist interpretations of wage labor can trace these core contradictions but cannot capture the experiences or ethics of work because these contain their own narrow, secular, and materialist ethical framings of its productivity. Central to these framings are understandings both of human fertility as part of nature rather than as part of the ethical language of kinship and of labor as an act on a secular world. Marx, and Arendt following him, placed laboring and begetting under the sign of a single, natural, and fertile life process.[3] Yet, this ethical move makes their approach analytically limited in relation not only to global capitalist experiences but also to the history and present of capitalism in Europe and the United States.

Many analysts have shown the centrality of Christian ethics and idioms of kinship to nineteenth- and twentieth-century corporate and state paternalism. Historians have long argued that paternalism rests on rearrangements of sexuality, kinship, and masculinity (Rose 1992; Stoler 2002). I have shown for the colonial and postcolonial Indian railways that arrangements of labor were governed by a polyvalent sense of work as a biomoral act supported by nature, family arrangements, and Protestant religious practices (Bear 2007a). But we have still not used these insights widely to examine the complexity of the act of labor within capitalism; the theories of materiality, immanence, and the divine that affect the interpretations of this act; or the ways in which kinship provides a language for concepts of social debt. Instead, we have relied on theories of alienation from the product of labor, or animal laborans, derived from Marx and Arendt, and we have understood paternalism as a control mechanism. Paternalism is much more than this. It is a practice of the economy that exceeds the secular, material definition of the act of labor and that supports the continuation of wage relations without partaking of their stripped-down, secular, materialist evaluation of the act of work. Its centrality to the formation of capitalism in empires and nations across the globe in the nineteenth and twentieth centuries (see Shever, chapter 4, this volume) demonstrates quite clearly how idiosyncratic and misleading Marxist definitions of the productive power of labor are.

These issues are also relevant to current approaches to neoliberalism that often analyze definitions of life, ethics, and productivity as if they were entirely encompassed by nature and by secular understandings of productivity and the market—even if they are now critical of these as a particular historical and social product (Dunn 2004; Ong and Collier 2005; Rose 1999). Works addressing religion and sentiment in relation to neoliberalism mark an important move away from this, but they still emphasize a uniform management vision that provides a spirit of capitalism, as in Weber, "to facilitate neoliberal transformation" (Richard and Rudnyckyi 2009).

Neither approach fully grapples with the fundamental contradiction of wage labor or the complexity of the act of labor, both of which contribute to the emergence of recalcitrant, diverse, nonsecular understandings of human productivity and expressions of social debt. Only by taking these seriously can we finally break out of our narrow analytical parochialism to comprehend the experiences of the world produced by the contradictory market transactions of wage labor. It is by focusing on the nostalgias for—and the practices and obdurate presence of—kinship and nonsecular idioms of the material world in contemporary workplaces that we can rupture these limited interpretations of the vital substance and spirit of neoliberalism. Since neoliberalism is defined by the increasing denial of social obligations between workers and capitalists, these attributions of productive powers are likely to become more diverse rather than more standardized. Certainly, it is only by deploying a broadened, open question about what productive powers are manifested in acts of capitalist labor that we can trace current social experiences of work.

Notes

1. See Yanagisako 2002:11 on the productive powers of the bourgeoisie, which I draw on by borrowing her phrase.

2. Markers are paid monthly about 10,000 rupees. Fitters get 200 rupees per day, welders 100–200 rupees, grinders 150–160 rupees, khalasies 160–180 rupees, and helpers 70–90 rupees.

3. Brennan (2000) also deconstructs Marx's model of labor as "like" a natural process. She suggests that we should not see labor as Marx did: as a subjective life-giving act that makes dead nature alive. She wants us to reject the split between humans and nature that Marx creates by his valorizing the human act of labor as giving life to nature. This chapter contributes a critique that would challenge Brennan to go further in her exploration of modernity. It shows that this split between humans as life-giving agents and nature as dead raw material is not omnipresent in capitalist modernity, although it is central to Marx. We therefore need to move beyond a theoretical critique of Marx and explore diverse understandings of productive powers that place humans in relation to the energetic forces of the world in very different ways. These have been historically significant to the politics of life and labor in previous forms of capitalism and remain so within neoliberalism.

8

Placing the Dead

Kinship, Slavery, and Free Labor in Pre– and Post–Civil War America

Gillian Feeley-Harnik

Lewis Henry Morgan's foundational study of kinship, *Systems of Consanguinity and Affinity of the Human Family*, was published by the Smithsonian Institution in Washington, DC, in 1871, shortly after Nathaniel Harris Morgan, his third cousin once removed, published *Morgan Genealogy: A History of James Morgan, of New London, Conn. and His Descendants* (1869) in Hartford, Connecticut. They carried out their research independently from the early 1840s into the mid-1860s, when their paths somehow crossed. Might their works be related?

Lewis's *Systems* was to reveal "'the hole of the pit whence [we have been] digged' by the good providence of God" (L. H. Morgan 1871:xxiii, quoting Isaiah 51:1). Nathaniel's *Genealogy* was "written for the generations to come" (N. H. Morgan 1869:title page, quoting Psalms 102:18). Nathaniel's work commemorated their first American forebear, James Morgan of New London (formerly Pequot), and his descendants, including Nathaniel's nineteen-year-old daughter, Harriet Emeline, who had died suddenly in 1863. Lewis dedicated his work on the "human family" to his two young daughters, Mary Elizabeth and Helen King, who had died within a month of each other in 1862, at six and a half and two years old, respectively. Joseph Henry, secretary of the Smithsonian, struck out the dedication as unscientific. Nathaniel established a family burial plot for his daughter in Hartford's first commercial cemetery (1845), to which he added stones commemorating their American paternal forebears. Lewis designed a family crypt for Rochester's Mount Hope, the most expensive tomb built since 1838, when Mount Hope was founded as the country's first municipal cemetery. Lewis saved the drafts of his dedication and his sketches for the crypt and his daughters' sarcophagi with his manuscripts of *Systems* and other papers, and he willed them with money for the education of women to the University of Rochester, where they can still be found.

In dedicating *Systems* to his daughters, Lewis described the work as his and "equally their contribution...to the Science of the Families of Mankind" (Morgan Papers, box 12:2, 7). Nathaniel's *Morgan Genealogy* was among the earliest family histories aspiring to be a "science" of genealogy as defined by the New England Historic Genealogical Society, incorporated in Boston in 1845 (Sheppard 1862:4). Yet, the Morgans' books were not simply genealogies, tracing ever-branching families from their roots out to their newest twigs and blasted buds with scrupulous accuracy. They were memorials, even tombs. The Morgans' contemporary William Whitmore, a leading member of the society, called such works "ancestral tablets" (1868b). Whitmore's "absorption in his chosen interests was of a character bordering on derangement," recalled a friend in an obituary (Gordon 1902). Yet, the interests he shared with the Morgans were widespread. Genealogical books, tablets, and burial plots coexisted with family Bibles made to hold family histories and images; embroidered, painted, engraved, and lithographed family records and registers, with the ancestral names of descendants listed therein; the ancestral names conferred on their descendants; memorial portraits and prints; letterpress broadsides; and bedcovers, towels, hair woven into jewelry, and many other remains of the dead among the living (Allen 1989; McDannell 1995:67–102; Simons and Benes 2002).

Had the Dyaks of Borneo sent emissaries to America—like the missionaries, government officials, and businessmen who wrote L. H. Morgan about the "Malays"—they would have spotted the Americans' propensity for secondary burials like their own, as Hertz (1907) later described them. Had the famed Merina statesman and scholar Raombana (1809–1855) lived long enough to meet Whitmore in Madagascar in 1862, they could have talked about their common interests in ancestors. Whitmore, on route to Calcutta, visited Madagascar when stopping in Mauritius to negotiate sugar prices for his father's Boston firm. In Port Louis, he completed the preface for his *Handbook of American Genealogy* (1862). Raombana had written an eight-thousand-page history of Madagascar in English. He could have asked how the names of the ancestors in Whitmore's book related to their tombs and which of those tombs they had chosen for their burial, and where and why, or was it their reburial? These were the questions that Maurice Bloch asked in *Placing the Dead* (1971), his study of burial practices in Imerina, an inspiration for many later anthropologists and historians of Madagascar, including myself.

Some of the small, but significant, signs of the international world of the eastern American states in the years after the Revolutionary War include Raombana's education in England in the mid-1820s; Nathaniel's early years as a sailor, then a captain, in the West Indies trade in the 1820s and 1830s; his son's travels as a sixteen-year-old sailor on a whaling ship in the Atlantic, Indian, and Pacific oceans in 1849–1851; Whitmore's cosmopolitan travels as a commission merchant in the 1850s and 1860s; and the worldwide contacts that Lewis made when he sent his questionnaires to his far-flung countrymen in the 1860s.

Great Britain's abolition of slavery in all its territories in 1833 led to the collapse of the West Indies trade even before the boom in city-to-city railroads such as the Boston-Albany Railway, which had to cut out Hartford in 1836. With the passage of the Thirteenth Amendment at the end of the Civil War in 1865, "free labor" became the law throughout the industrializing United States. The lifetimes of Nathaniel Harris Morgan (1805–1881), Lewis Henry Morgan (1818–1881), and William Whitmore (1836–1900) span the decades in which the political economy of the United States shifted from its coastal ports inland to the expanding western frontier through such channels as the Mohawk River valley, which made Rochester one of the fastest growing cities in the United States by the late 1820s. By 1900, "the political economy of continental industrialization [had] won out over the political economy of Atlantic trade" in the United States (Beckert 2004:1435; see Martin 1939:70–73).

The genealogies of Lewis and Nathaniel Morgan and William Whitmore were histories of generational relations, and they were ancestral tablets commemorating the dead interred in a succession of burial grounds as homestead plots and Protestant churchyards gave way to municipal and commercial cemeteries. They also documented the places where these forebears lived and died as their "British" antecedents became ever more "American" and more "modern." Lewis identified "modern civilization" with industrial technologies such as "the electric telegraph...the power loom...[and the] railway" and with "the modern sciences; religious freedom and the common schools," "representational and constitutional forms of government," "modern privileged classes," and the "monogamian family," which was to be "improved" further by "the equality of the sexes" (L. H. Morgan 1877:30,

468–492). By taking into account the web of political, economic, and religious connections through which these Anglo American Protestants were related, what more can we learn about their several modes of placing the dead in what they considered "modern" times and places? Following Lewis's lead, what are the "systems" involved in these modernizing practices, the "memorials of human thought and experience...deposited and preserved" (L. H. Morgan 1871:xxii), and what can they tell us about the presumed shift from kinship to contract so closely associated with modernity, then and now?

My argument is this: Lewis Henry Morgan's "invention of kinship" (Trautmann 1987) and the popular genealogical works of Nathaniel Morgan and William Whitmore to which it is related spanned one of the most critical periods of debate about the abolition of slavery, its replacement by "free labor," and extension of the right to vote. During this period, debates about "representational and constitutional forms of government"—for example, whether a loose federation of slave and nonslave states could, or should, become one republic, and who was to be a full citizen of that republic—became inseparable from debates about the organization and legitimacy of labor, the ideology and reality of "free contracts." In the words of historian Amy Dru Stanley, "in the age of slave emancipation contract became a dominant metaphor for social relations and the very symbol of freedom" (1998:x). If you were an Africanist or a scholar of Madagascar, you would say that these debates about citizenship and labor epitomized in free contracts were ultimately about redefining the status of a person as a certain kind of agent—that is, about kinning and dekinning. In Madagascar then—because these antecedents were not forgotten—free people had ancestors, whereas slaves were "people without ancestors" (*olo tsy raza*), tantamount to nonpersons (Feeley-Harnik 1991).[2] This continues today.

My hypothesis is that the interpersonal and professional practices of kinship that developed in the dawning modernity of the nascent United States were means of reckoning who counted as a "free" person and who did not. According to the first volume of John Codman Hurd's two-volume survey, *The Law of Freedom and Bondage in the United States* (1858)—published in the wake of *Dred Scott v. Sandford* (1857)—a free person was a "*natural person*" (that is, a human being, not a "legal person" such as a corporation or state) having "a *natural* capacity for choice and action." By contrast, "chattel bondage or chattel slavery" was a legal contradiction, "recognizing [in a person] a natural capacity for choice and action, and at the same time attributing [to that person] that incapacity for rights which belongs to the nature of a *thing*."[3] Hurd's purpose, as a counselor-at-law, was to explain how

American courts dealt with these contradictions in practice, for example, by "inquir[ing] into the absoluteness or extent of such legal recognition of mankind as persons [or as] *things*" (Hurd 1858:40–41; see also 106, 108).

Drawing mainly on archival data from Hartford, I argue first that "American genealogy" (Whitmore 1868a) as a growing means of placing the dead in time from the 1840s onward was tied to the efforts of living descendants to create moral exemplars of the self-made person distinguished by freedom of contract. These new forms of placing the dead and living in time were inextricable from new forms of placing them in space: separating the growing number of corporate workplaces of the living from their suburbanizing homes and shifting the places of their dead from inner-city churchyards to suburban garden cemeteries, resulting in patterns of urban segregation in life and death that hardened in the post–Civil War period. I suggest that a closer examination of the cemeteries might give us some preliminary answers to what kinds of "natural persons" with what kinds of "natural capacit[ies] for choice and action" the Morgans, Whitmore, and their contemporaries created in their genealogies. Finally, I return to the question that Cannell and McKinnon pose: how can the comparative study of kinship help us rethink the shift from kinship to contract that is identified with modernity in the American heartland?

COSMOPOLITAN WORLDS: HARTFORD

Hartford was founded in 1636 in the lowland between the Connecticut River on the east, the source of its maritime and upcountry shipping, and the Little River on the south, the source of waterpower for its mills and tanneries (figure 8.1). From roughly 1750 to the early 1830s, especially in the years following independence from Great Britain, its economy was dominated by the transoceanic and West Indies trades: produce, domestic animals, and flour were sent to sugar and tobacco plantations in exchange for goods ranging from sugar, rum, molasses, tobacco, and indigo to Málaga and Smyrna raisins, sperm and refined whale oils, and slaves (until 1774, when the state of Connecticut outlawed their importation).

Rowland Swift, president of Hartford's American National Bank at the time he contributed to Trumbull's *Memorial History of Hartford County* (1886), wrote: "Connecticut might be called the soul of the West India Trade, and imported at this time more spirit in proportion to its trade than any other State. One half of the horses, cattle, and mules exported the previous year from the United States were from Connecticut, and the principal article returned in payment for them was rum, and the molasses received is mostly distilled into new rum after it arrives. Into Connecticut therefore

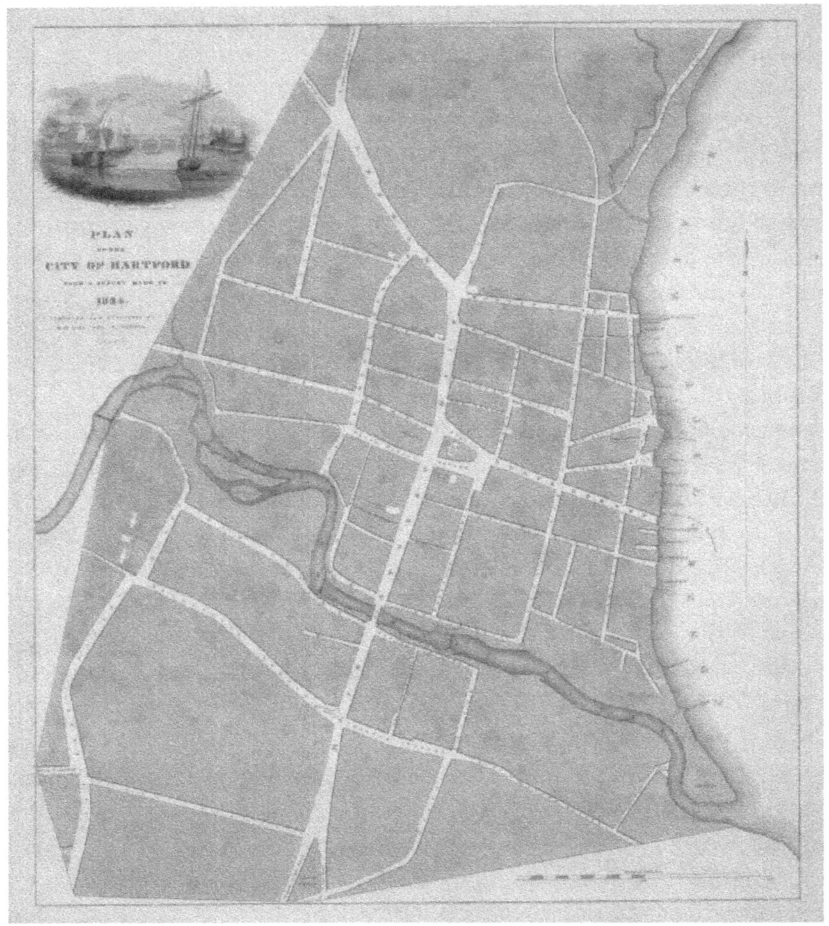

FIGURE 8.1
Plan of the City of Hartford, *1824. Surveyed and published by D. St. John and N. Goodwin, engraved by A. Willard, Hartford, 1824. Courtesy of the Connecticut Historical Society.*

are brought large amounts of West India goods which pay heavy duties, while at the same time the cash from the State goes to New York for supplies of dry goods" (Swift 1886:330).

The West Indies trading companies, or "houses," were family businesses. Several of the Morgans in Nathaniel's branch, including his father, Nathaniel, and other men of their generations, were farmers and merchants in the West Indies trade. Nathaniel's entry on Uncle John, his father's father's brother's son—he and Nathaniel's father were "old and early friends"—states proudly: "His air and bearing would appear peculiar in this day, but he had several compeers in Hartford then; princely merchants of the old English school; highly educated and of polished culture; bearing themselves with all the proud dignity of lords and nobles 'to the manor born.' Common men approached them with great deference and with heads uncovered; and we boys were hushed as they passed in the streets, with their gold-headed canes, short breeches, and silver shoe-buckles. Uncle John was one of the 'last of the Plantagenets'" (N. H. Morgan 1869:93).[4] According to Nathaniel, Uncle John in 1785 (at age thirty-two, four years after his marriage) imported from China on the *Empress of China*, "the first American vessel that ever entered the Chinese waters," a "rich and extensive" set of china dinnerware, made to his order with "his name and the family coat of arms, (a lion rampant, with a demi-griffin crest)" (92). His younger brother, Elias, later did the same.

In the next generation, in 1825, wholesalers in the West Indies trade had nineteen houses on Commerce Street parallel to the river and seventeen on Ferry Street from Commerce east to the dock where ferries crossed the river. Nathan and Denison Morgan (Nathaniel's older brothers, his father's first wife's sons), who had separate stores on Commerce Street, were "among the most prominent and successful of all the merchants engaged in the West India trade" and were "prominent members of Christ Church [Episcopal]," which would have been a sign of their rising social status. In 1824, they had built two "substantial brick houses" next to John's mansion on the south side of Morgan Street, just around the corner from Christ Church at Morgan and Main. They were so large that they had to be placed sideways on the lots to fit, gable ends facing the street (Talcott 1886:661, 663; figure 8.2).[5]

Nathaniel said that he began working on a "hard farm several years" in Lebanon, Connecticut (N. H. Morgan 1869:145). He was about thirteen years old in 1818 when he moved to Hartford to work for his brothers; twenty-one years old (ca. 1826) when "he was given the command of a merchantman and for a number of years followed the ocean" (Anonymous 1881b); and about twenty-nine years old in 1834 when his one surviving record book shows that he owned the schooner *Echo*, trading between Hartford and Boston.[6] He had married Harriet Emeline Saxton in 1830, and the first of their three children, Nathaniel Saxton, was born in 1833, so perhaps Nathaniel had begun restricting himself to the coastal trade at that point. However, Hartford's West Indies trade also dwindled after 1833 when Great Britain emancipated the slaves in all its colonies (with salient exceptions). Nathaniel had been the county jailer, living with Harriet Emeline and their

FIGURE 8.2
House of Elias Morgan on Prospect Street, Hartford, which he built and occupied ca. 1790–1812. Photograph by Fred D. Berry, ca. 1894. Courtesy of the Connecticut Historical Society.

two children (little Harriet Emeline was born in 1843) at the jail at 60 Pearl Street, for some ten years when he apprenticed Nathaniel Saxton, age sixteen, as a sailor on the whaling ship *Hannibal* in September 1849. He gave his son a box, to be opened at sea. Nathaniel Saxton wrote in his log on September 17: "[In the box was] a long letter of advice and council to me, and all our family daguerreotypes—The Daguerreotypes look natural & remind me of home."

Nathaniel Saxton's log covers the first six months of his voyage from New London to the Azores, the Cape Verde islands, south around the Cape of Good Hope, and into the Indian Ocean.[7] Pasted in front is a color-coded engraving of *The World* (figure 8.3) showing below the left hemisphere symbols for "the different forms of Government...Republics / Absolute Monarchies / Limited Monarchies / Confederacies / Dependencies / Independent Chiefs / Missionary Stations" and below the right hemisphere the colors for "the Religion of different Countries...Protestant–Yellow / Catholic–Red / Mahometan–Green / Greek Church–Brown / Pagan–Blue."

The *Hannibal* was heading toward Timor in January 1850 when Nathaniel Saxton started carving domestic scenes into a huge walrus tusk (figure 8.4). On one side he put, from top to bottom, a girl reading under a tree with a dog lying at her side (perhaps his sister, little Harriet Emeline, then six and a half years old?); a couple in a horse-drawn carriage passing a tree (his parents?); a house and tree behind a little fence (their home at

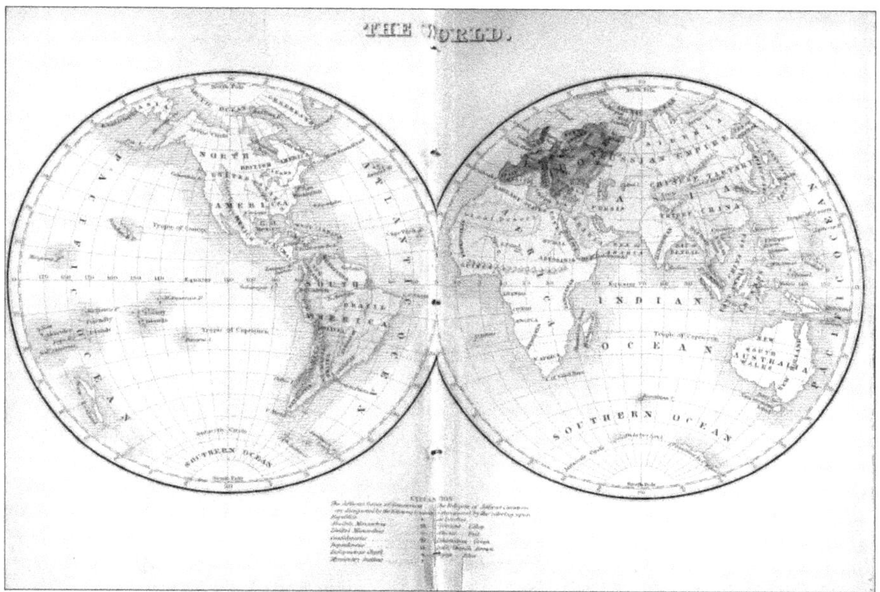

FIGURE 8.3

The World, *ca. 1849–1850. Hand-colored engraving pasted into the front of the journal kept by sixteen-year-old Nathaniel Saxton Morgan during his voyage around the world as a seaman on the New London whaling ship* Hannibal *in 1849–1851. Courtesy of the Mystic Seaport Museum.*

60 Pearl Street?); a three-masted schooner (the *Hannibal*, his current abode?); and a thatched shelter next to palms, as he would have seen in Dilly (now Dili, East Timor), where he went ashore in late January. Several months later, he made a large sketch on the other side of the tusk, a full-length portrait of an elegant woman. Most likely, she was from the Kamschatka Peninsula, where the *Hannibal* moored in late April 1850 for almost four months of whaling and where canoe loads of "Natives" came on board to trade.[8]

Nathaniel Saxton became a commander in the US Navy, active on the Union side in the Civil War, as his father must have been proud to record (N. H. Morgan 1869:206). The elder Nathaniel responded preemptively "to any curious kinsman who may [have] demand[ed] that the family Registrar should show also his own personal record," undoubtedly aware that compared with Uncle John (who got a BA at Yale College), his elder brothers, and other male kinsmen depicted in his "13 illustrative portraits," he had little education and relatively little wealth. Although "for a brief period, engaged in merchandizing," Nathaniel was quick to emphasize his being "generally

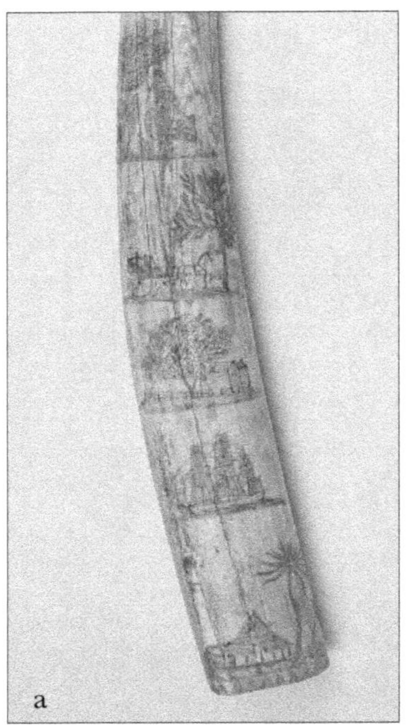

FIGURE 8.4
Scenes that Nathaniel Saxton Morgan carved on the (a) *front (five vignettes) and* (b) *back (full-length portrait of a woman) of a walrus tusk, 26 in. x 3 in. diameter at the base. Courtesy of the Mystic Seaport Museum.*

in the public service": "Alderman, City Sheriff, Prison Warden; first Pres.—Phoenix Insurance Co., &c.; and at present, State Commissioner on tax laws and taxation; President Board of Trustees of the 'Hartford Home,' &c. &c." Nathaniel wrote: "In broken health and great physical debility and suffering, which has reduced my ordinary weight of 165, to a skeleton of 110 pounds, [I am now] devoting my chief attention to the preparation of this family record, in honor of the Morgan sept and clan" (145).

Nathaniel documented the many Morgan "pioneers" who began moving from "the Groton hive [on the Thames River in the county of New London on Connecticut's south coast] to Western New York State" around 1800 either because farmland was becoming scarce or because they did not want their sons to die at sea (N. H. Morgan 1851:3; 1869:59). Christopher, his father's brother's son, was his most notable example. Having been a schoolteacher in Groton, Christopher became a wealthy merchant in Aurora on the banks of Lake Cayuga. At his death in 1834, he had amassed "one of the largest estates in western New York," and his business was in the hands of his eldest son, who later became a member of Congress (N. H. Morgan 1869:139; see Tarbox 1886:203–206).

Lewis Morgan was born on his family's farm in nearby Ledyard, settled by Connecticut migrants whom his father, Jedediah, joined when he moved from North Groton (later named Ledyard) in 1799. Lewis grew up in nearby Aurora after his father gave the farm to the eldest son, by his first wife (a Stanton, most likely from Lebanon), and moved to Aurora in 1823 with the youngest children of his second wife, Harriet Steele. Her paternal forebears had been among the "original proprietors" of Hartford (Trumbull 1886:261–262). Somehow, perhaps from descendants of the paternal cousin Christopher, Lewis learned about Nathaniel's genealogy and wrote him to insist on being included. Lewis succeeded. Nathaniel stated at the end of his entry on Lewis: "I have to confess that my own notes led me, at first, to challenge his claim to a niche in our fraternity, but he charged resolutely and gallantly through all my defenses, turned my own ample store of gathered facts and circumstances fairly against myself, and succeeded, not only with convincing, but demonstrative evidence in establishing his clear right by lineal descent, to his present place in our family camp" (N. H. Morgan 1869:179).

KINSHIP AND POLITICS: "A PROGRESSIVE CONFEDERACY"

Janet Carsten asks in her introduction to *Ghosts of Memory* (2007): "In what circumstances do people try to record and pass on knowledge about their ancestors to future generations? In what circumstances is such knowledge unimportant or not the subject of concern? When is it forgotten or suppressed? And how can we, as actors or as social analysts, tell the difference? How do these processes occur, and what are their political implications?" (23).

Nathaniel notes in passing that Christopher's younger brother, Colonel William, who settled in Ledyard, Connecticut, was for many years until his death in 1859 "the very discrete and efficient agent appointed by the State, to oversee and manage the estate of the Ledyard Pequots, a remnant of that ancient tribe of Indians, for whom the State had made a reservation of about 1,000 acres of land" (N. H. Morgan 1869:139).

Lewis Henry Morgan's interest in kinship was inspired by the research he did with Ely S. Parker in western New York state in the 1840s, published as *League of the Ho-dé-no-sau-nee, Iroquois* (1851). The league was a confederacy of nations whose remnants were also confined to small reservations, such as Tonawanda, where Parker was born and raised. Lewis assumed that a "tribe being in the nature of a family" was the simplest form of social organization until "rendered unnecessary by the adoption of a form of government" in which "the substitution of other ties [would] answer the same ends of protection and security" (78). However, despite the later entrenchment of that view in kinship-to-contract theories, including his own *Ancient Society* (1877), Lewis stated in 1851 that the "wisdom" of the league's founders was not to follow that historical path: "On the contrary, they rested the League itself upon the tribes, and through them, sought to interweave the race into one political family," led by male sachems crosscut by matrilineal relations, interwoven to create "one Family, dwelling together in one Long House [and bound] together in one common, indissoluble brotherhood," "one political family," "an extraordinary specimen of Indian legislation" (L. H. Morgan 1851:55, 60, 79, 82–83). And, arguably, he returned to that view at the end of *Ancient Society* (1877:551–554).

The striking similarities in the system of relationships of the patrilineal, Algonquian-speaking Ojibwe around Lake Superior—with whom Lewis worked while negotiating rights to their land for mine and railroad owners in the area—convinced him to expand the scope of his inquiry. The historical-philological derivation of the diversity of relationship terminologies from a single source would substantiate the monogenetic origin of all humankind.[9] Lewis did more fieldwork with Indians still farther west in 1859–1862 and, assisted by Joseph Henry at the Smithsonian Institution, sent questionnaires worldwide. Finally, he followed the advice of Henry's reader, the Reverend Joshua H. McIlvaine, who had been the Morgans' pastor at the Presbyterian church in Rochester, and revised his analysis of *Systems* from a historical-geographical to an evolutionary argument (Trautmann 1987).

Lewis Morgan's file on *Systems* at the University of Rochester includes both drafts of the book and five drafts of the dedication he intended for his daughters (figure 8.5). He had just begun his fourth summer of fieldwork in the far western territories when he heard about his daughter Mary's illness in May 1862. Returning home in July, a month early, he learned that both Mary and her younger sister, Helen, were dead. His designs are marked with detailed notes to the engraver because his dedication was to be framed by woodcuts of the family crypt in Connecticut brownstone at the top and his daughters' marble sarcophagi at the bottom. The book itself was to be "an offering upon their tomb" (Morgan Papers, box 12:2, 7).[10]

Whereas the aim of Lewis's memorial was to prove the unity of the "human family" through consanguinity and affinity, Nathaniel's was to document the unity of the Morgan family, "scattered widely over nearly or quite every state and territory of the United States" (N. H. Morgan 1869:17). Like

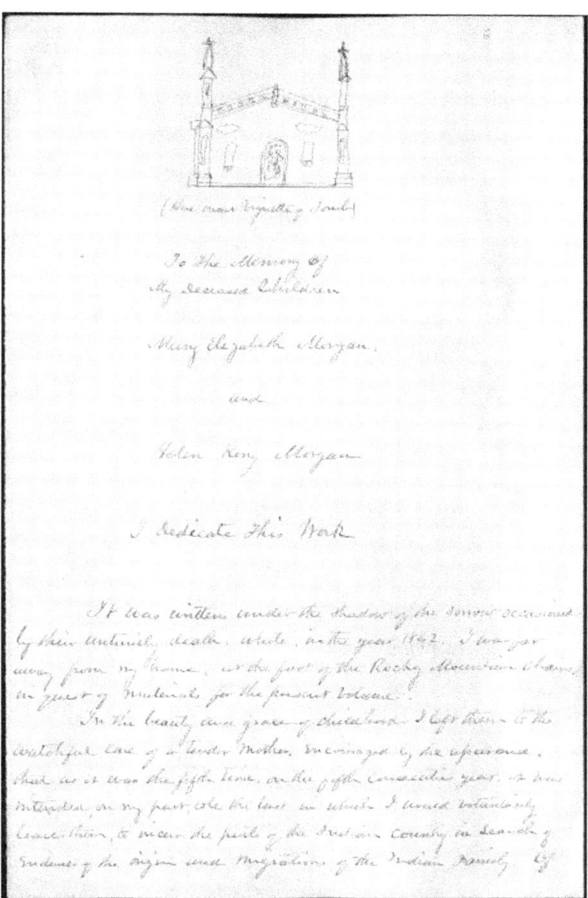

(Over main Vignette of Tomb)

To the Memory of
My deceased Children

Mary Elizabeth Morgan,

and

Helen King Morgan

I Dedicate this Work

It was written under the shadow of the sorrow occasioned by their untimely death, which, in the year 1862, I was far away from my home, at the foot of the Rocky Mountain chain, in quest of materials for the present volume.

In the beauty and grace of childhood I left them to the watchful care of a tender Mother, encouraged by the appearance that as it was the fifth time, and the fifth consecutive year, it was intended, on my part, to be the last in which I would voluntarily leave them, to incur the perils of the Indian Country in search of evidence of the origin and migrations of the Indian family. Of

FIGURE 8.5

The first page of Lewis Henry Morgan's dedication to his two dead daughters. Written for his first full draft of Systems, *sent to Joseph Henry at the Smithsonian in 1865, but never published, it was retained in his papers. Courtesy of the Department of Rare Books and Special Collections, University of Rochester Library.*

Lewis, Nathaniel had begun his genealogical inquiries back in the 1840s, perhaps after his father died in 1842. In 1851 he printed a booklet on the genealogy of James Morgan and his descendants, dedicated as a memorial to his father (N. H. Morgan 1851). In his later published work, he commemorated his young daughter's death and her parents' grief:

> HARRIET EMELINE, grad. of Hartford High School, class of 1862, died instantly and without any premonition, on the morning

> of April 28, 1863, at Hartford, aged nineteen years, six months and fifteen days. Four months prior she had a fearful fall, which for a few moments stunned her into unconsciousness, but from which she soon recovered, and no further effects of it were afterwards manifested, until the fatal morning when, in a second of time, she passed from life, to life eternal, in the presence of her astonished, bewildered and heart-riven parents, without a word or sign. One of the liveliest of earth's daughters, her whole life and character in the world below, seemed better adapted to the world above, and surely a father's heart and hand may be indulged in recording here this brief memorial, and saying of her early exit—*Suddenly, but safely.* (N. H. Morgan 1869:145)

For Harriet Emeline's burial, Nathaniel bought a family plot at the front of Spring Grove, founded in 1845 as Hartford's first commercial cemetery on upper Main Street just north of the municipal North Burying Ground (founded in 1807).[11] Nathaniel's older brother and his wife had already been buried there in 1860 and 1861, as had children of two other brothers in Hartford. To Harriet Emeline's memorial stone Nathaniel added stones for his father and the four forefathers, including James, who were all buried elsewhere. He marked the place with a house- or church-like monument in Connecticut brownstone, three of its walls engraved with their ancestral and present genealogical relationships and the fourth open to their future (figure 8.6).

In placing memorials of all five of his paternal forebears on his family plot, Nathaniel seems to have taken his personal efforts to be a general charge to restore the American Morgans as a whole. Acknowledging that "nothing seems, at first sight, less interesting, or less instructive, than a genealogical table—a mere register of names and dates" (N. H. Morgan 1869:10), he argued that his reader must understand that each story, even a name alone,

> when it occurs in the midst of these dry records, throws out an electric light at every link in the chain of the generations. Each of these names, in the table, is the memorial, perhaps the only memorial, of a human heart that once lived and died—a heart that kept its steady pulsations through some certain period of time, and then ceased to beat, and mouldered into dust. Each of these names is the memorial of an individual human life, that had its joys and sorrows, its cares and burdens, its affections and hopes, its conflicts and achievements, its opportunities,

FIGURE 8.6
Nathaniel Harris Morgan's family tomb, southeast corner of Spring Grove cemetery, North Main Street, Hartford, Connecticut. The south face commemorates Nathaniel Harris Morgan, his wife, their eldest daughter, their only son, and his wife; the west face commemorates the two of their three grandsons who died before their parents and grandparents; the north face commemorates N. H. Morgan's five American paternal forebears buried elsewhere; the east face is blank. Photograph by Gillian Feeley-Harnik, May 2010.

> wasted or improved, and its hour of death. Each of these dates of "birth," "marriage," "death!" Oh! how significant! What a day was each of these to some human family, or to some circle of loving human hearts. (N. H. Morgan 1869:11)[12]

He concluded his *Morgan Genealogy* with an appeal to his kin "to consecrate anew this ancient Necropolis of our family," the first James's burial ground in Groton, Connecticut, now lost among "tangled thorns" (16).

Lewis stated in *League of the Ho-dé-no-sau-nee, Iroquois* (L. H. Morgan 1851:78–79, 92–93) that familial relationships structured the earliest forms of human social organization ("tribes") until "the adoption of some form of government" substituted new ties of protection and security. Yet, the founders of the league had rested their confederacy on their "stupendous system of relationships" in order to create "one common family...a progressive confederacy...with vast capacities for enlargement, and remarkable durability of structure." Nathaniel's genealogical and burial practices display the same unexpected reversal by revealing, beneath crumbling town records and thorn-shrouded graves, the generative familial ties through which a "few feeble colonists, scattered along the wild shore of a strange wilderness, [had] sprung, as if by magic, into a Nation" (N. H. Morgan 1869:225). In short, families and nations are inextricably related.

THE CREATION OF "AMERICAN GENEALOGY" BEGINNING IN THE 1840S

Nathaniel announced to the readers of *Morgan Genealogy* (N. H. Morgan 1869:5–6), "The task of the genealogist, in groping his way amid the dusty records of the past, is much like that of the American Indian, in pursuing an obscure trail through a tangled wilderness." However, the "most formidable and vexatious embarrassments" that plagued his path came from his own kin. "Not one in five" responded to his many letters and "a thousand or more circulars." "The prevailing indifference to ancestry or kinship... seems to be a peculiar mark of our family...that frame of mind which is entirely careless as "*To whom related, or by whom begot*" (16).[13]

Nathaniel marked his genealogy as "American" by tracing the Morgans' common descent from James Morgan of New London, Connecticut, the first of their forebears to settle in the United States. In Whitmore's *Handbook of American Genealogy* (finished in Mauritius in 1862), he listed by year all the American genealogies published in the United States between the Revolutionary and Civil wars. They numbered about one a year from 1771 until the mid-1830s, increased to around three a year in the next decade, with a jump of nine to sixteen being published annually in 1847–1851 (which included the memorial genealogy that Nathaniel made for his father) and further growth into the early 1860s.

Whitmore published a revised and enlarged edition after the Civil War, *The American Genealogist* (1868a), showing a more substantial rise from about eleven to twenty-two genealogies a year in the mid-1850s through the 1860s, when the Morgans were researching and publishing their work. Whitmore published a third edition in 1875 and a fourth in 1897, shortly before his death. By 1897, the entries were so numerous that he cataloged them alphabetically by family rather than chronologically. An electronic search by date shows a jump from an average of about four per year in the 1840s to about fifteen per year in 1847–1852, about twenty-two per year in 1853–1863, around thirty-eight per year following the Civil War, around forty-two per year in 1877, about sixty-six per year in 1885, and around eighty-five per year in 1897.[14]

Like the Morgans, Whitmore's Americans tied their genealogies in time to their burials in certain places (the locations of some family reunions). Alongside *The American Genealogist* (1868a), Whitmore wrote *Ancestral Tablets: A Collection of Pedigrees, So Arranged That Eight Generations of the Ancestors of Any Person May Be Recorded in a Connected and Simple Form* (1868b). This, too, seems to have been a bestseller. Whitmore drew on the double meaning of a tablet: first, as a slab of stone, metal, or wood carved with words and images and set in place as a memorial and, second, as a notebook or table. Just as a tablet was like a second gravestone—allowing for the commemoration in a new place of an ancestor buried elsewhere—so Whitmore's tables for pedigrees were, effectively, portable tablets suited to even greater mobility and capable of encompassing the many generations since the earliest settlers in the new world and thus expanding the number of places across the country where dead forebears might be remembered.

For Whitmore, these new forms of placing the dead were "scientific" in scrupulously documenting the wealth self-made in America, not fantasies of English fortunes. More of their distinctive features emerge from an account of the New England Historic Genealogical Society written by its librarian, J. H. Sheppard (1862). The five merchants and book dealers in Boston who founded the society met in their homes in 1844 before moving in 1845 to the City Building in Court Square, where old records of the country's settlement—familial, governmental, legal, and religious—were to be gathered, stored, and published (Sheppard 1862:3–4, 511).[15] Sheppard compared the men's creation of the society to birthing a baby boy. The "little Genealogical stranger," an infant in swaddling clothes, struggled in its poor, rude "nursery" for many years before achieving its "strong, healthy and vigorous manhood" and deserving "the 'freedom suit' of a fire-proof building."[16]

The new genealogies commemorate the men "who first settled this country" and their descendants (Sheppard 1862:3, quoting a member of the society). Further, he claims, "This Genealogical Society is the first one, particularly devoted to the Pedigree of families in the world." It was followed only "some years later" by the creation of one in London. Whitmore indirectly explains the striking absence of "the ladies" in the society's works in his entry on a genealogy published by Sarah Robinson in 1837:

> It is so seldom that we have been called on to acknowledge the assistance of the ladies *in preserving family records by means of the press,* however many "old women's tales" may have crept into books, that we should be inclined to be very lenient. But in reality, Mrs. Robinson's history needs no apology, for it is evidently the result of much patient investigation. As it is of so early a date, we do not expect to see any attempt at a system of classification of families, but we do find a very strict attention to the precept of dating every fact. The female branches are traced in several cases; and we regret that so creditable an example has found so few imitators in Vermont. (Whitmore 1862:37; emphasis added)[17]

In short, the genealogies "preserv[ed]...by means of the press" that sprang up in the lifetimes of the Morgans and Whitmore were records of "families in the world," that is, not royalty or nobility, as in Europe, but ordinary merchants and tradespeople in America. They were not about the mysteries of inherited wealth but rather about earned wealth. They were to be not fantasies but plain accounts of how a person whose beginnings could be as humble as those of the "Genealogical stranger," on whom "no rich patron, nor beneficent donor smiled...as it stretched out its little arms" (Sheppard 1862:4), achieved wealth and esteem by his own talent and hard work, thereby contributing to the wealth and esteem of his country, in whose streets and cities his name might be commemorated (see, for example, Washburn and Buck 1911 for many such cases in Hartford). The labors of daughters, wives, mothers, and grandmothers crept in only between the lines. The genealogies were formally organized around men's generative familial-political-economic lines and were overwhelmingly by and about men (figure 8.7).[18]

Through the work of a founder and first vice president of the society, Lemuel Shattuck, the society's familial-political-economic principles of genealogy were incorporated into new schedules for Boston's census in 1845 so that the census would embrace, as he stated in the title of his report to Boston's city council, "collateral facts and statistical researches, illustrating the history and condition of the population, and their means of progress and prosperity" (Shattuck 1846). The US government took Shattuck's approach in the federal census for 1850 (Greenwood 2000:234, fig. 6). The 1850 census was still organized around the categories of "free" and "slave"

FIGURE 8.7

Engraving of Nathaniel Harris Morgan signed "Sincerely Your Friend," a typical salutation of the photographic cartes-de-visites *exchanged among men as tokens of their personal and professional relations. This engraving was used for N. H. Morgan's "13 Illustrative Portraits" in his* Morgan Genealogy *(1869), frontispiece. Courtesy of the Connecticut Historical Society.*

and, within these, "households" in which "males" and "females" resided. But the new forms now included data on every individual in a household (rather than gender- and age-based clusters of unnamed persons), as well as their births, marriages, deaths, causes of deaths, lengths of illnesses, and access to drinking and washing water.

In Shattuck's *Memorials* (1855), covering the descendants of his American progenitor, he drew on his expanded measures of morbidity and mortality to argue for distinguishing two kinds of genealogy. "Historical Genealogy" would "ascertain and record the most important facts in the history of generations, families and individual persons." "Philosophical Genealogy" would "abstract, analyze, and classify these facts so that they [would] illustrate the Natural History of the race to which they refer," taking genealogical and a broader range of "natural" factors into account (31–32). In short, familial history should constitute "natural" and national history. With that in mind, let us turn to the places in which the living settled themselves and their dead.

AMERICAN GENEALOGIES AND URBAN GENTRIFICATION: CEMETERIES AND PARKS

I have argued that the genealogical books of the Morgans, Whitmore, and their contemporaries were not only memorials of the dead; they were also—as Whitmore said—"ancestral tablets." They evoked the places where the dead were buried, and they were commonly decorated with epigraphs and poetic interludes akin to the epitaphs on gravestones where the genealogical identities of the dead were inscribed. The spatiotemporal dimensions of American genealogies are also evident in that they relate the histories of families to their settlements: each contributes to the growth of the other. Whitmore's collections include both. Nathaniel Morgan documents many particular instances. Lewis Morgan's developmental (if not chronological) account of the Ganowánian, or "Indian," systems of relationships had a spatial counterpart in his analysis in *Houses and House-Life of the American Aborigines* (1881), which he published separately when *Systems* and then *Ancient Society* each got too large to hold it. What more might we learn about the significance of genealogies in the pre– and post–Civil War United States if we shift from the places of the dead in books to their places in cemeteries and the changing places of the cemeteries in the settlements where the dead's survivors still lived?

City officials founded Mount Hope as a municipal cemetery along the Genesee River at the eastern edge of Rochester in 1838, following an outbreak of cholera in 1832. It was one of the earliest examples (after Mount Auburn in 1831 in Cambridge, Massachusetts) of a "rural" cemetery, so called because it was located at the city's edge. Mount Hope, like Mount Auburn, replicated the structure of the neighborhoods from which its dead residents came, refined in terms of local social classes because the intervening poor were set on the margins or dropped. Within two generations, rural cemeteries began to inspire the creation of urban parks, often designed by the same landscape architects. It would be premature to suggest that the relationship between the rural cemetery and the urban park formed the leading edge of the segregation of cities in the northeastern United States after the Civil

War, because these relations varied, as did their consequences, but the patterns in the cases of Rochester and Hartford are worth examining.

The rural cemeteries of Mount Auburn and Mount Hope were located in already well-off areas that became the core of wealthy suburbs, leaving poor inner-city neighborhoods behind.[19] Rochester's Highland Park—founded on land adjacent to Mount Hope that was donated in 1840 by the nurserymen Ellwanger and Barry, who supplied municipal officers and relatives of the dead with cultivated trees, shrubs, and plants—was designed by Frederick Law Olmsted in 1888. Olmsted, born and raised in Hartford, would have created Hartford's downtown City Park in the late 1850s had he not been working on Central Park in New York City. He sent instead a junior co-worker, Swiss-born Jacob Weidenmann, whose success prompted members of Hartford's board of directors for the park to ask him to design a "rural" cemetery—Cedar Hill (incorporated in 1864)—at the Hartford-Newington-Wethersfield town lines (Favretti 2007).[20]

Spring Grove, where Nathaniel put his family plot in 1863, was Cedar Hill's predecessor by roughly a generation, founded in 1845 just beyond Hartford's northern border. Hartford's first municipal burying ground—succeeding the ancient churchyard of the First Church of Christ (Congregational), built at the center of Hartford in 1630—was the Old South Burying Ground, established in 1801 on farmland south of the Little River. The second, the North Burying Ground, was established in 1807 on farmland along the Windsor Road (later North Main Street) bought from a merchant in the West Indies trade. It stood opposite the town's poorhouse, to which was joined a workhouse in 1812 where persons "reduced to want, or likely to be reduced to want, by Idleness, Mismanagement, or Bad Husbandry" were to be "bound in Service" (in the original language of the statute, which also stipulated, "The Conduct of the Negroes in this Town is to be inspected" for same) (quoted in Talcott 1886:362). A third municipal cemetery was established at Zion Hill in 1843 about a block north of the old site of Hartford's gallows.

The municipal burial grounds were nominally nonsectarian but seem in practice to have mingled only Protestants. A Catholic cemetery was established at the back (west) end of the North Burying Ground in 1839 (enlarged in 1848), and the Cathedral Cemetery was established at the back end of Spring Grove in 1852. Jewish burial societies established grounds at several locations in Hartford, including the Hebrew Cemetery (later Beth Israel Cemetery) adjoining Zion Hill in 1886 and, later, eight tiny adjacent plots fenced off along the southwest edge of Spring Grove in the 1920s.[21]

Stephen Page was the sexton at the North Burying Ground when he bought the farmland north of it to make Spring Grove.[22] Perhaps he thought to buy the land on the cheap. A memoir of the area, "*Up Neck*" *in 1825*—written in 1890 by Gurdon Wadsworth Russell, MD, who had grown up there in the days when Nathan and Denison Morgan had just built their brick houses on Morgan Street—identifies what was then Pine Street and formerly Cemetery Lane, along the south edge of the north cemetery, as "'Nigger Lane,' because there were a few houses upon it occupied by negroes." The slur in the name was commonplace, and he adds, "I don't remember that it was ever called 'Negro Lane,' or that it was ever said that 'negroes' lived there; the word was not current in that region...a 'nigger' was well known" (Russell 1890:12). This lane was a "pent road," a narrow strip of land left open by owners of adjacent lands to provide access to one or more of them (in this case, the property of one of Russell's forebears) and thus rare in a tight mosaic of private properties. North of the North Burying Ground (and opposite the poorhouse and workhouse) was "the house of Joseph Cook, a very respectable colored man, whose property was afterwards purchased by Stephen Page... and is now included in the cemetery [Spring Grove]" (82). Russell gives his reader the epitaph on Cook's gravestone in the north cemetery, perhaps as a history he could not otherwise supply: "Mr. Joseph Cook, A Man of Colour, was born in Virginia, free, came to Hartford about 1802, and died March 25, 1832. He had a sound mind, was industrious and honest, but more than all he was a Christian" (ibid.). Then Russell mocks Cook for his fruitless efforts to raise money for his church from his impoverished "friends."[23]

Hartford's City Park was planned and built in the years spanning the Civil War. The idea for the park was conceived by a prestigious Protestant clergyman, the Reverend Horace Bushnell, the pastor at North Church (Third Congregational) at the corner of Main, Village, and Morgan streets; Nathaniel and his family were among Bushnell's congregants. His proposal was accepted by a vote of 1005–682 in the election of January 5, 1854, though it took some time for the city to acquire the private properties involved. In an article on the park for Harriet Beecher Stowe's *Hearth and Home*, Bushnell (1869) named "Mr. N. H. Morgan, Esq., and another gentleman of the then dominant political party" as the city council members who helped, in the face of property owners who refused to sell, to "slide in[to an otherwise unrelated bill] a provision allowing the city to take ground for a public park by appraisal, in the same way as ground is taken for railroads" (101) thus giving the city of Hartford the power of eminent domain to clear the neighborhood.[24] Within a year, "all the properties were brought in by contract with the owners; as, of course, they never could have been but for the new statute right of the charter pressing them from behind.... The city now had a *full right in fee* in the new property" (102).

Baldwin's (1999:11–33) analysis of the reorganization of downtown Hartford in 1850–1930 emphasizes that Bushnell and his fellow reformers were motivated by communitarian ideals of creating a park for everyone in the city. Bushnell's vision was motivated by his theology of "the organic unity of the family" and the importance of children, outlined in his *Discourses on Christian Nurture* (1847, first delivered in 1846 at North Church, where Nathaniel Morgan and his wife could have heard the talks).[25] The park was to put this vision of familial unity into the heart of Hartford; it was to be the green carpet of the city's parlor. However, as Baldwin points out, Hartford's park was built upon the evacuation of some 220 people from their homes and livelihoods, and its ultimate result—evident already by the end of the century—was, in Baldwin's view, the intensification of segregation in Hartford.Bushnell described the situation from his perspective in *Hearth and Home*:

> On the north side [of the New Haven Railroad running south of the Little River], into the low bend of the river, as by common law right, all the garbage and truck of the city were dumped as in a Gehenna without fire—shavings, leather-cuttings, cabbage stumps, rags, hats without tops, old saddles, stove-pipes rusted out—everything, in short, that had no right to be anywhere else. There were besides on the premises two old tanneries—one falling to pieces, the other barely managing to stand upon a slant; and on a high clay-bank, just in front of the present Park-Row block was a little African Methodist chapel, looking out for prospect on the general litter of the region. And, finally, there was a back-side frontage of filthy tenements, including a soap-works, that ran completely round upon the east and north-east bank of the river, and projected their out-houses over it on brackets and piers—saying, as it were, to the coming ornament [the park]: "We give you such help as we can." (Bushnell 1869:101)

The tenements farther east along the river, at Main Street Bridge closest to Hartford's remaining mills and its commercial district, were left standing (figure 8.8). However, the land along the park's south side was zoned for large residential lots, almost all occupied by the mid-1880s, when a wealthy banker, Albert Harry Olmsted, built a mansion there. Albert was the brother, financial contributor, and advisor to Frederick Law Olmsted, who began designing three city parks for Rochester in 1888 (Brocklesby 1886:480 [engraving], 483; Olmsted and Ward 1912:60).

Who were the people displaced by the park, and where did they go?

FIGURE 8.8
Multi-family dwellings along the banks of the Park River, near the mills still operating on the north side's Mill Street and adjacent to downtown's Main Street Bridge, from which the photograph was taken, ca. 1890–1909. Bushnell Park, for which such buildings were cleared, is visible in the background. Courtesy of the Connecticut Historical Society.

Geer's Hartford City Directory (1842–1866), which succeeded *Gardner's Directory* in 1842, kept a separate section for "Colored" residents, including occupations and addresses, at the back of its listings from 1843 through 1865–1866. *Geer's* lists of churches in these years included the "African" or "Colored" churches at the end (out of alphabetical order).[26] These data show that (1) "Colored" persons were concentrated in eight to ten streets in Hartford's seaport, commercial, and mill districts before the demolition and reconstruction associated with the park; (2) already by 1852–1853, some people had settled just north of the official city limits, by far the majority on Cemetery Lane, the southern boundary of the North Burying Ground; (3) the granting of the permit to build the park coincided with the first of two new laws to increase the city's tax revenues by extending the city limits, thus encompassing the North Burying Ground and Spring Grove cemetery just beyond it; (4) this area was settled en masse by "Colored" residents from the center city to the blocks immediately around the two cemeteries; (5) the park project also involved the relocation in 1856–1857 of one of the two main African churches in the city since the 1820s (the African Methodist Church was relocated to the north side of the Little River to a lot on Pearl

Street near the county jail, where Nathaniel had been the jailer ten years earlier); and (6) both of the biggest African, or "Colored," churches in the mid-1900s in Hartford—the African Methodist Episcopal (Zion) Church and the (African or Colored) Talcott Street Church (Congregational) between Main Street and the river—moved to the Windsor Road area in the mid-1920s. The Metropolitan African Methodist Episcopal Zion Church in 2010 was adjacent to the entrance to Spring Grove cemetery on what is now Upper Main Street; the Talcott Street Congregational Church, now Faith Congregational Church, moved directly across from it. Eight other major churches serving African Americans and two churches serving Puerto Ricans are within the same two blocks around the North and Spring Grove cemeteries, with an American Legion center, a Save-A-Lot, and a Family Dollar Store among them.

Most of the mill owners—the latest in generations of owners dating back to the late 1600s—moved west along Hartford's Farmington Road to where the earlier sea merchants had also cleared land for farms. William Imlay, owner of one of the largest mills in the area, died where he lived on Pearl Street in 1858, but not before selling his Nook Farm in 1857 to Francis Gillette and Gillette's brother-in-law John Hooker, whose improved subdivision, also called Nook Farm, eventually counted Harriet Beecher Stowe (Hooker's wife's half sister) and Samuel Clemens (Mark Twain) among its lot owners. Gillette, an abolitionist, invited the Reverend J. W. C. Pennington, former pastor of Hartford's Talcott Street Church (African), to Gillette's Grove to give an address titled "The Reasonableness of the Abolition of Slavery at the South: A Legitimate Inference from the Success of British Emancipation" on August 1, 1856 (Pennington 1856). Pennington rented a place at 3 Baker Street (now Ward Street) in Frog Hollow in south Hartford, "still one of the poorest neighborhoods in the state" (*Geer's Hartford City Directory* 1856–1857:222; Partnership for Strong Communities 2012; figure 8.9).

In Hartford, the places of the dead commemorated in Nathaniel Morgan's and others' genealogies shifted geographically from churchyards in the city's center to cemeteries at its north and south borders beginning in the early 1800s as the center of its economy shifted from the coastal and oceanic trade associated with the Connecticut River on its east side to the banking and insurance companies located downtown and the manufacturing increasingly associated with the railroads on its west side. The North and Spring Grove cemeteries were built on farmland owned by West Indies traders as part of their mercantile operations, with the exception of the entrance drive to Spring Grove, which seems to have been set on Joseph Cook's lot. In the years immediately before, during, and after the Civil War, the old mills,

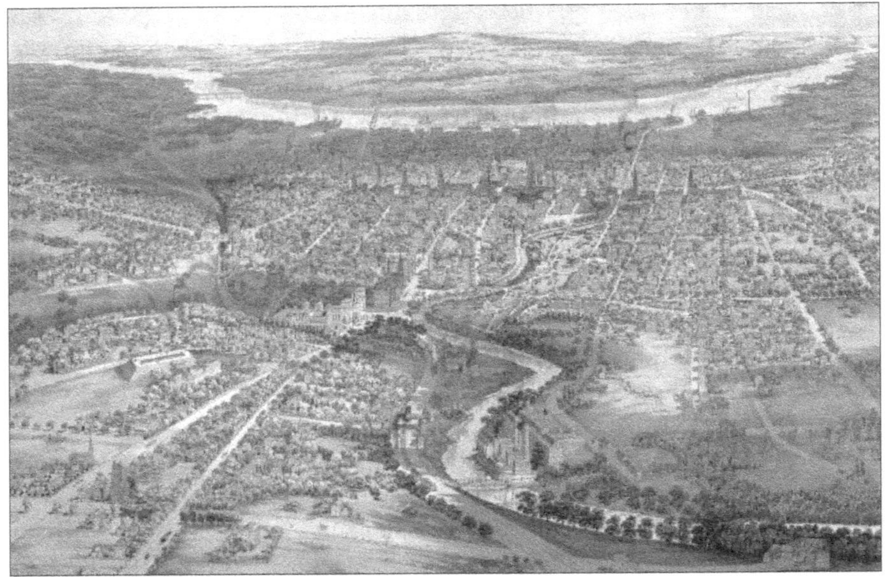

FIGURE 8.9
Bird's-eye view of Hartford, Connecticut, looking east toward the Connecticut River. Drawn and lithographed by John Bachmann, printed by F. Heppenheimer, and published by Jacob Weidenmann in 1864 as he was completing City Park, which is at the center of the picture. Courtesy of the Connecticut Historical Society.

tanneries, workers' housing, and workers, all associated with the West Indies trade, were also cleared out of the city's center. The workers to the north were moved around the cemeteries; the owners living in the city center were moved mainly to the farmlands in the west. The stuff covered over by the City Park was, as Bushnell said in *Hearth and Home* (1869), "all the garbage and truck of the city...everything, in short, that had no right to be anywhere else...the general litter of the region" (101).

A "NATURAL PERSON"

By "natural person," Hurd (1858) meant to distinguish a human person from the various kinds of *persona ficta*—artificial or juristic persons—introduced to define corporate forms such as railroad companies, banks, and insurance companies, which were increasingly common in industrializing capitalist systems in Europe and North America, compared with merchant capitalists' reliance on familial associations, partnerships, sole proprietorships, and the like (see Martin 1939:102–169).[27] Yet, Hurd's documentation of the contradictory laws of freedom and bondage in the United States shows that what constituted "natural persons" and their "nature" was as intensely debated in legal matters in the mid-nineteenth century as in science, medicine, and more broadly.

Whereas Lewis Morgan seemed to take seriously the idea that the semantic patterns of relationship terminologies he called "systems of consanguinity and affinity" were "handed down as transmitted systems, through the channels of the blood, from the earliest age of man's existence upon the earth" (L. H. Morgan 1871:xxii), Nathaniel derided "pride of blood" as "a baseless, shallow conceit" without a shadow of foundation for its support (N. H. Morgan 1869:12–13). "In twenty generations, or a period of about 600 years...the consanguinity, or relationship by blood, becomes less than one drop in a million; the distinctive name alone remaining.... Surely this fact ought effectually to silence every vain-glorious boast of nobler physical, mental or moral endowments,—or 'better blood,' derived from any mere agnatic or paternal line of ancestry, than mingles in common veins" (ibid.).[28] How might the new rural burial grounds associated with American genealogies of the self-made and the new urban forms with which they were associated illuminate these debates about the nature of persons? For example, where *does* blood come from? The data from the cemeteries suggest a combination of clean fertile ground plus improved methods of breeding.

The historian Gary Laderman argues that rural cemeteries gave the middle and upper classes private lots and monuments, "allowing them to mark the end of their journey in a manner representative of their economic status" (1996:44). Thus, they were similar to suburban subdivisions such as Hartford's Nook Farm; Gillette's Grove was a remnant of the forest there (Washburn and Buck 1911:35). Rochester's Mount Hope was created in the wake of a cholera epidemic to draw contagion out of the city to its periphery, yet this contagion could be purified by the restorative measures Lemuel Shattuck hoped to introduce to urban dwellers through his revised census registers, incorporating "Natural History": clean water, clean air, more paths than roads, flowering and fruiting deciduous and evergreen plants and trees, like new cultivated gardens but retaining some old trees and other features of bygone times, like the glacial kettles in Mount Hope, strikingly intertemporal places, both ancient and modern and neither (see Rutherford, chapter 11, this volume).

The trees almost certainly had a distinctive chronotopic significance in the American context, striking to British visitors in the years following the Revolutionary War, especially from the 1820s into the 1840s. They all commented on Americans' treatment of their land and trees, in which they saw more graphically than in any written document the radical transformation of time and person that the revolution had wrought in people who were still their kin (albeit migrants from their British homelands) but who now acted like strangers. Niagara Falls was a must-see, which meant that many of them traveled from Albany on the Hudson through the Mohawk Valley out to Rochester and then to Buffalo.

Like Lewis Morgan (1851) and his contemporaries, who still perceived the Iroquois trails and settlements immanent in the land, the British visitors saw the roads, farms, and towns of western New York as a chronometer of human history. For Basil Hall and Margaret Hall in the late 1820s, a single day's journey presented them with decades, if not generations, of "progress" requiring the utmost imagination to comprehend. Basil Hall wrote of their trip toward Syracuse on June 19, 1827: "During the drive we had opportunities of seeing the land in various stages of its progress, from the dense, black, tangled, native forest—up to the highest stages of cultivation, with wheat and barley waving over it: or from that melancholy and very hopeless-looking state of things, when the trees are laid prostrate upon the earth, one upon top of another, and a miserable log-hut is the only symptom of man's residence—to such gay and thriving places as Syracuse" (1829a, vol. 1:126–127, 131).

Although Hall remarks twice on "these poor remains of the former absolute masters of the territory—the native burghers of the forest!" (that is, the "Oneyda tribe of Indians"; 1829a, vol. 1:127) and those "extinct, or nearly extinct" (Seneca; ibid., 138), he does not dwell on them. Rather, both Basil and Margaret Hall comment repeatedly on the "murder," "attack," and "subversion" of trees and whole forests that the houses and towns entail, as if the number of settlers in "cleared space" were to be measured inversely to the number of trees killed to make way for them:

> The cleared spaces, however, as they are called, looked to our eyes not less desolate, being studded over with innumerable great black stumps; or, which was more deplorable still, with tall scorched, branchless stems of trees, which had undergone the barbarous operation known by the name of girdling. An American settler can hardly conceive the horror with which a foreigner beholds such numbers of magnificent trees standing round him with their throats cut, the very Banquos of the murdered forest! The process of girdling is this: a circular cut or ring, two or three inches deep, is made with an axe quite round the tree at about five feet from the ground. This, of course, puts an end to vegetable life; and the destruction of the tree being accelerated by the action of fire, these wretched trunks in a year

FIGURE 8.10
Skeleton of a Burnt Tree in the Middle of a Ploughed Field near Lockport, New York, 28th June 1827. *Courtesy of the Lilly Library, Indiana University, Bloomington. See also Hall's drawing* Newly Cleared Land in America *(also 1827, depicting a scene forty miles north of Rochester), which he captioned: "The newly-cleared lands in America have, almost invariably, a bleak, hopeless aspect.... The whole scene has no parallel in old countries" (Hall 1829b:pl. IX).*

> or two present the most miserable objects of decrepitude that can be conceived. (Hall 1829a:128–129; figure 8.10)

Hall finally concluded from the settlers' treatment of the land in western New York that they had no "local attachments" in British terms and that every son would be bound to move farther west to "attack...the wilderness" and "subvert other forests" as his father did before him (1829a:146–147). In contrast to Syracuse, he and Margaret Hall found Rochester still so filled with old stumps of oak, hemlock, pine, and other trees—on lots and roads alike—that they could scarcely move around them (160–162).

Beginning in the mid-1830s in the paintings of Thomas Cole, felled trees, cut stumps, axes, and woodcutters became distinctive allegorical elements in American art. By the mid-1850s, sculptures of cut stumps had become common as grave markers (Cikovsky 1979:611, 626). Some "family tree" images for genealogies were created by lithographers in the mid-1840s—for example, Edwin Hubbard's *Ancestral Tree* template of 1845, a hand-colored lithograph produced by Kellogg and Hammer in Hartford (Barnhill 2009; Brashears and Shortell 2009:138–139, no. 17). But the vast majority appeared after the end of the Civil War in 1865. Stumps and broken or sawed-off branches signified those who died without issue (Taylor 2002:75–76).

The Horticultural Society of Massachusetts was a major contributor to the creation of the Mount Auburn cemetery (French 1974; see Bender 1974). George Ellwanger and Patrick Barry, who supplied most of the new trees, shrubs, and plants for Mount Hope, also supplied the growing number of house yards and farms in and around Rochester with plants and, later, the plots of land on which new houses were built. Following the decline of the flour-milling industry in the 1850s (as wheat lands moved farther west), Rochester grew from the commercial reproduction of plant and animal species. Ellwanger and Barry's Mount Hope Botanical and Pomological Garden, founded in 1840, had become the largest nursery in the United States by the 1850s (McKelvey 1940; 1945:329). Ward's Natural Science Establishment, founded in Rochester around 1865, quickly became the nation's leading supplier of rocks, fossils, skeletons, anatomical models, and stuffed animals to schools, museums, and circuses (Ward 1948).

Hartford's city council hired Weidenmann to create the City Park, then Cedar Grove cemetery, in part because he was a botanist, as well as a horticulturalist and landscape architect. Although photographs from the time (for instance, Henney 1905:570) show the newly built park with just a few young trees, it was quickly repopulated. Within a generation, it had 150 cultivated species of trees, reckoned to be "perhaps the largest variety to be growing in open air within equal limits" (Ayres 1886:448), together with old elms from among the mills and two seedlings from Hartford's "charter oak," an ancient white oak identified with the city's founding. Its black-bordered obituary appeared on the front page of the *Hartford Courant* on the day it died (August 21, 1856; figure 8.11).

City Park soon became a repository of dead forebears on a citywide scale. Three days before Bushnell's death in 1876, it was renamed Bushnell Park to memorialize its genitor (Ayres 1886:449). By 1886, it held a massive Soldiers and Sailors Memorial Arch dedicated to the city's young men who died in the Civil War. The Corning Fountain—a New York banker's memorial to his father, who had been a wealthy Hartford merchant, commissioned in 1899 from sculptor John Massey Rhind—was one of the first in the country to bring "Indians" into the city parks. The stag (hart) at its peak is ringed by "Oneida maidens" and shy woodland animals and encircled at the base by "Saukiog braves" and lions as if in collective support (Anonymous 1900; SIRIS 2001–2004).

In northwestern Madagascar, old hardwood trees are periodically cut—when dead but not fallen to the ground—to remake the fence surrounding a particular royal tomb. Their hard, durable heartwood (*teza*), soft, sap-filled flesh, and bark covering evoke different elements of the human

FIGURE 8.11

The "charter oak" at Main Street and Charter Oak Avenue, Hartford, famed as the hiding place of the Royal Charter of Connecticut when it was threatened with revocation in October 1667. Photograph by Nelson Augustus Moore, taken on the morning of its fall, August 21, 1856. Courtesy of the Connecticut Historical Society.

beings who surround and protect the ancestral royals within (Feeley-Harnik 1991). Such ideas, combined with historian Philip Pauly's examination in *Biologists and the Promise of American Life* (2000), suggest the possibility of a deeper analysis that might cast light on the changing "nature" of the human persons—dust returning to dust—buried in the shelter of the tree persons in these would-be rural cemeteries. Pauly argues for the historical importance of agricultural technology in biologists' involvement in the development of America—especially practices of domesticating plants and animals (exemplified for him in the work of the self-trained horticulturalist Luther Burbank)—and in shaping the engineering ideal now dominant in the contemporary United States.[29] He describes his work as a cultural history of biology, but he goes further to argue that the very concept of culture in US history has been profoundly influenced by the work of biologists. He points out that the definition of "culture" in *The Century Dictionary and Cyclopedia* (1889–1900, vol. 2:1393)—"one of the major American intellectual products of the late nineteenth century"—begins with "tillage," then "the act of promoting growth in animals or plants.... specifically the process of raising plants with a view to the production of improved varieties," which is extended to "the systematic improvement and refinement of the mind," and only at the end does it include the equation of "culture with learning and civilization" that was associated with "British anthropologist E. B. Tylor and American biologist W. K. Brooks" (Pauly 2000:8).

Sixteen-year-old Nathaniel Saxton Morgan, writing on December 31, 1849, as the *Hannibal* sailed through the Indian Ocean, expressed the moral dimensions of improvement, and perhaps the new ideas of time that its cultivation involved: "The last day of the year—Breeze fresh fore part—light latter part.—Those of us who have neglected properly to improve the past year. Can never recover it. It has gone forever.—May we all remember our past negligence, and make amends in the future—and improve the coming year to our advantage and honor." In circulars of 1859 and 1865, John Humphrey Noyes, the founder and leader of the Oneida Perfectionists, explicitly drew on the example of breeding sheep to improve the quality of their wool to argue for the application of the same scientific principles of breeding to improve the spiritual stock of people, which he first called "scientific propagation," then "stirpiculture" (Robertson 1970:341–344, see 334–355, writing as a "stirpicult"). Many of the new spiritualist and socialist utopian communities in and beyond western New York state experimented in visionary reproductive biology to transform their families and communities (see Cannell, chapter 9, this volume, and 2007). The genealogical cultivation that the Morgans, Whitmore, and their fellow practitioners of American genealogy sought in ancestral lines and in the tree-filled grounds of rural cemeteries at the edge of newly reordered cities warrants closer attention in this light.

CONCLUSION

Theories of a shift from kinship to contract developed exactly during the years between the 1830s and 1880s in the United Kingdom and the United States, when scholars were debating the significance of the "division of labor" in specialized workplaces already defined by their separation from the home places, where laborers reproduced themselves on their own time and at their own cost. Susan McKinnon (chapter 2, this volume) shows that this shift is now so taken for granted as to provide the basis for theories of economic and social change in so-called developing countries. Yet, it must be seen as peculiar, from the comparative perspective of the mixed economy in which it originated, precisely because it omits the middle term that makes the freedom to contract meaningful, namely, slavery. The supposed separation of kinship and contract is clear and definitive only in relation to Great Britain's Act for the Abolition of Slavery throughout the British Colonies

(1833) and in the United States in 1865 in relation to the passage of the Thirteenth Amendment to the Constitution abolishing slavery and involuntary servitude throughout the United States (as Lincoln had done in the eleven Confederate states with the Emancipation Proclamation in 1863).

What is the significance of the elision of the "peculiar institution" in the swift movement from kinship to contract, in which kinship takes up the cultural and social work of clarifying the new, soon-to-be-"modern" form of work called "labor," rather than slavery, which had been its historical antithesis? Inspired by Malagasy ethnography and, more broadly, Africanist scholarship on slavery and power, I have made use of the maxim "Look to the ancestors." Kinship makes all the difference between being recognized as a human or not and, beyond that, as a particular kind of human, part of the "people," however these may be defined. People without kin—"without ancestors" (*tsy raza*), as people in northwestern Madagascar say—are slaves. The Malagasy perspective draws attention to the source of power inherent in being socially recognized as a person; slaves are those most vulnerable to the person-making and -breaking efforts of others. In this sense, kinship is not only a "moral philosophy," as McKinley (2001) has argued, but inextricably a political philosophy, in which cutting is just as significant as the binding by "trust" that McKinley emphasizes. Remembering is entwined with forgetting, expelling, and striking from the record.

The genealogies in the books by Lewis Morgan, Nathaniel Morgan, and William Whitmore in their new era of free labor exemplify genealogies made by men precisely about the development of personhood through work and, through work, the creation of wealth and esteem, earned, not inherited. If we take the genealogies together with the other forms of placing the dead in relation to the living that they and their contemporaries practiced—specifically, the new forms of rural burials—they mark the reorganization of northeastern American cities from mixed use to separate business and residential sectors in which workers are segregated by kind. And I have suggested more tentatively that they also seem to be about new conceptions of humanity—expressed in one way by Lewis Henry Morgan's "consanguinity," that all human beings all over the world share a common humanity, and in another, that they share it very differently, as articulated in notions of breeding and crossing strongly influenced by rural but more specifically by agrarian, and, increasingly, industrial agrarian, ideas and practices of how organisms work and can be made to work.

How did Americans' modernizing practices in the nineteenth century spread to the world at large? Or did they? Beckert argues that the abolition of slavery that (briefly) decimated cotton production in the United States led to the expansion of "strikingly similar systems of labor" worldwide in which the "new growers of cotton owned themselves, but their freedom continued to be severely limited by contractual relations between borrowers and lenders, tenants and landlords," typically by forms of debt bondage supported by "the enclosure of capital and capitalists in nation-states [with] a much greater claim on their citizens and subjects than ever before" (2004:1428, 1433).[30]

If we take this argument further, we see the outcome of kinning and dekinning (as moral-political-economic processes) in the nineteenth and twentieth centuries to be the formation of multiple coexisting and competing forms of kinship inextricable from new forms of contractual relations (which are both coproductive and destructive)—analogous to what the historian Willie Lee Rose (1982) called the "three domesticities" of slavery in the antebellum American South—but far more extensive. Provincializing the historical and geographical heartland of kinship-to-contract theory and practice in this larger context is one way to establish a broader theoretical foundation for the study of kinship and capitalism, recognizing that they are inseparable.

Acknowledgments

This chapter is based on archival research in the Lewis Henry Morgan Papers, Department of Special Collections and Rare Books, Rush Rhees Library, Rochester University; the Mystic Seaport Museum; the Connecticut Historical Society; and the Clements Library, University of Michigan; and on footwork in the Spring Grove cemetery of Hartford and Mount Hope cemetery of Rochester and surrounding neighborhoods. Heartfelt thanks to Nancy Finlay, Judith Ellen Johnson, Karl Sanford Kabelac, Richard C. Malley, Diana Ross McCain, Sierra Nixon, Paul O'Pecko, and John Potter for their archivist expertise; to Thomas R. Trautmann for his reading of an earlier draft of this chapter; to the School for Advanced Research for hosting "The Difference Kinship Makes"; to my fellow participants for their insights; and, above all, to Fenella Cannell and Susan McKinnon for bringing us together and "throw[ing] out an electric light at every link in the chain of the generations."

Notes

1. Whitmore's father, Charles Octavius, clerked for Boston commission merchants in the West Indies trade before specializing in groceries in 1830, first with Israel Lombard, then in 1855 with his elder son and then his younger son. In 1862, C. O. Whitmore and Sons moved into sugar, building the Union Sugar Refinery in Charlestown with an office at 1 Central Wharf in Boston. They were still in business when the second edition of Whitmore's "American genealogy" was published in 1868 (Anonymous 1907; Appleton 1901:96; *Boston Directory* 64[1868]:693).

2. Bloch's analysis of placing the dead focused on the Merina, who identified themselves as white (*fotsy*), that is, as freeborn, not as black (*mainty*), like the descendants of former slaves who lived in a nearby village and constituted half the population in the area (1971:3, 4, 35, 198–201 and pls. 1a, 1b).

3. Hurd understood the "positive law" (that is, man-made laws by comparison with "natural laws" based on inherent rights, a distinction derived from British law) he practiced as being "necessarily understood to be a rule of action for mankind" (1858:41). See Michael Lambek's discussion of law and agency (chapter 10, this volume).

4. Compare historian David Hancock's (1995:279–319) account of the British merchants of the Atlantic trade in 1735–1785 who sought to better their marginal standing outside the peerage and baronetage by their "urge to improve" themselves, from their land under cultivation to their art-filled houses and gardens.

5. According to Nathaniel, his five surviving brothers by his father's first wife (one died at sea) were merchants or farmers in the West Indies trade, and five of his surviving sisters were married to prosperous merchants in Hartford (N. H. Morgan 1869:81–84, 141–144). At least in John and Elias's generation, West Indies merchants also dealt in ships, bonds and notes, land, houses, stores, some small-scale manufacturing, and eventually banking, marine insurance, and transportation (Martin 1939:170–198).

6. N. H. Morgan record book (1834), Connecticut Historical Society, Account Books (manuscript stacks).

7. See Nathaniel Saxton Morgan's log, 1849–1851 (Mystic Seaport Museum, log no. 862, MC84.34). His shipmate Daniel Way took over on February 10, 1850, as they left New Guinea and sailed into the Pacific.

8. Daniel Way noted one visit on June 16: "3 large canoes came off loaded with Natives in their fur and skin dresses, for trade. They were the most healthy and robust looking race of people that I ever saw—Very stout built and of a light copper color" (ibid.).

9. In Lewis Morgan's paper "Agassiz: Theory of the Diverse Origin of the Human Race," presented at his men's club in 1859, he stated, "The new science of Ethnology [has] come into existence...with the avowed object of making herself the champion of the old theory of unity of origin" (1859:22); see the "Essay on Classification" in Agassiz's *Contributions*, vol. 1 (1857).

10. Morgan explained to Joseph Henry, secretary of the Smithsonian: "The dedication.... It is unusual in such publications as yours but certainly not improper. The circumstances are peculiar. I have ever felt that I lost my children, in some sense by following this investigation, and I cannot divest my mind of the sense of justice which prompts[?] the dedication" (Morgan Papers, box 4:1, letter from Morgan to Henry, February 21, 1867). Henry responded that Morgan could insert the dedication into "say fifty (50) copies, to be distributed among [his] friends and Correspondents...but it would not be consistent with the usages of Scientific Institutions to introduce anything of the kind

in a Memoir of its Transactions" (Morgan Papers, box 4:7, letter from Henry to Morgan, December [?], 1867). In any event, Henry printed his version, to which Morgan—under pressure from Henry's assistant Spencer Fullerton Baird—ultimately acceded, but documenting their dispute yet again (see his journal entry of July 20, 1871, in White 1937:369–70).

11. Stephen Page—the city's sexton of Old North and an undertaker—founded Spring Grove in 1845; his wife was the first burial, and his sons the heirs of the business (*Geer's Hartford City Directory* 1845:76, 128; 1897:714).

12. Nathaniel cites "a writer in the *N.Y. Evangelist*" as the source of these words, but they appear, usually unattributed, in several other contemporary genealogies. The original source is an anonymous article, "Genealogies and Their Moral," published a generation earlier in one of the first issues of the *New England Historical and Genealogical Register* (Anonymous 1847), which concludes by linking genealogies and burial grounds.

13. Nathaniel apparently assumed that his readers would know the sources of most of his quotes, in this case, Alexander Pope's *Elegy to the Memory of an Unfortunate Lady* (1717, l. 71). The lady's fate could be theirs if they persisted in their thoughtless ways: "How loved, how honored once, avails thee not, / To whom related, or by whom begot; / A heap of dust alone remains of thee; / 'Tis all thou art, and all the proud shall be!" His *Genealogy* includes, usually as chapter headings, many such quotes, which were also found on contemporaneous tombstones.

14. The fifth edition of 1900 was republished in 1971 and 1976 by the Genealogical Publishing Company in Baltimore. See also Daniel Steele Durrie's *Bibliographia Genealogica Americana* (1868); Durrie was related to L. H. Morgan through Morgan's mother.

15. See Shattuck's *Memorials* (1855) for a long list of his "extensive and authentic sources of information," including family lore and papers. Genealogical work is "a sacred duty...due to our ancestors, and to our posterity...a memorial of our own existence.... What legacy could we transmit to our children and our children's children which they would more highly prize?" However, he advised against the "immemorial custom" of entering family records in the blank pages between the Old and New Testaments of a family Bible. There are too many Bibles around for any one of them to be recognized as a "family Bible"; they do not include blank forms (though many publishers did introduce them); and "by their frequent use," they suffer "injury and loss." He recommended instead that everyone keep a separate "Family Register," based on forms he published in 1841 and again in 1856 (Shattuck 1855:2–3, 6–7, 305). In fact, the only vestige of Nathaniel's *Morgan Genealogy* in Lewis's papers are the disbound pages about himself and his siblings and the concluding page, which he or his wife tucked—with the newspaper clipping on his brother Alfred's death in California in 1860—into the back of their family Bible, which also held daguerreotypes of them and their children set into the inside front cover (see photo in Feeley-Harnik 1999). This Bible (American Bible Company, 1848) is

the first of 1,244 entries in the "Inventory of Books of L. H. Morgan & Wife, 1851," kept from the year of their marriage to Lewis's death in 1881 and, at $20 (in 1851), the most costly single volume among them (Trautmann and Kabelac 1994:62, 117). See Fenella Cannell (chapter 9, this volume) for Mormons' responses to the abstraction of genealogies from familial, female, and religious life.

16. A "freedom suit" could refer to the suit a master gave his apprentice at the end of his indenture or the "best Sunday suit of black broadcloth" a boy in "Old Boston" would be given when he came of age at twenty-one years and his earnings were his own (Wright 1878:202; Douglas 1898:234, whose female character jokes that "girls [get] a wedding gown"). "Freedom suit" was also used to refer to suffragettes' clothing in the years 1848–1875 (Kesselman 1991) and to the legal process by which a slave petitioned for his or her freedom in court.

17. In "Indian country," Lewis seems generally to have started his inquiries with men, but he wrote, "It was not always possible to complete a schedule without consulting the matrons of the tribe. They are skilled in relationships beyond the males, and can resolve, with facility, questions of remote consanguinity," an observation he included with other "singular illustrations of Indian character." (L. H. Morgan 1871:136).

18. See McKinnon's discussion of Morgan's *Ancient Society* (1877) in this volume (chapter 2).

19. Most of Mount Auburn is actually in Watertown, but its main entrance is in Cambridge.

20. Weidenmann's landscape design for City Park is printed in his first book, *Beautifying Country Homes* (1870). Weidenmann's *Modern Cemeteries* (1888) uses Cedar Hill cemetery in Hartford as its prototype.

21. See *Geer's Hartford City Directory* 1861–1862:411; McManus 1886:413; Cohen-Goldfarb Collection n.d.

22. See *Geer's Hartford City Directory* 1842:11. His wife was his first burial. On his death, Spring Grove went to his sons (Stephen B. and William H.), who transformed it into a stock company and sold it in 1867. Incorporated as Spring Grove Association, the owners had sold some twenty acres as building lots by 1872 (*Geer's Hartford City Directory* 1872), perhaps suggesting that commercial cemeteries could deal in real estate more broadly.

23. Russell found bills of sale for slaves in his great-grandfather's papers and heard "the women…boasting" of the numbers of slaves their ancestors owned (Russell 1890:12–13).

24. Denison Morgan was one of the city's three appraisers (Adams 1895:68).

25. Lewis and Mary Morgan's library included Bushnell's *God in Christ* (1849), which Mary got before their marriage, and many of his sermons in pamphlet form (Trautmann and Kabelac 1994:129, 2008).

26. See, for example, *Geer's Hartford City Directory* 1845:142.

27. In the early 1840s in US Supreme Court cases dealing with railroad companies,

corporations defined as *persona ficta* began to acquire rights of citizenship and residence (see Dewey 1926), whereas the US Supreme Court ruling in the case of *Dred Scott v. Sandford* in 1857 held that a "free negro of the African race, whose ancestors were brought to this country and sold as slaves, is not a 'citizen' within the meaning of the Constitution of the United States" (transcript, Library of Congress, http://www.ourdocuments.gov/doc.php?flash=old&doc=29&page=transcript, accessed January 22, 2011).

28. Based on very slim evidence (his enthusiastically remembered support of Henry Clay's presidential campaign in 1832; see Anonymous1881a), Nathaniel might have been "positively antislavery, but non-abolitionist," as Bushnell's daughter described her father in his collected correspondence (Bushnell and Cheney 1880:80). Lewis might have been both antislavery and pro-abolitionist on the grounds that owning slaves as property promoted the "propagat[ion]" of "this black race [having] no independent vitality among us [in the North]" (Morgan to William Seward, February 2, 1850, William Henry Seward Papers, Rare Books and Manuscripts, Rush Rhees Library, Rochester University). Yet, as Lewis explained to colleagues in his paper on Agassiz's work, he held a "long cherished belief in the unity and consequent brotherhood of the human race," which he hoped to substantiate through his ethnological research (L. H. Morgan 1859:9). Lewis's language in his letter to Seward, in his paper on Agassiz, in his rare references to "experiments" in "interbreeding" between "Indians" and "Whites" in his entry of June 4, 1859, in his Kansas-Nebraska journal (L. H. Morgan 1959:46–49), and in the brief footnote on his Indian research in *Systems* (L. H. Morgan 1871:206–207n2) is drawn from contemporary work in zoological and agricultural sciences. See Feeley-Harnik 1999 for controversies over blood in the Morgans' time and place, including sources of and forces on blood; Carsten's discussion (chapter 5, this volume) of contemporary debates about blood in Malay hospitals.

29. In a discussion of the "nature-making" involved in the "eugenic landscapes" of California's parks system, Stern (2005) singles out Burbank as a eugenicist. Pauly's work (2000) suggests that the ideas and practices of biological engineering were then and remain widely shared.

30. See the chapters by Bear, Shever, Yanagisako, and Bodenhorn in this volume for similar circumstances in shipbuilding, oil production, textile and clothing manufacture, and migrant labor, respectively. To my mind, Marx, in his historical analysis of capital, moved too quickly from his early focus in the 1840s on the estrangement of labor as a productive power, or life force, in human beings to his later *Capital*, volume 1 (1867)—post–Civil War from an Americanist perspective—in which he focused more narrowly on the estrangement of the product as commodity fetishism, in which work/labor figures in a far more attenuated form. We would still benefit from a systematically comparative, historical approach to the concurrent globalizing processes of production and consumption outside what he took to be their heartland.

9

The Re-enchantment of Kinship

Fenella Cannell

> American kinship is built on the same set of premises.... The relative in nature is at one extreme, the relative in law is at the other extreme. The first is but a relationship of nature, fundamental as that is. The second is but a set of artificial rules...for conduct, without substantive or natural base. But the blood relative, related in nature and by law, brings together the best of nature modified by human reason; he is thus the relative in the truest and most highly valued sense.
>
> —*David Schneider,* American Kinship: A Cultural Account

This chapter is concerned with ways in which US Mormonism might reconfigure our understanding of American kinship and its articulations with religion and what we call "modernity." Sociological and popular paradigms assume that modernity is characterized by the separating of aspects of life into the progressively objectified domains of politics, economics, religion, and kinship. In modernization stories, these disembedded domains are then ranked, with economics and politics viewed as becoming more crucial to the workings of the world than either religion or kinship.

Not all aspects of the complex relations between religion and kinship—or between either one of these and the state—can be addressed here. However, one framing context for this chapter is the secularization debates. Secularization theories are, of course, presented as an analysis of religion and its supposed withdrawal or diminishment in modernity. Its most positivist variants assert that religion declines both as institution and as experience, losing salience as increasing religious fragmentation relativizes the claims of any particular faith.[1] One response is to claim, with Charles Taylor (2007), that the phenomenological "normality" of the secular world is itself a historical artifact. Secularization theories do not usually explicitly address the question of kinship, although some critical interpretations acknowledge a connection with the changing boundaries between state and private life (Casanova 1994:64) or with the implicit ideas of human nature adduced in secular law (Asad 2003:57–58). This chapter shares with others in this volume—most explicitly, Lambek and Feeley-Harnik but, implicitly, also Carsten, Shever, and Rutherford—the aim of shedding light on the complex interplay between the ideas and practices of kinship and the rhetoric and institutions of secularization.

The case of historical and contemporary Mormonism bears in several ways on these debates. First, it speaks to a moment in American political thinking when kinship came to be cast as "private," definitions of what was permissible in public religion were becoming narrower, and the relationship between religion and public life was less transparent. Second, it highlights the fact that anthropological theories of kinship themselves have become unintentionally limited by unexamined assumptions about secularization. I focus, in particular, on the work of David Schneider and especially on his 1968 classic, *American Kinship: A Cultural Account* (2nd ed., 1980). I choose Schneider for several reasons. Although in many ways sui generis, Schneider's account has enormously influenced at least two generations of anthropologists and sociologists of kinship. Schneider demonstrated the fundamental limitations of assuming that kinship studies could simply trace the interactions between those who are related by blood; instead, he stressed the ways in which the American category of "blood relative" is itself a complex symbol, composed by a folding together of culturally specific claims about humanity's place in nature and the relationship between nature and law. The effects of Schneider's work—and his recognition of the culturally made status of categories of natural substance and natural linkage—were far-reaching in kinship and gender studies, feminist anthropology, queer theory, sociology of the family, studies of new reproductive technologies, and the anthropology of the laboratory. It especially inspired those writing about the United States but was also widely taken to be a model for a loosely defined category of "Western kinship."[2]

I choose Schneider also because I believe that the characteristic ahistoricism of his approach to kinship can be productively read against the empirical material on Mormonism I present. My argument is that Schneider's central constitutive categories—the famous "blood" and "law" by which, for him, American kinship is identified as a symbolic system—cannot be decontextualized in the way that he assumes. Janet Carsten (2001:31) has acutely commented that Schneider's category of blood is underspecified and that many different ideologies of blood may be present in America. I entirely concur with that insight, but I wish to frame it in a particular way. I suggest that Schneider's terms have no meaning separable from specific historical referents and that, in the case of the United States, neither "blood" nor "law" has a meaning separable from the particular *religious* formations through which US modernity was constituted (Feeley-Harnik 1999, 2001a, 2001b, and chapter 8, this volume). This observation runs counter to Schneider's placement of religion as a purely second-order phenomenon in his discussion of American kinship—a positioning that reflects his own secularist assumptions, which, due to the influence of his work, reinforced the secularist assumptions of others. In a later section of the chapter, I illustrate some of what is entailed through the example of contemporary American Mormon ideas about adoption, understood as one privileged locus for observing the intersections between "blood" and "law."

THE RELIGIOUS CONSTRUCTION OF AMERICAN MODERNITY

For the first empirical section of this chapter, I rely in particular on the work of the historian Sarah Barringer Gordon (2002). Gordon provides an outstanding discussion of the development of the US Constitution in relation to nineteenth-century Mormonism. The key to this story is the sequence of Mormon attempts to establish legal status for the religious commandment of celestial marriage (religiously motivated polygamy) between the 1840s and the 1880s. None of these attempts was successful. Eventually and painfully, the Latter-day Saints (LDS) would relinquish plural marriage in exchange for Utah's recognition as a state in the union, following a new revelation to the then prophet and president, Wilford Woodruff.[3]

The commandment that some Mormon men were to practice celestial marriage was a revelation given to the founding prophet and leader of Mormonism, Joseph Smith Jr., in 1831. However, it was so repugnant to Smith's followers—almost all of whom came from Methodist and other mainstream Christian backgrounds—that it initially was kept secret from all but a few. Even Smith's wife, Emma, was not told (Brodie 1996; Newell and Avery 1984). Yet, the importance of the commandment was insisted upon by Smith and by the second prophet, Brigham Young. Paradoxically, the great sacrifice and difficulty required in order to live in plurality made it increasingly recognized as a legitimate mark of the spiritual elite and, by the 1850s, as the sign and trial of those destined for Mormon leadership. As has been clearly shown by historians (Daynes 2001), by no means all Mormons entered celestial marriage even at the height of the institution, but it occupied tremendous symbolic importance even for those who did not. Celestial marriage was also connected to the theocratic and millenarian tendencies of early Mormonism because it was understood to be required of the Mormon faithful in preparation for the imminent return of Christ (Underwood 1993).

As Gordon adeptly shows, the specter of polygamy aroused a steady resistance in the American mainstream, but the grounds for opposition constantly shifted. In the earlier part of the century, polygamy stood as a proxy for the even more fraught issue of slavery; eventually, the federal government would refuse to allow the states latitude on either aspect of "domestic relations" (Gordon 2002:57). In the 1870s, one key rallying point against polygamy was the concern over rising national divorce rates. This focused on Mormons in Utah, where converts whose spouses did not also join the Saints were permitted ready divorce and remarriage within the faith (175). Toward the end of the nineteenth century, polygamy in Utah came to be associated in the mind of the American public with fears about the control of both property and votes by private cartels (217ff.).

Since the US Constitution supposedly guaranteed freedom of religious conscience, it was by no means a foregone conclusion that any marital arrangement justified by religion would be outlawed. However, the persecution of the Saints and their expulsion in 1839 from Missouri, whence they fled to Nauvoo, Illinois, had begun to undermine the Saints' confidence in the powers of the Constitution to protect them. Federal law and the laws of individual states were in fundamental tension, and the theoretical federal protection of religious conscience proved unenforceable, given that mainstream public opinion in most states was against bigamy. Smaller and less well-organized religious groups making experiments in marital arrangements had existed for some time in the United States (Cross 1950), but the sheer numbers of Mormon converts and their success in making permanent settlements attracted greater attention, jealousy, and suspicion.

The prophet and founder of Mormonism, Joseph Smith Jr., attempted to run for the office of US president as an alternative means to secure the Latter-day Saints' ways of life, including polygamous marriage, but this attempt ended in and partially provoked his assassination at the Carthage jail in Missouri in 1844 (Gordon 2002:188; see also Bushman 2006). Smith's successor, Brigham Young, then pursued legal security for the Saints through a succession of different means. When opinion once again turned against the Saints in Illinois and they were forced to abandon their town and temple at Nauvoo, Brigham Young took his followers to Utah with the intention of having the new Mormon settlements in the territory recognized as a state and thereby sheltering polygamy under a new state law that would enshrine Mormon principles as the wish of the majority.

The church's leaders began openly to acknowledge plural marriage from 1852, and this—combined with the growing population of Utah—provoked continued opposition. By 1856, the Republicans were building their campaign against the "twin relics of barbarism" said to exist in the United States: polygamy and slavery. In 1862, the Morrill Act passed by Congress declared bigamy illegal in all the states of the union, thus creating a double bind for the Utah Mormons, whose attempt to found a legal polygamous state was now blocked.

Brigham Young then shifted his campaign to the judiciary, hoping to create a ruling in favor of the Saints through the Supreme Court by arguing that the Morrill Act overreached the Constitution and exceeded the proper limits of federal interference in local democracy. However, the church's test case ended in failure, and the ruling in *Reynolds v. United States* (1879) insisted that although the Constitution protected the rights of all citizens to freedom of belief, it did not guarantee its citizens the freedom to act on those beliefs against national or state law.[4] This ruling was followed by a campaign of federal prosecutions of polygamous Mormons in Utah. Women, formerly seen as victims of polygamy, were arrested alongside men (Gordon 2002:182).

As Gordon shows, central to the *Reynolds* judgment was the crystallization of a particular American majority view on the relation of law to religion and on the definition of religion that was to be entertained as valid. Although *Reynolds* in many ways represented an unprecedented extension of federal powers at the expense of the states, it simultaneously drew on a body of legal opinion developed earlier in state courts. In particular, it had recourse to a notion of "general Christianity" that had already gained wide acceptance in state common law. The key precedent here was the decision by Justice James Kent in 1811, in an appeal by John Ruggles against the state of New York. Ruggles had been found guilty of blasphemy,[5] and his lawyer appealed based on the idea that offenses against Christianity could not be prosecuted by the state under a disestablished constitution. Justice Kent ruled against this, however, finding, "We are a Christian people and the morality of the country is deeply engrafted upon Christianity" (Gordon 2002:72), although *not* upon any other religion. Therefore, although religious opinion was entirely free, public utterances that offended the sensibilities of the Christian majority were liable to disturb the order of the community and were therefore punishable under the law. This view was eventually invoked in *Reynolds*; it was found that polygamy "obviously" offended against general American Christian principles and thus tended toward the "subversion of good order" (133).

As Gordon points out, the definition of "religion embraced in such... court opinions was a democratically constructed yet indelibly Protestant public morality" (2002:135). The assumptions of the majority outweighed alternative views of what Christian public morals might be; thus, Mormon claims to be following a revealed and restored Christianity were ignored.[6] It is especially interesting to note the relation of this mainstream definition of "essential Christianity" to the relative spheres of influence of the churches and courts as they were being redrawn. Many Protestant churchmen of the time were wary of the fact that marriage was increasingly being defined as a civil contract rather than as a sacrament. The developments of the 1880s could be described as one form of "secularization" as the churches lost jurisdiction relative to the state. Yet, if America was becoming institutionally more secular, this was clearly a "Protestant secularism." The national government was not tied to any church, but, implicitly, Protestant values shaped its claims and interests.[7]

Mainstream nineteenth-century American opinion had come to see a clear and apparent link between monogamous marriage and democratic government. For many commentators, types of marriage that did not conform to the Protestant norm must lead ineluctably to the abusive subjugation of dependents by patriarchs and to impediments to independent judgment and free competition in matters of business, choice of religion, and the exercise of the electoral franchise.[8] Thus, the state came to articulate its claim to have "valid political interests in the monogamous structure of the household" (Gordon 2002:227), on which it expected to command public support. This claim was also expressed from early on through statements that claimed monogamy as an essentially *American* institution while casting Mormon polygamy as ineradicably "foreign" and also as deeply "barbarous" by contrast with American "civilization."

As Gillian Feeley-Harnik has shown (1999, 2001a, 2001b, and chapter 8, this volume), religious worldviews were foundational in the construction of ostensibly nonreligious aspects of scientific and political culture in nineteenth-century America. Recognition of the powerful Protestant bias in supposedly secular US government thinking and policy in the nineteenth century and later is by no means new; indeed, it has been raised in a number of contexts by various authors.[9] Protestant bias in the construction of ideas of interiority—which transform and objectify both kinship and religion—has been extensively discussed by Webb Keane (2007) for a European (Dutch) colonial context, as well as for sociological theory more generally. In the context of the battle over Mormon polygamy, I suggest that the issue of interiority was again to the fore, although this remains implicit in Gordon's text. What the Protestant majority appeared to fear from Mormon polygamy was, above all, that the "wrong" sort of kinship arrangements would engender the "wrong" sort of person—a person insufficiently autonomous, self-governing, individuated, transparent, and "sincere" (Keane 2007; Trilling 1972). It was not only that the products of Mormon kinship might have allegiances running counter to those of the nation-state but also, and more fundamentally, that the person so produced would be an "uncanny" counterpart to the kind of person Protestantism envisaged as rightly populating and safeguarding the modern world.

The first argument I want to draw out from this discussion of Gordon's work concerns the evidence that "law"—in the sense of both formal law and moral norms—is made in nineteenth-century US history through the progression of, and conflict between, different religious ways of thinking and is inseparable from these. For me, this renders problematic the whole approach that Schneider takes to the definition of American kinship. As those who have been versed in the anthropology of kinship will know, Schneider's famous account, though brief, is difficult to grasp in its entirety. This difficulty arises because Schneider describes American kinship as a paradoxical system, a system that has its cake and also eats it, that proceeds in terms of "contradictions and their resolutions" (1980:110n2). At times, Schneider's own analysis seems to mirror these contradictions descriptively rather than resolve them. Thus, "blood," for Schneider, is a symbol of natural substance and is opposed to "law"; however, Schneider claims that, in most spheres of life, American culture enjoins humanity to "dominate nature" (107) but simultaneously represents people as part of nature, obeying the natural destiny of animals to care for their offspring yet distinguished from animals by the exercise of "natural" human reason (that is, law). Kinship, Schneider (28) suggests, is a symbolic space of repose between these contradictions in which nature/biology/substance and law/choice/code for conduct can become one and the same. The symbol of the "blood relative" is so powerful because it achieves an apparently seamless conjunction of the criteria of "nature" and the criteria of "law." But, as others have implied, Schneider's treatment of marriage is less clear; its symbolically "natural" element is an act (sex) and not a substance, as Michael Lambek (chapter 10, this volume) points out, and the referents and equivalences of the sets of terms Schneider groups together are not self-evident. "Code for conduct" is an extremely wide category, which seems rather like a catchall in Schneider's analysis, and "law" could mean either familial ethical norms or formal state law. At other points, Schneider speaks instead of "destiny" and "morality" (1980:110), although these terms are not fully integrated into his schema.

For Schneider, this lack of concretion and specificity is not important since he aims to describe the general shape of a symbolic system that, he wants to argue, can occur in many registers. However, as others have noted, the approach he takes is deeply ahistorical in that it treats such terms as "blood," "law," "nature," and "culture" as if the social conditions in which they are formed are not important facts about them. This ahistoricism coincides with and permits Schneider's disregard for the role of religion in the formation of American kinship. Although religious communities or ethnic groups may have their own, local variations on a code for conduct, for Schneider these are purely secondary to the underlying consistencies in the arrangement of symbols that he discerns. Indeed, one might argue that Schneider's whole method precluded any other conclusion, since he was looking for what was *shared* between these different groups and this was what he termed "American kinship" (1980:13–15). Schneider does not appear to set much store by informants' claims that religious variation was important in their kinship arrangements, even where he does discuss these (70–71), but he is attentive to the points where claims of religious or ethnic specificity turn out to be replicated across many groups (15). One might say that Schneider worked from an already secularized assumption that "religion" is simply a subcategory of citizenship.[10] The historical evidence reviewed so far argues powerfully that Schneider was mistaken in treating a symbol such as "law" as an ahistorical category or as one that functions independently of the specifics of different American religious beliefs. In ignoring the historical making of these categories, Schneider also ignores the real tensions and conflicts involved in this making.

Powerfully persuasive musings on the oxymoronic place of "nature" in America, for instance, appear in Schneider's text:

> In American culture man's fate...follows the injunction, Master Nature! But...where kinship and family are concerned, American culture appears to turn things topsy-turvy. For this is one part of nature with which man has made his peace.... Kinship is the blood relationship.... Kinship is...maternal instinct.... These are the ways of nature.
>
> [But] Reason selects the good and rejects the bad in nature.
>
> The order of law is the outcome of the action of human reason on nature. (Schneider 1980:107–109)

Yet, the idea that "natural" kinship should be lived through the exercise of reason is *not*, as he implies, uniformly held throughout American culture.

Rather, this is the idea of the Protestant majority and is inseparable from the development of both Protestant thought and majoritarian interpretations of US constitutional rights in the period 1830–1890. Such ideas about nature-combined-with-reason are certainly descriptive of the "civilized" kinship of Protestant monogamy, but they are certainly not descriptive of the "revealed" kinship of the American Mormons, who were considered by antipolygamy campaigners as "barbarous." Thus, Schneider presents as "American culture" in toto what is actually the ideology of the winners in a historical conflict of ideals, and he excludes from anthropological consideration the many Americans—including but not limited to American Mormons—over whom this victorious logic prevailed. At the same time, Schneider rules out serious consideration of the divergent religious logics that were actually the central dynamic in the making of American culture and American kinship. Although Gordon's evidence speaks first to the category of law, my objection obviously applies equally to the historical formation of blood, which develops in relationship to the legal parameters of kinship and affinity to which she attends.

I return later to the possible implications of Gordon's story for the theme of disembedding and modernity. First, however, I consider the issue of American kinship through the material that particularly problematized it for me—that is, through discussions I have had with American Latter-day Saints in research conducted since 2001. I show that the blood and law of contemporary Mormon kinship are not only different from those of the Protestant mainstream, and religiously constructed, but are also in a different relationship to each other than the "blood" and "law" (or nature-culture, etc.) of Schneider's work, since Mormon ontology does not oppose the material and the immaterial to each other in any simple fashion.

MORMON ADOPTION AS RECOGNITION: THE IDENTIFICATION OF BLOOD AND THE LAW

Let me begin with part of a letter posted on a current website, Adoption Network Law Center. It is headed "Letters from Birthmothers: Cristal" and reads, in part:

> My Dearest Matthew,
> I have a strong belief that we get to choose our family before we are born. That we live with God before we become a flesh and blood person and He offers us a number of people to be our families on earth. As a result of this belief, I wrote you a short story. (www.adoptionnetwork.com, accessed June 2007)

The short story written by Cristal concerns a little boy who is with God before he is born. The child is eager to jump into the Pool of Life, but God calls him to come and choose his family from the Great Tree first. The little boy searches along its many branches in vain; then, he is drawn to the leaves at the very top of the tree and asks God to let him look there.

> Heavenly Father smiled a warm and comforting smile. "Those are the adopting families," He thought. He did not say a word but simply moved to the highest and most center part of the tree.... Matthew looked and looked.... He...saw one of the leaves sparkle. He reached out and touched the branch, and he knew that was his home. Excited, he turned his little head to God and exclaimed, "This is it! This is my family! They are the ones I want to be with! They are waiting for me!"

God tells Matthew that this is a "very special" family and that he "will not be able to get there the traditional way" and will have to choose another mother, a birth mother. "She will be guided to your parents and you will end up in their arms as you have chosen to be."

> After another long while, Matthew found someone, he believed, would be a great birthmother. Beaming he touched another branch and said, "This one! She will love me and she will want me to be happy with my family, I choose her." Again God smiled. Thank you for choosing me. Much love always and forever ~ Your Birthmother,
>
> Cristal

In citing this letter, I do not want to imply that it is simple or transparent. The story appears as part of a website for a private adoption agency specializing in LDS adoptions. It is therefore embedded in the institutional processes and political economy of American adoption, which are complex, the more so because the LDS Church also has its own adoption service and strong views on adoption protocols. Birth mothers' attitudes are also not uniform. The prototypical situation is that of a very young woman who cannot marry the baby's father, but there are also many variations in age and financial circumstance. Even among the "typical" teenage mothers, some choose to keep their babies and bring them up with the help of their natal families, despite the church's strong advice that every child should be brought up by a married man and woman. Nor do I wish to suggest that when babies are given up for adoption by Mormon birth mothers, this decision is somehow made bland or easy by religious teachings. The circumstances, attitudes, and experiences of birth mothers vary considerably, but the intense social and religious value ascribed to motherhood within Mormonism means that giving up a baby for adoption is understood as a very difficult sacrifice.

Nevertheless, Mormon thinking about adoption contains the potential of a distinctive interpretation that is not available to other Americans in quite the same way. Mormon doctrine posits that just as we proceed to another life after death, so at birth we do not come out of nothing, but from a heaven in which we are already individuated and where we are known to one another.[11] Although at birth we largely forget this prior existence, from time to time we may have glimpses of it in this life, including through kinship. Babies and very young children are sometimes said to show in various ways that they have not yet quite forgotten where they have come from. For adults, intimations often take the form of a momentary feeling of closeness to another person—perhaps a future close friend or spouse—that is experienced as a strong sense of recognition, of having known that person somewhere else before. For this reason, although the language of kinship "choice" is not devoid of the implications it might have in non-Mormon circles—including both the responsibility attached to personal agency and the risks and freedoms of consumerism—it is not delimited by them either. "Choosing" kin in this world implies recognizing the prior truth of a premortal belonging. Yet, as Cristal's story shows, choosing kin in the premortal existence is imagined not as arbitrary selection but as an agentive recognition of connections that *already existed*.[12]

It might seem tempting to describe premortal kinship as metaphysical, were it not that, in LDS doctrine, spirit and matter are not opposed to each other. The spirit beings who populate the premortal existence are earthly-matter-in-potential, themselves a form of matter,[13] waiting for their opportunity to develop through the acquisition of a mortal body in this life. Only through the physical life can individuals attain the highest level of the Mormon afterlife, the celestial kingdom. Those who reach it will still continue as physical beings, although their bodies will be of refined and perfected matter, they will still live in families, and they will continue to bear and parent children in heaven.[14] Thus, as I have argued elsewhere (Cannell 2005b), a genealogical sensibility is not confined to the present life for Latter-day Saints but stretches forward into an infinite future of postmortal existence.

In LDS adoption circles, paradigmatic stories illustrate the imaginative power of these propositions. Pregnant women who intend to give up their babies for adoption and prospective adoptive parents often meet each other in LDS agency settings, looking for a match. One hopeful couple was certain that the baby of a particular woman was meant to be brought up by them. When the baby was born, however, the young mother decided to bring up the baby, took him home, and cared for him lovingly. Unbeknown to her, the couple refused to consider other infants. Four months later, the young mother sought out the couple as adoptive parents, saying that she had come to recognize through prayers and signs that the baby boy was "theirs": "Not mine."

Latter-day Saints are not in any way indifferent to other registers of relatedness found in American society, including the claims of "biological" relatedness or of kinship founded in law or in social convention. The idea of premortal relatedness, however, at times complicates these definitions and at other times may be used as a frame of reference by which competing claims of other kinship paradigms can be judged.

Joan (all names in this section are pseudonyms) is the mother of five children by birth and three by adoption and lives in a small Mormon town south of Salt Lake. Her adoptive children were found at orphanages in an East African country; Joan and her husband had taken the step of going out to look for children to help after experiencing powerful and unexpected spiritual promptings to do so. The children were between five and ten years old at the time of adoption. Joan might have been expected to emphasize the idea that all eight of her children were premortally destined to be together as a family. Her experience, however, was more complex. Despite initial difficulties, she and the family had bonded with the two adopted sons, but her relations with the adopted daughter, Mary, remained distant and strained, causing Joan a lot of questioning. She worried because evidence had emerged after the adoption that Mary actually had living family members, including a half brother to whom she was close but whose existence had been concealed by the orphanage.

It is a distinctive aspect of Mormon teaching that bonds between living family members can be eternalized through Mormon temple rituals; thus, families can truly "be together forever." For children not "born in the covenant," including adoptive children, the parent-child bond is ritually "sealed" in the temple. Joan worried about whether to seal Mary, because of a strong, persistent feeling that Mary "was really her [birth] mother's" and ought therefore to be ritually joined to her birth mother for eternal time. Eventually, Joan went ahead with the temple ritual and was reassured by the "sweet" sensations they shared during it (understood as promptings of the Holy Spirit) that she had made the right decision. But she reached this point only after being assured by LDS temple officials that the sealing would not preclude Mary from being reunited with her birth mother in eternity. Although this is the standard official position, it continued to be puzzling to Joan, given the LDS emphasis on the absolute efficacy of temple ritual. But, as Joan said, she was confident that if there had been any mistake, "Heavenly Father would sort it all out" in the life to come.[15] Joan also noted that her suggestion that Mary be sealed to her birth mother had been refused by the church on the grounds that the adoption had made Mary legally Joan's daughter and "they had to go by the law of the land on that one." Yet, the sense that Mary was really her birth mother's persisted.

Joan's interpretation was that Heavenly Father intended some children to be adopted into families eternally and other children were there to be looked after for this lifetime only—despite what national law or the church's consequent regulations might suggest to the contrary. The sense of real kinship could not be determined in this way. Yet, neither was it dependent simply on "biology," since Joan feels that her adopted sons are "meant to be part of [her] family" forever. She suggests, however, that the situation could still change; perhaps sometime in the mortal or postmortal future, she will discover that Mary *is* meant to be her daughter eternally after all. At that time, presumably, she will experience the bonding to Mary that still eludes her; that is, she will "recognize" Mary for the daughter she always was. Such an outcome is entirely imaginable within Mormonism because one of the purposes of mortal existence is moral testing and the gaining of experience. One way to view even difficult relationships is that we are locked together because there is something we are meant to be learning from one another.

Although much else could be said about Mormon adoption, these brief examples may be sufficient to establish my claim that LDS conceptions of kinship run counter to Schneider's pan-American symbolic categories of "blood" and "law." The Mormon teaching that kinship is recognition thus challenges not only Schneider's understandings of kinship but also those of others in the anthropological literature on so-called Western kinship that he helped inspire.

Schneider assumed that "blood" (as opposed to "blood relative") was a clear-cut symbol in which equal maternal and paternal contributions mingle at conception and create a child with enduring links to both parents. He later stated that, with scientific innovation, the symbolic workings of "blood" would be mapped onto "biological substance," however it was then understood (Schneider 1980:23).

Much of the important work on the new reproductive technologies

(Edwards 2000; Thompson 2005) and other innovative literature on kinship in "the West" has focused on actual instabilities in the mapping of biogenetic material and in the constitution of the "biological" versus the "social" or "technological." Thus, Sarah Franklin's work (2001, 2007) develops the insights of Strathern, Rabinow, and others into the increasing preoccupation of science with animal and human heredity, the production of "second natures," and the visible modeling of the new genetics on cultural practices. This work has moved the discussion forward in immensely valuable ways, but it will be readily apparent that Mormon recognition raises an additional difficulty with Schneider's paradigm because it fits into neither the category of biogenetic substance nor that of man-made social law and convention. It occupies the space of a third term, suggesting that real kinship rests on something powerful but ineffable and certainly not simply material, as the term is generally employed.[16] This is especially clear in the case of adoption practices, which in other Western contexts are often put forward as the paradigmatic case in which tensions arise as the dual components of kinship (blood and law or the biological and social) come into a conflict (Carsten 2000, 2001, 2007; Howell 2001).

Mormonism holds that all creation is, in some sense, material, and it does not place spirit and matter in opposition to each other. It therefore stands in contrast not only to many other Christian religious traditions but also to much anthropological discussion, which assumes that the meaning and status of the material and the physical are obvious, conceiving them in a dualistic relation with the mind or, in some contexts, with what is assumed to be the "unreal." Thus, the point so well anticipated by Carsten—that there might not turn out to be one single template for the American symbol of blood—finds evidence here of a radical kind.

THE SECULARIZATION OF WESTERN KINSHIP?

This leads me to wonder whether the discussion of "Western" kinship has not, quite unintentionally, reproduced part of the cultural bias it is analyzing. Insofar as several of these studies take direction from a development or critique of Schneider, they reinforce the focus on the biological-social or blood-law axis as the space of kinship, and they thus inadvertently reproduce Schneider's assumptions that kinship is delimited by secularity.

I am thinking, in particular, of the whole field of studies of new reproductive technologies and other medical perspectives on so-called Western kinship. The originality and fruitfulness of these studies are beyond question. However, the work has been firmly located in the clinic.[17] In IVF (in vitro fertilization) treatment (as in other medical situations), the immediate concern of informants is with the physical processes they are undergoing and what these entail for their lives, and the dominant discourse is that of specialists who couch their professional speech in terms of a materialist science. Anthropologists have, of course, recognized this, but their responses have tended to place these scientific views in contrastive tension with *social* understandings of relatedness, which (especially after Schneider) already assume the subordinate status of the religious.[18] For example, Charis Thompson's admirable *Making Parents* (2005) refers to the "ontological" problems of IVF and to the image of the "sacred" fetus but treats these terms as merely metaphorical.[19] For Thompson, the real story is about "the biomedical mode of reproduction operating within standard capitalism" (2005:258), and religion is important primarily as it defines interest group voting on embryology in the US Congress. Margaret Lock's brilliant study of "brain death," *Twice Dead* (2002), explicitly discusses the role of religious belief in organ donation in the United States. Interestingly, Lock finds that many of her informants are highly ambivalent about whether they believe in an afterlife or define themselves as "religious" and that they have things to say on this issue. Yet, Lock's main conclusion is that in the modern West "the *body* is the site of tragedy" (2002:203) and is also the idiom of the postmortal survival of individuals. For Lock, post-Christian reformulations continue to inflect organ donation; some kind of transcendence of death is sought through the gift of life to another person, but that transcendence is only in material form.

The topic of religion has also been addressed by other important writers on American kinship: Faye Ginsburg's (1989) memorable and pioneering study of "pro-life" and "pro-choice" women in North Dakota, for instance, where religious affiliations are a crucial factor. Rayna Rapp's (1999) work is similarly attentive to religious factors affecting attitudes to amniocentesis. Such studies respond to the realities of the American political scene and, in this sense, give more space to the issue of religion than Schneider's model would seem to invite. However, even these ethnographies ultimately treat religion as a factor that conditions opinion formation among citizens, rather than as a fundamental determinant of American kinship categories. Conversely, Susan Harding's (2000) superb account of Jerry Falwell's Liberty Baptist Church and of the turn toward social activism in fundamentalist Christian thinking is attentive to the place of both pro-family and pro-life rhetorics in the Moral Majority. Harding's central argument is that the apparently clear demarcation lines between modern, liberal, secular opinion and antimodern, religious opinion in the United States are partly a chimerical effect of the political and media battles won and lost around the time of the Scopes trial. In this sense, Harding's book and this chapter are closely in tune in questioning the obviousness of the secular in the contemporary United States. Certainly, conservative Baptists have a distinctive view of the religious meaning of life and conception. Yet, although Harding writes most evocatively about the meanings of the pro-life turn in conservative Protestantism, her central focus is on the production of "born-again Christian subjectivity out of materials provided by the feminist...movement" (2000:185)—that is, on the production of the distinction between liberal and conservative opinion. To that extent, even Harding's work focuses more closely on the ways in which the changing categories of the "religious" and the "secular" help define American *political* constituencies and less closely on the ways in which understandings of *kinship* and their limitations derive from the same historical processes.

Perhaps even more than Falwell's Baptists, American Mormons are not, in any stereotypical sense, rightly viewed as "antimodern." They are decidedly not antitechnological, for instance, and their views on matters related to scientific innovations affecting human reproductive life are less predictable than those of conservative Protestants. Thus, all five LDS members of the US Senate voted in favor of stem cell research in 2001 (Clark 2001), invoking an LDS ambiguity about when life enters the fetus.[20] As in the case of the meaning of adoption described above, Mormon teaching is distinctive precisely in refusing to make "matter" and "spirit" or "body" and "soul" into each other's opposites. In this, it contrasts with most major bodies of American Christian and Jewish opinion *and* with mainstream secular discourse. It thus throws into relief what the latter may share with the former and confirms the suggestion that the character of the American secular is Protestant.

For Latter-day Saints, the idea and the lived practice of kinship are saturated with explicit religious meaning; salvation is thought of as a collective endeavor in which both hope and anxiety are invested in the idea that all members of an extended family should find each one another again in the celestial kingdom. LDS teaching permits vicarious baptism for the dead, through which deceased family members can also be offered membership in the church and thus potentially be united with their kin. Kinship bonds are conceived as being eternal in the hereafter and also, as we saw, as being chosen before mortal birth. Therefore, all kinship relations are invested with a sacred quality, and quite ordinary family activities partake in this sacredness. The LDS institution of Monday night "family home evenings"—during which family recreations such as playing a game or sharing a snack are combined with a moral and religious lesson—is one expression of this tendency.

Latter-day Saints are not alone among religious Americans in reaching for ways to articulate kinship relationships as sacred. This is suggested, for instance, by Pamela Klassen's (2001) account of Christian, Jewish, and pagan women in the home birthing movement and by Linda Layne's (2011) ethnography of the construction of children lost through miscarriage as "angel babies." It would appear that the difficulty of separating "religious" from "scientific" views of kinship described by Gillian Feeley-Harnik (1999, 2001a, 2001b, and chapter 8, this volume) for contemporaries of Lewis Henry Morgan did not end in the nineteenth century in the United States but has, in some ways, persisted. Indeed, in my view, the Latter-day Saints' ontology both attracts and (sometimes) repels non-Mormon American Christians precisely because it explicitly articulates certain ideas that, in some ways, "feel right," but it does so through a theology they find unacceptable. This ambivalent relation has, of course, a historical dimension: Mormonism emerged in the 1830s out of a Christian culture on the eastern seaboard that was shared with the traditional denominations. Then, the LDS Church and mainstream values became differentiated, as this chapter has shown, through a series of painful clashes over the course of the nineteenth century. In several ways, therefore, Mormon thinking figures as the "path not taken" by mainstream American churches (Cannell 2005b; cf. Bloom 1992).

At the same time, we can also see a hypervalorization of kinship taking place in self-defined "secular" circles in the United States and the United Kingdom. This occurs in many registers, for example, in avowedly secular expressions of care for and interest in the related dead (Bennett 1999; Day 2009) and in relation to the heightened meanings ascribed to contemporary childhood (Zelizer 1994[1985]). I have argued elsewhere, in an account of the way these expressions of care are articulated in hobbyist popular genealogy (Cannell 2011), that the analytically secular status of such practices in the UK context does not follow automatically from the important fact that people may not wish to describe what they do as "religion." Connectedly, we might suggest that certain lacunae in secular thought speak loudly of the explicitly Christian ideas that recently preceded them (Mauss 1985[1938]). Much of Jeanette Edwards's ethnography, for instance, with its fine ear for the significant in what people say, shows her northern English informants pondering the complexities of kinship transmission. Her informants muse on how characteristics understood as inherited can "[skip] a generation" (Edwards 2009:138). They linger over the interplay between physical inheritance and the inheritance of behavioral traits acquired from one's upbringing (Edwards 2000:217). Or, as

Edwards says, the assertion that human characteristics are passed on "in the blood" can be made one moment and contradicted the next. People call on alternative modalities of envisaging kinship, especially those that derive from the work of care and nurturance, love, and sympathy. This range of modalities, for Edwards, gives English kinship its resilience as a way of speaking about social connections of all kinds.

In Edwards's approach to English kinship, we see, above all, the theoretical influence of Marilyn Strathern (1992b). But it also recalls Schneider in the assumption that these tensions and tautologies primarily works to make a certain kinship system, one viewed as a secular object located on the axis social–physical. For Edwards, as for several other scholars attending to the new reproductive technologies, the expression of contradictions is intensified by the novelty of these interventions. But what if the work being done in these conversations is also, or instead, the production of a space of mystery? That is, what if one aspect of the tautologies of this kind of kinship is not that it signifies a clash between two structuring principles (blood and law) but that it permits the expression of feelings about kinship as what is mysterious, yet intimate, in the human condition; the sense of connectedness to and yet separateness from others, both past and present, living and dead; the sense of something patterned, not arbitrary, yet too complex to be amenable to any complete or reductive explanation?

My own view is that Edwards's informants' sense of mystery about how a person is made is a soul-shaped space in contemporary discourse. Indeed, since Edwards tells us that some residents of her field site attend Catholic and Baptist churches (although she does not tell us more about this), it may be that her informants might still call on that vocabulary more explicitly from time to time.

Strangely, Schneider never discusses the concept of the soul, which surely as much as "reason" is a crucial aspect of American theories about what makes humans human. Nor does he discuss the injunction quoted above to "Master Nature" in relation to the postlapsarian interpretations of the Fall, which, according to Sahlins (1996), have decisively influenced all American culture, kinship, and economic thought. The only direct engagement Schneider offers with the formative role of religion in US culture appears to be in an essay of 1969. This is rather adumbrated but includes the claim that whereas in Judaism one is a member of the religion by both blood and law, Christianity in the United States has developed by separating out kinship by blood from membership in a religion under the law (Schneider 1969). Leaving aside the fact that Mormon thinking does not follow this pattern, the general logic of this argument seems to me highly questionable. Surely, it is more likely (and perhaps empirically demonstrable) that the particular kinds of symbolic interplay envisaged between the "given" and the "made" in American kinship derive in part from the strong influence of Christian (and Judaic) models in the history of the culture?

My argument, therefore, draws on Lock, Edwards, and others who go a little against the grain, to shed light on the restrictions that a purely secular reading of American kinship (Schneider's, among others) may confer. Rather, I suggest that in avowedly secular contexts, kinship may be an acceptable locus for ineffable meaning when explicitly religious framings are not. However, kinship treated as what Lambek (chapter 10, this volume) powerfully describes as something akin to Arendt's "romanticized object"—as something "immoderate" and "immodern"—also appears to be a central constitutive feature of avowedly religious opinion, albeit differently framed.

DISEMBEDDED KINSHIP?

One conclusion that could be drawn from this chapter is that the material considered here tends to support those who question the applicability of the term "secularization," in the European sense, to describe the relationship between the state and religion as it has developed in the United States (Casanova 1994:9). In contrast to European states—with their history of what Casanova calls "caesaropapism"—the US Constitution formally espouses a position of neutrality toward different faiths, which, however, has never amounted to the attempt to create a formal separation between religion and public debate, as in some European settings. In addition, the brilliant historical account offered by Gordon offers support to those analyses of supposedly neutral state or legal spaces in American culture that discern in them a decidedly specific Protestant bias. Insofar as America became secular at all, it was a Protestant secularity.

In this framing, other forms of religiosity were consigned to spaces of activity that did not overtly challenge the developing federal state, and the Constitution, in turn, exerted a surprising pressure toward conformity in this respect on the individual states of the union. Both religion and kinship were to be modeled on one particular kind of Protestant idea, which set limits to the institutional freedoms of both. What was specifically disallowed, of course, was the prospect of theocracy, or rather the multiple proto-theocracies that had belonged to an earlier phase of American religious, legal, and political life. Insofar as such ideas continued to be pursued institutionally (and they were), they had to be framed within new limits.

At the same time, it may be supposed that this restriction of the religious character of the state, while eliciting conformity even from Mormon Utah, at one level, only added to the imaginative power of the interdicted, at another. I am always struck by how many people I meet who assume, if the topic of my research comes up, that I must be working with polygamists and that most Latter-day Saints still practice plural marriage today. In fact, as we saw, official church sanction for the practice lasted only sixty years and ended twice as long ago, in 1890. Intensive media interest in the small groups of present-day breakaway polygamists is, of course, part of the reason for this misconception; often, it is not made clear that these groups are excommunicated from the mainstream LDS Church. Nevertheless, the media coverage itself evidences a public fascination with the transgressive attraction of polygamy that I assume is not only a sexual frisson but also a political one.

Most contemporary Mormons have no thoughts of a literal theocracy. Yet, even in Mormonism's present, politically integrated form, it always retains a millenarian element. The time horizon of Mormon kinship is distinctive, not only bringing in flashes of memory from the premortal existence but also creating a context in which present actions prefigure and help create the postmortal future of eternal togetherness and progression. In the sense that Latter-day Saints are empowered and obliged to act to make families who will achieve salvation together, their religion implicitly relativizes the claims of the nation-state. Every ordinary Mormon necessarily helps to make a community that will far outstrip America.[21]

Simultaneously, Mormon time—through its focus on the premortal existence—emphasizes not only the ultimate alternative collectivity but also the ultimately irreducible individual. The being who comes into this world at birth is not simply a vulnerable little physical creature but is the instantiation of a person who was always already himself or herself in another form before and will be so again in a form to come after this life. Since Mormonism also refuses to make an opposition between spirit and matter, we can see that, for Latter-day Saints, birth and motherhood, as well as death, are moments of an intense integration of religious and familial concerns, in which ordinary relatedness is literally identified with the stuff of divine salvation. These ideas, which constitute central experiential facets of Mormon piety, are not necessarily widely understood among people outside the Mormon church. Yet, I argue, they seem to have elective affinities with tendencies toward utopian or romanticized treatments of kinship in both religious and secular culture. Indeed, Harold Bloom (1992) has argued that Mormonism's tendency to suggest that each individual is, in some way, always co-present with God prior to birth (as in Cristal's story about her son, above) is characteristic of "gnostic" tendencies widely found in American Christian churches with quite different explicit theologies. If so—and ethnographies such as Luhrmann's (2004) seem to support this interpretation—then it is not surprising that Mormon kinship fascinates both LDS members and non-LDS observers.

Each contribution to this volume questions the default posititioning of kinship as a less significant structuring force in modern life than politics or economics. This, of course, does not mean that the political economy of kinship ideology is unimportant; indeed, Feeley-Harnik's work (chapter 8, this volume) is exemplary in showing the joint emergence of new structures of property with new ways of thinking about descent. The developments she charts in relation to Lewis Henry Morgan's family took place just a decade or two after the Mormons had left the eastern states in their search for a permanent home. Several astute commentators on American kinship have drawn attention to the ways in which contemporary investments in family sentiment can distort reality and permit an evasion of real social responsibility for the vulnerable (Ivy 1995; Zelizer 1994[1985]). I would not disagree. Indeed, the economic context of adoption is one of several aspects of LDS practices that require more exploration than I am able to supply in this short account. At the same time, I would not wish to suggest that Mormon kinship thinking or practice can be accounted for solely in terms of economic factors.

If, from the point of view of the expansion of legal power, both kinship and religion are subordinated to the modern state (Lambek, chapter 10, this volume), then the relationship between kinship and religion remains perhaps the least clearly specified area of modernization narratives, whether in practical politics or in academic theory. From the perspective of material science and medicine, I suggest, religion is perhaps subordinated to kinship, insofar as kinship is treated as a physical reality and religion is not. I argue that secularist trends in kinship analysis—including Schneider's theories—effected a parallel maneuver. Another tradition of literature has derived ultimately from Weber's (1978b) suggestion that in a disenchanted world the search for meaning and value—which, for many, could only with difficulty continue to be pursued in formal religious contexts—might be displaced onto a range of other settings, including art, intellectual life, and the erotic.

The notion of re-enchantment as it is generally discussed, however, has less to say about intense religious investments in familial, rather than sexual, love.[22] Bellah (1997) is very much in the minority in taking up Weber's discussion not of erotic love but of kin and neighborly love and Weber's implication that these are the values least distinguishable from the development of salvationist religions. Indeed, Bellah suggests that Weber never described kinship in this sense as an objectified value sphere in competition with religion in the rationalized modern world, as economics and politics came to be objectified. Rather, "brotherly love" was transformed and universalized within world-denying religions (8), and there are some suggestions that Weber thought this form of love could also be understood as informing modern companionate marriage (Weber 1998).

Whether or not we wish to use Weber's terminology, I find it difficult not to return to the trains of thought provoked by these two diverse insights. On the one hand, the process of disenchantment would, he thought, produce a new "polytheism" in modernity, a world of bizarrely objectified domains, increasingly and rivalrously incompatible in their values (Kippenberg 2005). On the other hand, he suggested that religion and kinship never came to be completely objectified in opposition to each other, even in the West. I illustrate here the possibility of a particular irony in the way that Mormon kinship has meaning in the modern context. Certainly, religious kinship ideas can be used to conceal social realities and can be deployed to mask them. But even so, they may also reveal something truthful about the modern world that is otherwise difficult to see, precisely by evoking a world in which the domains of human experience are not fully divided from and against one another. In this sense, modern disenchantment may be partially transcended through a language and practice of kinship understood as ineffable, a third term, one that escapes from the polarity of substance and legality and remains embedded, like an anti-fetish, hidden in our metaphors of human transmission.

Acknowledgments

A conversation with Professor Janet Bennion in 2001 provided, in part, the stimulus to think about the relationship between Mormon kinship and Schneider's work, and I thank her for her inspiration and her scholarship. The research on which this article is based was funded by Economic and Social Research Council of Great Britain Research Competition Award R000239016 and by the London School of Economics Seed Money Staff Research Fund. Both are gratefully acknowledged. Susan McKinnon provided incisive editing, and she and other colleagues at the SAR advanced seminar "The Difference Kinship Makes" and the London School of Economics Department of Social Anthropology provided many insightful comments. All errors are, of course, my own.

Notes

1. For an overview of the anthropology of secularism, see Cannell 2010. On secularization theory, see Casanova 1994; Dobellaere 1998; Martin 2005.

2. That is, for kinship in the United Kingdom, mainland Europe, and former colonies where the influence of either is considered to be dominant.

3. A scholarly and insightful account of contemporary ("fundamentalist") Mormon polygyny is given by Janet Bennion (1998). Since polygamy is now forbidden by the Church of Jesus Christ of Latter-day Saints, all such groups are excommunicated from the church and constitute independent organizations. None of my own LDS informants were polygamous.

4. Gordon notes that by the late 1870s, the Supreme Court "had reined in the applicability of the Reconstruction amendments to the daily lives of those who claimed that the federal government should now protect their rights.... The development of an alternative body of limitations on affirmative government power lay in the future.... *Reynolds v. United States* lies on this fault line between constitutional interpretations" (2002:120).

5. Having opined that "Jesus Christ was a bastard and his mother must be a whore" (Gordon 2002:71).

6. In the *Reynolds* case, the church's lawyer, George Washington Biddle, argued that the Ten Commandments were a sufficient basis for a minimal, public, consensual Christianity. His opponent, Charles Devens, insisted that the New Testament clearly prohibited polygamy. Biddle and the Saints disagreed and claimed that this was a theological and not a legal issue (Gordon 2002:141).

7. Compare the possibility of a distinctively Muslim secular being defined in Malaysia, as discussed by John Bowen (2010).

8. As Gordon rightly notes, these formulations avoided dwelling on the abusive exercise of patriarchal power outside Mormonism.

9. On the otherwise unaccountable unfolding of policies toward the (Roman Catholic) lowland Philippines in the US colonial period, see Cannell 2005a. See also Casanova's (1994:9) analysis of the contrasts between Europe (where formerly established churches were often superseded by the state) and the United States (where there was no established church but a greater public role was retained for religion). On American "civil religion," see Bellah 1967.

10. Raymond T. Smith (n.d.) also notes the limitations of Schneider's attention to class variations.

11. For details on Mormon concepts of the war in heaven, the spirit world, and the question of whether being precedes gender, see www.lds.org.

12. This kind of always-already logic is part of what Harold Bloom means when he refers to Mormonism's "gnostic" tendencies. There is obviously a tension between the idea of agency (Matthew has to search hard for his family) and the idea of the predestined character of kin bonds. This tension is central to Mormon thought and is epitomized, for instance, by the phrase "choose the right" (or CTR), which is used on

youth jewelry and other items. The right already exists, but our free agency is required to discern and select it; it is quite possible to make wrong choices.

13. The prophet of Mormonism, Joseph Smith Jr., taught, "There is no such thing as immaterial matter. All spirit is matter" (Doctrine and Covenants 131:7, see also 93:33). For an example of gospel doctrine commentary on this, see Woodford 1998.

14. These children will be born in spirit form and will eventually go on to populate other worlds when their turn comes for mortal existence. The celestial kingdom is, as has often been noted, a form of apotheosis.

15. The position of last resort is often taken by Latter-day Saints and is sometimes accompanied by the reflection that things may look different in the life to come anyway. This kind of response is typical of situations in which ritual and social kinship (or kinship of the heart) may be in conflict.

16. It might be argued that Latter-day Saint kinship bonds follow some principle of divine law, but this would be misleading. As already noted, the fulfillment of the mysterious connections between kin rests on the deployment of human free agency. Besides, it is clear that, for Schneider, "law" is a category of man-made convention (for instance, laws governing embryology research and surrogacy or the legal status of marriage) linked to man's imperative to "conquer nature," as he says. The question of divine law is not discussed.

17. Jeanette Edwards's important study, *Born and Bred* (2000), is the exception. However, the questions Edwards asks are still provoked by the imagined clinic and its innovative procedures, although people are asked to reflect on these at home or in the pub.

18. Compare Kath Weston's insight that "the critique of kinship has provided a tonic for the fetish" (2001:151).

19. Compare Lynn Morgan's *Icons of Life* (2009).

20. This teaching is rarely adduced to justify abortion.

21. Radical comparative perspectives on the current world order are, of course, potentially available in any Christian tradition and were discussed by Weber as one motivation for conversion to Christianity (see Hefner 1993); however, only for Mormons is Zion clearly and immediately made through earthly kinship.

22. Except in their standard Protestant forms, which Weber mentioned as a compromise between religious universalism and familial or local idioms of a more normative kind than the material discussed here.

10

Kinship, Modernity, and the Immodern

Michael Lambek

There is no critique of the place of kinship in narratives of modernity that could be completely objective, and no single correct historical narrative to be discerned and distinguished from the ideological variants. This is not to argue that all narratives are equally justifiable or compelling but rather that how one understands the situation depends on how one defines or conceptualizes the central terms. I suggest that there is much to learn from the way anthropologists of religion and politics have debated similar questions under the rubric of secularism, by which I mean here, primarily following Talal Asad (2003), the retraction, objectification, and subsumption of religion by the state. Not only can one make arguments concerning kinship parallel to those made about religion in relation to secularism, but one can also conceptualize kinship as a central part of the same story, insofar as acts of kinship are or have been understood as ritual or religious acts. Moreover, just as the more empiricist debates around secularism move between the possible privatization, objectification, or shrinkage of religion and the recognition of its unruly resurgence, so, too, the story of kinship is surely one of simultaneous absence and presence, retraction and expansion. Thus, one can observe both growing detachment from kin and retraction of the sphere of kinship *and* excessive attachment, for instance in the United States, to "family values."

Following the secularism literature, for the purposes of this chapter, I identify modernity roughly with the ostensibly rational, jural, and bureaucratic state.[1] I identify the modern (liberal) state primarily by means of its self-identification and self-constitution via the rule of law. By emphasizing the jural dimension, my argument may appear to reiterate a point long ago discerned by Henry Maine (McKinnon, chapter 2, this volume). However, what is at issue is less a full shift from status to contract (or kinship to law) than the ways in which status becomes defined explicitly by state law alongside tradition or religion. It is less that the significance of kinship declines than that law becomes ever more important (pervasive and encompassing) and, in the process, ostensibly and progressively disembeds itself from kinship and religion, distinguishes them from each other, and perhaps encapsulates them, simultaneously becoming ever more entangled with them.

I propose framing kinship in a specific (and relatively novel) way, as constituted through a series of definitive acts—or, more precisely, performative acts—and then as the histories such acts produce (Lambek 2011). Such a model of kinship foregrounds a historical narrative of the interface or contestation between state law and bureaucracy, on the one side, and religious or traditional authority, on the other (as they become distinguished from each other), to effect such enactments and to manage, order, evaluate, legitimate, record, remember, acknowledge, and possibly celebrate them. At the same time, these acts themselves can be understood as domaining practices. Hence, if kinship is one of the grounds on which state law establishes its superior authority and encapsulation of "religion," then "kinship," like "religion," becomes constituted in the process. Thus, "kinship," "religion," and "law" are mutually implicated in one another.

Nevertheless, anthropology is not reducible to genealogy and must also acknowledge what is outside, as well as inside, scare quotes. Thus, if kinship and religion come to be identified as discrete entities subject to recognition, regulation, and even constitution by the law, then they also inevitably precede and exceed it. For one thing, as they become vehicles for idealized worlds beyond the state or the market, they may take on features of what Hannah Arendt (1958b) called romanticized objects,[2] to which all kinds of excess causality are attributed. The story of modernity is, in part, a story of anxiety over the ostensible loss of kinship (as much as or irrespective of its actual loss). The surfeit of meaning, relations, and sentiment that kinship brings—whether the joy and conflict in its presence or the anxiety and grief in its feared absence—is an expression of what I will call the immodern.

I coin "immodern" as an alternative to such implicitly historicist terms as "traditional," "premodern," and "postmodern." I take immodern—like immeasurable, immemorial, immense, and immortal—as a negation by means of an excess or a transcendence. Kinship is immodern, in part, because not simply in modernity (under state law, in the present) does it fall to kinship to symbolize or evoke a wholeness that is always already compromised or lost. Every generation looks back with nostalgia to the imagined richness of interaction experienced by the preceding generation.[3] Indeed, insofar as kinship indexes kindness, care, intimacy, solidarity, and mutual respect (the last a key feature of African kinship, if not of Euro American kinship), it sustains a utopian vision in which everyone is kin or fully treats others as kin, counterpoised to everyday reality, which is found lacking and in which actual kin relations may be riven with conflict. Conversely, a dystopian vision is one of anti-kinship, in which the positive attributes are entirely replaced—by selfishness, loneliness, witchcraft, the market, technology, big government, and so on. However, it is not the case that everyone everywhere would like to see utopia realized. In the Comoro Archipelago island of Mayotte, in the western Indian Ocean—where I have conducted research among Muslim Kibushy (Malagasy) speakers—during the mid-1970s, the question was less whether people were or were not (literally) one another's kin than whether they treated one another as kin. This is not a question asked with the same frequency or intensity in North America. Indeed, the fact that we are afraid to consider the consequences may be one of the sharpest indexes of the different role that kinship has come to play (and signify).

FAMILY AND KINSHIP

Just as some secularization theorists have argued that belief and worship become private matters within modernity, so, too, some kinship theorists have assumed the dissolution of the public, political side of kinship depicted by authors such as Meyer Fortes (1969) in African societies. In reconsidering the validity of this dominant narrative concerning kinship and modernity, it might clarify matters to make a distinction between "family" and "kinship," taking the former as a potent symbol and central part of lived experience and the latter as an analytical concept in the anthropological repertoire. Whereas the ostensibly bounded family is almost by definition "private" with respect to what is outside its boundaries (as it was for Aristotle), and yet empirically visible, kinship in anthropological thinking is much broader and deeper than the family, specifically neither public nor private, and is latent as a structure, model, or structuring force. Indeed, in contemporary Euro American public discourse, one senses that the greater the emphasis on "the family," the less visible "kinship" in its wider senses becomes.

Within social science, we could speak of Malinowskian and Morganic positions, the former emphasizing the boundedness and reality of discrete empirical units, the latter the significance of underlying interconnectivity.[4] The former, which is closer to Euro American ideology, begins with differentiated individual atoms, the latter with structure and an undifferentiated whole. In the latter view, families are products or precipitates of kinship systems rather than their building blocks. I draw here on a salient article by the formidable trio of Jane Collier, Michelle Rosaldo, and Sylvia Yanagisako, who write, "The Family as we know it...is a sphere of human relationships shaped by a state that recognizes Families as units that hold property, provide for care and welfare, and attend particularly to the young—a sphere conceptualized as a realm of love and intimacy *in opposition* to the more 'impersonal' norms that dominate modern economies and politics" (1992:40).

In this cultural "opposition" lies the gist of the problem in analyzing the obscurity of kinship in modernity, since surely we need to take the realm of intimacy seriously (and not restrict it to the heteronormative family); yet, kinship, too, operates by means of "impersonal norms," including the recursivity of terminological systems (as manifested in both American componential analysis and Lévi-Straussian structuralism) and the material ways in which the state shapes and recognizes the family. Consider the demographic transition in which the size of families has rapidly declined. This is not simply a matter of freeing women from continual reproduction, or both parents from the burden of supporting many children. A longer-term effect lies in the shrinking sibling group. Not only do the constituent units become smaller and thus look more private—possibly also encouraging greater psychological intimacy and conflict between children and parents—but there is also an inevitable reduction in the public reach of kinship. There are fewer siblings and collaterals with whom to align politically, to engage in economic activities, to network, or to arrange marriages. Moreover, the span of births being shorter, there are less likely to be uncles and aunts overlapping in age with nieces and nephews. The historical picture so strikingly painted by Leonore Davidoff (2004) of the early twentieth-century European bourgeois family—in which households frequently contained adult unmarried siblings (especially, after World War I, sisters) of the married couple—is simply not true of recent generations in the Euro American middle class.[5]

The forces of change can be quite complex; thus, the demographic transition currently under way in officially recognized families in Mayotte, shaped by both economic conditions and state policies, is offset by the additional children local men have with undocumented Comorian migrants.[6]

If historical events such as wars and historical processes such as shifts in state policy have demographic effects, the broader point is that matters of numerical scale and proportion do influence kinship's public role and visibility. At the same time, the *meaning* of all of this remains critical. The thing that older people in Mayotte still find most difficult to understand about me is that I have intentionally limited the number of my offspring to two. There remains for them something disturbing, not only ostensibly irrational but also fundamentally unethical, in restricting family size. This has little to do with contraception or the value of individual human life and much to do with the good of reproduction and "wealth in people" as ends in themselves.

Given the visibility yet constriction of the ostensibly private yet empirical family, where are we to discover or locate the underlying structures or forces of kinship more broadly? As evident in the quotation from Collier, Rosaldo, and Yanagisako, this entails the state's role in procreation and other aspects of life, including the way the state legalizes and medicalizes specific acts of kinship, classifies and counts family members, regulates family size and functioning by means such as child benefits and taxation, punishes or rewards certain forms of preferential treatment of kin ("corruption"), curtails immigration, and, as I will discuss shortly, engages in the production of new persons and relationships. From Michel Foucault (1980) we learn not about the shrinkage, privatization, or disembedding of kinship but rather about its embeddedness within and emergence from a broader set of biopolitical practices as a site and product of a specific nexus of power/knowledge. The emphasis on law—which, from a different angle, David Schneider (1968) also notes—counters any direct privatization of kinship: it is public law that ensures the privacy of the family (and law that constitutes private-public distinctions in the first place).

Perhaps part of the ideology of modernity is to conceal or downplay the state's role in kinship.[7] However, it is not as if comparable practices did not shape kinship in smaller-scale societies. Perhaps one of the shortcomings of Foucault's original analyses and their interpretations by others was the implication that biopolitical disciplinary practices are specific or unique to the modern state. What else are we to consider the interests of many so-called tribal societies, with their focus on initiation and marriage rituals and on social reproduction more generally? Persons and relations are here produced and reproduced by disciplinary practices as well, but we call these ritual rather than bureaucracy or law. We speak of ritual adepts rather than regimes of experts, authority rather than power, and symbolism rather than rational calculation. Yet, Victor Turner (1969) describes Ndembu (Luunda) ritual associations penetrating the most intimate aspects of people's lives, much as psychiatrists, social workers, and immigration boards do. An infertile Ndembu woman had recourse, and was subject, to intrusive disciplinary practices much as a woman seeking in vitro fertilization (IVF), the procedures havin,g in each case, decisive consequences for the identity of subsequent offspring and exemplifying, in each case, a particular cultural theory of procreation. Similarly, birth (filiation) and the ascription of collective and personal identity are linked in societies where descent groups are salient, just as birth (filiation) and the ascription of citizenship and personal identity are intimately connected in modernity.

I am not suggesting that we conflate legal, bureaucratic, and scientific modes of biopolitics with ritual ones. What we need to think about more clearly are the similarities and distinctions in the *means* by which modern states and other kinds of societies define and carry out such tasks and hence the distinctive kinds of groups, persons, relations, and sentiments they produce.[8]

ACTS OF KINSHIP

Anthropologists sometimes confuse kinship as a field of study or branch of anthropology with kinship as a social practice or dimension of human being, the object of their study. In considering the fate of kinship in modernity, it is important to distinguish or disentangle its fate within anthropology from its fate, as we say, in the real world. That David Schneider (1984) and Rodney Needham (1971) may have pronounced kinship dead in anthropology says nothing one way or the other about the significance of kinship or the family, for example, in or for the Schneider or Needham households or the societies in which they lived.

Although we cannot see kinship in modernity or elsewhere unmediated by an anthropological model, its trajectory looks different depending on which model we draw from, whether we emphasize descent or alliance, symbolic analysis or practice theory. Each has a different story to tell about modernity. To these main approaches (Good 2010) I add a performative model, perceiving kinship as constituted through certain kinds of acts and the ethically saturated conditions established by means of acts. This is offered as an additional rather than ostensibly mutually exclusive, alternative model, yet I do see enactment as fundamental (obviously not exclusive) to what kinship is. Hence, my model is ambitious insofar as it is meant to apply not only to modernity but also to kinship everywhere and also to provide a wedge by which we might describe part of what is distinctive to modernity.

To start with what is universal to kinship in human society risks naturalizing kinship. But Claude Lévi-Strauss (1969[1949]; see also Freud 1999[1913]) showed how one could speak universally and at the same time distinguish human kinship, or culture, from nature (in the sense of neither essentializing nor reducing the former).[9] As intentional performances rather than as expressions of drive, instinct, or other forms of necessity, elementary acts of kinship are humanly social, cultural, and indeed ethical. And, as acts, they are not static, but subject to differential construction over time and in different language games. Such acts include recognizing and accepting children (as one's own; as members of one's group, class, or society; as human), marrying (getting married, marrying someone off, officiating at the enactment of marriage, forming an alliance through marriage), and succeeding (identifying with and differentiating from, displacing, acknowledging, receiving from or handing over to members of the adjacent generation). In all cases, we can speak of agents and patients, the acted and the acted upon, and also of mediators, officiates, and witnesses (as well as alternative candidates and those excluded from consideration).

In this view, kinship does not simply convey meaning as a symbol or set of symbols—nor is it simply constituted as a local domain through abstract symbols and meanings—but is also carried out in acts that are *meant* and that have meaningful consequences, including retroactive assignments of meaning. Kinship (models, persons, relationships, groups, boundaries, meanings, structure, acts) is (re)produced in explicitly performative (illocutionary) acts that identify, name, introduce, acknowledge, relate, unite, separate, bless, bestow property, and so on. As rituals, such acts entail the conjunction of the "canonical" (the previously encoded message) with the "indexical" (the message relevant to the immediate context; Rappaport 1999), such that, for example, the child who is baptized is not any child, but *mine*. Such acts may include the transfer of substances, but they cannot be reduced to such transfers in a mechanical sense, such as the simple deposition of semen, sprinkling of holy water, and so on. Acts are explicit, declared, and acknowledged; they connect intention with consequence. They also occur less explicitly or elaborately in the course of everyday life and may be as simple and as common as addressing someone by a kin term. This is not a subjective view, because, following J. L. Austin (1965[1955]) and Roy Rappaport (1999), the intention is embedded in the form and kind of action, as part of a larger order of acts, irrespective of the subjectivity of particular actors. Performance, as Rappaport puts it with respect to religious ritual, entails acceptance but not necessarily belief. Or as Austin sees it, the performer's word is a matter of her public statements, not of inner mental conditions such as "sincerity." Put another way, acts of kinship entail submission to an order of kinship, irrespective of personal sentiment; they are simultaneously active and passive, and the actors are simultaneously agents and patients.

What such acts do is constitute persons and relations according to a prior order or structure and set up the criteria by which, in this instance, subsequent practice is shaped and evaluated (Lambek 2010c). To become a parent or a spouse is to establish the terms by which a particular relationship is constituted and understood. Acts produce commitments and inform people with, and of, their commitments to one another, thereby determining not practice itself but the meanings that are attributed to it. In other words, such acts establish kinship as an ethical domain. Not only are they to be understood as felicitous or infelicitous in and of themselves, but they also establish the criteria for what is good and bad, just and unjust, right and wrong with respect to specific persons and relationships. They do not, of course, determine that people will be good parents or good children all the time; they produce not behavior but criteria. In this model—and in contrast to some practice theory (but true to Aristotle)—ethics is not extrinsic but rather intrinsic to action, as action is to ethics.[10] Hence, kinship can never be reduced either to biology or to interest and calculation.

I come to this approach, in part, from ethnographic experience in Mayotte, where acts of kinship are highlighted and celebrated. Marked acts occur around births and at circumcisions, weddings, funerals, and blessing ceremonies for the deceased, but they include many other rituals carried out across the life span and after death by kin and community members for one another. These rituals simultaneously perform transitive acts on, over, or with respect to individuals and (intransitively) reproduce, reiterate, confirm, and instantiate the relationships among the participants, as well as the broader order or structure from which they are generated. Although some acts take place among members of the community at large, many are both logically entailed and highly salient in and as kinship—as children and grandchildren are acknowledged and as filiation, paternity, maternity, conjugality, affinity, siblingship, succession, and ancestrality are established across the life cycle.

These acts—from carrying a newborn infant to the mosque porch and leaving it to be carried back home by someone else, to inviting community members to pray for one's deceased parents—are productive and reproductive of persons and relationships. They are intrinsically ethical, not only in being right and good in and of themselves—or marking the good and right unfolding of the life cycle—but also in establishing the criteria for right identification and action, for how subsequent acts and practice will be produced and construed by means of situated judgment (phronesis) and evaluated, as right or wrong, adequate or inadequate, and so forth. Such acts announce specific relationships and establish or reiterate commitments to them. Elsewhere in the world, acts of kinship and acts producing kinship also happen not only around the beginning of life but also across the life cycle and in processes of separation and departure, as well as of arrival and connection. This is nicely captured in the image of *dexiosis*, the parting handshake with the dead, evident in Greek funerary sculpture.[11] This may be at once an act of greeting, a sign of respect or affection, and a farewell. (People who shake hands are at arm's length.) The memory work characteristic of Euro American kinship (Carsten 2007; Feeley-Harnik and Cannell, chapters 8 and 9, respectively, this volume; Young 1996), the untying of relations in Melanesian kinship (Bamford 2007; Battaglia 1990; Strathern 1988; Weiner 1976), the emphasis on separations and reunions in China (Stafford 2000), and the reburial of and other mortuary practices concerning the Vietnamese war dead (Kwon 2008) are other examples.[12]

RELIGION AND THE STATE

The theory of performative acts provides a means by which to understand the relationship of kinship to religion within the so-called modern state. In Mayotte, the primary acts of kinship are simultaneously religious, unfolding by means of an Islamic idiom, especially the utterance of sacred verse and with respect to Islamic tradition concerning such things as (male) circumcision and mortuary practices. In fact, decisive acts of kinship throughout the world are marked and formalized and hence can be considered "rituals" (*rites de passage*) and likely also, in some sense, "religious." Yet, the practice of carrying a newborn to the mosque, which was enacted at the end of the postpartum period in Mayotte during the 1970s, has substantially declined in appearance and saliency since then. This is because birth has become a matter for state regulation and surveillance; it has become medicalized and legalized. Today, a woman must give birth in a hospital or clinic. In the first phase of implementation, she had to do so in order for her infant to qualify for a birth certificate and subsequent identity documents. In the second phase, she had to show her own documentation (of citizenship and insurance) in order to enter. At the beginning, many women resisted these procedures (Lambek 1993), but after the hospital was upgraded, the staff professionalized, and the necessity for identity papers made evident, women began to accede. Yet, we can say that their entries into a hospital (including showing up for prepartum checkups) and the practices carried out therein (including signing birth certificates) are still acts of kinship. Here, religious idioms and order and "traditional" or "popular" practices have been marked as such and displaced by the bureaucratic and technological idioms and order of the state, but not exactly at the expense of kinship itself.

Acts surrounding birth make the infant simultaneously a member of both family and state. Insofar as birth entails citizenship, citizenship is an aspect of kinship. Indeed, consequent to the birth of a child in Mayotte, a migrant woman could seek the right to permanent residence and citizenship. Biopolitics is thus not a replacement of kinship per se but a relocation and supplementation of certain significant acts, as well as the authority for carrying out these acts and the commitment to standing by their consequences. Documentation by means of a birth certificate is basic to the constitution of personhood and relationality no less than the "documentation" entailed in depositing and fetching the infant at the mosque.[13] Nevertheless, there are differences between these practices. From the action perspective that I have been elucidating, the shift to new forms of authorization or recognition is the biggest transformation of kinship to take place under modernity and is a major way in which modernity itself can be understood. This shift is often described as "secularism."

Secularism is currently at the center of debates in the anthropology of religion and in political anthropology but is not much applied in the literature on kinship. However, it is highly relevant for several reasons. First, insofar as one influential model of secularism concerns the state's encapsulation of religion—the state regulates and defines what religion is and what degree of autonomy religious acts and groups have within it—the same process applies to kinship. Second, the debate about privatization is of long standing with respect to religion; indeed, another influential way that secularism has been defined or described has been with respect to privatization—and the critiques of the privatization model are more advanced in the field of religion than they are in the field of kinship. But, third, insofar as acts of kinship are also religious acts, the relationship to secularism is not one of simple analogy; rather, what has been happening with respect to kinship is continuous with secularism and, indeed, constitutes a large part of its actual substance. This is perhaps most easily seen in contemporary struggles between particular religious groups and the state over issues such as polygyny or female circumcision. But, as Fenella Cannell (chapter 9, this volume) indicates, it has been a fact of life in North America and Western Europe for a long period.

In this respect, the study of kinship has not only much to learn from the analysis of secularism but also much to contribute to it. As the state gets involved in acts of kinship, it does not merely encapsulate or privatize kinship; rather, it comes to play a significant role in the very enactment, production, and reproduction of kinship. Many acts of kinship are simultaneously acts of the state. One question to ask, then, is whether (and to what degree) the state supplants religion in the production of kinship or works alongside it. A second question is whether there is within the sphere of kinship something analogous to the resurgence of religion in the public sphere. Or, to put this another way, is the "religious" response to or reaction against secularism not also a resistance or reaction on the part of (or with respect to) "kinship"? Are not "religious" debates now phrased as much over issues of "kinship" (such as marriage and celibacy) as over more purely "theological" matters, such as the nature of God? Is it in light of such conflicts that we can most readily recognize kinship's public and political dimensions and saliency? Another question is whether the close ethnographic inspection of acts of kinship might provide lessons for the analysis of secularism, for example, by noting how significant acts of kinship are often constituted by articulating a series of components authorized, respectively, by the state, institutionalized religion, and a third domain one could refer to as popular or traditional. In practice, this articulation is often harmonious rather than conflictual. Conversely, the presence or possibility of conflict should remind anthropologists of kinship that they need always keep questions of pluralism at hand.

SECULARISM AND THE FATE OF KINSHIP

From the perspective taken here, the question of kinship in modernity is the question of the articulation of state-produced or state-authorized acts of kinship with those produced or authorized by other orders, whether these are explicitly orders of religion or simply of a tradition. To put it slightly differently, the issue is the articulation of different kinds of authority in the joint production of acts of kinship. Such articulation, of course, differs over time and from state to state, religious community to religious community, with respect to majority and minority populations, and with respect to which particular acts of kinship are at issue. It is fair to say that most of the major acts of kinship, the so-called life-crisis rituals, have been addressed or harnessed by the modern state, fall within its purview, or have consequences with respect to the state. Such encapsulation of kinship by the state could be considered a form of deprivatization but, as noted, is more likely a shift in locus and form of authorization. Questions include, when, how, and with what arguments, incentives, penalties, and consequences does the state intervene? Does the state require the presence of religious authority at acts of kinship, and when and how does it limit religion or constitute the domain of kinship differently than do religious or traditional orders?

This articulation has a long history, and it has not been uncontested. If the story of Oedipus has become the central myth of modern kinship, his daughter Antigone illustrates the articulation in its sharpest terms, in this instance, in the struggle over burial.[14] As Mayfair Yang (1994) has shown, contestations over the respective roles of kinship ethics and state bureaucracy go back for millennia in China.[15] In this respect, the central issue is less modernity per se than the state's power, reach, and interests. The effects of the state on kinship may have to be disentangled from those of capitalism and scientific reason and technology, though, doubtless, they draw upon and reinforce one another. The degree of confrontation depends, in part, on how kinship is defined and whether the state's role in authorizing, producing, and drawing from life-crisis rituals is understood as an intrinsic part of kinship or as external and possibly opposed to it.

The point very often is not the direct opposition of the state to religion but their changing relationships and the encapsulation of one within the other. Thus, in the 1940s it was required by law in the province of Québec that weddings be conducted only by religious officials, the state determining and also affirming what counted as "religion" and, in effect, forcing people to submit to a religious order. Perhaps this was no less "secular," in Asad's sense (2003), than the outcome of the "quiet revolution" in Québec during the 1960s, in which the influence of the church shrank radically and it became legally possible to conduct activities such as weddings (or schooling) entirely outside the purview of religious authority. Although religion shifted from being necessary to optional, at neither time could one marry legitimately outside the authority of the state.

Needless to say, Québec was quite late in rendering the religious component unnecessary to acts of kinship. A sign once posted at the entrance to the cathedral square in the city of Basel indicated that civil marriages were legalized in 1871 in the first Swiss canton to do so. The first civil marriage in Basel took place on September 19, 1872, and in 1876 a national register of marriages and a set of regulations for marriage were established.[16] In contemporary Geneva, the church can marry a couple only after they have completed a civil marriage.[17] In these societies, it is thus possible to get married outside the gaze of religion and even in the absence of kin, so long as it is within the gaze of the state. But as an act of citizenship, marriage remains equally a significant act of kinship.[18]

There are certainly differences between enacting kinship by means of ritual constituted through bureaucracy (Herzfeld 1992) as authorized by a jural order and ritual constituted by means of a liturgical order.[19] Recognizing that this, too, is a distinction that could be deconstructed, without developing a systematic comparison, I suggest a few places to examine their respective means and effects. One concerns questions of truth. To overgeneralize and oversimplify, whereas science makes its truths by correspondence, experiment, and logic, religion establishes them by means of performativity, such that, as Rappaport (1999) has shown, the facts are expected to conform to the performative utterance, rather than the reverse. The law stands between these two regimes of truth. On the one hand, it seeks or demands empirical evidence and submits its hypotheses to scrutiny, like science, but on the other, it both executes performative judgments and draws interpretively on precedent, somewhat like religion.[20] Furthermore, liturgical rituals form a hierarchy with respect to the perdurance of their effects (ibid.), such that the primary anchorage of a person in one dimension of his or her identity can enable much play in others. The lively indexicality of ritual performance can be contrasted with the ostensible atomism, decontextualization, and exactitude of bureaucratic files.[21] The need for fixity and exclusive rights is reinforced by capitalist notions of property; for example, land registration has had a huge impact on kinship in parts of the world under some form of World Bank governance.

Central to the ideology of modernity is individual freedom, and it is sometimes asserted (generally, by non-anthropologists) that modernity affords much more freedom of mobility than "tradition," in which people are born and die within fixed kinship groups and positions. If the contrast is with small-scale societies, nothing could be further from the truth. The modern state fixes identity, making it difficult to change such things as one's name or one's citizenship. Since 9/11, bureaucratic identification and surveillance have only increased, now drawing on biological markers in addition to photographs and paper documents. Children in the United States are told to grow up to be themselves, but this has come to mean acknowledging a given biological and jural destiny. Being "yourself" means being the person into whose family you were born (except when the family is viewed as "deviant"). You can be "born again," but, ideally, you do not change (conceal, deny) your name, gender, family, or citizenship. When you do change these things, you have to go through the state bureaucracy or legal system.[22] Ideally, at any given time, you claim only one name, nationality, and the like. You should be a single, specified person, clearly identifiable from your driver's license. You should have one primary set of parents (for life) and one spouse or partner (at a time). "Freedom" comes (ostensibly) with voting, education, profession, love, income, and, above all, consumption and choice of lifestyle, but not from identity.

In sum, the state demands clarity, exclusivity, and relatively decontextualized forms of personhood. Thus, one attribute of modern kinship is the weight placed on bureaucratic exactitude, precision, and permanence. This is different from the precision produced or performed in rituals. Compare the relative fixity of the Euro American person with the contextual or indexical expression of kinship among the Nuer (Evans-Pritchard 1940; cf. Lambek 2008), in which the segmentary logic exists, as Mary Douglas (1980) noted, in people's heads rather than being fixed on paper or in architecture. Modern identity is understood as bounded and exclusive from the state's perspective, even as its lability is praised in ideologies of freedom, desire, and self-realization with respect to life therein or thereafter. Compare also the kind of multiplicity and hence pervasive ambiguity found in northwestern Madagascar. I characterize kinship there by means of irony, in the sense of the dramatic irony proposed by Kenneth Burke (1945), namely, that there are multiple simultaneous voices or positions and no final or ultimate one. As in all kinship systems, not only is the position one holds (such as father or son) always relative and contingent to the context, but also—given bilateral reckoning several generations back combined with wide exogamy (complex, in Lévi-Strauss's sense)—one is constituted by multiple relations and multiple identities. When the demands of the various non-exclusive identities (including religious affiliation) conflict, the outcome is uncertain, clarified not by applying a rule or checking a file but by such things as getting sick consequent to the breaking of taboos associated with particular ancestors. Here, the indexical, embodied dimension is critical. Identity is channeled over the course of the life cycle by various forms of interpellation by living and ancestral kin, but it remains multiple and labile until it is fixed by the mode and place of burial. Such burial, in turn, forms a constraint upon the members of the next generation. Ambiguity is thus also partly a function of timing. Whereas marriage (and jural paternity) in many African societies has been described as a continuous process—taking many years and possibly a lifetime to complete and therefore at any given moment possibly ambiguous under "customary" law (Comaroff 1980; Goody 1973; Solway 1990)—under state law, ideally if not in practice, it becomes instantaneous and precise.

Bureaucracy ascribes singularity, whereas, in practice, kinship is rarely a single order and many societies provide alternative ways to ascertain it. Multiplicity of a striking quality is found among the Inuit of Greenland (Nuttall 1992), where one takes on kinship positions relative to one's family of birth, that of the person one is recognized as reincarnating, and those of all others who are reincarnating that person. Since kinship is inherently relational, rather than autonomous, this entails relations with relations. The result is that everyone can justifiably call everyone else by virtually the whole panoply of kinship terms available in the system. Such play is, of course, undermined when the state bureaucracy registers only one set of relations.

A brief illustration from North America illustrates how this limitation can work. In correspondence from an editor whom I do not know personally, she announced an addition to her last name and hence email address. Assuming a marriage, I expressed congratulations. To my surprise, she replied that her conjugal relationship was of some standing. What had changed was that their daughter had come of school age. Not only does the state take over the right to authorize names, but also coming under the state's gaze in a new way is what impels certain kinds of rationalization of names.

If kinship is public in the sense of being legitimated by state institutions, ritual acts are public insofar as they occur as a spectacle, with witnesses who are often simultaneously guests. Kinship here is publicly on record in a different way from the bureaucratic register (which can contain relatively secret files), immediately visible and drawing on the acquiescence of multiple witnesses who themselves commit to the act through gifts, congratulations, prayers, and the like.[23] This illustrates also that kinship qua reproduction is always also a product of and a moment for exchange.

Finally, the dominant semiotic ideology (Keane 2007) of bureaucracy is referential and atemporal, whereas religion and kinship emphasize ongoing practice. Bureaucracy looks at people from outside and above and emphasizes fixed external and internal boundaries; religious ritual maintains the salience of embodied presence and emphasizes various kinds of movement and connectivity, including that of touch, from within.

KINSHIP AND THE IMMODERN

Despite encapsulation within the order of the state, kinship always manages to be something more. Kinship, I argue, is both immoderate and immodern. It is immoderate (from the perspective of rationalized bureaucracy) because it contains a superfluity and an excess: a superfluity of people who could count as kin; an excess in the number of ways kinship can be calculated and hence the names and relationships we have for and with one another; a surfeit of meaning, feeling, and presence. It is immoderate insofar as the demands of care and love can be inexhaustible. There is no necessary give-and-take, no balancing of the gift here (Sahlins 1972), at least not within kinship at its core; kinship can embrace sacrifice and selflessness but also hierarchy and exploitation. Kinship is characterized by a superfluity of ceremonies that have the tendency to inflate or exaggerate, whether in purity of form, excess of elaboration, or number of participants. Whatever the rationalizations entailed in restricting exchange relations to a small number of kin, when it comes to major acts of kinship, expenses are often high.

Kinship is immodern insofar as it is immoderate in all these ways and insofar as it exceeds (rather than simply precedes) modernity. It does not offer or accept parsimony, uniformity, exclusivity, or fixity. It escapes laws that attempt to pin it down, that discern and decide according to mutually exclusive choices: biological paternity or not, rights or no rights, one right but not another. Bureaucracy ostensibly abhors superfluity and ambiguity and attempts to tame kinship, but kinship is an aspect of life that cannot be rationalized, in any sense of that word.

CONCLUSION

I have taken kinship as acts and their consequences for the production of relations and persons. In modernity, kinship is found alongside many other disciplines or discourses of person-making (Hacking 1999), but it is perhaps the only one that is intrinsically relational. Kinship does not "make up persons" as monads but as always already invested in webs of relatedness. It is so thoroughly relational because new kin are related not only to those who produce them but also to those people's relations, in turn. Kin relations are ever ramifying and auto-productive. Although kinship occurs in a particular nexus of biopolitics, it cannot be reduced to an effect of biopolitics.

Kinship is never the sole discourse and practice of person-making in any society. The big shift in modernity comes less with respect to abandoning kinship for other forms of personhood than with the state's role in legitimating the making of new persons, a role it appropriates largely from what has been called religion but which, from a certain angle and in some societies more than others, could be seen simply as undifferentiated from kinship in the first place. Marked in the anthropological literature as *rites de passage*, the elementary acts of kinship establish and affirm the beginnings, transformations, and endings of persons, relationships, criteria, and commitments. If we take ritual seriously, as an intrinsic part of kinship, then we sharpen our understanding of what is lost—and perhaps gained—when the state steps in and replaces religious ritual with law. If kinship is grounded in ritual acts, then it is significant when the state appropriates them, entailing a shift from ethical responsibility to legal obligation. In this respect, secularism has striking implications for kinship.

It is a fact of modernity that kinship is partially encapsulated in and by the state. This is, in the first instance, why it is pure ideology to see kinship as private and disengaged from other institutions. Encapsulation does not entail "a separate and subordinate domain" (McKinnon and Cannell n.d.:2). Kinship is not separate, because it is embedded in the fundamental actions of the state, and it is not subordinate, because it is part and parcel of what the state is and means. The state is constituted in and through such acts as making citizens, providing birth and death certificates, registering property, taxing households, and, more generally, producing and authorizing the means by which people are related to one another as parents, offspring, spouses, siblings, and the like (in addition to regulating such relations). Insofar as we can distinguish the modern state from other political systems, it is evident that the state has appropriated functions with respect to kinship that were otherwise within the domain of what we can broadly call religion or tradition.[24] Conversely, then, the political debates around secularism very much concern the struggle for control over the articulation and legitimation of kinship.

When a birth register is signed, is this a matter of "kinship" or "the state"? It would be a category error to select only one or the other as if these were discrete phenomena, separate domains. To think of them as distinct, as if kinship were ever independent of state or society, is to start with a Malinowskian, atomistic, rather than a Morganic, holistic, conception of kinship—that is, to start with the biological family rather than the collective. It is this ideology that has been so prominent.

Nevertheless, ideology has effects. One shift I have observed in Mayotte is from kinship conceived as an open web—descent creeping, as someone once said to me, like a squash vine (*razaña mandady kara antsirebiky*)—to kinship conceived as bounded units. These are, of course, ideal types, and this is, of course, both a matter of relative weight and a discontinuous and incomplete process. But fixed, bounded units are much better for accounting purposes, fitting into the state bureaucracy, the legal system, and the policing, medicalizing, and sanitizing gaze. They also fit much better as owners of property, where land and other material goods are registered under specific names. Thus, in Mayotte there has been a shift from collective, open-ended estates (*shirika*), shared on the basis of bilateral kinship, to the legal inscription of private ownership under individual names, with bureaucratic registration and formal means of transmission. Kinship's salience partially shifts from networks of siblings and cousins to atomistic enclosures, from what underpins the social world to what divides it into competing units. With Mayotte's integration into the French state, this has occurred step-by-step: the surveying and registration of land, the introduction of title deeds under individual names, citizenship papers, birth and marriage certificates, the introduction of patrilineally reproducible family names for passports, personalized bank accounts in which salaries and benefit checks are deposited, and the like. Relations of contract between possessive individuals are the result. But, at the same time, ritual enactments of kinship—including ever-larger ceremonies of marriage and commemoration—and the ethical states of relationship they acknowledge and bring into being are flourishing.

Acknowledgments

This chapter, once longer by a third, has benefited from extremely helpful suggestions from Jackie Solway while in the making and from remarkably comprehensive and perspicacious comments from Fenella Cannell, Susan McKinnon, and Danilyn Rutherford on the first draft, as well as extensive discussion with other seminar participants. I have not been able to do justice to their attempts to curtail the unruliness and idealist tendencies or sharpen the analysis. I am also indebted to the Social Sciences and Humanities Research Council of Canada and the Canada Research Chairs program.

Notes

1. Hence, I do not consider modernity with respect to its geographic scope, singularity or multiplicity, historical phases, representational versus indexical nature, or the centrality of either capitalism or science.

2. I borrow the concept from Handler (1988:189–190) on the nation; see also Lambek 2003:210 on memory.

3. The parallel with the psychoanalytic mother is not accidental.

4. Compare the distinction between social organization and social structure (Firth 1963). I do not pursue here the question of the relations of the terms "family" and "kinship" in domaining practices, either with respect to modernity or with respect to disciplinary distinctions between anthropology and sociology.

5. See chapter 8 in this volume by Gillian Feeley-Harnik on the rise of family genealogies and work by Adam Kuper (2009) and Susan McKinnon (n.d.; chapter 2, this volume) on cousin marriage in the United Kingdom and United States, respectively.

6. After a long campaign and much social transformation, Mayotte is becoming a full *département* of France, in which polygyny is forbidden.

7. But see the interesting analysis by Andrea Muehlebach (2011) concerning the role of the neoliberal state in inciting certain ideals of citizenship as kinship (or kinship as citizenship) in voluntary acts of care.

8. Compare Foucault 1985 on the modes and means of the constitution of ethical subjects.

9. I am guided here also by an early essay of Clifford Geertz (1973a) in which he argues that, with respect to human culture, it is a category error to try to distinguish the universal from the particular (nature from culture) as distinct objects. This lesson is exceedingly difficult to follow, and I will probably fail to do so, but it is something to keep in mind. It is evident that there is something simultaneously, deeply universal about human kinship and intrinsically particular about any given cultural manifestation.

10. For further elaboration, see Lambek 2010a, 2010c.

11. I refer to classical mortuary pillars found in the Archaeological Museum in Athens on which the living are pictured clasping hands with deceased parents, children, or spouses.

12. Elsewhere, I discuss Isaac's blessing in Genesis of his son Jacob, an act of kinship that transpires in later life and moreover reverses the ostensibly natural hierarchy of seniority indexed by sibling birth order, showing that human "acts" trump natural "facts" (Lambek 2011). This text also illustrates how a focus on acts of kinship can lead to a historical account of the unfolding of specific families.

13. Interestingly, whereas the French state began by interfering in the first acts of the life cycle, in Mayotte, subsequent acts hold more saliency. A history of kinship in Mayotte would emphasize how the components of marriage and circumcision rituals have been disaggregated and recombined. The most important and the least changed ritual is undoubtedly burial. This has a logic unfolding from Islam but is also true to the pre-Islamic Malagasy background, in which burial is the most important act in the production of kinship. As numerous studies from Madagascar have shown (Astuti 1995; Bloch 1971; Middleton 1999), it is in burial that the multiple identities and relationships one has maintained or juggled in life are resolved. One comes, finally, to belong to the kin group in whose tomb or burial ground enclosure one is interred. The salience is evident in a twenty-first-century dispute over royal succession in Mahajanga. To simplify a long, complex story (Lambek 2010b), the son of the preceding king was declared ineligible to rule when the king was buried with his commoner father rather than his royal mother. This broke the continuity of the descent line (royal status having precedence over unilineality). Acts at death rather than at birth declare who you fundamentally are and therefore who your offspring are and what you can or cannot pass on to them.

14. Compare contemporary Vietnam, where people "have been torn between the familial obligation to attend to the memory of the war dead related in kinship and the political obligation not to do so for those who fought against the revolutionary state" (Kwon 2010:410).

15. See Feuchtwang, who suggests that state and family law "inhabit different temporalities and set different standards." However, he continues, "yhey are incommensurate, but they co-exist, neither can replace the other, but each inflects the other" (2011:212).

16. Until 2000, marriage notices had to be publicly posted. According to the signboard, this was replaced by classes in which prospective brides and grooms are "invited to participate in a preparatory phase."

17. Moreover, many church weddings in Geneva are now described as "ecumenical," including the participation of officiants from more than one religion, most frequently, a Roman Catholic priest with a Protestant pastor.

18. For an anthropological discussion of this history in England, see Wolfram 1987.

19. These might be seen as distinct modalities of Schneider's (1968) "code." Of course, religion can have laws and bureaucracy of its own, just as states can appropriate rituals or develop civil religion. The distinction between state and religion is not absolute and is often contested. The ways in which secular-nonsecular distinctions have been constituted were the subject of a conference organized by Trevor Stack and Tim Fitzgerald at the British Academy in January 2010.

20. In ritual, Rappaport argues, the existence, realization, acceptance, and morality of conventions are joined indissolubly. He contrasts this with the "principles, rules, procedures or understandings established by proclamation, or legislation on the one hand or by daily practice on the other" (1999:137).

21. Compare Marcel Mauss's (1985[1938]) distinction between the jural and the dramatistic as sources of the person. These could also be seen as poles of an ongoing dialectical relationship between objectification and embodiment.

22. I realize that I have been conflating "law" and "bureaucracy"; the point here is merely their connection and their differentiation from ritual order. I have ignored both the different modes and manifestations of law and the complex questions concerning the nature of law in nonstate societies and outside the Western tradition. For a comparative analysis of names and naming, see Bruck and Bodenhorn 2006.

23. Consider villagers in Mayotte observing the placement of the infant on the mosque porch. An anecdote from Sudan (Boddy, personal communication 2012) makes the converse point: collateral kin who had not witnessed the bureaucratic transaction were able to challenge an adoption.

24. Consider also the meaning of "the nation" for the state (Handler 1988).

11

Kinship and Catastrophe

Global Warming and the Rhetoric of Descent

Danilyn Rutherford

> The future whispers while the present shouts. Somehow we have convinced ourselves that we care far less about what happens to our children than about avoiding the inconvenience and discomfort of paying our own bills.
>
> —Al Gore, *Earth in the Balance*

This chapter takes a cliché seriously. In the contemporary United States, as elsewhere, the exhortation to think of future generations is a mainstay of political rhetoric, not to mention camp humor: "What about the children?" the comedians and politicians ask. In times of crisis, "our children" figure both as the beneficiaries of today's wise policy decisions and as the judges who will condemn "us" for our faulty ones. So familiar, so trite, so ubiquitous on the left and right—and yet this way of speaking about the future raises a question. What imperatives are mobilized when public figures trot out "our children" in an effort to turn up the volume on the future, to shape our present choices by making the future shout?

Al Gore wrote the lines of this epigraph in *Earth in the Balance,* his 1992 foray into popular writing on climate change and other environmental threats. In this Nobel Prize–winning work on global warming, Gore reminds us that our "choice" of responses to environmental problems will "bind not only ourselves, but our grandchildren and their grandchildren, as well" (1992:92). In the following pages, I focus less on how choices bind descendants than on how descendants bind choices, especially in the face of impending doom. I investigate the workings of a modern rhetoric of descent: a way of talking and writing designed to persuade readers and listeners to follow a particular course of action by locating them in an emerging genealogy. I focus on the use of this rhetoric in two twenty-first-century treatments of global catastrophe: *The Stern Review on the Economics of Climate Change* (Stern 2006) and Cormac McCarthy's post-apocalyptic novel, *The Road* (2006), both of which I consider in the company of Gore's environmental writings. My analysis draws on an eclectic set of sources, from eighteenth-century philosophy to anthropological treatments of what Hildred Geertz and Clifford Geertz (1964:105) described as "downward looking" descent. The rhetoric of descent elicits an intergenerational form of what David Hume (1896) called "sympathy": the bringing of another's passions and perspectives into intimate proximity with one's own. It works to foreground what anthropologist Rupert Stasch has referred to as "the cultural fact of intertemporality": "difference of time and connection across times" (2009:141). This rhetoric puts a pleat in history, creating a shortcut between now and then. Those who feel the force of this rhetoric choose the future, as it were: what is to come seems close at hand. As a result, the rhetoric of descent has a role to play in modern policymaking and fiction that address the prospect of catastrophic change.

When economists, politicians, and fiction writers deploy the rhetoric of descent, they are not simply repeating well-worn phrases. This way of talking about relationships raises profound questions about the extent of people's responsibilities, given the fact of their mortality—questions of the sort that activists like Gore have posed in raising the alarm about the crises that future generations will face. In investigating this bond between kinship and catastrophe, I hope to further our understanding of the prominence of the nuclear family in US political discourse (see Berlant 1998; Masco 2008, 2009). Lee Edelman's scathing polemic, *No Future: Queer Theory and the Death Drive* (2004), takes a close look at the conceit that our children are our future. According to Edelman, by providing an alibi for attacks on sexual minorities and by encouraging gay men and lesbians to embrace mainstream models of family life, this conceit distracts our attention from present-day sufferings and pleasures and compels Americans to sacrifice for a future that might never arrive. Like Edelman, I am interested in the temporality of this rhetoric: the ways it gives shape to the lived experience of duration and transience that David Couzens Hoy (2009) calls "the time of our lives." But in the cases that I consider, the rhetoric of descent does not foster a sense of continuity but rather a sense of potential rupture. One of my aims is to account for why this rhetoric proves so powerful at moments when time seems out of joint.

Bringing David Hume's concept of sympathy into dialogue with writings on kinship, I show how difference infects the rhetoric of descent—and, indeed, people's very experience of time—especially when catastrophe seems near at hand. At such times, the rhetoric of descent interrupts the homogeneous, empty time associated with modernity and the modern nation (Anderson 1991[1983]:24; Benjamin 1968:263). It encourages its modern addressees to "engage with the noncontemporaneity of actors who are in other ways mutually contemporary" (Stasch 2009:141) in ways that Rupert Stasch and other anthropologists can help us to understand. In examining how children direct adults' minds to the "past, future, and hypothetical times" (ibid.), even as they stand with them in the present, I follow Stasch's ethnography of the Korowai of West Papua, offering a semiotic reading of this rhetoric, one that approaches lived temporality as dependent on both signs and bodies—signs that are material objects and bodies that are signs. This approach helps us grapple with the deeper imperatives tapped into by the rhetoric of descent. These jut prominently to the fore in Cormac McCarthy's bestselling novel *The Road*, which both exemplifies and dismantles the conceit that our children are our future. In the dying world depicted by McCarthy, it is not merely the rhetoric of descent but also the force of signification that makes the past and future whisper and shout. Not only children but also tools, commodities, landscapes, and the ashen husks of living things elicit awareness of what Stasch calls the "otherness" of time.

Stasch describes people who have a highly elaborated sense of time's passage and the transience of social bonds. Stern, Gore, and McCarthy conjure situations that bring this aspect of lived temporality to the fore. Yet, in focusing on the future, their treatments of global crisis fail to capture the range of ways in which people experience the relationship between kinship and catastrophe, including the disasters that many are living through right now. In the conclusion, I return to this question of what the rhetoric of descent excludes and obscures. To get started, I consider some writings on global warming that insert the rhetoric of descent into the politically powerful policy discourse of environmental economics, whose models depend on certain presumptions about the nature of compelling times and choosing subjects.

ETHICS AND ARTIFICE IN THE DEBATE OVER GLOBAL WARMING

On October 30, 2006, the British economist Nicholas Stern unleashed a salvo in the debate over what to do about global warming. The chancellor of the exchequer, Gordon Brown, had asked Stern for a survey of the scholarly literature on the economics of climate change, and Stern produced a report that challenged previous studies of the costs and benefits of mitigating climate change by mathematically modeling the relationship between global warming and gross domestic product (GDP).[1] *The Stern Review* (2006), as the bulky document was dubbed, established that the damage done by unchecked climate change over the long run would far outweigh the cost of slowing its advance now; in essence, he demonstrated that what was good for the planet was good for the pocketbook. As Stern's supporters and critics were quick to point out, the secret to this encouraging outcome lay in Stern's adjustments to something that economists call "discounting," an analytic tool that boils down to a simple adage: for most people, to one degree or another, a bird in the hand is worth more than two in the bush.

Discounting enables economists to calculate the relative value of things depending on how long consumers must wait to enjoy them. In estimating the benefits of mitigating climate change, Stern used a discount rate that assigned a higher worth to birds in bushes—that is, benefits to be received in the future—than the discount rates used by other economists would. Rather than try to quantify people's "impatience" and fear of death, theft, and loss, Stern (2006:45) derived the number he used from the projected growth in consumption and the probability that the world will end—the probability, that is, that there will be no one around to enjoy anything at a particular date. But when it came to estimating the cost of mitigating global warming, Stern followed convention and used a discount rate that assigned a low worth to future expenses. Stern's critics called foul. By overvaluing future benefits and undervaluing future costs, Stern had cheated in order to make preventing climate change seem like a good deal (Mendelsohn 2006–2007).

The argument between Stern and his critics might seem at first glance to have been a matter of technicalities. And yet, serious moral issues were at stake. Drawing a distinction between "descriptive" and "prescriptive" approaches to economic modeling, Stern defended his approach to discounting by declaring that it would have been "unethical"—in his view, a violation of individuals' rights—to discount benefits at a higher rate, which would have involved "discrimination between individuals by date of birth" (Yale Symposium 2007:9). But Stern did not simply refer to "individuals"; he also wrote of "the welfare of future generations" as a factor that should shape policy decisions today. So did his critics. Robert O. Mendelsohn (2006–2007:42–43), for example, argued that using low discount rates would lead to bad (read "anti–free market") policy decisions that would leave no generation unscathed. To think of future generations is not the same as to think of one's relationship with one's own children (Cole 2007, 2009:14–17). Stern and his opponents were not speaking in relational terms: they sorted individuals by birthday rather than place them in family trees (Yale Symposium 2007:9). Yet, I would argue, Stern's approach to discounting was made compelling by the prevalence of rhetoric that does just this relational work.

The Stern Review invited policymakers and the broader public to sympathize with future generations in the sense that David Hume (1896) gave the term (see also Deleuze 2001[1953]). For Hume, sympathy is an inferential process; it results from the interpretation of another's behavior. Those who sympathize posit an origin for this behavior in a perspective or passion that the force of habit leads them to reproduce in themselves. According to Hume (1896:602), sympathy begins with those most proximate to the individual—his or her immediate family—and then extends outward. Typically, this process entails the interpretation of embodied reactions, but sympathy also results from the reading of signs made available in texts, talk, and institutions. Hume described the "enlivening" of sympathy-at-a-distance as the aim of modern governance, achieved through "artifices" ranging from laws to political speeches to popular writings (491). Hume's account offers us a way to grasp the role of the rhetoric of descent in the turn from the calculation of probabilities to the scenario-based initiatives designed to increase "preparedness" that have characterized twenty-first-century policy in biosecurity, as described by Lakoff and Collier (2008:14). Successive US administrations have managed to spur high investments in the "war on terror" through sympathy-enlivening artifices that enable people to imagine their families being victims of an attack. When Stern appeals to the "welfare of future generations," he can count on the help of other artifices, such as Al Gore's well-publicized books, films, and lectures, that conjure scenarios linking our children's fate to the fate of the world.

The rhetoric of descent appears in a disguised form in *The Stern Review*, but it is ever present in Gore's work on climate change. A quick look at the first few pages of Gore's glossy companion volume to *An Inconvenient Truth* reveals this rhetoric in action. The cover folds out to a picture of Gore on a blackened stage and, behind him, an image of the earth as seen from space. We turn past the title page to find a two-page photograph of the Caney Fork River in Carthage, Tennessee, in 2006, resplendent in green. The book's dedication reads, "For my beloved wife and partner, Tipper, who has been with me for the entire journey" (Gore 2006:7). The dedication is illustrated with a 1973 photograph of the same Caney Fork River, this time showing Gore and his wife in a canoe—Al smiling and paddling, Tipper cradling her pregnant belly—"one month before the birth of their first child" (6). Moving from the earth to a river that flows through the years and generations, the opening pages bring together the time of the planet, the time of a place, and the time of a family, whose "journey" is documented in the book. These opening pages telegraph the film's goal: to change how people think about the environment by changing how they situate themselves in time.

In *Earth in the Balance* (1992:238), which set the tone for Gore's later work, the rhetoric of descent is an equally important resource. A close look at the book reveals the rhetoric of descent functioning in four different guises. The first is the conventional one I have already flagged: kinship appears in the form of ties that extend downward through the generations. "Too often we are unwilling to look beyond ourselves to see the effects of our actions today on our children and grandchildren" (2) is Gore's repeated refrain. In the second guise, Gore deploys the rhetoric of descent to evoke connections that extend horizontally. One example appears in the foreword to the paperback version of *Earth in the Balance.* Gore describes the participants in the Rio Summit as seeming "to share…a recognition that we are all part of something much larger than ourselves, a family related only distantly by blood but intimately by commitment to each other's common future and to the global environment of which we are all a part" (1993:xiii).

In the third and most idiosyncratic guise, Gore uses the rhetoric of descent as the source of some minutely detailed and often far-fetched analogies that he almost compulsively draws to build his case. Although Gore's passion for comparison sends him in many different directions—good public policy resembles a fuel-efficient vehicle (1992:326), the media industry is like a coal company, "strip-mining" our interests and desires (241)—Gore's most extended trope comes from the field of family therapy. Our civilization is a dysfunctional family, ruled over by a domineering father—science and the Cartesian worldview—whose unquestioned rule has forced people to sever their emotional ties to the natural world. Those who suffer the greatest harm are the family's most vulnerable members: "the wetlands, the rainforests, the oceans," indigenous people, the poor, "those who cannot speak for themselves," "those who will come after us" (235). The future itself belongs to this category: "In philosophical terms, the future is, after all, a vulnerable and developing present [a child, as it were], and unsustainable development is therefore what might be called a form of 'future abuse'" (ibid.).

Gore's most striking deployment of the rhetoric of descent occurs when he is writing in confessional mode. "Some experiences are so intense, while they are happening, that time seems to stop altogether," Gore (2006:8), notes in the first words of the companion volume to *An Inconvenient Truth.* Gore goes on to describe an episode recounted in the first chapter of *Earth in the Balance*, in which he explains why he wrote the book: a "single horrifying event [that] triggered a big change in the way I thought about my relationship to life itself" (1992:13). In April 1989, Al and Tipper's son, Albert Gore III, who was then six, suffered severe injuries when a car struck him outside a baseball stadium. Months of hospitalization followed, and it was not clear whether the boy would survive. Gore's depiction of the accident is a vivid illustration of how *Earth in the Balance* acts as what Hume would call a sympathy-enlivening artifice. Gore's account of the trauma invites sympathy: the passage, ideally, infects readers with Gore's commitment to do something about the environment. The sympathetic reader's mind turns to his or her own children; in a typical response to trauma, he or she resolves to forestall risk. It matters that this story concerns a father and a son. It also matters that it concerns a brush with death. Mobilizing proximity in gender and relatedness in the face of mortality, the conceit compels listeners to leap through time.

Make no mistake: Gore is writing as an American politician, and American politicians understand the power of kinship talk. And yet, in Gore's writings, as in *The Stern Review*, the rhetoric of descent calls to mind rupture, not continuity, as Edelman and other critics of this tendency would lead us to expect. Gore's near loss of his son leads him to realize that there could be no future, that the future could fall prey to future abuse, could never get to mature into its potential. Hume's account of sympathy gives us a sense of how Gore's strategy works. But there is more to say about how the rhetoric of descent makes the future shout. To illuminate what, besides the family's nearness, is involved, I now turn to the anthropological literature on future-oriented forms of kinship. I focus, in particular, on Rupert Stasch's analysis of the meaning and value of children among the Korowai of West Papua, where the transience and vulnerability of social relationships is a fact of everyday life.

DOWNWARD-LOOKING DESCENT AND THE OTHERNESS OF TIME

The anthropological literature on kinship suggests that the sense of temporality embedded in the conceit that children are our future is neither as straightforward nor as universally held as one might expect. Only certain kinship systems are "downward looking," to borrow Hildred and Clifford Geertz's (1964:105) term: focused less on a determining past than on an open-ended future. In certain situations, a future-oriented approach to relationships makes particular sense.

The Geertzes' analysis of teknonymy among Balinese commoners in the 1950s describes one such situation. Teknonymy is the practice of referring to adults by one of their children's names—calling a man "Ralph's father" or a woman "Veronica's mother," for example. For Balinese commoners, teknonymy served as a strategy for maintaining "elasticity" in the reckoning of common descent (Geertz and Geertz 1964:94; see also Carsten 1995a:325). Referring to adults by their descendants' names leads a "curtain of genealogical amnesia" to "steadily descend over each generation in turn" (Geertz and Geertz 1964:94). Commoners stop using an individual's personal names as soon as he or she reaches adulthood and becomes known as the "father or mother of X" or the "father or mother of Y." Members of the Balinese gentry, by contrast, do use personal names, a practice that the Geertzes associate with their "more strongly corporate, larger, more enduring" kin groups, which "are buttressed by lengthy genealogical traditions" (ibid.). The Geertzes do not, however, imply that commoners do not participate in "corporate groups." Rather, commoners have many to choose from, and "genealogical amnesia" enables them to divide their allegiances when the occasion and need arise. This tendency expresses itself not simply in everyday social life but also in ritual. One effect of this downward-looking logic is to equate great-grandparents and great-grandchildren: the very old and the very young appear as near to the world of the gods (102).

Whereas the Geertzes focus on sociological differences, Janet Carsten's account of kinship practices among Malay fishing villagers provides a historical context for downward-looking descent. Southeast Asia's long "history of maritime trade and the movement of people" and the "stress on siblingship rather than filiation" that arose in these conditions have led kinship in Langkawi, Carsten's field site, to "focus on the future rather than on the past" (Carsten 1995a:325, 326). My writings on Biak, a coastal group in the troubled Indonesian territory of West Papua, show how kinship practices oriented to the future can provide a means of domesticating foreign influences, including, in the case of Biak, an intrusive Indonesian state (Rutherford 1998, 2003). Biak brothers and sisters love each other, but they must lose each other to marriage. And yet, throughout their adult lives, these divided siblings engage in exchanges that anticipate the day when their descendants will marry and have children who will reproduce the original cross-sex pair. This longing drives brothers to attempt to succeed in the Indonesian bureaucracy, but only as a means of serving familial ends. Moving from regional history to biography, Rita Astuti (2000) shows that people's perspectives shift over the life course, through her analysis of the changing viewpoints of Dadilahy, an elderly Vezo man from the area in Madagascar where she did fieldwork. It was only in old age that Dadilahy "no longer looked at the vast but flat expanse of relations centered on him" and began to view himself as the "genealogical source" of what Astuti calls a "kindred": a broad network of descendants below him (2000:101). As Astuti makes clear, what we could call Dadilahy's sympathy for those relatives who might survive his death represents one of a range of possible ways in which Vezo create an orientation to lived time through their attachments to kin.

These different examples of where downward-looking descent comes from and what it does provide a comparative perspective on the rhetoric used by Stern and Gore. Looking downward enables people to expand their networks, since descendants generally tend to outnumber antecedents. This effect suits the purposes of environmentalists, who are eager to encourage people to care more deeply about more people and things. Equally important, the anthropological literature suggests that certain conditions in the life of an individual or a society will make people more likely to feel the pull of relationships that project them forward in time. The specter of death or environmental catastrophe can have this effect—"the prospect of hanging in a fortnight serves to concentrate the mind wonderfully," as Gore (1992:9), quoting Samuel Johnson, points out—and it often serves to concentrate the mind on future kin. But in addition to the effects of the rhetoric of descent, the anthropological literature sheds light on its mechanics. Rupert Stasch's ethnography of the Korowai helps us grasp the practices of sign use and interpretation that turn children into a sign of what is to come.

When Stasch asked Korowai men and women why they had children—not as silly a question as one might think—the following answer was typical: "A guy lives, has children and dies. They stay, have children, and die. The children that initially grow and live, these people don't live, they die" (2009:140). Children stand for and against both "generational succession" and "human transience"—for and against both life and death. The child who "initially grows and lives" is destined to die—and, in dealing with this growing and living child, one cannot help but anticipate this deathly horizon. "Relations to children are made of temporal otherness," Stasch (141) remarks. He then elaborates: "In Korowai social relations, a time is not a self-standing element that precedes its engagement with other times, but is made out of its relations with times external to it. Different people have disparate memories and futures, and this otherness of time is central to people's mutual attachments" (142).

A range of historical and social factors may well be responsible for the heightened sensitivity of Korowai to this temporal Otherness and the fragility of human relationships more generally. Stasch writes of people who live, quite literally, in the middle of West Papua's lowland forests: much to the delight of the adventure tourists who visit them, the Korowai build their houses in trees. The population is dispersed across the landscape in shifting domestic groups. The events that create relationships—with spouses, Indonesian soldiers, German tourists, and local guests—initiate a process that turns an experience that is unexpected or disturbing into the basis of a social bond. Korowai know that this process can be problematic: the prevalence of witchcraft, witch killings, and other acts of violence among previous generations prevented many Korowai men from reaching old age. The tension between intimacy and estrangement that pervades all social relationships becomes especially evident when it comes to relationships with children. Korowai love their children: their antics, their emerging skills, their weight on one's lap. But, historically, rates of infanticide have been remarkably high. Korowai call newborns "demons," using a term that also designates both foreigners and malignant corpse-like monsters who come back to kill their relatives. Women deliver babies on the ground in holes filled with leaves. In the past, until the birth occurred, no one knew whether the infant would be kept or killed. A mother's initial reaction to her newborn was often revulsion. She became attached to her baby only when she and others at the birth scene imagined the future that they and the newborn might someday share.

Stasch's discussion offers fodder for a rich account of the temporal orientations involved in the debate over discounting and environmentalism more generally. The choices made at the birth scene juxtaposed short-term urges against long-term considerations. Different times came together in people's imaginations as they decided whether to keep a baby. The person who cut the baby's umbilical cord and carried it into the house was sometimes a parent but often a more distant relative. The considerations that led someone to pick up the child—or leave it behind—all resulted from an anticipation of the future. A father's sister mused upon the fish that the child might someday catch for her. A mother imagined that the child might replace her by surviving her death or slowly kill her by increasing her toils. One argument in favor of infanticide focused on the state of the world. "A view that the world is turning 'bad' (*lembul*) could be expressed by denying the desirability of raising a child at all" (Stasch 2009:155). Countering this view was the argument that, by having children, one could make the world "good." The Korowai homeland is filled with "extinction territories"—sites where houses stand abandoned or have vanished altogether, with the forest taking over the sago groves on which most Korowai depend for food. "If people die without children," the Korowai say, "the land will disappear" (144).

Like Stern's "future generations," Korowai children invite those who engage with them to stand in the shoes of a future Other. They do this effectively because relations with children foreground a form of sympathy—the reciprocal exchange of passions and perspectives on which all Korowai social bonds rest—and extend it forward in time. On the one hand, children signify change: "Children *are* their potential for future abilities and actions" (Stasch 2009:143). On the other hand, children signify continuity: they appear to parents as their "body doubles," a way of thinking that makes relations between a child and its same-sex parent—say, a father and son—a source of particular delight. But children not only replace parents (and keep the forest at bay) but also remind others of what their parents did. Korowai take a strongly epistemological interest in birth and death; they want to know who and what is responsible for these events. Children, like dead bodies, are evidence of someone else's actions, living proof of others' acts of care (147). Children elicit anticipated retrospection; they are contemporaries that conjure a hypothetical future in which noncontemporaries will recognize them as traces of what once was (see Derrida 1995; Hoy 2009). If children are also valued for their companionship—"a child is for going around together," the Korowai say—then the "human transience" they call to mind may heighten the pleasure of such moments (Stasch 2009:143–144). The Korowai may well "weep for having," as Adela Pinch (1998:134), quoting Wordsworth, has put it—experiencing their children's co-presence as doubly precious precisely because they know that it is not going to last.

Stasch offers us powerful tools for dissecting the rhetoric of descent along the lines suggested by Hume's (1896) account of sympathy as an inferential process, that is, one requiring the positing of an affective cause behind a behavioral cue. "Kinship attachment is for Korowai a discipline of signification and sign-interpretation," "an indigenous semiotics," as Stasch (2009:142) puts it. He has access to this semiotics by virtue of his own semiotics, drawn from the work of Charles Sanders Peirce (1991), whose work foregrounds the interpretation of relationships of contiguity and causality. A sign, for Peirce, is an object that stands for another object to a mind (see also Keane 1997; Parmentier 1994). For Peirce, signs stand for objects in three possible ways: by virtue of the perceived similarity of the two objects (the sign as icon), by virtue of the perceived contiguity or causal relationship between the two objects (the sign as index), or by virtue of a convention linking the two objects (the sign as symbol). In all three cases, these perceptions become possible only because of a sign's embeddedness in a history of interpretation—and this embeddedness itself depends on the sign's status as a material object. For Peirce, interpretation itself is an event; it produces a sign whose object is the relationship between two objects. By breaking down rather than taking for granted Korowai understandings of kinship, Stasch opens his readers' eyes to broad networks of intertemporal, intersubjective, and, indeed, causal relationships grounded in a world of things that is also a world of signs.

The forests of West Papua may seem far from the settings that gave rise to *The Stern Review* and Gore's prolific writings. Yet, in all these settings, engagements with the noncontemporaneity of contemporaries both stem from and bring into focus questions about times to come. Stasch helps us understand why the rhetoric of descent proves so compelling in times of crisis. In the spirit of Hume, he does so by revealing the semiotic forces at work in this way of extending sympathy over time. In the next section of this chapter, I return to the English-language world and another, rather different kind of "artifice." Cormac McCarthy's story of a father and son at the end of time does much to affirm mainstream visions of the family, not to mention American-style masculinity. Along the way, *The Road* indicates the limits of the rhetoric of descent by setting it within a wider world of dying signs.

A FATHER, A SON, AND OTHER SIGNS

The Road was, in many respects, an unlikely bestseller. In March 2007, when the Oprah Book Club endorsed the Pulitzer Prize–winning book, its seventy-three-year-old author scarcely seemed suited for popularity.[2] Cormac McCarthy wrote in the Southern Gothic tradition before turning to the American West, where he set novels such as *Blood Meridian* (1985), which many critics consider his finest work, and *No Country for Old Men* (2005), which became an Oscar-winning movie. McCarthy's novels have never made for easy reading, treating such topics as incest, infanticide, necrophilia, scalp hunting, and serial killing, all rendered in excruciatingly vivid, hauntingly beautiful prose (see, for instance, McCarthy 1968, 1973, 1985, 2005).

Yet, *The Road* found an enthusiastic audience. In the *Guardian*, British environmental journalist George Monbiot named McCarthy (along with Al Gore) as one of "fifty people who could save the planet" (*Guardian* 2008). *The Road* "could be the most important environmental book ever," Monbiot noted, echoing an earlier promise to readers "[This novel will] change the way you see the world" (*Guardian* 2008; Monbiot 2007). In a 2009 interview in the *Wall Street Journal*, McCarthy reflected on the novel's popularity. Asked how fathers had reacted to his book, McCarthy described getting "the same letter from six different people" in different parts of the world. They all said the same thing: "I started reading your book after dinner and I finished it 3:45 the next morning, and I got up and went upstairs and I got my kids up and I just sat there in the bed and held them" (Caesar 2010; Jurgenson 2009). The depiction of a father and son's journeys through a devastated landscape clearly enlivened sympathy, and the novel sold more than a million copies in the United States alone.

Literary critics have made much of McCarthy's debt to Faulkner, Melville, and other American authors; McCarthy himself has referred to the "ugly fact that books are made of other books" (Woodward 1992). But McCarthy's relationship with his son, to whom he dedicated the novel, and his discussions with scientists also left their mark on *The Road*, as interviews with McCarthy suggest. The impetus for *The Road* "came a few years [before] when he was in a hotel room in El Paso, Texas, with his young son who was asleep. In the middle of the night he stared out the window wondering what the city might look like in 50 or 100 years" (Conlon 2007). Although McCarthy was thinking of his son, the future that came to mind stemmed, in part, from conversations with McCarthy's brother, a biologist and lawyer, about "hideous end-of-the-world scenarios" (Jurgenson 2009). This future also stemmed from McCarthy's experience as a fellow at the Santa Fe Institute, where his colleagues included physicists, biologists, and anthropologists.[3] McCarthy deliberately left the cause of the catastrophe in the book vague—it could be a meteor or a nuclear war. *The Road* belongs to the environmental literature not because it was intended to depict the outcome of global warming but because it delves into the experience of nature's loss. Much like the computerized creation of "life" pioneered by other Santa Fe Institute fellows (Helmreich 2000), the novel is a thought experiment—a "hideous" exercise in imagining a scenario—that subjects existing forms to extreme conditions. *The Road* examines the workings of the rhetoric of descent in a world with a high probability of ending. What choices and imperatives would remain for a father whose son signifies the future at a time when time is running out?

Not many choices, but the imperatives would be strong. The book follows the father and son—known simply as the man and the boy—in the eastern United States as they travel south across the Appalachians to the sea in search of warmer weather. At 1:17 a.m. some ten years earlier, there was a bright flash in the sky, the lights went out, and the world the man had known fell apart. In the flashbacks that punctuate the tale of travel, the man recalls the catastrophe's immediate aftermath, along with scenes of happiness from his life before. Looming large in the man's memory is his son's birth shortly after the fateful day. The man is keenly aware that his son has no memory of the world as it once was—no past, as it were—and that he is not likely to have much of a future. The book is filled with wrenching decisions—what to eat, where to go, what to take along, who to trust—but, above all, whether to go on living.

McCarthy's unblinking look at the relationship between kinship and catastrophe reveals the force of the rhetoric of descent even with the erasure of modern domains. The world, as depicted in the novel, has become deeply inhospitable. There are no states—just state roads—and no modern social identities. "Are you a doctor?" the man is asked. "I'm nothing," he replies. "The last instance of a thing takes the class with it," the narrator observes, "turns out the light and is gone" (McCarthy 2006:28). The named social groups in the novel are mostly scary ones: the "blood cults" and gangs of "road agents" who make up the category of "bad guys" whom the father opposes to the "good guys," those who "carry the fire." The natural world is even more impoverished. Nothing lives except humans and an insect or two: no crops, no trees, no mammals, no fish, no birds. The man and the boy step into fields of ferns; the plants crumble into ash. The book is filled with reminders of the world that once existed, reminders of everything that is vanishing or already gone.

All that is left to sustain life is the dwindling detritus of a vanished consumer economy: shopping carts for transport, discarded motor oil for fueling "slutlamps," a can of Coke stuck in the back of a vending machine, old cans and jars of food. To recall my discussion of discount rates, there are few birds in this bush. The man and the boy dress in piles of blankets and wrap plastic over their shoes, burning dead trees for warmth as the climate grows cooler and the rain turns to gray snow. Merely surviving is hard enough without the threat posed by the bad guys, who at first seem to have sacrificed humans for ritual purposes but who now kill for food. The man and the boy barely escape after finding a cellar filled with half-dead captives, who are being eaten limb by limb. In a particularly horrific scene, the man and boy stumble upon the carcass of a newborn infant, evidence that some of the bad guys are reproducing for food.

In this dismal setting, the bad guys display what the economists would call extremely high time preference—a deep aversion to deferring consumption. Compelled by hunger and desperation, they literally eat their young rather than engage in intertemporal sympathy with the person whom the infant will become. With time running out, cannibalism accompanies the vanishing of social identities: the person—even the descendant—becomes meat. But the fact that the bad guys violate their victims before eating them suggests that their actions are a form of desecration, as well as a way of staying alive.

At the other extreme, the boy's mother takes the opposite tack: having assessed her predicament, she commits suicide. "We're survivors," the man tells her in a flashback set not long before the action that makes up the story. "'Survivors?' she said. 'We're not survivors, we're the walking dead in a horror film.'" The man objects, and the woman continues: "'They are going to rape us and kill us and eat us and you won't face it. You'd rather wait for it to happen. But I can't. I can't'" (McCarthy 2006:57). The boy's mother has run the math and drawn her own conclusions; the "right thing to do" is to kill herself, and ideally, her child as well. Much like that of Judge Holden, the villain of McCarthy's earlier novel *Blood Meridian*, hers is an orderly sensibility. "Always so deliberate, hardly surprised by the most outlandish advents. A creature perfectly evolved to meet its own end" (58).

That leaves the man, who seemingly heeds the woman's parting words: "'The one thing I can tell you is that you wont [*sic*] survive for yourself.... A person who had no one would be well advised to cobble together some passable ghost'" (McCarthy 2006:57). The man lives on fiction, telling his son that they will find warmth and the good guys on the coast. Yet, he retains the option of accepting the woman's version of reality. He has two bullets left in the pistol he is carrying at the start of the book: one for himself and one for his son. The choice the man faces in confronting his own death, which becomes more imminent as the story proceeds, is whether he will kill his son to protect him from a more painful end. Unlike his wife, he is not "deliberate" and is often "surprised"—unsure of whether he can carry through with this plan.

But in addition to the force of the rhetoric of descent, the novel documents the price paid by those who follow its dictates. This choice—to live or to die, to kill or to let survive—also dogs the relationships that the man and boy form with the few other people they encounter in the story. Alongside the pathos of the man's efforts to care for his son, the novel explores a developing moral conflict between the boy and the man. The man trusts no one and is ready to leave others to die if it will serve the purpose of protecting his son. The boy fears that his father and he are no longer the "good guys," given their refusal to help anyone they meet. In the end, the boy is right: he survives by trusting a stranger. Critics have focused on the tender bond between the father and son, who are "each the other's world entire" (McCarthy 2006:6). But equally striking is the novel's ambivalence about the exclusivity of this relationship. In light of the novel's surprisingly happy ending, the woman seems almost satanic in her insistence on "meeting her own end" rather than welcoming what the man calls "luck."

Patriarchal as it seems, McCarthy's account of what compels the man takes us beyond the mysterious forces posited by early scholars of kinship, according to David Schneider (1984). What Schneider calls the "Fundamental Assumption" that "Blood is Thicker than Water" does not hold. "Consanguinity doesn't mean that much," McCarthy has said, claiming that he is close to his son and his brother because they are "[this] kind of guy" (Jurgenson 2009).[4] Recalling Stasch's ethnography, *The Road* celebrates the father-son relationship as a source of pleasurable companionship and the outcome of acts of care (McCarthy 2006:13). *The Road* is filled with descriptions of such acts, with the man fixing a wheel on the shopping cart or fashioning masks to protect their lungs from dust. The novel manages to be moving without being sentimental because we sense the contingency of the man's attachment to the boy, which, as is the case for the Korowai, is haunted by alternatives: choosing death or choosing to eat one's young.

At the same time, appearances notwithstanding, *The Road* is not a celebration of the nuclear family—the "little genealogy" of modern societies that, according to anthropologist Elizabeth Povinelli (2002), displaced the "big genealogy" of the absolutist king. The father-son pair in the novel is not one family unit among others; the boy is, to all appearances, "the last instance of a thing." "'I never thought to see a child again. I didn't know that would happen,'" remarks an old man whom the man feeds at the boy's urging (McCarthy 2006:172). To look downward in this context is not to look outward to an expanded pool of significant others; it is to see the flow of life running dry. The scenario looks more like Povinelli's "premodern" alternative, in which only the king—the Divine King—is one in a line of kin. This element of the novel is in unexpected harmony with the nineteenth-century French historian Numa Denis Fustel de Coulanges's (2006[1874]) account of how descent—and the relations with the dead that it entails—gave the ancient Greeks and Romans their first taste of transcendence. Like the Geertzes' Balinese informants, the characters in *The Road* equate the very old and the very young with gods. Yet, this equation is equivocal; it is as if the end of time and descent suddenly opened a space for a divinity that cannot quite exist. The man's orientation to his son verges—but only verges—on the religious. "He knew only that the child was his warrant. He said: 'If he is not the word of God, God never spoke'" (McCarthy 2006:6). The old man mentioned above says that he thought he had died when he saw the boy. The man replies, "'What if I said that he's a god?'"

Instead, *The Road* moves beyond the mainstream version of the rhetoric of descent by linking relations between parents and children to "the cultural fact of intertemporality" more generally. *The Road* recalls the Korowai litany—"the child has children, dies, the children have children, die"—only with the cycle of regeneration grinding to a halt. The old man plumbs the depths of this rupture: "'When we're gone at last, then there'll be nobody here but death and his days will be numbered, too'" (McCarthy 2006:172–173). The novel links the impending death of nature—and of death itself—with the death of the United States: there are no states, no identities, no groups. In the context of British debates over genetically modified crops, Ben Campbell (2009) has described how the emergence of "fields of post–human kinship" united the English with the winged denizens of the hedgerow. McCarthy's book conjures a keen sense of attachment between a disappearing society and the dying natural environment. "Why all these trees?" one is tempted to ask, just as Campbell asks, "Why all these birds?" Yet, the significance of "all these trees" extends beyond the nation. *The Road* ponders the fate of fatherhood in a setting where one's son has little chance of survival. But the novel is equally concerned with the fate of signs.

Lost pasts and lost futures become compellingly present by virtue of the boy, but other things possess a similar power. The novel presents the experience of living without a future as both excruciating and strangely clarifying. The narrator describes it thus: "No lists of things to be done. The day providential to itself. The hour. There is no later. This is later. All things of grace and beauty such that one holds them to one's heart have a common provenance in pain. Their birth in grief and ashes. So, he whispered to the sleeping boy. I have you" (McCarthy 2006:54). The pain, like the grace and beauty, is that of impending loss, made all the more pressing by the sleeping boy's presence. The boy crystallizes what is strikingly evident not only in the plot but also throughout McCarthy's prose. This fictional world is filled with intimations of the Otherness of time. All the things that make up this dying world are compelling signs of what was and what will be: contemporaneous and noncontemporaneous at once.

The Russian linguist Mikhail Bakhtin's (1981) notion of the "chronotopes" or spatiotemporal horizons elicited by literary works helps us understand this aspect of McCarthy's writing. In analyzing *Blood Meridian*, Dana Phillips (2002) has pointed out that McCarthy's spatiotemporal horizons are often cosmic in scale. What looks like a history of the West in *Blood Meridian* is really "natural history" inscribed in the "optical democracy" of a Western landscape where "all preference is made whimsical and a man and a rock become endowed with unguessed kinships" (McCarthy 1985:247, quoted. in Phillips 2002:29). This reading challenges the premise that McCarthy's novels are symbolic. Rather, to use Peirce's language, they are indexical, filled with objects that point to other objects, to which they bear a relationship of causality and contiguity, brought to the reader's attention by similes that accentuate their vividness.

The same is true of the *The Road*, but here, natural history is ending. The novel stylistically signals the dwindling of time; many paragraphs consist less of sentences than of lists: no movement, just a description of what is. This brings to mind chronotopes of different scales. On the one hand, the cold gray landscape calls to mind the time of the cosmos and "the absolute truth of the world": "The cold relentless circling of the intestate earth. Darkness implacable. The blind dogs of the sun in their running. The crushing black vacuum of the universe" (McCarthy 2006:130). On the other hand, the various objects that remain on earth call for framing within an immediate past or future. The man is constantly reading his surroundings for signs of others' presence and striving to avoid leaving such signs himself. It is a matter of survival, but some of these signs also conjure national and biographical spatiotemporal horizons. The man and the boy experience this empty landscape as filled with ghosts: from the "chattel slaves" who once had walked the floors of old plantations to the friends and families who had lived in the neighborhoods through which they pass. The boy is frightened when the father takes him to the father's childhood home, haunted by a past he never knew. Signs that point to no visible origin are a source of terror for the boy: his worst nightmare is of a toy penguin that moves without anyone winding it up (36).

But at the same time that the novel stresses the capacity of signs to signify, it also suggests that this capacity is slipping away. The things of the world call to mind fading pasts and futures. In doing so, they call to mind vanishing addressees: the other minds for which one object stands for another object, which have their own existence in time. The man and the boy stumble upon a library: "Shelves tipped over. Some rage at the lies arranged in their thousands row on row. He picked up one of the books and thumbed through the heavy bloated pages. He'd not have thought the value of the smallest thing predicated on the world to come. It surprised him. That the space which these things occupied was itself an expectation" (McCarthy 2006:187). With time ending, there soon will be no one to read these books. The loss of the future brings into focus the futurity built into signs—signs including not only children but also texts. As the earth empties of humans, it is becoming difficult to imagine any moment from the vantage point of another—to anticipate retrospection—by perceiving things as they will have been perceived. Earlier, the narrator describes the world "shrinking down about a raw core of parsible entities. The names of things slowly following those things into oblivion. Colors. The names of birds. Things to eat. Finally the names of things one believed to be true" (88–89). The narrator links this "drawing down" of the "sacred idiom shorn of its referents and so of its reality" to the end of descent. "Do you think that your fathers are watching? That they weigh you in their ledgerbook? Against what? There is no book and your fathers are dead in the ground" (196).

The man contradicts himself a few pages later. "'I think maybe they are watching,' he said. 'They are watching for a thing that even death cannot undo and if they do not see it they will turn away from us and they will not come back'" (McCarthy 2006:210). Overall, the novel is as uncertain and ambivalent about the fate of signs and their addressees as the father is about his own fate and that of his child. Uncertainty and ambivalence extend to God's existence, however often he appears as a possible audience for the man and the boy. The old man they meet puts this ambivalence in a nutshell. "'There is no God and we are his prophets,'" he declares (170).

The book's conclusion remains poised between these alternatives of survival and death, marking the stubborn persistence, yet impending demise, of both descent and signs. As the man dies, he tells his son to speak to him everyday—to use him as a "passable ghost." The family that takes in the boy at the end of the book concurs with this request. "The woman would talk to him sometimes about God. He tried to talk to God but the best thing was to talk to his father and he did talk to him and he didn't forget. The woman said that was all right. She said that the breath of God was his breath yet though it pass from man to man through all time" (McCarthy 2006:286). The novel jarringly restores the conventional version of the rhetoric of descent as a new "little genealogy" incorporates the boy. And yet, the cosmic perspective—of an "all time" that extends beyond and excludes human relationships—has the final say. "Once there were brook trout in the streams in the mountains. You could see them standing in the amber current where the white edges of their fins wimpled softly in the flow. They smelled of moss in your hand. Polished and muscular and torsional. On their back were vermiculate patterns that were maps of the world in its becoming. Maps and mazes. Of a thing which could not be put back. Not be made right again. In the deep glens where they lived all things were older than man and they hummed of mystery" (286–287). The maps and mazes point and mislead. They signify the transience of their referents.

Mystery shrouds what is ending with the end of the world, for with the world goes the key to its signs.

The Road illuminates why it has proven so effective to use children and grandchildren as signs that make the future shout. Yet, in doing so, it reveals the power of natural and man-made things and places to extend people's passions and perspectives across time. The rhetoric of descent may seem to speak in the language of the nuclear family. But what looks like kinship in the novel bleeds into the domains of science and theology by way of McCarthy's insights into the life and death of signs.

CONCLUSION: REWRITING THE RHETORIC OF DESCENT

It is not always easy for people to think and care about what will happen when they are gone. But relations with children and other companions who are contemporaneous and noncontemporaneous at once can force people to do just that. We see this happening in *The Road* and among the Korowai, albeit for different reasons, and when politicians and economists contemplate the climate catastrophes to come. By reading very different texts together, I explore how the rhetoric of descent evokes the Otherness of time. I part ways with early scholars of descent, who left us with an image of "primitives," who were forced to submit to kin-based hierarchies, and "moderns," who were free of such constraints (Engels 1972[1884]; Morgan 1877; see also Kuper 1988; Watson 1985). I also part ways with critics of descent theory who have explained away the "mysterious force" associated with what some called the "fact of blood relations" as an artifact of American culture or modernity writ large (Povinelli 2002, 2006; Schneider 1980, 1984). As the ethnographic literature considered here suggests, perspectives sometimes associated with "primitive" descent can lead a secret life in the seemingly most "modern" sectors of social life.

In attending to the cultural fact of intertemporality mobilized by the rhetoric of descent, I also move beyond Edelman's easy dismissal of the conceit that children are our future. To grasp the power of this rhetoric in *The Stern Review* and in environmentalism more generally, we have to grasp the forms of difference and connection from which kinship is made. Once we begin this operation, it becomes difficult to maintain firm boundaries between kinship and other social domains. The kinship literature is filled with portraits of the intertemporal nature of relationships with intimate others, from Gillian Feeley-Harnik's (2001a) discussion of Lewis Henry Morgan's "rivers of blood" connecting humans, animals, landscapes, and spirits, to Fenella Cannell's (2005b:349) account of how Mormon kinship "is also the very nature of God." The Otherness of time that haunts these relationships can point to natural history or a transcendent deity. But not only our relationships with kin possess this capacity; everything we encounter stands both within and beyond our shared time. As McCarthy makes plain, there are "unguessed kinships" that connect rocks and men.

The texts considered here are useful in illuminating this broader sense of the temporality of human experience, which could create the basis for a new, more affirmatively empirical approach to kinship. Descent is, arguably, about the interpretation of evidence. To ask about genealogy is to ask about causes: how did these people get here? Any particular response impoverishes a broader reality. "How did you get to Carnegie Hall?" someone asked a famous musician. "By bus," the joke goes, but the answer could just as easily be "by birth" or "by the big bang" and make just as much or as little sense. This new, more affirmatively empirical approach to kinship could open up new ways of thinking about what the rhetoric of descent excludes. Gore and McCarthy privilege a highly truncated form of filiation: a descent group consisting of a father and a son. The conceit that our children are the future may or may not speak to the childless and to those whose most important companions—contemporaneous and noncontemporaneous at once—may consist of books, artwork, and traditions of practice or homes, landscapes, friends, and pets. But this new approach also alerts us to the temporal dimensions of what is left out of this rhetoric. Worrying about one's children's future on a dying earth is, arguably, the luxury of those who can take for granted their children's welfare today. McCarthy's novel describes the present-tense existence of the urban homeless. It describes the current lot of hunters and gatherers, for whom the loss of biodiversity is an apocalypse that is happening now. Likewise, *The Stern Review*'s treatment of discounting has little room for those who cannot afford to consume much, either now or in the future. However often Gore refers to current suffering, he privileges the disasters yet to come.[5]

To rewrite the rhetoric of descent is to call for a broader vision of ethics and temporality, a broader vision of what we owe not only to the "emancipated heirs" of the future, as Walter Benjamin put it, but also to the "enslaved forebears" of the past. Advocates for environmental justice have argued that any policy designed to mitigate global warming must pay heed to who benefited from industrialization and who paid the price (Been 1992–1993; Bullard 1994; Mobilization for Climate Justice 2009; Pressend 2010). The lines of descent leading to the world's current woes extend from markets to dead trees, from DNA to spoken and written texts, from today's pleasures to yesterday's misdeeds. The "fact of blood relations" has proven compelling in times of catastrophe. But we "moderns" are—and should be—moved by other mysterious forces as well.

Notes

1. A former senior vice president of the World Bank, Stern was then serving as an advisor to the British government.

2. Early on, McCarthy had enjoyed critical acclaim and public recognition, in the form of a MacArthur fellowship and the National Book Award, among other honors. Yet, he had refused to give lectures, pursue academic positions, or grant interviews, living in relative poverty despite his comfortable upbringing as the son of an attorney for the Tennessee Valley Authority. Before the interview that appeared on *The Oprah Winfrey Show* in June 2007, McCarthy had granted only one interview in his entire career (Woodward 1992).

3. McCarthy's colleagues at the Santa Fe Institute provided commentary on the novel (see Erwin 2006; Lansing 2006; Wilkins 2006).

4. McCarthy's orientation to consanguinity is, arguably, reflected in *Blood Meridian*, a novel that depicts the shedding of blood ties to family and origins on the violent American frontier (Parkes 2002).

5. Novels by Jones (1975) and Robinson (2004) offer contrasting accounts of the relationship between children, futurity, and justice. See also Spillers 2003.

References

Abrams, Philip

1972 The Sense of the Past and the Origins of Sociology. Past and Present 55 (May):18–32.

Act for the Abolition of Slavery

1833 An Act for the Abolition of Slavery throughout the British Colonies; for promoting the Industry of the manumitted Slaves; and for compensating the Persons hitherto entitled to the Services of such Slaves. August 28, 1833. 3–4 Wil1.4 c.73.

Adams, Julia

2005 The Familial State: Ruling Families and Merchant Capitalism in Early Modern Europe. Ithaca, NY: Cornell University Press.

Adams, Julia, Elisabeth S. Clemens, and Ann Shola Orloff

2005 Introduction: Social Theory, Modernity, and the Three Waves of Historical Sociology. *In* Remaking Modernity: Politics, History, and Sociology. Julia Adams, Elisabeth S. Clemens, and Ann Shola Orloff, eds. Pp. 1–72. Durham, NC: Duke University Press.

Adams, Sherman W.

1895 The Hartford Park System. Connecticut Magazine 1(1):67–71.

Agassiz, Louis

1857–1862 Contributions to the Natural History of the United States of America. 4 vols. Boston: Little, Brown.

Alberdi, Juan Bautista

1979[1852] Bases y Puntos de Partida para la Organización Política de la República Argentina. Buenos Aires: Centro Editor de América Latina.

Allen, Gloria Seaman

1989 Family Record: Genealogical Watercolors and Needlework. Washington, DC: Daughters of the American Revolution Museum.

References

Alonso, Ana Maria

1994 The Politics of Space, Time and Substance: State Formation, Nationalism and Ethnicity. Annual Review of Anthropology 23:379–405.

Anderson, Benedict

1991[1983] Imagined Communities: Reflections on the Origin and Spread of Nationalism. Rev. edition London: Verso.

Anonymous

1847 Genealogies and Their Moral. [Attributed to Lemuel Shattuck]. New England Historical and Genealogical Register 1(3):290.

1881a Golden Wedding: Fiftieth Anniversary of the Marriage of Mr. and Mrs. N. H. Morgan. Brief Account of Mr. Morgan's Life in Hartford. Evening Post (Hartford), May 4.

1881b Death of Mr. Nathaniel H. Morgan. Hartford Courant, July 13.

1900 The Corning Fountain. Munsey's Magazine, April 23.

1907 Charles Octavius Whitmore. Memorial Biographies of the New England Historic Genealogical Society 8[1880–1889]:229.

Anzaldua, Gloria

1987 Borderlands/La Frontera: The New Mestiza. San Francisco: Aunt Lute Books.

Appadurai, Arjun

1981 Gastro-politics in Hindu South Asia. American Ethnologist 8(3):494–511.

1996 Modernity at Large: Cultural Dimensions of Globalization. Minneapolis: University of Minnesota Press.

Appleton, William S.

1901 Memoir of William H. Whitmore. Proceedings of the Massachusetts Historical Society, 2nd ser., 15:96–104.

Arendt, Hannah

1958a The Human Condition. Chicago: University of Chicago Press.

1958b The Origins of Totalitarianism. New York: Meridian.

Asad, Talal

1993 Genealogies of Religion: Discipline and Reasons of Power in Christianity and Islam. Baltimore, MD: Johns Hopkins University Press.

2003 Formations of the Secular: Christianity, Islam, Modernity. Stanford, CA: Stanford University Press.

Astuti, Rita

1995 People of the Sea: Identity and Descent among the Vezo of Madagascar. Cambridge: Cambridge University Press.

2000 Kindreds and Descent Groups: New Perspectives from Madagascar. *In* Cultures of Relatedness: New Approaches to the Study of Kinship. Janet Carsten, ed. Pp. 90–103. Cambridge: Cambridge University Press.

Austin, J. L.

1965[1955] How to Do Things with Words. New York: Oxford University Press.

Axtell, James

1985 The Invasion Within: The Contest of Cultures in Colonial North America. Oxford: Oxford University Press.

2000 Babel of Tongues: Communicating with the Indians in Eastern North America. *In* The Language Encounter in the Americas, 1492–1800. Edward G. Gray and Norman Fiering, eds. Pp. 15–60. Oxford: Berghahn.

Ayres, William A.

1886 Parks and Public Works. *In* The Memorial History of Hartford County, Connecticut, 1633–1884, vol. 1. James Hammond Trumbull, ed. Pp. 447–462. Boston: Edward L. Osgood.

Bakhtin, Mikhail

1981 Forms of Time and of the Chronotope in the Novel. *In* The Dialogic Imagination: Four Essays. Michael Holquist, ed. Caryl Emerson and Michael Holquist, trans. Pp. 84–258. Austin: University of Texas Press.

Baldwin, Peter C.

1999 Domesticating the Street: The Reform of Public Space in Hartford, 1850–1930. Columbus: Ohio State University Press.

Bamford, Sandra

2007 Biology Unmoored: Melanesian Reflections on Life and Biotechnology. Berkeley: University of California Press.

Bandieri, Susana

2005 Asuntos de Familia: La Construcción del Poder en la Patagonia; El Caso de Neuquén. Boletín del Instituto de Historia Argentina y Americana "Dr. Emilio Ravignani" 28(2):65–94.

Barnhardt, Ray, ed.

1976 Cross-Cultural Issues in Alaskan Education. Fairbanks: University of Alaska, Center for Northern Education Research.

Barnhill, Georgia B.

2009 Written on Stone: Family Registers, Family Trees, and Memorial Prints. *In* Picturing Victorian America: Prints by the Kellogg Brothers of Hartford, Connecticut, 1830–1880. Nancy Finlay, ed. Pp. 61–71. Hartford: Connecticut Historical Society.

Basch, Linda, Nina Glick Schiller, and Cristina Szanton Blanc

1994 Nations Unbound: Transnational Projects, Postcolonial Predicaments and Deterritorialized Nation-States. Longhorn, PA: Gordon and Breach Science.

Basso, Keith

1990 To Give Up on Words. *In* Western Apache Language and Culture. Pp. 80–98. Tucson: University of Arizona Press.

Basu, Paul

2006 Highland Homecomings: Genealogy and Heritage Tourism in the Scottish Diaspora. London: Routledge.

References

Battaglia, Debbora

1990 On the Bones of the Serpent: Person, Memory, and Mortality in Sabarl Island Society. Chicago: University of Chicago Press.

Bear, Laura

2007a Lines of the Nation: Indian Railway Workers, Bureaucracy, and the Intimate Historical Self. New York: Columbia University Press.

2007b Ruins and Ghosts: The Domestic Uncanny and the Materialization of Anglo-Indian Genealogies in Kharagpur. *In* Ghosts of Memory: Essays on Remembrance and Relatedness. Janet Carsten, ed. Pp. 36–57. Oxford: Blackwell.

Beckert, Sven

2004 Emancipation and Empire: Reconstructing the Worldwide Web of Cotton Production in the Age of the American Civil War. American Historical Review 109(5):1405–1438.

Been, Vicki

1992–1993 "What's Fairness Got to Do with It?" Environmental Justice and the Siting of Locally Undesirable Land Uses. Cornell Law Review 78:1001–1085.

Belini, Claudio

2006 El Grupo Bunge y la Política Económica del Primer Peronismo. Latin American Research Review 41(1):27–50.

Bellah, Robert N.

1967 Civil Religion in America. Daedelus: Journal of the American Academy of Arts and Sciences 96(1):1–21.

1997 Max Weber and World-Denying Love: A Look at the Historical Sociology of Religion. Humanities Center and Burke Lectureship on Religion and Society, University of California, San Diego, October 30, 1997. http://www.robertbellah.com/articles_3.htm, accessed January 14, 2011.

Bellah, Robert N., Richard Madsen, William M. Sullivan, Ann Swidler, and Steven M. Tipton

2007[1985] Habits of the Heart: Individualism and Commitment in American Life. 3rd edition Berkeley: University of California Press.

Bender, Thomas

1974 The "Rural" Cemetery Movement: Urban Travail and the Appeal of Nature. New England Quarterly 47(2):196–211.

Benjamin, Walter

1968 Theses on the Philosophy of History. *In* Illuminations: Essays and Reflections. Pp. 253–264. New York: Schocken.

Bennett, Gillian

1999 Alas Poor Ghost! Traditions of Belief in Story and Discourse. Logan: Utah State University Press.

Bennion, Janet

1998 Women of Principle: Female Networking in Contemporary Mormon Polygyny. Oxford: Oxford University Press.

Benson, Susan N.

1981 Ambiguous Ethnicity: Interracial Families in London. Cambridge: Cambridge University Press.

2006 Injurious Names. *In* The Anthropology of Names and Naming. Gabriele vom Bruck and Barbara Bodenhorn, eds. Pp. 177–199. Cambridge: Cambridge University Press.

Berlant, Lauren

1998 The Queen of America Goes to Washington City: Essays on Sex and Citizenship. Durham, NC: Duke University Press.

Birla, Ritu

2009 Stages of Capital: Law, Culture, and Market Governance in Late Colonial India. Durham, NC: Duke University Press.

Birmingham, Steve

1967 "Our Crowd": The Great Jewish Families of New York. New York: Harper and Row.

Bloch, Maurice

1971 Placing the Dead: Tombs, Ancestral Villages, and Kinship Organization in Madagascar. London: Seminar Press.

Bloom, Harold

1992 The American Religion: The Emergence of the Post-Christian Nation. New York: Simon and Schuster.

Bodenhorn, Barbara

1988 Iñupiat Family Continuities in Changing Times, vols. 1 and 2. Report written for the Iñupiat History, Language and Culture Commission, Barrow, Alaska.

1990 The Animals Come to Me, They Know I Share: Iñupiaq Kinship, Changing Economic Relations and Enduring World Views on the North Slope of Alaska. PhD dissertation, University of Cambridge.

1992 "I'm Not the Great Hunter, My Wife Is": Iñupiat and Anthropological Models of Gender. Etudes/Inuit/Studies 12(1–2):55–74.

2000 "He Used to Be My Relative": Exploring the Bases of Relatedeness among Iñupiat of Northern Alaska. *In* Cultures of Relatedness: New Approaches to the Study of Kinship. Janet Carsten, ed. Pp. 128–148. Cambridge: Cambridge University Press.

2004a "It's Good to Know Who Your Relatives Are, but We Were Taught to Share with Everyone": Shares and Sharing among Iñupiaq Households. *In* The Social Economy of Sharing: Resource Allocation and Modern Hunter/Gatherers. George Wenzel, Greta Hovelsrude Broda, and Noburo Kishigami, eds. Pp. 13–41. Osaka, Japan: SENRI.

2004b Is Being "Really Iñupiaq" a Matter of Cultural Property? *In* Properties of Culture, Culture as Property. Eric Kasten, ed. Pp. 35–50. Berlin: Dietrich Reimer.

2006 Calling into Being: Names and Speaking Names on the North Slope of Alaska. *In* The Anthropology of Names and Naming. Gabriele vom Bruck and Barbara Bodenhorn, eds. Pp. 139–156. Cambridge: Cambridge University Press.

Boon, James A.

1977 The Anthropological Romance of Bali 1597–1972: Dynamic Perspectives in Marriage and Caste, Politics and Religion. Cambridge: Cambridge University Press.

Boon, James A., and David M. Schneider

1974 Kinship vis-à-vis Myth: Contrasts in Lévi-Strauss' Approaches to Cross-Cultural Comparison. American Anthropologist 76(4):799–817.

Borneman, John

1992 Belonging in Two Berlins: Kin, State, Nation. Cambridge: Cambridge University Press.

Bott, Elizabeth

1971[1957] Family and Social Network: Roles, Norms and External Relationships in Ordinary Urban Families. London: Tavistock.

Bowen, John

2010 Secularisms in Crisis? First Leverhulme Lecture, London School of Economics, February 2.

Brashears, Candice C., and Michael Shortell

2009 Checklist of Kellogg Lithographs in the Connecticut Historical Society. *In* Picturing Victorian America: Prints by the Kellogg Brothers of Hartford, Connecticut, 1830–1880. Nancy Finlay, ed. Pp. 137–222. Hartford: Connecticut Historical Society.

Brennan, Theresa

2000 Exhausting Modernity: Grounds for a New Economy. London: Routledge.

Briggs, Jean

1970 Never in Anger: A Portrait of an Eskimo Family. Cambridge, MA: Harvard University Press.

1998 Inuit Morality Play: The Emotional Education of a Three-Year-Old. New Haven, CT: Yale University Press.

Brioschi, Francesco, Luigi Buzzacchi, and Massimo G. Colombo

1990 Gruppi di imprese e mercato finanziario: La struttura di potere nell'industria italiana. Rome: Nuova Italia Scientifica.

Brocklesby, William C.

1886 Architecture in Hartford. *In* The Memorial History of Hartford County, Connecticut, 1633–1884, vol. 1. James Hammond Trumbull, ed. Pp. 463–498. Boston: Edward L. Osgood.

Brodie, Fawn M.

1996 No Man Knows My History: The Life of Joseph Smith, the Mormon Prophet. 2nd edition New York: Vintage.

Brøsted, Jens

1985 Native Power: The Quest for Autonomy and Nationhood of Indigenous Peoples. Bergen, Norway: Universitatsverlaget.

Brower, Arnold, Sr.

1981 Testimony in *ICAS v. U.S.*, appendix 1:7. Ninth District Court.

Bruce, Steve

2002 God Is Dead: Secularization in the West. Oxford: Blackwell.

Bruck, Gabriele vom, and Barbara Bodenhorn, eds.

2006 The Anthropology of Names and Naming. Cambridge: Cambridge University Press.

Bryceson, Deborah, and Ulla Vuyorela, eds.

2002 The Transnational Family: New European Frontiers and Global Networks. Oxford: Berg.

Bullard, Robert D.

1994 Unequal Protection: Environmental Justice and Communities of Color. San Francisco: Sierra Club Books.

Burch, Ernest S., Jr.

1975 Eskimo Kinsmen: Changing Family Relations in Northwest Alaska. St. Paul, MN: West Publishing.

1998 Boundaries and Borders in Early Contact North-Central Alaska. Arctic Anthropology 35(2):19–48.

2005 Alliance and Conflict: The World System of the Iñupiaq Eskimos. Lincoln: University of Nebraska Press.

2006 Social Life in Northwest Alaska: The Structure of Iñupiaq Eskimo Nations. Anchorage: University of Alaska Press.

Burke, Kenneth

1945 Four Master Tropes. *In* A Grammar of Motives. Pp. 503–517. New York: Prentice Hall.

Bushman, Richard Lyman

2006 Joseph Smith, Rough Stone Rolling: A Cultural Biography of Mormonism's Founder. New York: Random House.

Bushnell, Horace

1847 Discourses on Christian Nurture. Boston: Massachusetts Sabbath School Society.

1849 God in Christ. Hartford, CT: Brown and Parsons.

1869 Hartford Park. Hearth and Home 1(7):101–102.

Bushnell, Horace, and Mary A. [Bushnell] Cheney

1880 Life and Letters of Horace Bushnell. New York: Harper.

Caesar, Ed

2010 Cormac McCarthy and the Road to Poetry. Sunday Times, January 3. http://entertainment.timesonline.co.uk/tol/arts_and_entertainment/books/article6971682.ece, accessed January 4, 2010.

Campbell, Ben

2009 Fields of Post-human Kinship. *In* European Kinship in the Age of Biotechnology. Jeanette Edwards and Carles Salazar, eds. Pp. 162–178. Oxford: Berghahn.

Cannadine, David

1981 War and Death, Grief and Mourning in Modern Britain. *In* Mirrors of Mortality: Studies in the Social History of Death. Joachim Whaley, ed. Pp. 187–242. New York: St. Martin's.

Cannell, Fenella

2005a Immaterial Culture? "Idolatry" in the Lowland Philippines. *In* Spirited Politics: Religion and Public Life in Contemporary Southeast Asia. Andrew C. Willford and Kenneth M. George, eds. Pp. 159–185. Ithaca, NY: Southeast Asia Program, Cornell University.

2005b The Christianity of Anthropology: Malinowski Memorial Lecture, May 20, 2005. Journal of the Royal Anthropological Institute, n.s., 11(2):335–356.

2007 "Loving the Dead": Mormon Genealogy, Kinship and Religion. Paper presented at the Department of Anthropology Seminar, University of Virginia, January.

2010 The Anthropology of Secularism. Annual Review of Anthropology 39:85–100.

2011 English Ancestors: The Moral Possibilities of Popular Genealogy. Journal of the Royal Anthropological Institute 17(3):462–480.

Carsten, Janet

1995a The Politics of Forgetting: Migration, Kinship, and Memory. Journal of the Royal Anthropological Institute, n.s., 1(2):317–335.

1995b The Substance of Kinship and the Heat of the Hearth: Feeding, Personhood, and Relatedness among Malays in Pulau Langkawi. American Ethnologist 22(2):223–241.

1997 The Heat of the Hearth: The Process of Kinship in a Malay Fishing Community. Oxford: Clarendon.

2000a "Knowing Where You've Come From": Ruptures and Continuities of Time and Kinship in Narratives of Adoption Reunions. Journal of the Royal Anthropological Institute, n.s., 6(4):687–703.

2001 Substantivism, Antisubstantivism, and Anti-antisubstantivism. *In* Relative Values: Reconfiguring Kinship Studies. Sarah Franklin and Susan McKinnon, eds. Pp. 29–53. Durham, NC: Duke University Press.

2004 After Kinship. Cambridge: Cambridge University Press.

Carsten, Janet, ed.

2000b Cultures of Relatedness: New Approaches to the Study of Kinship. Cambridge: Cambridge University Press.

2007 Ghosts of Memory: Essays on Remembrance and Relatedness. Oxford: Blackwell.

Casanova, José

1994 Public Religions in the Modern World. Chicago: University of Chicago Press.

Cashin, Joan E.

1990 The Structure of Antebellum Planter Families: "The Ties That Bound Us Was Strong." Journal of Southern History 56(1):55–70.

Ceisel, Christina M.

2009 Checking the Box: A Journey through My Hybrid Identity. Cultural Studies Critical Methodologies 9(5):661–668.

Censer, Jane Turner

1984 North Carolina Planters and Their Children: 1800–1860. Baton Rouge: Louisiana State University Press.

Chakrabarty, Dipesh

1989 Rethinking Working Class History: Bengal 1890–1940. New Delhi: Oxford University Press.

2000 Provincializing Europe: Postcolonial Thought and Historical Difference. Princeton, NJ: Princeton University Press.

Chance, Norman

1990 Iñupiat and Arctic Alaska: An Ethnography of Development. London: Holt, Rinehart and Winston.

Chandler, Alfred D.

1980 The United States: Seedbed of Managerial Capitalism. *In* Managerial Hierarchies: Comparative Perspectives on the Rise of the Modern Industrial Enterprise. Alfred D. Chandler and Herman Daems, eds. Pp. 9–40. Cambridge, MA: Harvard University Press.

Chen, Calvin

2008 Some Assembly Required: Work, Community and Politics in China's Rural Enterprises. Cambridge, MA: Harvard University Press.

Chock, Phyllis Pease

1999 "A Very Bright Line": Kinship and Nationality in U.S. Congressional Hearings on Immigration. PoLAR 22(2):42–52.

Cikovsky, Nicolai, Jr.

1979 "The Ravages of the Axe": The Meaning of the Tree Stump in Nineteenth-Century American Art. Art Bulletin 61(4):611–626.

Clark, Drew

2001 The Mormon Stem-Cell Choir. Slate, August 3, 2001. http://www.slate.com/?id=112974, accessed October 18, 2010.

Cohen, Jeffrey H.

2002 Migration and "Stay at Homes" in Rural Oaxaca, Mexico: Local Expression of Global Outcomes. Urban Anthropology 31(2):231–259.

2004 The Culture of Migration in Southern Mexico. Austin: University of Texas Press.

Cohen-Goldfarb Collection

N.d. http://www.iajgsjewishcemeteryproject.org/connecticut-ct/hartford-hartford-county.html, accessed October 25, 2010.

Cole, Jennifer

2007 Fresh Contact in Tamatave, Madagascar: Sex, Money, and Intergenerational Transformation. *In* Generations and Globalization. Jennifer Cole and Deborah Durham, eds. Pp. 74–101. Bloomington: Indiana University Press.

2009 Sex and Salvation: Imagining the Future in Madagascar. Chicago: University of Chicago Press.

Colli, Andrea

2003 The History of Family Business, 1850–2000. Cambridge: Cambridge University Press.

Colli, Andrea, and Mary B. Rose

2003 Family Firms in Comparative Perspective. *In* Business History around the World at the End of the Twentieth Century. Franco Amatori and Geoffrey Jones, eds. Pp. 339–352. Cambridge: Cambridge University Press.

Collier, Jane, Michelle Rosaldo, and Sylvia Yanagisako

1992 Is There a Family? New Anthropological Views. *In* Rethinking the Family: Some Feminist Questions. Barrie Thorne and Marilyn Yalom, eds. Pp. 31–48. Boston: Northeastern University Press.

Collier, Jane Fishburne, and Sylvia Junko Yanagisako, eds.

1987 Gender and Kinship: Essays toward a Unified Analysis. Stanford, CA: Stanford University Press.

Comaroff, John

1987 Sui genderis: Feminism, Kinship Theory, and Structural "Domains." *In* Gender and Kinship: Essays toward a Unified Analysis. Jane Fishburne Collier and Sylvia Junko Yanagisako, eds. Pp. 53–85. Stanford, CA: Stanford University Press.

Comaroff, John, ed.

1980 The Meaning of Marriage Payments. London: Academic Press.

Conlon, Michael

2007 Writer Cormac McCarthy Confides in Oprah Winfrey. Reuters, June 5. http://www.reuters.com/article/idUSN0526436120070605, accessed February 4, 2010.

Constable, Nicole, ed.

2005 Cross-Border Marriages: Gender and Mobility in Transnational Asia. Philadelphia: University of Pennsylvania Press.

Contreras, Carlos Alberto

N.d. Cutralco: Historia de su origen relato del Doctor Víctor Ezio Zani a Carlos Alberto Contreras. Unpublished manuscript in the author's possession.

Conway, Dennis, and Jeffrey Cohen

2003 Local Dynamics in Multi-local Transnational Spaces of Rural Mexico: Oaxacan Experiences. International Journal of Population Geography 9:141–161.

Copeman, Jacob

2005 Veinglory: Exploring Processes of Blood Transfer between Persons. Journal of the Royal Anthropological Institute, n.s., 11(3):465–485.

Cornelius, Wayne, and Jessa M. Lewis

2006 Impacts of Border Enforcement on Mexican Immigration. Boulder, CO: Lynne Rienner.

Cott, Nancy F.

1977 The Bonds of Womanhood: "Women's Sphere" in New England, 1780–1835. New Haven, CT: Yale University Press.

Coutin, Susan Bibler

2006[2003] Cultural Logics of Belonging and Movement: Transnationalism, Naturalization, and US Immigration Politics. *In* The Anthropology of the State: A Reader. Aradhana Sharma and Akhil Gupta, eds. Pp. 310–336. Malden, MA: Blackwell.

Coward, Rosalind

1983 Patriarchal Precedents: Sexuality and Social Relations. London: Routledge and Kegan Paul.

Cross, Whitney R.

1950 The Burned-Over District: The Social and Intellectual History of Enthusiastic Religion in Western New York, 1800–1850. Ithaca, NY: Cornell University Press.

Daems, Herman

1980 The Rise of the Modern Industrial Enterprise: A New Perspective. *In* Managerial Hierarchies: Comparative Perspectives on the Rise of the Modern Industrial Enterprise. Alfred D. Chandler and Herman Daems, eds. Pp. 203–223. Cambridge, MA: Harvard University Press.

Daniel, E. Valentine

1984 Fluid Signs: Being a Person the Tamil Way. Berkeley: University of California Press.

Daniels, Jonathan

1972 The Randolphs of Virginia. Garden City, NY: Doubleday.

Das, Veena

1995 National Honor and Practical Kinship: Unwanted Women and Children. *In* Conceiving the New World Order: The Global Politics of Reproduction. Faye D. Ginsburg and Rayna Rapp, eds. Pp. 212–233. Berkeley: University of California Press.

2006 Secularism and the Argument from Nature. *In* Powers of the Secular Modern: Talal Asad and His Interpreters. David Scott and Charles Hirschkind, eds. Pp. 93–112. Stanford, CA: Stanford University Press.

2007 The Figure of the Abducted Woman: The Citizen as Sexed. *In* Life and Words: Violence and the Descent into the Ordinary. Pp. 18–37. Berkeley: University of California Press.

Davidoff, Leonore

2004 The Legacy of the Nineteenth-Century Bourgeois Family and the Wool Merchant's Son. Transactions of the Royal Historical Society 14:25–46.

Davidoff, Leonore, and Catherine Hall

1987 Family Fortunes: Men and Women of the English Middle Class, 1780–1850. Chicago: University of Chicago Press.

Day, Abby

2009 Believing in Belonging: An Ethnography of Young People's Construction of Belief. Culture and Religion 10:263–278.

Daynes, Kathryn M.

2001 More Wives Than One: The Transformation of the Mormon Marriage System, 1840–1910. Urbana: University of Illinois Press.

DeBernardi, Jean

2004 Rites of Belonging: Memory, Modernity, and Identity in a Malaysian Chinese Community. Stanford, CA: Stanford University Press.

2006 The Way That Lives in the Heart: Chinese Popular Religion and Spirit Mediums in Penang, Malaysia. Stanford, CA: Stanford University Press.

Delaney, Carol

1995 Father State, Motherland, and the Birth of Modern Turkey. *In* Naturalizing Power: Essays in Feminist Cultural Analysis. Sylvia Yanagisako and Carol Delaney, eds. Pp. 177–199. New York: Routledge.

Deleuze, Gilles

2001[1953] Empiricism and Subjectivity. Constantin V. Boundas, trans. New York: Columbia University Press.

Demos, John

1986 Past, Present, and Personal: The Family and the Life Course in American History. New York: Oxford University Press.

Derrida, Jacques

1995 Archive Fever: A Freudian Impression. Eric Prenowitz, trans. Chicago: University of Chicago Press.

Dewey, J.

1926 The Historic Background of Corporate Legal Personality. Yale Law Journal 35(6):655–673.

Dobellaere, Karl

1998 Secularization. *In* Encylopedia of Religion and Society. William H. Swatos Jr., ed. http://hirr.hartsem.edu/ency/secularization.htm, accessed December 19, 2009.

Dolgin, Janet

1997 Defining the Family: Law, Technology, and Reproduction in an Uneasy Age. New York: New York University Press.

Dorow, Sara, and Amy Swiffen

2009 Blood and Desire: The Secret of Heteronormativity in Adoption Narratives of Culture. American Ethnologist 36(3):563–573.

Douglas, Amanda Minnie

1898 A Little Girl in Old Boston. New York: Dodd, Mead.

Douglas, Mary

1966 Purity and Danger: An Analysis of Concepts of Pollution and Taboo. London: Routledge and Kegan Paul.

1980 Evans-Pritchard. Brighton, UK: Harvester.

Dumont, Louis

1970 Religion, Politics, and Society in the Individualistic Universe. *In* Proceedings of the Royal Anthropological Institute of Great Britain and Ireland, pp. 31–45.

Dunn, Elizabeth C.

2004 Privatizing Poland: Baby Food, Big Business, and the Remaking of Labor. Ithaca, NY: Cornell University Press.

Durrie, Daniel Steele

1868 Bibliographia Genealogica Americana: An Alphabetical Index to American Genealogies and Pedigrees Contained in State, County and Town Histories, Printed Genealogies, and Kindred Works. Albany, NY: Joel Munsell.

Edelman, Lee

2004 No Future: Queer Theory and the Death Drive. Durham, NC: Duke University Press.

Edwards, Jeanette

2000 Born and Bred: Idioms of Kinship and the New Reproductive Technologies in England. Oxford: Oxford University Press.

2009 Skipping a Generation: Genealogy and Assisted Conception. *In* Kinship and Beyond: The Genealogical Model Reconsidered. Sandra Bamford and James Leach, eds. Pp. 138–174. Oxford: Berghahn.

Ellison, James

2009 Governmentality and the Family: Neoliberal Choices and Emergent Kin Relations in Southern Ethiopia. American Anthropologist 111(1):81–92.

Engels, Friedrich

1972[1884] The Origins of the Family, Private Property, and the State. New York: Pathfinder.

Englund, Harri, and James Leach

2000 Ethnography and the Meta-narratives of Modernity. Current Anthropology 41(2):225–239.

Erwin, Doug

2006 The End of the World: Extinction and the Reemergence of Life. Themes in *The Road*: Where Science and Fiction Meet. Oprah.com, January 1. http://www.oprah.com/oprahsbookclub/Fiction-and-Scientific-Themes-in-The-Road-by-Cormac-McCarthy/2, accessed February 5, 2010.

Evans-Pritchard, E. E.

1940 The Nuer. Oxford: Clarendon.

Faber, Bernard

1972 Guardians of Virtue: Salem Families in 1800. New York: Basic Books.

Farrell, Betty G.

1993 Elite Families: Class and Power in Nineteenth-Century Boston. Albany: State University of New York Press.

Favaro, Orietta, and Mario Arias Bucciarelli

1999 La Conformación de una Provincia Exportadora de Energía: Neuquén, 1950–1980. *In* Neuquén: La Construcción de un Orden Estatal. Orietta Favaro, ed. Pp. 225–251. Neuquén, Argentina: CEHEPYC.

Favaro, Orietta, and Graciela Iuorno

1999 Entre Territorio y Provincia: Libaneses y Sirios; Comercio y Política en el Neuquén. *In* Neuquén: La Construcción de un Orden Estatal. Orietta Favaro, ed. Pp. 57–80. Neuquén, Argentina: CEHEPYC.

Favretti, Rudy J.

2007 Jacob Weidenmann: Pioneer Landscape Architect. Middletown, CT: Wesleyan University Press.

Feeley-Harnik, Gillian

1981 The Lord's Table: Eucharist and Passover in Early Christianity. Philadelphia: University of Pennsylvania Press.

1991 A Green Estate: Restoring Independence in Madagascar. Washington, DC: Smithsonian Institution Press.

1999 "Communities of Blood": The Natural History of Kinship in Nineteenth-Century America. Comparative Studies in Society and History 41(2):215–262.

2001a The Ethnography of Creation: Lewis Henry Morgan and the American Beaver. *In* Relative Values: Reconfiguring Kinship Studies. Sarah Franklin and Susan McKinnon, eds. Pp. 54–84. Durham, NC: Duke University Press.

2001b "The Mystery of Life in All Its Forms": Religious Dimensions of Culture in Early American Anthropology. *In* Religion and Cultural Studies. Susan Mizruchi, ed. Pp. 140–191. Princeton, NJ: Princeton University Press.

Feldman, Eric A., and Ronald Bayer, eds.

1999 Blood Feuds: AIDS, Blood and the Politics of Medical Disaster. Oxford: Oxford University Press.

Ferguson, James

1999 Expectations of Modernity: Myths and Meanings of Urban Life on the Zambian Copperbelt. Berkeley: University of California Press.

Fernandes, Leela

1997 Producing Workers: The Politics of Gender, Class, and Culture in the Calcutta Jute Mills. Philadelphia: University of Pennsylvania Press.

1998 Culture, Structure, and Working Class Politics. Economic and Political Weekly 33:52–60.

Feuchtwang, Stephan

2011 After the Event: The Transmission of Grievous Loss in Germany, China and Taiwan. Oxford: Berghahn.

Firth, Sir Raymond

1963 Elements of Social Organization. 3rd edition. Boston: Beacon.

Fogel-Chance, Nancy

1993 Living between Both Worlds: "Modernity" and "Tradition" among North Slope Iñupiaq Women in Anchorage. Arctic Anthropology 30(1):94–108.

Fortes, Meyer

1958 Introduction. *In* The Developmental Cycle in Domestic Groups. Jack Goody, ed. Pp. 1–14. Cambridge: Cambridge University Press.

1969 Kinship and the Social Order: The Legacy of Lewis Henry Morgan. Chicago: Aldine.

Fortes, Meyer, and E. E. Evans-Pritchard, eds.

1940 African Political Systems. Oxford: Oxford University Press.

Foster, Robert J.

1991 Making National Cultures in the Global Ecumene. Annual Review of Anthropology 20:235–260.

2002 Bargains with Modernity in Papua New Guinea and Elsewhere. *In* Critically Modern: Alternatives, Alterities, Anthropologies. Bruce M. Knauft, ed. Pp. 57–81. Bloomington: Indiana University Press.

Foucault, Michel

1980 The History of Sexuality, vol. 1. New York: Vintage.

1985 The History of Sexuality, vol. 2: The Use of Pleasure. Robert Hurley, trans. New York: Pantheon.

1991 Governmentality. *In* The Foucault Effect. Graham Burchell, Colin Gordon, and Peter Miller, eds. Pp. 87–105. London: Harvester Wheatsheaf.

Franklin, Sarah

2001 Biologization Revisited: Kinship Theory in the Context of the New Biologies. *In* Relative Values: Reconfiguring Kinship Studies. Sarah Franklin and Susan McKinnon, eds. Pp. 302–325. Durham, NC: Duke University Press.

2007 Dolly Mixtures: The Remaking of Genealogy. Durham, NC: Duke University Press.

Franklin, Sarah, and Susan McKinnon

2001a Relative Values: Reconfiguring Kinship Studies. *In* Relative Values: Reconfiguring Kinship Studies. Sarah Franklin and Susan McKinnon, eds. Pp. 1–25. Durham, NC: Duke University Press.

Franklin, Sarah, and Susan McKinnon, eds.

2001b Relative Values: Reconfiguring Kinship Studies. Durham, NC: Duke University Press.

Freeman, Caren

2005 Marrying Up and Marrying Down: The Paradoxes of Marital Mobility for Chosŏnjok Brides in South Korea. *In* Cross-Border Marriages: Gender and Mobility in Transnational Asia. Nicole Constable, ed. Pp. 80–100. Philadelphia: University of Pennsylvania Press.

2011 Making and Faking Kinship: Marriage and Labor Migration between China and South Korea. Ithaca, NY: Cornell University Press.

French, Stanley

1974 The Cemetery as Cultural Institution: The Establishment of Mount Auburn and the "Rural Cemetery" Movement. American Quarterly 26(1):37–59.

Freud, Sigmund

1999[1913] Totem and Taboo. London: Routledge.

2003[1919] The Uncanny. *In* The Uncanny. David McLintock, trans. Pp. 121–162. London: Penguin.

Fustel de Coulanges, Numa Denis

2006[1874] The Ancient City: A Study of the Religion, Laws, and Institutions of Greece and Rome. Mineola, NY: Dover.

Gallagher, Mary E.

2005 Contagious Capitalism: Globalization and the Politics of Labor in China. Princeton, NJ: Princeton University Press.

Gaonkar, Dilip Parameshwar, ed.

2001 Alternative Modernities. Durham, NC: Duke University Press.

Geertz, Clifford

1973a The Impact of the Concept of Culture on the Concept of Man. *In* The Interpretation of Cultures. Clifford Geertz, ed. Pp. 33–54. New York: Basic Books.

1973b The Integrative Revolution: Primordial Sentiments and Civil Politics in the New States. *In* The Interpretation of Cultures. Clifford Geertz, ed. Pp. 255–310. New York: Basic Books.

Geertz, Clifford, ed.

1963 Old Societies and New States: The Quest for Modernity in Asia and Africa. New York: Free Press.

Geertz, Hildred, and Clifford Geertz

1964 Teknonymy in Bali: Parenthood, Age-Grading, and Generational Amnesia.

Journal of the Royal Anthropological Institute 94(2):94–108.

Genova, Nicholas de, and Ana Y. Ramos-Zayas

2003 Latino Crossings: Mexicans, Puerto Ricans, and the Politics of Citizenship. London: Routledge.

Ginsburg, Faye D.

1989 Contested Lives: The Abortion Debate in an American Community. Berkeley: University of California Press.

Gittins, Diana

1993[1985] The Family in Question: Changing Households and Familiar Ideologies. London: Macmillan.

Glenn, Evelyn Nakano

1983 Split Household, Small Producer and Dual Wage Earner: An Analysis of Chinese-American Family Strategies. Journal of Marriage and the Family 45(1):35–46.

Good, Anthony

2010 Kinship. *In* The Routledge Encyclopedia of Social and Cultural Anthropology. 2nd edition. Alan Barnard and Jonathan Spencer, eds. Pp. 395–404. New York: Routledge.

Goody, Esther

1973 Contexts of Kinship. Cambridge: Cambridge University Press.

1982 Parenthood and Social Reproduction: Fostering and Occupational Roles in West Africa. Cambridge: Cambridge University Press.

Gordon, G. A.

1902 William Whitmore. New-England Historical and Genealogical Register (January):68.

Gordon, Sarah Barringer

2002 The Mormon Question: Polygamy and Constitutional Conflict in Nineteenth-Century America. Chapel Hill: University of North Carolina Press.

Gore, Al

1992 Earth in the Balance: Ecology and the Human Spirit. New York: Penguin.

1993 Earth in the Balance: Ecology and the Human Spirit. New York: Plume.

2006 An Inconvenient Truth: The Planetary Emergency of Global Warming and What We Can Do about It. New York: Rodale.

Gorelik, Adrián

1987 La Arquitectura de YPF, 1934–1943: Notas para una Interpretación de las Relaciones entre Estado, Modernidad e Identidad en la Arquitectura Argentina de los Años 30. Anales del Instituto de Arte Americano 24:97–107.

Grassby, Richard

2001 Kinship and Capitalism: Marriage, Family, and Business in the English-Speaking World, 1580–1740. Cambridge: Cambridge University Press.

Green, Linda

2006 Study Explores Social Effects of TB in Southwest Alaska. Grassroots Science. http://ykalaska.wordpress.com/2006/08/07/study-explores-social-effects-of-tb-in-southwest-alaska, accessed April 4, 2012.

Greenwood, Val D.

2000 The Researcher's Guide to American Genealogy. 3rd edition. Baltimore, MD: Genealogical Publishing.

Grishop, James I.

2006 The Envios of San Pablo Huixtepec, Oaxaca: Food, Home, and Transnationalism. Human Organization 65(4):400–406.

Grossberg, Michael

1985 Governing the Hearth: Law and the Family in Nineteenth-Century America. Chapel Hill: University of North Carolina Press.

Guardian

2008 50 People Who Could Save the Planet. January 5. http://www.guardian.co.uk/environment/2008/jan/05/activists.ethicalliving, accessed January 4, 2010.

Hacking, Ian

1999 The Social Construction of What? Cambridge, MA: Harvard University Press.

Hall, Basil

1829a Travels in North America, in the Years 1827 and 1828. 3 vols. Edinburgh: Cadell.

1829b Forty Etchings, from Sketches Made with a Camera Lucida, in North America, in 1827 and 1828. Edinburgh: Cadell.

Hall, Peter Dobkin

1977 Family Structure and Economic Organization: Massachusetts Merchants, 1700–1850. *In* Family and Kin in Urban Communities, 1700–1930. Tamara K. Hareven, ed. Pp. 38–61. New York: New Viewpoints.

1978 Marital Selection and Business in Massachusetts Merchant Families, 1700–1900. *In* The American Family in Social-Historical Perspective. 2nd edition. Michael Gordon, ed. Pp. 101–114. New York: St. Martin's.

1982 The Organization of American Culture, 1700–1900: Private Institutions, Elites, and the Origins of American Nationality. New York: New York University Press.

Hancock, David

1995 Citizens of the World: London Merchants and the Integration of the British Atlantic Community, 1735–1785. Cambridge: Cambridge University Press.

Handler, Richard

1988 Nationalism and the Politics of Culture in Quebec. Madison: University of Wisconsin Press.

Hansen, Thomas Blom, and Finn Stepputat

2006 Sovereignty Revisited. Annual Review of Anthropology 35:295–315.

Hansen, Thomas Blom, and Oskar Verkaaik

2009 Introduction: Urban Charisma on Everyday Mythologies in the City. Critique of Anthropology 29:5–26.

Haraway, Donna J.

1997 Modest_Witness@Second_Millennium.FemaleMan©_Meets_OncoMouse™. New York: Routledge.

Harding, Susan Friend

2000 The Book of Jerry Falwell: Fundamentalist Language and Politics. Princeton, NJ: Princeton University Press.

Harris, Jose

2001 General Introduction. *In* Community and Civil Society, by Ferdinand Tönnies. Jose Harris, ed. Pp. ix–xxx. Cambridge: Cambridge University Press.

Harvey, David

1989 The Condition of Postmodernity. Oxford: Basil Blackwell.

Hefner, Robert W., ed.

1993 Conversion to Christianity: Historical and Anthropological Perspectives on a Great Transformation. Berkeley: University of California Press.

Helmreich, Stefan

2000 Silicon Second Nature: Culturing Artificial Life in a Digital World. Berkeley: University of California Press.

Heng, Geraldine, and Janadas Devan

1992 State Fatherhood: The Politics of Nationalism, Sexuality, and Race in Singapore. *In* Nationalisms and Sexualities. Andres Parker, Mary Russo, Doris Sommer, and Patricia Yaeger, eds. Pp. 343–364. New York: Routledge.

Henney, William Franklin

1905 The Making of a Model Municipality, as Exemplified by the Growth of Hartford, Capital of Connecticut. Connecticut Magazine 9:557–609.

Hertz, Robert

1907 Contribution à une etude sur la représentation collective de la mort. Année Sociologique 10:48–137.

Herzfeld, Michael

1992 The Social Production of Indifference: Exploring the Symbolic Roots of Western Bureaucracy. New York: Berg.

Heyman, Josiah M., ed.

1999 States and Illegal Practices. Oxford: Berg.

Ho, Engseng

2006 The Graves of Tarim: Genealogy and Mobility across the Indian Ocean. Berkeley: University of California Press.

Honig, Emily

1986 Sisters and Strangers: Women in the Shanghai Cotton Mills, 1919–1949. Stanford, CA: Stanford University Press.

Howell, Signe

2001 Self-Conscious Kinship: Some Contested Values in Norwegian Transnational Adoption. *In* Relative Values: Reconfiguring Kinship Studies. Sarah Franklin and Susan McKinnon, eds. Pp. 203–223. Durham, NC: Duke University Press.

2006 The Kinning of Foreigners: Transnational Adoption in a Global Perspective. New York: Berghahn.

Hoy, David Couzens

2009 The Time of Our Lives: A Critical History of Temporality. Cambridge, MA: MIT Press.

Huang, Yasheng

2003 Selling China: Foreign Direct Investment during the Reform Era. Cambridge, MA: Harvard University Press.

Hume, David

1896 A Treatise on Human Nature. L. A. Selby-Bigge, ed. Oxford: Clarendon.

Hurd, John Codman

1858 The Law of Freedom and Bondage in the United States, vol. 1. Boston: Little, Brown.

Inda, Jonathan Xavier

2005 Analytics of the Modern: An Introduction. *In* Anthropologies of Modernity: Foucault, Governmentality, and Life Politics. Jonathan Xavier Inda, ed. Pp. 1–20. Oxford: Blackwell.

Ivy, Marilyn

1995 "Have You Seen Me?" Recovering the Inner Child in Late Twentieth-Century America. *In* Children and the Politics of Culture. Sharon Stephens, ed. Pp. 79–103. Princeton, NJ: Princeton University Press.

Jones, Gayle

1975 Corregidora. Boston: Beacon.

Jurgenson, John

2009 Hollywood's Favorite Cowboy. Wall Street Journal, November 20. http://online.wsj.com/article/SB10001424052748704576204574529703577274572.html, accessed February 4, 2010.

Kapferer, Bruce

1989 Nationalist Ideology and a Comparative Anthropology. Ethnos 54(3–4):161–199.

Karakasidou, Anastasia N.

1997 Fields of Wheat, Hills of Blood: Passages to Nationhood in Greek Macedonia. Chicago: University of Chicago Press.

Keane, Webb

1997 Signs of Recognition: Powers and Hazards of Representation in an Indonesian Society. Berkeley: University of California Press.

2007 Christian Moderns: Freedom and Fetish in the Mission Encounter. Berkeley: University of California Press.

Kearney, Michael

1972 Winds of Ixtepeji: Worldview and Society in a Zapotec Town. New York: Holt, Rinehart and Winston.

1995a The Local and the Global. Annual Review of Anthropology 24:547–565.

1995b The Effects of Transnational Culture, Economy and Migration on Mixtec Identity in Oaxacalifornia. *In* The Bubbling Cauldron: Race, Ethnicity and the Urban Crisis. Michael P. Smith and Joe R. Reagin, eds. Pp. 226–243. Minneapolis: University of Minnesota Press.

Kelly, John D.

2002 Alternative Modernities or an Alternative to "Modernity": Getting out of the Modernist Sublime. *In* Critically Modern: Alternatives, Alterities, Anthropologies. Bruce M. Knauft, ed. Pp. 258–286. Bloomington: Indiana University Press.

Kelly, John D., and Martha Kaplan

2001 Nation and Decolonization: Toward a New Anthropology of Nationalism. Anthropological Theory 1:419–437.

Kesselman, Amy

1991 The "Freedom Suit": Feminism and Dress Reform in the United States, 1848–1875. Gender and Society 5(4):495–510.

Khurana, Rakesh

2007 From Higher Aims to Hired Hands: The Social Transformation of American Business Schools and the Unfulfilled Promise of Management as a Profession. Princeton, NJ: Princeton University Press.

Kierner, Cynthia A.

2004 Scandal at Bizarre: Rumor and Reputation in Jefferson's America. Charlottesville: University of Virginia Press.

Kim, Eleana

2003 Wedding Citizenship and Culture: Korean Adoptees and the Global Family of Korea. *In* Transnational Adoption. Toby Volkman, ed. Special issue, Social Text 74:57–82.

2010 Adopted Territory: Transnational Korean Adoptees and the Politics of Belonging. Durham, NC: Duke University Press.

Kippenberg, Hans G.

2005 Religious Communities and the Path to Disenchantment: The Origins, Sources, and Theoretical Core of the Religion Section. *In* Max Weber's Economy and Society: A Critical Companion. Charles Camic, Phillip S. Gorski, and David M. Trubek, eds. Pp. 162–182. Stanford, CA: Stanford University Press.

Klassen, Pamela

2001 Blessed Events: Religion and Home Birth in America. Princeton, NJ: Princeton University Press.

Klausner, Samuel Z., and Edward F. Foulks

1982 Eskimo Capitalists: Oil, Politics, and Alcohol. Totowa, NJ: Allanheld.

Kleinfeld, Judith, and James Bloom

1973 A Long Way from Home: Effects of Public High Schools on Village Children Away from Home. Anchorage, AK: Institute of Social, Economic and Government Research.

Knauft, Bruce M.

2002 Critically Modern: An Introduction. *In* Critically Modern: Alternatives, Alterities, Anthropologies. Bruce M. Knauft, ed. Pp. 1–54. Bloomington: Indiana University Press.

Knight, Christopher

1991 Blood Relations: Menstruation and the Origin of Culture. New Haven, CT: Yale University Press.

Kolko, Beth E., Lisa Nakamura, and Gilbert B. Rodman

2000 Introduction. *In* Race in Cyberspace. Beth E. Kolko, Lisa Nakamura, and Gilbert B. Rodman, eds. Pp. 1–14. London: Routledge.

Kulikoff, Allan

1976 "Throwing the Stocking": A Gentry Marriage in Provincial Maryland. Maryland Historical Magazine 71(4):516–521.

1986 Tobacco and Slaves: The Development of Southern Cultures in the Chesapeake, 1680–1800. Chapel Hill: University of North Carolina Press.

Kumar, Krishan

1991 Maine and the Theory of Progress. *In* The Victorian Achievement of Sir Henry Maine: A Centennial Reappraisal. Alan Diamond, ed. Pp. 76–87. Cambridge: Cambridge University Press.

Kuper, Adam

1982 Lineage Theory: A Critical Retrospect. Annual Review of Anthropology 11:71–95.

1983 Anthropology and Anthropologists: The Modern British School. London: Routledge and Kegan Paul.

1988 The Invention of Primitive Society: Transformations of an Illusion. London: Routledge.

1991 The Rise and Fall of Maine's Patriarchal Theory. *In* The Victorian Achievement of Sir Henry Maine: A Centennial Reappraisal. Alan Diamond, ed. Pp. 99–110. Cambridge: Cambridge University Press.

2001 Fraternity and Endogamy: The House of Rothschild. Social Anthropology 9(3):273–287.

2009 Incest and Influence: The Private Life of Bourgeois England. Cambridge, MA: Harvard University Press.

Kurtz, Stanley

2002 Root Causes. *Review of* What Went Wrong? Western Impact and Middle

Eastern Response, by Bernard Lewis. Policy Review Online 112 (April–May): 1–8. http://www.hoover.org/publications/policy-review/article/6942, accessed August 18, 2005.

2007 Marriage and the Terror War. Parts 1 and 2. National Review Online, February 15 and 16. http://www.nationalreview.com/articles/219989/marriage-and-terror-war/stanley-kurtz; and http://www.nationalreview.com/articles/220002/marriage-and-terror-war-part-ii/stanley-kurtz, accessed September 7, 2007.

Kwon, Heonik

2008 Ghosts of War in Vietnam. Cambridge: Cambridge University Press.

2010 The Ghosts of War and the Ethics of Memory. *In* Ordinary Ethics: Anthropology, Language, and Action. Michael Lambek, ed. Pp. 400–413. New York: Fordham University Press.

Laderman, Gary

1996 The Sacred Remains: American Attitudes toward Death, 1799–1883. New Haven, CT: Yale University Press.

Lakoff, Andrew, and Stephen J. Collier

2008 The Problem of Securing Health. *In* Biosecurity Interventions: Global Health and Security in Question. Andrew Lakoff and Stephen J. Collier, eds. Pp. 7–32. New York: Columbia University Press.

Lambek, Michael

1993 Knowledge and Practice in Mayotte: Local Discourses of Islam, Sorcery, and Spirit Possession. Toronto: University of Toronto Press.

2003 Memory in a Maussian Universe. *In* Regimes of Memory. Susannah Radstone and Katharine Hodgkin, eds. Pp. 202–216. London: Routledge.

2008 Provincializing God? Provocations from an Anthropology of Religion. *In* Religion: Beyond a Concept. Hent de Vries, ed. Pp. 120–138. New York: Fordham University Press.

2010a Introduction. *In* Ordinary Ethics: Anthropology, Language, and Action. Michael Lambek, ed. Pp. 1–36. New York: Fordham University Press.

2010b Succession or Secession? Initial Reflections on Recent Conflicts over Leadership of the Sakalava Bemihisatra of Mahajanga. Paper presented at the Madagascar Symposium, Toronto, January.

2010c Towards an Ethics of the Act. *In* Ordinary Ethics: Anthropology, Language, and Action. Michael Lambek, ed. Pp. 39–63. New York: Fordham University Press.

2011 Kinship as Gift and Theft: Acts of Succession in Mayotte and Israel. American Ethnologist 38(1):1–15.

Lambert, Helen

2000 Sentiment and Substance in North Indian Forms of Relatedness. *In* Cultures of Relatedness: New Approaches to the Study of Kinship. Janet Carsten, ed. Pp. 73–89. Cambridge: Cambridge University Press.

References

Lampland, Martha

1994 Family Portraits: Gendered Images of the Nation in Nineteenth-Century Hungary. East European Politics and Societies 8(2):287–316.

Lansing, Stephen

2006 Man versus Nature: Coevolution of Social and Ecological Networks; Themes in *The Road*: Where Science and Fiction Meet. Oprah.com, January 1. http://www.oprah.com/oprahsbookclub/Fiction-and-Scientific-Themes-in-The-Road-by-Cormac-McCarthy/7, accessed February 5, 2010.

Laqueur, Thomas

1999 Pint for Pint. London Review of Books, October 14.

Lardy, Nicholas R.

2002 Integrating China into the World Economy. Washington, DC: Brookings Institution Press.

Laslett, Peter

2004[1965] The World We Have Lost: England before the Industrial Age. London: Methuen.

Latour, Bruno

1993 We Have Never Been Modern. Catherine Porter, trans. Cambridge, MA: Harvard University Press.

Layne, Linda L.

2011 Of Fetuses and Angels: Fragmentation and Integration of Narratives in Pregnancy Loss. Paper presented at the Cambridge Senior Seminar.

Layne, Linda L., ed.

1999 Transformative Motherhood: On Giving and Getting in a Consumer Culture. New York: New York University Press.

Leinaweaver, Jessaca B.

2007 On Moving Children: The Social Implications of Andean Child Circulation. American Anthropologist 34(1):163–180.

Lévi-Strauss, Claude

1969[1949] The Elementary Structures of Kinship. Boston: Beacon.

1982 The Way of the Masks. Seattle: University of Washington Press.

1984 The View from Afar. New York: Basic Books.

1987 Anthropology and Myth: Lectures, 1951–1982. Oxford: Basil Blackwell.

Liu, Haiming

2005 The Transnational History of a Chinese Family: Immigrant Letters, Family Business, and Reverse Migration. New Brunswick, NJ: Rutgers University Press.

Lock, Margaret

2002 Twice Dead: Organ Transplants and the Reinvention of Death. Berkeley: University of California Press.

Lock, Margaret, Julia Freeman, Rosemary Sharples, and Stephanie Lloyd
2006 When It Runs in the Family: Putting Susceptibility Genes in Perspective. Public Understanding of Science 15:277–300.

Lockhart, James
1994 Sightings: Initial Nahua Reactions to Spanish Culture. *In* Implicit Understandings: Observing, Reporting, and Reflecting on the Encounters between Europeans and Other Peoples in the Early Modern Era. Stuart B. Schwartz, ed. Pp. 218–249. Cambridge: Cambridge University Press.

López Beltrán, Carlos
2007 Hippocratic Bodies: Temperament and Castas in Spanish America (1570–1820). Journal of Spanish Cultural Studies 8(2):253–289.

Luhrmann, Tanya
2004 Metakinesis: How God Becomes Intimate in Contemporary U.S. Christianity. American Anthropologist 106(3):518–528.

MacCormack, Carol, and Marilyn Strathern, eds.
1980 Nature, Culture, and Gender. Cambridge: Cambridge University Press.

Mahmood, Saba
2006 Secularism, Hermeneutics, and Empire: The Politics of Islamic Revolution. Public Culture 18(2):323–352.

Maine, Henry Sumner
1970[1861] Ancient Law: Its Connection with the Early History of Society and Its Relation to Modern Ideas. Gloucester, MA: Peter Smith.

Majumdar, Rochona
2009 Marriage and Modernity: Family Values in Colonial Bengal. Durham, NC: Duke University Press.

Marcus, George E.
1980 Law in the Development of Dynastic Families among American Business Elites: The Domestication of Capital and the Capitalization of the Family. Law and Society 14:859–903.

Marcus, George E., ed.
1998 Corporate Futures: The Diffusion of the Culturally Sensitive Corporate Form. Chicago: University of Chicago Press.

Marcus, George E., with Peter Dobkin Hall
1992 Lives in Trust: The Fortunes of Dynastic Families in Late Twentieth-Century America. Boulder, CO: Westview.

Marriott, McKim
1976 Hindu Transactions: Diversity without Dualism. *In* Transaction and Meaning: Directions in the Anthropology of Exchange and Symbolic Behavior. Bruce Kapferer, ed. Pp. 109–142. Philadelphia: Institute for the Study of Human Issues.

Martin, David

2005 On Secularization: Towards a Revised Theory. Aldershot, UK: Ashgate.

Martin, Emily

1998 Anthropology and the Cultural Study of Science. Special issue, Science, Technology and Human Values 23:24–44.

Martin, Margaret E.

1939 Merchants and Trade of the Connecticut River Valley, 1750–1820. Northampton, MA: Department of History, Smith College.

Marx, Karl

1992[1885] Capital, vol. 2. London: Penguin Classics.

Masco, Joseph

2008 Survival Is Your Business: Engineering Ruins and Affect in Nuclear America. Cultural Anthropology 23(2):361–398.

2009 Life Underground. Anthropology Now 1(2):13–29.

Mauer, Bill

1996 The Land, the Law, and Legitimate Children: Thinking through Gender, Kinship, and Nation in the British Virgin Islands. *In* Gender, Kinship, Power: A Comparative and Interdisciplinary History. Mary Jo Maynes, Ann Waltner, Birgitte Soland, and Ulrike Strasser, eds. Pp. 351–363. New York: Routledge.

Mauss, Marcel

1985[1938] A Category of the Human Mind: The Notion of Person, the Notion of Self. *In* The Category of the Person: Anthropology, Philosophy, History. Michael Carrithers, Steven Collins, and Steven Lukes, eds. Pp. 1–25. Cambridge: Cambridge University Press.

1990[1950] The Gift: The Form and Reason for Exchange in Archaic Societies. W. D. Halls, trans. New York: Norton.

McCarthy, Cormac

1968 Outer Dark. New York: Random House.

1973 Child of God. New York: Random House.

1985 Blood Meridian; or, The Evening Redness in the West. New York: Random House.

2005 No Country for Old Men. New York: Knopf.

2006 The Road. New York: Knopf.

McDannell, Colleen

1995 Material Christianity: Religion and Popular Culture in America. New Haven, CT: Yale University Press.

McKelvey, Blake

1940 The Flower City: Center of Nurseries and Fruit Orchards. Rochester Historical Society Publications, vol. 18, part 2, pp. 121–169.

1945 Rochester: The Water-Power City, 1812–1854. Cambridge, MA: Harvard University Press.

McKinley, Robert

2001 The Philosophy of Kinship: A Reply to Schneider's Critique of the Study of Kinship. *In* The Cultural Analysis of Kinship: The Legacy of David M. Schneider. Richard Feinberg and Martin Ottenheimer, eds. Pp. 131–167. Urbana: University of Illinois Press.

McKinnon, Susan

1991 From a Shattered Sun: Hierarchy, Gender, and Alliance in the Tanimbar Islands. Madison: University of Wisconsin Press.

1995 Houses and Hierarchy: The View from a South Moluccan Society. *In* About the House: Lévi-Strauss and Beyond. Janet Carsten and Stephen Hugh-Jones, eds. Pp. 170–188. Cambridge: Cambridge University Press.

2000 Domestic Exceptions: Evans-Pritchard and the Creation of Nuer Patrilineality and Equality. Cultural Anthropology 15(1):35–84.

2001 The Economies in Kinship and the Paternity of Culture: Origin Stories in Kinship Theory. *In* Relative Values: Reconfiguring Kinship Studies. Sarah Franklin and Susan McKinnon, eds. Pp. 277–301. Durham, NC: Duke University Press.

2008 Afterword: Adoptive Relations in Theories of Kinship and Modernity. *In* Relative Power: Changing Interpretations of Fosterage and Adoption in Pacific Island Societies. Jeanette Dickerson-Putman and Judith Schachter, eds. Special issue, Pacific Studies 31(3–4):232–247.

N.d. What's Cousin Marriage Have to Do with Modernization? Unpublished manuscript in the author's possession.

McKinnon, Susan, and Fenella Cannell

N.d. The Difference Kinship Makes: Rethinking the Ideologies of Modernity. SAR advanced seminar proposal.

McManus, Thomas

1886 The Roman Catholic Church. *In* The Memorial History of Hartford County, Connecticut, 1633–1884, vol. 1. James Hammond Trumbull, ed. Pp. 410–419. Boston: Edward L. Osgood.

Mendelsohn, Robert O.

2006–2007 A Critique of the Stern Report. Regulation (Winter):42–46.

Merrill, Boynton, Jr.

1976 Jefferson's Nephews: A Frontier Tragedy. Princeton, NJ: Princeton University Press.

Middleton, Karen, ed.

1999 Ancestors, Power and History in Madagascar. Leiden: Brill.

Mintz, Sidney Wilfred

1986 Sweetness and Power: The Place of Sugar in Modern History. New York: Penguin.

Mintz, Steven, and Susan Kellog

1988 Domestic Revolutions: A Social History of American Family Life. New York: Free Press.

Mobilization for Climate Justice

2009 Indigenous People Lead Massive Demonstration in Copenhagen. Act for Climate Justice! http://www.actforclimatejustice.org/2009/12/indigenous-peoples-lead-massive-demonstration-in-copenhagen, accessed September 15, 2010.

Modell, Judith S.

1998 Rights to the Children: Foster Care and Social Reproduction in Hawai'i. *In* Reproducing Reproduction: Kinship, Power, and Technological Innovation. Sarah Franklin and Helena Ragoné, eds. Pp. 156–172. Philadelphia: University of Pennsylvania Press.

Mody, Perveez

2008 The Intimate State: Love-Marriage and the Law in Delhi. London: Routledge.

Mollona, Massimiliano

2005 Factory, Family and Neighbourhood: The Political Economy of Informal Labour in Sheffield. Journal of the Royal Anthropological Institute 11(3):527–548.

Mombello, Laura

2005 La "Mística Neuquina": Marcas y Disputas de Provincianía y Alteridad en una Provincia Joven. *In* Cartografías Argentinas: Políticas Indigenistas y Formaciones Provinciales de Alteridad. Claudia Briones, ed. Pp. 151–178. Buenos Aires: Antropofagia.

Monbiot, George

2007 Civilization Ends with a Shutdown of Human Concern: Are We There Already? Guardian.co.uk, October 30. http://www.guardian.co.uk/commentisfree/2007/oct/30/comment.books, accessed February 4, 2010.

Monnig, Laurel A.

2008 Adoption Is Blood: Understanding Chamorro Poksai as Chamorro Authenticity within Racialized Decolonization Politics on Guam. *In* Relative Power: Changing Interpretations of Fosterage and Adoption in Pacific Island Societies. Jeanette Dickerson-Putman and Judith Schachter, eds. Special issue, Pacific Studies 31(3–4):182–210.

Morgan, Lewis Henry

1851 League of the Ho-dé-no-sau-nee, Iroquois. Rochester, NY: Sage and Brother.

1859 Agassiz: Theory of the Diverse Origin of the Human Race. Read before "The Club" on May 16. Morgan Papers, MSS, no. 44. Department of Rare Books and Special Collections, Rush Rhees Library, University of Rochester.

1871 Systems of Consanguinity and Affinity of the Human Family. Washington, DC: Smithsonian Institution Press.

1877 Ancient Society; or, Researches in the Lines of Human Progress from Savagery through Barbarism to Civilization. New York: Henry Holt.

1881 Houses and House-Life of the American Aborigines. Washington, DC: Government Printing Office.

1959 The Indian Journals, 1859–62, by Lewis Henry Morgan. Leslie A. White, ed. Ann Arbor: University of Michigan Press.

Morgan, Lynn M.

2009 Icons of Life: A Cultural History of Human Embryos. Berkeley: University of California Press.

Morgan, Nathaniel Harris

1851 Our Family Genealogy. Hartford, CT: Press of Case, Tiffany and Co. Connecticut Historical Society, open stacks, box 929.2 M8470.

1869 Morgan Genealogy: A History of James Morgan, of New London, Conn. and His Descendants; From 1607 to 1869. Hartford, CT: Case, Lockwood & Brainard. Connecticut Historical Society, open stacks, box 929.2 M848m b.

Mosconi, Enrique

1984 Obras del General Enrique Mosconi. Buenos Aires: Yacimientos Petrolíferos Fiscales.

Muehlebach, Andrea

2011 Labor in Post-Fordist Italy. Cultural Anthropology 26(1):59–82.

Nader, Laura

1990 Harmony Ideology: Justice and Control in a Zapotec Mountain Village. Stanford, CA: Stanford University Press.

Nash, Catherine

2008 Of Irish Descent: Origin Stories, Genealogy, and the Politics of Belonging. Syracuse, NY: Syracuse University Press.

Nash, June C.

1979 We Eat the Mines and the Mines Eat Us: Dependency and Exploitation in Bolivian Tin Mines. New York: Columbia University Press.

Needham, Rodney

1971 Rethinking Kinship and Marriage. London: Tavistock.

Nevins, Joseph

2002 Operation Gatekeeper: The Rise of the "Illegal Alien" and the Making of the US-Mexican Border. London: Routledge.

Newell, Linda King, and Valeen Tippetts Avery

1984 Mormon Enigma: Emma Hale Smith. Garden City, NY: Doubleday.

Nicoletti, María Andrea, and Pedro Floria Navarro

2000 Confluencias: Una Breve Historia del Neuquén. Buenos Aires: Dunken.

2002 Building an Image of the Indian People from Patagonia during the Eighteenth and Nineteenth Centuries: Science and Christening. *In* Archaeological and Anthropological Perspectives on the Native Peoples of Pampa, Patagonia and Tierra del Fuego to the Nineteenth Century. Claudia Briones and José Luis Lanata, eds. Pp. 133–143. Westport, CT: Bergin and Garvey.

Novas, Carlos, and Nikolas Rose

2000 Genetic Risk and the Birth of the Somatic Individual. Economy and Society 29(4):485–513.

Nugent, David

1999 State and Shadow State in Northern Peru circa 1900: Illegal Political Networks and the Problem of State Boundaries. *In* States and Illegal Practices. Josia M. Heyman, ed. Pp. 63–98. Oxford: Berg.

Nuttall, Mark

1992 Arctic Homeland: Kinship, Community and Development in Northwest Greenland. Toronto: University of Toronto Press.

Ochoa, Gilda L.

2004 Becoming Neighbors in a Mexican American Community. Austin: University of Texas Press.

Oi, Jean C., and Andrew G. Walder

1999 Property Rights and Economic Reform in China. Stanford, CA: Stanford University Press.

Olmsted, Henry King, and George Kemp Ward

1912 Genealogy of the Olmsted Family in America. New York: A. T. De La Mare.

Ong, Aihwa

1999 Flexible Citizenship: The Cultural Logics of Transnationality. Durham, NC: Duke University Press.

Ong, Aihwa, and Stephen J. Collier

2005 Global Assemblages: Technology, Politics, and Ethics as Anthropological Problems. Oxford: Blackwell.

Ong, Aihwa, and Donald Nonini, eds.

1997 The Cultural Politics of Modern Chinese Transnationalism. New York: Routledge.

Ottenheimer, Martin

1996 Forbidden Relatives: The American Myth of Cousin Marriage. Urbana: University of Illinois Press.

Oxfeld, Ellen

1993 Blood, Sweat, and Mahjong: Family and Enterprise in an Overseas Chinese Community. Ithaca, NY: Cornell University Press.

Palacios, María Susana, and Norma Paris

1993 Municipio y Sectores Dirigentes: El Caso de Cutral Có (1933–1955). *In* Historia de Neuquén. S. Bandieri, Orietta Favaro, and Marta B. Morinelli, eds. Pp. 320–331. Buenos Aires: PLUS ULTRA.

Panter-Brick, Catherine, and Malcom T. Smith, eds.

2000 Abandoned Children. Cambridge: Cambridge University Press.

Parkes, Adam

2002 History, Bloodshed, and the Spectacle of American Identity in *Blood*

Meridian. In Cormac McCarthy: New Directions. James D. Lilley, ed. Pp. 103–124. Albuquerque: University of New Mexico Press.

Parmentier, Richard J.

1994 Signs in Society: Studies in Semiotic Anthropology. Bloomington: Indiana University Press.

Parry, Jonathan

1986 The Gift, the Indian Gift, and the "Indian Gift." Man, n.s., 21(3):453–473.

Parsons, Talcott

1955 The American Family: Its Relations to Personality and to the Social Structure. *In* Family, Socialization and Interaction Process, by Talcott Parsons and Robert F. Bales. Pp. 3–33. Glencoe, IL: Free Press.

Partnership for Strong Communities

2012 Our Neighborhood, Frog Hollow. http://pschousing.org/our-neighborhood-frog-hollow, accessed March 25, 2012.

Pascoe, Peggy

2004 History of US Miscegenation Laws. National Public Radio interview with Robert Siegel, March 16. http://www.npr.org/templates/story/story.php?storyId=1771433, accessed December 24, 2010.

2009 What Comes Naturally: Miscegenation Law and the Making of Race in America. Oxford: Oxford University Press.

Pauly, Philip J.

2000 Biologists and the Promise of American Life: From Meriwether Lewis to Alfred Kinsey. Princeton, NJ: Princeton University Press.

Pedroso de Lima, Antónia

2000 Is Blood Thicker Than Economic Interest in Familial Enterprises? *In* Dividends of Kinship: Meanings and Uses of Social Relatedness. Peter P. Schweitzer, ed. Pp. 151–176. London: Routledge.

Peirce, Charles Sanders

1991 Peirce on Signs: Writings on Semiotics. James Hoopes, ed. Chapel Hill: University of North Carolina Press.

Pennington, J. W. C.

1856 The Reasonableness of the Abolition of Slavery at the South: A Legitimate Inference from the Success of British Emancipation; An Address, Delivered at Hartford, Conn., on the First of August, 1856. Hartford, CT: Case, Tiffany.

Phillips, Dana

2002 History and the Ugly Facts of *Blood Meridian. In* Cormac McCarthy: New Directions. James D. Lilley, ed. Pp. 17–46. Albuquerque: University of New Mexico Press.

Pieke, Frank

1995 Bureaucracy, Friends and Money: The Growth of Capital Socialism in China. Comparative Studies in Society and History 37(3):494–518.

Pina Cabral, Joao de
1989 L'héritage de Maine: Repenser de catégories descriptives dans l'étude de la famille en Europe. Ethnologie Française 19(4):329–340.

Pinch, Adela
1998 Stealing Happiness: Shoplifting in Early Nineteenth Century England. *In* Border Fetishisms: Material Objects in Unstable Spaces. Patricia Spyer, ed. Pp. 122–149. New York: Routledge.

Piore, Michael, and Charles F. Sabel
1984 The Second Industrial Divide: Possibilities for Prosperity. New York: Basic Books.

Plotkin, Mariano Ben
2003 Mañana es San Perón: A Cultural History of Peron's Argentina. K. Zahniser, trans. Wilmington, DE: Scholarly Resources.

Povinelli, Elizabeth
2002 Notes on Gridlock: Genealogy, Intimacy, Sexuality. Public Culture 14(1):215–238.
2006 The Empire of Love: Towards a Theory of Intimacy, Genealogy, and Carnality. Durham, NC: Duke University Press.

Pred, Allan, and Michael Watts, eds.
1992 Reworking Modernity: Capitalisms and Symbolic Discontent. New Brunswick, NJ: Rutgers University Press.

Pressend, Michelle
2010 South Africa: Copenhagen Accord Makes Shame of Global Environmental Justice. South African Civil Society Information Service, AllAfrica.Com, January 14. http://allafrica.com/stories/201001140623.html, accessed September 15, 2010.

Pugh, Allison J.
2008 Longing and Belonging: Parents, Children, and Consumer Culture. Berkeley: University of California Press.

Rabinow, Paul
1999 French DNA: Trouble in Purgatory. Chicago: University of Chicago Press.

Rapp, Rayna
1979 Review Essay: Anthropology. Signs: Journal of Women in Culture and Society 4(3):497–513.
1999 Testing Women, Testing the Fetus: The Social Impact of Amniocentesis in America. New York: Routledge.

Rappaport, Roy
1999 Ritual and Religion in the Making of Humanity. Cambridge: Cambridge University Press.

Ratanapruck, Prista
2008 Market and Monastery: Manangi Trade Diasporas in South and Southeast Asia. PhD dissertation, Harvard University.

Redfield, Robert

1960 The Little Community and Peasant Society and Culture. Chicago: University of Chicago Press.

Reed, Isaac Ariail, and Julia Adams

2011 Culture in the Transitions to Modernity: Seven Pillars of a New Research Agenda. Theory and Society 40(3):247–272.

Reiter, Rayna

1975 Men and Women in the South of France: Public and Private Domains. *In* Toward an Anthropology of Women. Rayna R. Reiter, ed. Pp. 252–282. New York: Monthly Review Press.

Richard, Analiese, and Daromir Rudnyckyi

2009 Economies of Affect. Journal of the Royal Anthropological Institute, n.s., 15(1):57–77.

Robertson, Constance Noyes, ed.

1970 Oneida Community: An Autobiography, 1851–1876. Syracuse, NY: Syracuse University Press.

Robinson, Marilynne

2004 Gilead. New York: Picador.

Rodriguez, Gregory

2008 Mongrels, Bastards, Orphans and Vagabonds: Mexican Immigration and the Future of Race in America. New York: Vintage.

Rodriguez, Richard

1992 Days of Obligation: An Argument with My Mexican Father. London: Penguin.

Rofel, Lisa

1999 Other Modernities: Gendered Yearnings in China after Socialism. Berkeley: University of California Press.

Roitman, Janet L.

2005 Fiscal Disobedience: An Anthropology of Economic Regulation in Central Africa. Princeton, NJ: Princeton University Press.

Rosaldo, Michelle Zimbalist

1974 Is Female to Male as Nature Is to Culture? *In* Woman, Culture and Society. Michelle Zimbalist Rosaldo and Louise Lamphere, eds. Pp. 67–87. Stanford, CA: Stanford University Press.

Rosaldo, Michelle Zimbalist, and Louise Lamphere, eds.

1974 Woman, Culture and Society. Stanford, CA: Stanford University Press.

Rose, Nikolas S.

1999 Governing the Soul: The Shaping of the Private Self. London: Free Association Books.

Rose, Sonya O.

1992 Limited Livelihoods: Gender and Class in Nineteenth-Century England. London: Routledge.

Rose, Willie Lee
1982 Slavery and Freedom. William W. Freehling, ed. New York: Oxford University Press.

Russell, Gurdon Wadsworth
1890 "Up Neck" in 1825. Hartford, CT: Case, Lockwood, and Brainard.

Rutherford, Danilyn
1998 Love, Violence, and Foreign Wealth: Kinship and History in Biak, Irian Jaya. Journal of the Royal Anthropological Institute 4(2):257–281.
2003 Raiding the Land of the Foreigners: The Limits of the Nation on an Indonesian Frontier. Princeton, NJ: Princeton University Press.

Sacks, Karen
1975 Engels Revisited: Women, the Organization of Production, and Private Property. *In* Toward an Anthropology of Women. Rayna R. Reiter, ed. Pp. 211–234. New York: Monthly Review Press.

Sahlins, Marshall
1972 Stone Age Economics. Chicago: Aldine.
1994 Cosmologies of Capitalism: The Trans-Pacific Sector of "the World System." *In* Culture/Power/History: A Reader in Contemporary Social Theory. Nicholas B. Dirks, Geoff Eley, and Sherry B. Ortner, eds. Pp. 412–455. Princeton, NJ: Princeton University Press.
1996 The Sadness of Sweetness: The Native Anthropology of Western Cosmology. Current Anthropology 37(3):395–428.

Sailer, Steve
2003 Cousin Marriage Conundrum: The Ancient Practice Discourages Democratic Nation-Building. American Conservative, January 13.

Sanjek, Roger
2003 Rethinking Migration, Ancient to Future. Global Networks 3(3):315–336.

Sartorio, Donata, ed.
2009 Italian Touch. Milan: Skira.

Schachter, Judith [Modell]
2008 "A Relationship Endeared to the People": Adoption in Hawaiian Custom and Law. *In* Relative Power: Changing Interpretations of Fosterage and Adoption in Pacific Island Societies. Jeanette Dickerson-Putman and Judith Schachter, eds. Special issue, Pacific Studies 31(3–4):211–231.

Schatz, Edward
2004 Modern Clan Politics: The Power of "Blood" in Kazakhstan and Beyond. Seattle: University of Washington Press.

Schiller, Nina Glick, Linda Basch, and Cristina Blanc-Szanton
1992 Towards a Transnational Perspective on Migration: Race, Class, Ethnicity, and Nationalism. New York: Annals of the New York Academy of Sciences.

Schneider, David M.
1968 American Kinship: A Cultural Account. Englewood Cliffs, NJ: Prentice Hall.

1969 Kinship, Nationality and Religion in American Culture: Toward a Definition of Kinship. *In* Forms of Symbolic Action: Proceedings of the 1969 Annual Spring Meeting of the American Ethnological Society. Robert F. Spencer, ed. Pp. 116–125. Seattle, WA: American Ethnological Society.

1980 American Kinship: A Cultural Account. 2nd edition. Chicago: University of Chicago Press.

1984 A Critique of the Study of Kinship. Ann Arbor: University of Michigan Press.

Schweitzer, Peter P.

2000 Introduction. *In* Dividends of Kinship: Meanings and Uses of Social Relatedness. Peter P. Schweitzer, ed. Pp. 1–32. London: Routledge.

Segre Reinach, Simona

2010 If You Speak Fashion You Speak Italian: Notes on Present Day Italian Fashion Identity. Critical Studies in Fashion and Beauty 1(2):203–215.

Sennett, Richard

2008 The Craftsman. New Haven, CT: Yale University Press.

Shao, Jing

2006 Fluid Labour and Blood Money: The Economy of HIV/AIDS in Rural Central China. Cultural Anthropology 21(4):535–569.

Shao, Jing, and Mary Scoggin

2009 Solidarity and Distinction in Blood: Contamination, Morality and Variability. Special issue, Body and Society 15:29–49.

Shapiro, Henry D.

1978 Appalachia on Our Mind: The Southern Mountains and Mountaineers in the American Consciousness, 1870–1920. Chapel Hill: University of North Carolina Press.

Shattuck, Lemuel

1846 Report to the Committee of the City Council Appointed to Obtain the Census of Boston for the Year 1845, Embracing Collateral Facts and Statistical Researches, Illustrating the History and Condition of the Population, and Their Means of Progress and Prosperity. Boston: John H. Eastburn.

1855 Memorials of the Descendants of William Shattuck, the Progenitor of the Families in America That Have Borne His Name. Boston: Dutton and Wentworth.

Sheppard, J. H.

1862 A Brief History of the New England Historic-Genealogical Society. Albany, NY: Joel Munsell.

Shever, Elana

2008 Neoliberal Associations: Property, Company, and Family in the Argentine Oil Fields. American Ethnologist 35(4):701–715.

2012 Resources for Reform: Oil and Neoliberalism in Argentina. Stanford, CA: Stanford University Press

Shils, Edward

1970 The Tyranny of Tradition. Encounter 34(3):57–61.

1991 Henry Sumner Maine in the Tradition of the Analysis of Society. *In* The Victorian Achievement of Sir Henry Maine: A Centennial Reappraisal. Alan Diamond, ed. Pp. 143–178. Cambridge: Cambridge University Press.

Shorter, Edward

1975 The Making of the Modern Family. New York: Basic Books.

Siegel, James T.

1998 A New Criminal Type in Jakarta: Counter-Revolution Today. Durham, NC: Duke University Press.

Simons, D. Brenton, and Peter Benes, eds.

2002 The Art of Family: Genealogical Artifacts in New England. Boston: New England Historic Genealogical Society.

SIRIS

2001–2004 Smithsonian Institution Research Information System, Smithsonian American Art Museum. Inventory of American Sculpture. http://sirisartinventories.si.edu/ipac20/ipac.jsp?uri=full=3100001~!4327!0#focus, accessed January 22, 2011.

Sivaramakrishnan, K., and Arun Agrawal, eds.

2003 Regional Modernities: The Cultural Politics of Development in India. Stanford, CA: Stanford University Press.

Skinner, G. William

1976 Mobility Strategies in Late Imperial China: A Regional Systems Analysis. *In* Regional Analysis, vol. 1: Economic Systems. Carol A. Smith, ed. Pp. 327–364. New York: Academic Press.

1977 Cities and the Hierarchy of Local Systems. *In* The City in Late Imperial China. G. William Skinner, ed. Pp. 279–294. Stanford, CA: Stanford University Press.

Smith, Daniel Blake

1980 Inside the Great House: Planter Family Life in Eighteenth-Century Chesapeake Society. Ithaca, NY: Cornell University Press.

Smith, Daniel Scott

1973 Parental Power and Marriage Patterns: An Analysis of Historical Trends in Hingham, Massachusetts. Journal of Marriage and the Family 35(3):419–428.

Smith, Raymond T.

N.d. American Kinship. Raymond T. Smith home page. http://home.uchicago.edu/~rts1/american.htm, accessed January 24, 2011.

Solberg, Carl E.

1979 Oil and Nationalism in Argentina: A History. Stanford, CA: Stanford University Press.

1982 Entrepreneurship in Public Enterprise: General Enrique Mosconi and the Argentine Petroleum Industry. Business History Review 56(3):380–399.

Solway, Jacqueline

1990 Affines and Spouses, Friends and Lovers: The Passing of Polygyny in Botswana. Journal of Anthropological Research 46(1):41–66.

Sommer, Doris

1991 Foundational Fictions: The National Romances of Latin America. Berkeley: University of California Press.

Spillers, Hortense J.

2003 Mama's Baby and Papa's Maybe. *In* Black, White, and in Color: Essays on American Literature and Culture. Chicago: University of Chicago Press.

Stafford, Charles

2000 Separation and Reunion in Modern China. Cambridge: Cambridge University Press.

Stanley, Amy Dru

1998 From Bondage to Contract: Wage Labor, Marriage, and the Market in the Age of Slave Emancipation. Chicago: University of Chicago Press.

Starr, Douglas

1998 Blood: An Epic History of Medicine and Commerce. New York: Knopf.

Stasch, Rupert

2009 Society of Others: Kinship and Mourning in a West Papuan Place. Berkeley: University of California Press.

Stephen, Lynn

1991 Zapotec Women. Austin: University of Texas Press.

2009 Expanding the Borderlands: Recent Studies on the US-Mexico Border. Latin American Research Review 44(1):266–277.

Stern, Alexandra Minna

2005 Eugenic Nation: Faults and Frontiers of Better Breeding in Modern America. Berkeley: University of California Press.

Stern, Nicholas

2006 The Stern Review on the Economics of Climate Change. London: HM Treasury. National Archives of the United Kingdom. http://webarchive.nationalarchives.gov.uk/+/http:/www.hm-treasury.gov.uk/sternreview_index.htm, accessed February 9, 2010.

Stewart, Alex

2003 Help One Another, Use One Another: Toward an Anthropology of Family Business. Entrepreneurship Theory and Practice 27(4):383–396.

2008 Who Could Best Complement a Team of Family Business Researchers: Scholars down the Hall or in Another Building? Family Business Review 21(4):279–293.

Stoler, Ann Laura

2002 Carnal Knowledge and Imperial Power: Race and the Intimate in Colonial Rule. Berkeley: University of California Press.

2004 Affective States. *In* A Companion to the Anthropology of Politics. David Nugent and Joan Vincent, eds. Pp. 4–20. Malden, MA: Blackwell.

2005 Intimations of Empire: Predicaments of the Tactile and the Unseen. *In* Haunted by Empire: Geographies of Intimacy in North American History. Ann Laura Stoler, ed. Pp. 1–22. Durham, NC: Duke University Press.

Strathern, Marilyn

1980 No Nature, No Culture: The Hagan Case. *In* Nature, Culture, and Gender. Carol MacCormack and Marilyn Strathern, eds. Pp. 174–222. Cambridge: Cambridge University Press.

1984 Domesticity and the Denigration of Women. *In* Rethinking Women's Roles: Perspectives from the Pacific. Denise O'Brien and Sharon W. Tiffany, eds. Pp. 13–31. Berkeley: University of California Press.

1988 The Gender of the Gift: Problems with Women and Problems with Society in Melanesia. Berkeley: University of California Press.

1991 Partial Connections. Lanham, MD: Rowman and Littlefield.

1992a Reproducing the Future: Essays on Anthropology, Kinship and the New Reproductive Technologies. Manchester, UK: Manchester University Press.

1992b After Nature: English Kinship in the Late Twentieth Century. Cambridge: Cambridge University Press.

2005 Kinship, Law and the Unexpected: Relatives Are Always a Surprise. Cambridge: Cambridge University Press.

Strong, Pauline Turner, and Barrik Van Winkle

1993 Tribe and Nation: American Indians and American Nationalism. Social Analysis 33:9–27.

Supple, Barry E.

1957 A Business Elite: German-Jewish Financiers in Nineteenth-Century New York. Business History Review 31(2):143–178.

Sutton, David E.

1997 Local Names, Foreign Claims: Family Inheritance and National Heritage on a Greek Island. American Ethnologist 24(2):415–437.

Swift, Rowland

1886 Commerce and Banking. *In* The Memorial History of Hartford County, Connecticut, 1633–1884, vol. 1. James Hammond Trumbull, ed. Pp. 308–348. Boston: Edward L. Osgood.

Talcott, Mary K.

1886 Prominent Business Men. *In* The Memorial History of Hartford County, Connecticut, 1633–1884, vol. 1. James Hammond Trumbull, ed. Pp. 353–372. Boston: Edward L. Osgood.

Tarbox, Increase N.

1886 Emigration. *In* The Memorial History of Hartford County, Connecticut, 1633–1884, vol. 1. James Hammond Trumbull, ed. Pp. 201–206. Boston: Edward L. Osgood.

Taussig, Michael T.

1980 The Devil and Commodity Fetishism in South America. Chapel Hill: University of North Carolina Press.

Taylor, Charles

2007 A Secular Age. Cambridge, MA: Harvard University Press.

Taylor, Maureen A.

2002 Tall Oaks from Little Acorns Grow: The Family Tree Lithograph in America. *In* The Art of Family: Genealogical Artifacts in New England. D. Brenton Simons and Peter Benes, eds. Pp. 75–89. Boston: New England Historic Genealogical Society.

Thompson, Charis

2005 Making Parents: The Ontological Choreography of Reproductive Technologies. Cambridge, MA: MIT Press.

Thompson, Stuart

1988 Death, Food and Fertility. *In* Death Ritual in Late Imperial and Modern China. James L. Watson and Evelyn S. Rawski, eds. Pp. 71–108. Berkeley: University of California Press.

Tierney, John

2003 Iraq's Family Bonds Complicate U.S. Efforts: Marriages of Cousins Help Insulate Kin from Outsiders. New York Times, September 28. http://www.zaxistv.com/sociology/values/iraqmarriage.htm, accessed August 18, 2005.

Tipps, Dean C.

1973 Modernization Theory and the Comparative Study of Societies: A Critical Perspective. Comparative Studies in Society and History 15(2):199–226.

Titmuss, Richard M.

1970 The Gift Relationship: From Human Blood to Social Policy. London: London School of Economics.

Tönnies, Ferdinand

2001[1887] Community and Civil Society. Jose Harris, ed. Cambridge: Cambridge University Press.

Trautmann, Thomas R.

1987 Lewis Henry Morgan and the Invention of Kinship. Berkeley: University of California Press.

Trautmann, Thomas R., and Karl Sanford Kabelac

1994 The Library of Lewis Henry Morgan. Transactions of the American Philosophical Society, vol. 84, parts 6 and 7.

2008 The Library of Lewis Henry Morgan and Mary Elizabeth Morgan: The Pamphlets. Rochester, NY: Department of Rare Books and Special Collections, Rush Rhees Library, University of Rochester.

Trilling, Lionel

1972 Sincerity and Authenticity. Cambridge, MA: Harvard University Press.

Triptree, Jill

2009 An Elegance beyond Fashion. Luxury Insider: A Fashion Blog. http://www.luxury-insider.com/reviews/2009/tods-the-italian-touch, accessed February 20, 2012.

Trumbull, James Hammond, ed.

1886 The Memorial History of Hartford County, Connecticut, 1633–1884, vol. 1. Boston: Edward L. Osgood.

Turner, Victor

1969 The Ritual Process: Structure and Anti-structure. Ithaca, NY: Cornell University Press.

Tutton, Richard

2002 Gift Relationships in Genetics Research. Science as Culture 11:523–542.

Underwood, Grant

1993 The Millenarian World of Early Mormonism. Urbana: University of Illinois Press.

Ungar, Steven, ed.

1977 The Destruction of American Indian Families. New York: Association on American Indian Affairs.

Velez-Ibañez, Carlos G.

1980 Through the Eyes of an Anthropologist. *In* The Chicanos: As We See Ourselves. Arnulfo Trejo, ed. Pp. 37–48. Tucson: University of Arizona Press.

Verdery, Katherine

1996 What Was Socialism, and What Comes Next? Princeton, NJ: Princeton University Press.

Wacquant, Loïc

2009 Prisons of Poverty. Minneapolis: University of Minnesota Press.

2010 The Penal State. Lecture given at Cambridge University, October.

Wank, David L.

1999 Commodifying Communism: Business, Trust, and Politics in a Chinese City. Cambridge: Cambridge University Press.

Ward, Roswell H.

1948 Henry A. Ward, Museum Builder to America. Rochester, NY: Rochester Historical Society.

Washburn, Albert L., and Henry Robinson Buck, comps.

1911 History of Hartford Streets, Their Names, with Origin and Dates of Uses. Hartford, CT: Municipal Art Society of Hartford.

Watkins, Evan, ed.

1995 Corporate Culture. Special issue, Social Text 44:1–68.

Watson, Rubie

1985 Inequality among Brothers: Class and Kinship in South China. Cambridge: Cambridge University Press.

Weber, Max

1946 From Max Weber: Essays in Sociology. H. H. Gerth and C. Wright Mills, eds. and trans. New York: Oxford University Press.

1978a Economy and Society, vol. 1: An Outline of Interpretive Sociology. Guenther Roth and Claus Wittich, eds. Ephraim Fischoff, Hans Gerth, A. M. Henderson, Ferdinand Kolegar, C. Wright Mills, Talcott Parsons, Max Rheinstein, Guenther Roth, Edward Shils, and Claus Wittich, trans. Berkeley: University of California Press.

1978b Religious Ethics and the World: Sexuality and Art. *Published as* Religious Groups (The Sociology of Religion). *In* Economy and Society, vol. 1. Guenther Roth and Claus Wittich, eds. and trans. Pp. 602–611. Berkeley: University of California Press.

1992 The Protestant Ethic and the Spirit of Capitalism. New York: Routledge.

1998 Religious Rejections of the World and Their Directions. *In* From Max Weber: Essays in Sociology. H. H. Gerth and C. Wright Mills, eds. and trans. Pp. 323–359. New York: Oxford University Press.

2003[1927] General Economic History. Frank H. Knight, trans. Mineola, NY: Dover.

Weidenmann, Jacob

1870 Beautifying Country Homes: A Handbook of Landscape Gardening; Illustrated by Plans of Places Already Improved. New York: O. Judd.

1888 Modern Cemeteries: An Essay upon the Improvements and Proper Management of Rural Cemeteries. Chicago: Monumental News Co. New York Public Library, Special Collections, Rare Books Division.

Weiner, Annette

1976 Women of Value, Men of Renown. Austin: University of Texas Press.

Weston, Kath

1991 Families We Choose: Lesbians, Gays, Kinship. New York: Columbia University Press.

2001 Kinship, Controversy, and the Sharing of Substance: The Race/Class Politics of Blood Transfusion. *In* Relative Values: Reconfiguring Kinship Studies. Sarah Franklin and Susan McKinnon, eds. Pp. 147–174. Durham, NC: Duke University Press.

White, Leslie A., ed.

1937 Extracts from the European Travel Journal of Lewis H. Morgan. Rochester, NY: Rochester Historical Society Publications.

Whitmore, William Henry

1862 A Handbook of American Genealogy: Being a Catalogue of Family Histories and Publications Containing Genealogical Information, Chronologically Arranged. Albany, NY: Joel Munsell.

1868a The American Genealogist: Being a Catalogue of Family Histories and Publications Containing Genealogical Information Issued in the United States, Arranged Chronologically. 2nd edition. Albany, NY: Joel Munsell.

1868b Ancestral Tablets: A Collection of Pedigrees, So Arranged That Eight Generations of the Ancestors of Any Person May Be Recorded in a Connected and Simple Form. Boston: published for the compiler.

Wiencek, Henry

1999 The Hairstons: An American Family in Black and White. New York: St. Martin's Griffin.

Wilkins, Jon

2006 Like Father, Like Son: Conflict, Negotiation, and Shared Fate; Themes in *The Road*: Where Science and Fiction Meet. Oprah.com, January 1. http://www.oprah.com/oprahsbookclub/Fiction-and-Scientific-Themes-in-The-Road-by-Cormac-McCarthy/6, accessed February 5, 2010.

Wilson, Tamar Diana

2009 Beyond Bounded Communities. Urban Anthropology 38(2–4):149–160.

Winter, J. M.

2005[1985] The Great War and the British People. 2nd edition. Basingstoke, UK: Palgrave Macmillan.

Wolf, Eric

1959 Sons of the Shaking Earth: The People of Mexico and Guatemala. Chicago: University of Chicago Press.

1966 Peasants. Englewood Cliffs, NJ: Prentice Hall.

Wolfe, Patrick

1999 Settler Colonialism and the Transformation of Anthropology: The Politics and Poetics of an Ethnographic Event. London: Cassell.

Wolfram, Sybil

1987 In-Laws and Outlaws: Kinship and Marriage in England. London: Croom Helm.

Woodford, Robert J.

1998 "In the Beginning": A Latter-day Perspective. Ensign, January. http://lds.org/ensign/1998/01/in-the-beginning-a-latter-day-perspective?lang=eng, accessed January 24, 2011.

Woodward, Richard B.

1992 Cormac McCarthy's Venomous Fiction. New York Times Magazine, April 19. http://www.nytimes.com/1992/04/19/magazine/cormac-mccarthy-s-venomous-fiction.html?pagewanted=1, accessed February 4, 2010.

Worl, Rosita, and Charles W. Smythe

1986 Barrow: A Decade of Modernization; The Barrow Case Study. Anchorage: US Department of Interior, Minerals Management Service, Alaska Outer Continental Shelf Region.

Wright, Caleb Earl

1878 Two Years behind the Plow; or, The Experience of a Pennsylvania Farm-Boy. Philadelphia: Claxton, Remsen, and Haffelfinger.

Wrightson, Keith

1982 English Society, 1580–1680. London: Hutchinson.

Wyatt-Brown, Bertram

1982 Southern Honor: Ethics and Behavior in the Old South. Oxford: Oxford University Press.

Yale Symposium

2007 Yale Symposium on the Stern Review. Yale Center for the Study of Globalization, February. http://www.ycsg.yale.edu/climate/forms/FullText.pdf, accessed February 9, 2010.

Yanagisako, Sylvia Junko

1985 Transforming the Past: Tradition and Kinship among Japanese Americans. Stanford, CA: Stanford University Press.

2002 Producing Culture and Capital: Family Firms in Italy. Princeton, NJ: Princeton University Press.

Yanagisako, Sylvia Junko, and Jane Fishburne Collier

1987 Toward a Unified Analysis of Gender and Kinship. *In* Gender and Kinship: Essays toward a Unified Analysis. Jane Fishburne Collier and Sylvia Junko Yanagisako, eds. Pp. 14–50. Stanford, CA: Stanford University Press.

Yanagisako, Sylvia, and Carol Delaney, eds.

1995 Naturalizing Power: Essays in Feminist Cultural Analysis. New York: Routledge.

Yang, Mayfair Mei-Hui

1994 Gifts, Favors, and Banquets: The Art of Social Relationships in China. Ithaca, NY: Cornell University Press.

Young, Donna

1996 Remembering Trouble: Three Lives, Three Stories. *In* Tense Past: Cultural Essays in Trauma and Memory. Paul Antze and Michael Lambek, eds. Pp. 25–44. New York: Routledge.

Young, Kate, Carol Wolkowitz, and Roslyn McCullagh

1981 Of Marriage and the Market: Women's Subordination in International Perspective. London: CSE Books.

Zaloom, Caitlin

2004 The Productive Life of Risk. Cultural Anthropology 19(3):365–391.

Zelizer, Viviana A.

1994[1985] Pricing the Priceless Child: The Changing Social Value of Children. Rev. edition. Princeton, NJ: Princeton University Press.

2005 The Purchase of Intimacy. Princeton, NJ: Princeton University Press.

Zlolniski, Christian

2006 Janitors, Street Vendors, and Activists: The Lives of Mexican Immigrants in Silicon Valley. Berkeley: University of California Press.

Index

School for Advanced Research Advanced Seminar Series

Published by SAR Press

Chaco & Hohokam: Prehistoric Regional Systems in the American Southwest
Patricia L. Crown & W. James Judge, eds.

Recapturing Anthropology: Working in the Present
Richard G. Fox, ed.

War in the Tribal Zone: Expanding States and Indigenous Warfare
R. Brian Ferguson & Neil L. Whitehead, eds.

Ideology and Pre-Columbian Civilizations
Arthur A. Demarest & Geoffrey W. Conrad, eds.

Dreaming: Anthropological and Psychological Interpretations
Barbara Tedlock, ed.

Historical Ecology: Cultural Knowledge and Changing Landscapes
Carole L. Crumley, ed.

Themes in Southwest Prehistory
George J. Gumerman, ed.

Memory, History, and Opposition under State Socialism
Rubie S. Watson, ed.

Other Intentions: Cultural Contexts and the Attribution of Inner States
Lawrence Rosen, ed.

Last Hunters–First Farmers: New Perspectives on the Prehistoric Transition to Agriculture
T. Douglas Price & Anne Birgitte Gebauer, eds.

Making Alternative Histories: The Practice of Archaeology and History in Non-Western Settings
Peter R. Schmidt & Thomas C. Patterson, eds.

Cyborgs & Citadels: Anthropological Interventions in Emerging Sciences and Technologies
Gary Lee Downey & Joseph Dumit, eds.

Senses of Place
Steven Feld & Keith H. Basso, eds.

The Origins of Language: What Nonhuman Primates Can Tell Us
Barbara J. King, ed.

Critical Anthropology Now: Unexpected Contexts, Shifting Constituencies, Changing Agendas
George E. Marcus, ed.

Archaic States
Gary M. Feinman & Joyce Marcus, eds.

Regimes of Language: Ideologies, Polities, and Identities
Paul V. Kroskrity, ed.

Biology, Brains, and Behavior: The Evolution of Human Development
Sue Taylor Parker, Jonas Langer, & Michael L. McKinney, eds.

Women & Men in the Prehispanic Southwest: Labor, Power, & Prestige
Patricia L. Crown, ed.

History in Person: Enduring Struggles, Contentious Practice, Intimate Identities
Dorothy Holland & Jean Lave, eds.

The Empire of Things: Regimes of Value and Material Culture
Fred R. Myers, ed.

Catastrophe & Culture: The Anthropology of Disaster
Susanna M. Hoffman & Anthony Oliver-Smith, eds.

Uruk Mesopotamia & Its Neighbors: Cross-Cultural Interactions in the Era of State Formation
Mitchell S. Rothman, ed.

Remaking Life & Death: Toward an Anthropology of the Biosciences
Sarah Franklin & Margaret Lock, eds.

Tikal: Dynasties, Foreigners, & Affairs of State: Advancing Maya Archaeology
Jeremy A. Sabloff, ed.

Gray Areas: Ethnographic Encounters with Nursing Home Culture
Philip B. Stafford, ed.

Pluralizing Ethnography: Comparison and Representation in Maya Cultures, Histories, and Identities
John M. Watanabe & Edward F. Fischer, eds.

American Arrivals: Anthropology Engages the New Immigration
Nancy Foner, ed.

Violence
Neil L. Whitehead, ed.

Law & Empire in the Pacific: Fiji and Hawai'i
Sally Engle Merry & Donald Brenneis, eds.

Anthropology in the Margins of the State
Veena Das & Deborah Poole, eds.

The Archaeology of Colonial Encounters: Comparative Perspectives
Gil J. Stein, ed.

Globalization, Water, & Health: Resource Management in Times of Scarcity
Linda Whiteford & Scott Whiteford, eds.

A Catalyst for Ideas: Anthropological Archaeology and the Legacy of Douglas W. Schwartz
Vernon L. Scarborough, ed.

The Archaeology of Chaco Canyon: An Eleventh-Century Pueblo Regional Center
Stephen H. Lekson, ed.

Community Building in the Twenty-First Century
Stanley E. Hyland, ed.

Afro-Atlantic Dialogues: Anthropology in the Diaspora
Kevin A. Yelvington, ed.

Copán: The History of an Ancient Maya Kingdom
E. Wyllys Andrews & William L. Fash, eds.

The Evolution of Human Life History
Kristen Hawkes & Richard R. Paine, eds.

The Seductions of Community: Emancipations, Oppressions, Quandaries
Gerald W. Creed, ed.

The Gender of Globalization: Women Navigating Cultural and Economic Marginalities
Nandini Gunewardena & Ann Kingsolver, eds.

New Landscapes of Inequality: Neoliberalism and the Erosion of Democracy in America
Jane L. Collins, Micaela di Leonardo, & Brett Williams, eds.

Imperial Formations
Ann Laura Stoler, Carole McGranahan, & Peter C. Perdue, eds.

Opening Archaeology: Repatriation's Impact on Contemporary Research and Practice
Thomas W. Killion, ed.

Small Worlds: Method, Meaning, & Narrative in Microhistory
James F. Brooks, Christopher R. N. DeCorse, & John Walton, eds.

Memory Work: Archaeologies of Material Practices
Barbara J. Mills & William H. Walker, eds.

Figuring the Future: Globalization and the Temporalities of Children and Youth
Jennifer Cole & Deborah Durham, eds.

Timely Assets: The Politics of Resources and Their Temporalities
Elizabeth Emma Ferry & Mandana E. Limbert, eds.

Democracy: Anthropological Approaches
Julia Paley, ed.

Confronting Cancer: Metaphors, Inequality, and Advocacy
Juliet McMullin & Diane Weiner, eds.

PUBLISHED BY SAR PRESS

DEVELOPMENT & DISPOSSESSION: THE CRISIS OF FORCED DISPLACEMENT AND RESETTLEMENT
Anthony Oliver-Smith, ed.

GLOBAL HEALTH IN TIMES OF VIOLENCE
Barbara Rylko-Bauer, Linda Whiteford, & Paul Farmer, eds.

THE EVOLUTION OF LEADERSHIP: TRANSITIONS IN DECISION MAKING FROM SMALL-SCALE TO MIDDLE-RANGE SOCIETIES
Kevin J. Vaughn, Jelmer W. Eerkins, & John Kantner, eds.

ARCHAEOLOGY & CULTURAL RESOURCE MANAGEMENT: VISIONS FOR THE FUTURE
Lynne Sebastian & William D. Lipe, eds.

ARCHAIC STATE INTERACTION: THE EASTERN MEDITERRANEAN IN THE BRONZE AGE
William A. Parkinson & Michael L. Galaty, eds.

INDIANS & ENERGY: EXPLOITATION AND OPPORTUNITY IN THE AMERICAN SOUTHWEST
Sherry L. Smith & Brian Frehner, eds.

ROOTS OF CONFLICT: SOILS, AGRICULTURE, AND SOCIOPOLITICAL COMPLEXITY IN ANCIENT HAWAI'I
Patrick V. Kirch, ed.

PHARMACEUTICAL SELF: THE GLOBAL SHAPING OF EXPERIENCE IN AN AGE OF PSYCHOPHARMACOLOGY
Janis Jenkins, ed.

FORCES OF COMPASSION: HUMANITARIANISM BETWEEN ETHICS AND POLITICS
Erica Bornstein & Peter Redfield, eds.

ENDURING CONQUESTS: RETHINKING THE ARCHAEOLOGY OF RESISTANCE TO SPANISH COLONIALISM IN THE AMERICAS
Matthew Liebmann & Melissa S. Murphy, eds.

DANGEROUS LIAISONS: ANTHROPOLOGISTS AND THE NATIONAL SECURITY STATE
Laura A. McNamara & Robert A. Rubinstein, eds.

BREATHING NEW LIFE INTO THE EVIDENCE OF DEATH: CONTEMPORARY APPROACHES TO BIOARCHAEOLOGY
Aubrey Baadsgaard, Alexis T. Boutin, & Jane E. Buikstra, eds.

THE SHAPE OF SCRIPT: HOW AND WHY WRITING SYSTEMS CHANGE
Stephen D. Houston, ed.

NATURE, SCIENCE, AND RELIGION: INTERSECTIONS SHAPING SOCIETY AND THE ENVIRONMENT
Catherine M. Tucker, ed.

THE GLOBAL MIDDLE CLASSES: THEORIZING THROUGH ETHNOGRAPHY
Rachel Heiman, Carla Freeman, & Mark Liechty, eds.

KEYSTONE NATIONS: INDIGENOUS PEOPLES AND SALMON ACROSS THE NORTH PACIFIC
Benedict J. Colombi & James F. Brooks, eds.

REASSEMBLING THE COLLECTION: ETHNOGRAPHIC MUSEUMS AND INDIGENOUS AGENCY
Rodney Harrison, Sarah Byrne, & Anne Clarke, eds.

IMAGES THAT MOVE
Patricia Spyer & Mary Margaret Steedly, eds.

Timeless Classics from SAR Press

Ancient Civilization and Trade
Jeremy A. Sabloff & C. C. Lamberg-Karlovsky, eds.

The Archaeology of Lower Central America
Frederick W. Lange & Doris Z. Stone, eds.

Chan Chan: Andean Desert City
Michael E. Moseley & Kent C. Day, eds.

The Classic Maya Collapse
T. Patrick Culbert, ed.

Demographic Anthropology: Quantitative Approaches
Ezra B. W. Zubrow, ed.

The Dying Community
Art Gallaher, Jr., & Harlan Padfield, eds.

Elites: Ethnographic Issues
George E. Marcus, ed.

Entrepreneurs in Cultural Context
Sidney M. Greenfield, Arnold Strickon, & Robert T. Aubey, eds.

Explanation of Prehistoric Change
James N. Hill, ed.

Explorations in Ethnoarchaeology
Richard A. Gould, ed.

Late Lowland Maya Civilization: Classic to Postclassic
Jeremy A. Sabloff & E. Wyllys Andrews V, eds.

Lowland Maya Settlement Patterns
Wendy Ashmore, ed.

Methods and Theories of Anthropological Genetics
M. H. Crawford & P. L. Workman, eds.

New Perspectives on the Pueblos
Alfonso Ortiz, ed.

The Origins of Maya Civilization
Richard E. W. Adams, ed.

Photography in Archaeological Research
Elmer Harp, Jr., ed.

Reconstructing Prehistoric Pueblo Societies
William A. Longacre, ed.

Shipwreck Anthropology
Richard A. Gould, ed.

Simulations in Archaeology
Jeremy A. Sabloff, ed.

Structure and Process in Latin America
Arnold Strickon & Sidney M. Greenfield, eds.

The Valley of Mexico: Studies in Pre-Hispanic Ecology and Society
Eric R. Wolf, ed.

Morleyana: A Collection of Writings in Memoriam, Sylvanus Griswold Morley—1883–1948

Published by Cambridge University Press

The Anasazi in a Changing Environment
George J. Gumerman, ed.

Regional Perspectives on the Olmec
Robert J. Sharer & David C. Grove, eds.

The Chemistry of Prehistoric Human Bone
T. Douglas Price, ed.

The Emergence of Modern Humans: Biocultural Adaptations in the Later Pleistocene
Erik Trinkaus, ed.

The Anthropology of War
Jonathan Haas, ed.

The Evolution of Political Systems
Steadman Upham, ed.

Classic Maya Political History: Hieroglyphic and Archaeological Evidence
T. Patrick Culbert, ed.

Turko-Persia in Historical Perspective
Robert L. Canfield, ed.

Chiefdoms: Power, Economy, and Ideology
Timothy Earle, ed.

Published by University of California Press

Writing Culture: The Poetics and Politics of Ethnography
James Clifford & George E. Marcus, eds.

Published by University of Arizona Press

The Collapse of Ancient States and Civilizations
Norman Yoffee & George L. Cowgill, eds.

Published by University of New Mexico Press

Sixteenth-Century Mexico: The Work of Sahagun
Munro S. Edmonson, ed.

Meaning in Anthropology
Keith H. Basso & Henry A. Selby, eds.

Southwestern Indian Ritual Drama
Charlotte J. Frisbie, ed.

Participants in the School for Advanced Research advanced seminar "The Difference Kinship Makes: Rethinking the Ideologies of Modernity" co-chaired by Fenella Cannell and Susan McKinnon, March 21–25, 2010. *Standing, from left*: Michael Lambek, Sylvia Yanagisako, Elana Shever, Danilyn Rutherford, Janet Carsten, Barbara Bodenhorn, Laura Bear, Gillian Feeley-Harnik; *seated, from left*: Fenella Cannell, Susan McKinnon. Photograph by Jason S. Ordaz.

www.ingramcontent.com/pod-product-compliance
Lightning Source LLC
Chambersburg PA
CBHW021111270326
41929CB00009B/834

9781938645013